PMP® Certification
FOR
DUMMIES®

PMP® Certification

FOR

DUMMIES®

by Peter Nathan
and Gerald Everett Jones

WILEY

Wiley Publishing, Inc.

PMP® Certification For Dummies®

Published by
Wiley Publishing, Inc.
111 River Street
Hoboken, NJ 07030
www.wiley.com

About the Authors

Peter Nathan, PMP, MBA is a career-veteran IT project manager who recently went through the process of obtaining the PMP certification. He hosted a PMP Exam Prep Training Class at Universal Studios sponsored by the Los Angeles Chapter of the PMI for 30 project managers. He took the long road getting certified. He read the books, took courses, got a practice CD, and worked through practice exams—on paper, interactively using the CD software, and online. After all that effort, the Project Management Institute certified Nathan as a PMP. He's glad he went through it, but is he ever glad it's over! He has strong opinions for anyone who wants to avoid the needless pain and suffering of repeating his mistakes. Using his experience in process reengineering, this book is his experience-proven shortcut method to passing the exam. Pete has 20 years experience working on IT projects. As a project manager himself, he has lead cross-functional teams in application development and integration, process improvement, organizational effectiveness, and change management. Besides Universal Studios, he has worked for Paramount Pictures, NBC, Chemical Bank, CitiBank, Shearson/American Express, and the Big 8 national consulting firm Laventhol & Horwath. He is currently implementing a project management center of excellence with BAE Systems for the USAR. He was the Chief Technology Officer of the Los Angeles Microsoft Project Users Group (MUPG) and a member of the Los Angeles and Atlanta Chapters of Project Management Institute. He's beta tested several versions of Microsoft Project, including the latest enterprise Project Server line.

Gerald Everett Jones has written more than 20 business and computer books, including the Sybex titles *Murphy's Laws of Excel, Guided Tour of Excel,* and *How to Lie with Charts*. He is an honors graduate of the College of Letters of Wesleyan University. He has held PM positions in educational program development (Coronet Instructional Media), industrial sales training (Sandy Corporation), and computer graphics software development (Creative Technologies, Inc. and The Reynolds Group). He is also co-author with movie director Pete Shaner of the forthcoming book *Real World Digital Video: Industrial-Strength Production Techniques.*

Dedication

For Stacy and Jay.

Authors' Acknowledgments

A dedicated team of professionals worked long and hard to bring you this book. When you pass the PMP Certification Exam, you owe with us a debt of gratitude to Melody Lane, Acquisitions Editor, and Pat O'Brien, Project Editor.

Heartfelt personal thanks to Georja Umano Jones for her sweetness, patience, and belief. Our most sincere thanks to Stacy Nathan for her cheerful support and encouragement throughout the entire project. A debt of gratitude is owed to Anne and Jay Saravo who enabled the writing of Parts II and III.

A special thanks is due to Dr. Daryn DeRose for assistance with the statistical portions for risk and quality. We would like to recognize the assistance of the PMI and various members of the Los Angeles, Orange County, and Atlanta chapters of PMI.

And thanks to our tireless literary agent, Matt Wagner of Waterside Productions, who puts it all together.

Publisher's Acknowledgments

We're proud of this book; please send us your comments through our online registration form located at www.dummies.com/register/.

Some of the people who helped bring this book to market include the following:

Acquisitions, Editorial, and Media Development

Project Editor: Pat O'Brien

Acquisitions Editor: Melody Layne

Senior Copy Editor: Diana Conover

Technical Editor: Hugh Cameron, PMP

Editorial Manager: Kevin Kirschner

Permissions Editor: Carmen Krikorian

Media Development Specialist: Megan Decraene

Media Development Manager: Laura VanWinkle

Media Development Supervisor: Richard Graves

Editorial Assistant: Amanda Foxworth

Cartoons: Rich Tennant (www.the5thwave.com)

Production

Project Coordinator: Regina Snyder

Layout and Graphics: Jacque Schneider, Janet Seib, Jeremey Unger

Proofreaders: TECHBOOKS Production Services, Carl Pierce, Andy Hollandbeck

Indexer: TECHBOOKS Production Services

Special Help
Roger Voight, PMP

Publishing and Editorial for Technology Dummies

Richard Swadley, Vice President and Executive Group Publisher

Andy Cummings, Vice President and Publisher

Mary C. Corder, Editorial Director

Publishing for Consumer Dummies

Diane Graves Steele, Vice President and Publisher

Joyce Pepple, Acquisitions Director

Composition Services

Gerry Fahey, Vice President of Production Services

Debbie Stailey, Director of Composition Services

Contents at a Glance

Introduction 1

Part I: PMP Certification Exam and PM Overview 7

Chapter 1: The PMP Certification Exam 9

Chapter 2: Exam Basics and Study Tips 21

Chapter 3: Project Management Basics 31

Chapter 4: Professional Responsibility 45

Part II: Initiating the Project 61

Chapter 5: Determining Goals, Deliverables, Scope, and Initiation Processes 63

Chapter 6: Identifying Boundaries 81

Chapter 7: Opening the Project 99

Part III: Planning the Project 111

Chapter 8: Refining the Project 113

Chapter 9: Creating the Work Breakdown Structure 139

Chapter 10: Establishing Project Controls 189

Part IV: Executing the Project 229

Chapter 11: Procuring Resources, Managing, and Reporting Progress 231

Part V: Controlling and Closing the Project 257

Chapter 12: Ensuring Plan Compliance 259

Chapter 13: Taking Corrective Action 281

Chapter 14: Closing the Project 299

Part VI: The Part of Tens 315

Chapter 15: Ten Test Preparation Tips 317

Chapter 16: Ten Tips for Exam Day 325

Part VII: Appendixes 331

Appendix A: Important Formulas 333

Appendix B: Practice Exam 369

Appendix C: About the CD-ROM 385

Index 391

Table of Contents

Introduction 1

About This Book...1
What This Book Is 1
What This Book Isn't...2
Who You Are 3
How This Book Is Organized..3
Chapter Structure 4
    Page one 4
    Quick Assessment 4
    Prep Test..4
Icons Used in This Book...4

Part 1: PMP Certification Exam and PM Overview 7

Chapter 1: The PMP Certification Exam 9

How the PMP Certification Gets You Ready for Prime Time 9
    Why PMI is the PMP overlord 10
    Focusing on practical PM skills 11
    Getting a handle on PM jargon 11
    Introducing the PMBOK...12
Finding Out about PMI..12
    Those influential people who wrote the test 12
    Getting in contact with PMI..13
    Studying the right materials 13
Getting PMP Certified 13
    Understanding exam requirements................................14
    Applying to take the exam...15
    Inspecting the test question structure 16
    What percentage of questions relate to each exam section? 17
    Criteria for passing the exam 17
What the Exam Measures..17
    Creating a study plan 18
    Memorizing key lists 18
    Study tips...18
Tracking Your Study Plan by Using PMI Methodology...............19
    Your exam is the product of your project 19
    Project scheduling tools to plan your exam baseline.............19
    Project controls on your study progress 20
    Measuring your earned value 20

Chapter 2: Exam Basics and Study Tips **21**

Thinking Horizontally and Vertically...21
The Secret Scheme of Tricks and Traps..22
Knowing the types of questions 22
Learning Tips...23
Memory aid tricks 23
Recognizing patterns in questions...23
Becoming test-wise 25
The Vocabulary of Project Management 27
The Breakdown of Exam Questions..28
Anticipating the Exam 29

Chapter 3: Project Management Basics **31**

Benefiting from PM Methodology 31
Project Management Context 31
Organizational culture and structure 32
General management skills 32
Social, economic, and environmental influences.........................32
Setting Your Sights on PM..33
Taking a closer look at projects...33
Defining the org chart 34
Understanding progressive elaboration..36
Understanding PM Models..36
What is a process?...36
Diving into the matrix 37
Distinguishing the Five Process Management Groups 38
Distinguishing the Nine Knowledge Areas 38
Correlating the Processes, Knowledge Areas, and Exam Parts 40

Chapter 4: Professional Responsibility **45**

Professional Responsibility 48
Professional Code of Conduct 49
Responsibilities to the Profession...50
Responsibilities to Customers and the Public..............................52

Part II: Initiating the Project *61*

**Chapter 5: Determining Goals, Deliverables, Scope,
and Initiation Processes** **63**

Conceiving Projects 66
Performing a Feasibility Study or Analysis...66
What is a feasibility study? 66
Conducting a project feasibility study..67
Organizing Project Plan Materials..67
Can the project deliver the results?..68
Should the company undertake this project? 68

Identifying the Need..69
Project Selection Criteria and Methods 70
Describing a Product or Service 71
Dividing the Project into Manageable Components 71
Introducing the knowledge area processes 72
Interlinking life-cycle processes 73
Determining and Defining Project Scope 74
Identifying requirements and expectations 74
Organizational policies and influences..................75
The basis of future decisions 75
Developing a Project Charter 76
Drafting the Project Charter/Letter of Engagement 76

Chapter 6: Identifying Boundaries **81**
Managing Expectations 84
Identifying Project Stakeholders 84
Expectations of Managers and Sponsors 86
What makes a good sponsor? 86
Working with sponsors 87
Measuring Project Benefits 89
Setting acceptance criteria 90
Determining project metrics 90
Setting Milestones...91
Setting Quality Standards..92
Coping with an Organization's Structure 93
Functional organization 94
Matrix organization 94
Projectized organization......................................95

Chapter 7: Opening the Project **99**
Authorizing the Project 102
Kicking off the project 102
Publishing the project charter............................103
Selecting the project manager 103
Documenting constraints and assumptions 104
Maintaining Project Records 106

Part III: Planning the Project........................*111*

Chapter 8: Refining the Project **113**
Project Integration Management.................................116
Project Plan Development...116
Establishing a PMIS...119
Growing the Project Plan 119
Using rolling wave planning 120
Developing the project plan................................120

Planning and Defining Scope 121
Creating the Scope Management Plan.....................................123
    Planning the scope...123
    Writing the scope statement...125
    Defining the scope...127
Understanding Formulas for the Time Value of Money.............128
    Benefit/cost ratio...129
    Payback analysis 129
    Discounting cash flow...131
    Internal rate of return 134

Chapter 9: Creating the Work Breakdown Structure 139

Using a Work Breakdown Structure.......................................142
    Decomposing the work..146
    Updating the scope statement from WBS 146
    Relating the WBS to the activity list 147
    Creating a responsibility assignment matrix....................147
    Planning for needed resources.......................................148
Creating a Staff Management Plan 150
    Organizational Planning..150
    Staff Acquisition 152
Planning for Procurement...154
    Procurement Planning 154
    Solicitation Planning 156
    Contracting for services and supplies..............................157
Developing the Schedule...159
    Defining activities 159
    Sequencing activities..161
    Sequencing and scheduling techniques 164
    Diagramming networks..166
    Estimating effort — Activity Durations 169
    Estimating techniques and formulas 170
    Developing the schedule 173
Building the Budget and Spending Plan 177
    Estimating costs 177
    Defining a budget..180
Harnessing Earned Value Management 182
    Planning for earned value analysis 182
    Analyzing formulas for earned value 183

Chapter 10: Establishing Project Controls 189

Creating the Project Plan 192
    Maintaining the plan as a living document 192
    Creating subsidiary plans..192
    Planning for future changes 193
    Obtaining written approvals for buy-in 193
Authorizing Work to Be Performed..194

Planning Stakeholder Communications 194
    Sharing findings with stakeholders.........................196
    Applying the formula for communications channels 197
Improving Quality 198
    Quality Planning 199
    Approaching quality..202
    Cost of quality..204
    Philosophies of the QC gurus 205
    Quality definitions from each guru 213
Identifying and Planning for Risk 213
    Identifying risk...216
    Qualifying risks...219
    Quantifying risks..220
    Developing responses for risks 223

Part IV: Executing the Project 229

Chapter 11: Procuring Resources, Managing, and Reporting Progress 231

Executing the Project Plan...234
Procuring Resources..236
Soliciting...236
    Selecting sources of materials 238
    Administrating contracts 239
Implementing Resources...241
    Developing the team 242
    Motivating the team 243
    Assuring your authority 246
    Tolerating conflicts 246
Communicating 247
Distributing Information...249
Assuring Quality...250
Measuring Progress with Metrics 252

Part V: Controlling and Closing the Project.....................257

Chapter 12: Ensuring Plan Compliance 259

Integrating Overall Change Control 262
Improving Quality 264
Measuring Compliance...267
    Inspecting tasks 267
Project Metrics 268
Verifying Scope and Work Results 272
Controlling Scope Changes 275
Updating Subsidiary Plans..277

Chapter 13: Taking Corrective Action 281

Controlling Risks 284
Mastering risk controls 286
Handling change requests 286
Taking corrective action 287
Controlling Schedule Changes 288
Controlling Cost Changes 290
Communicating Performance 292

Chapter 14: Closing the Project 299

Repeating Closeout at Each Phase 302
Evaluating Work Packages 303
Retaining the Knowledgebase 303
Closing Down Administrative Functions 304
Contract Closeout 307
Handling Staff During Closing 308
Releasing resources 309
Rewarding performance 309

Part VI: The Part of Tens *315*

Chapter 15: Ten Test Preparation Tips 317

Take Care of Admin Stuff 317
Define Your Study Plan 318
Stay Motivated 319
Do Your Homework 319
Look for Question Patterns 321
Remember the Process Interactions 322
Know the Component Process Interactions 323
Recognize Question Types 323
Do the Math 324

Chapter 16: Ten Tips for Exam Day 325

Before You Get to the Test Center 325
Day before 325
Exam day 326
At the Test Center 326
Registration 326
Exam tools 326
Settling in 327
Taking the tutorial 327
Beginning the Exam 328
Analyze the Question Patterns 328
Make Notes 329

Part VII: Appendixes 331

Appendix A: Important Formulas 333
The Quantitative View of Project Management...................................333
PM Statistics for Dummies 334
Estimating Time Formulas..344
Equivalent worth 362
Paybacks and benefits 363
Estimating Depreciation 365

Appendix B: Practice Exam 369

Appendix C: About the CD-ROM 385
System Requirements 385
Using this CD ROM with Microsoft Windows 385
Dummies Test Prep Tools 387
Practice test 387
Web site links 387
Commercial Demos 387
Template Files...388
If You Have Problems with the CD 388

Index...391

Introduction

You hold in your hands a quick, no-nonsense guide to passing the most important certification exams for project management (PM) — the Project Management Professional (PMP) certification for experienced people and the introductory-level Certified Associate in Project Management (CAPM). The exam's sponsor is the Project Management Institute (PMI).

About This Book

As project management becomes a distinct profession with its own career track, the job title of project manager will increasingly be awarded to highly trained specialists. To make that happen, hiring managers need to know how to select the right person for the PM role. The PMP certification is the global leader in achieving this goal — through a uniformly applied test open to all project managers with the required background and work experience.

Whatever your level of understanding of project management, this is the book for you. As we mention at the outset, one of two exams will be appropriate at this point in your career, depending on your level of experience:

✔ **Certified Associate in Project Management (CAPM):** This is the new *introductory level* certification demonstrating fundamental PM knowledge and experience.

✔ **Project Management Professional (PMP):** This *advanced level* certification is the major league exam for project managers. No other PM exam is as widely recognized. To sit for it, you must meet specific requirements for PM work experience.

What This Book Is

This book's goal is simple: to help you pass the PMP or the CAPM Certification Exam. You want those three (or four) magic letters after your name so you can get to the next step of both qualifying for better, more exciting jobs and managing projects more professionally. This book is organized to maximize your time investment and get you ready for the exam quickly as possible. Although we may sidetrack a few times to make a point, we don't pad the book with material not required for the exam.

Promoting ourselves shamelessly, we promise that *PMP Certification For Dummies* is the book you need to pass the PMP exam. This book includes

- ✔ **Explanations of the core methodology.** This helps you understand the key concepts and know them cold.

- ✔ **Chapter quizzes that help you master sample questions.** You'll learn to spot the most likely formats for tricky questions and exception questions. You'll be able to assess your own readiness to take the exam and identify where you need to study further.

- ✔ **Hundreds of practice test questions in the book and on the CD.** Feel free to cram before the test by reviewing the questions and answers.

If your goal is to pass the exam in minimal time and with minimal effort, this is the only book you need. (Okay, there's lots of other stuff on the CD — we're counting that!)

We've tried to make the book easy to follow. It steers a linear course though how you'd manage a project in the real world. That's actually a different approach from competing books — including the "official" ones published by the test sponsors. We hope you'll appreciate the care it took to make the material accessible and practical. We wrote the book that Pete wishes he'd had when he took the exam. We hope that you'll tell us how you like the book, how you did on the exam, and what improvements we can add in the next edition.

What This Book Isn't

This book is not a preview of the exam based on someone's guess of what the exam is about. It's based on the test sponsor's published Role Delineation Study, an authoritative description of what project managers do, and the test content itself. These methods and questions mirror tasks PMPs perform while practicing project management in the real world. The chapters are organized according to the task or practice competency statements described in the Role Delineation Study. As such, each chapter describes *what* a PMP does, *why* a task is being performed, and *how* a task should be completed. The emphasis on the what, the why, and the how is directly from the Role Delineation Study. Linked to the task statements are the specific PM knowledge and skills needed to complete each area. This serves as your road map for the PMP exam.

Although this is not the first PMP certification book on the market, the publisher and the writing team agree that we won't rush a product out the door unless we're confident that it is important, relevant, accurate, and critical.

We're not going to give you an MBA in project management or prepare a full project plan from scratch. Nor is this an intro class where you learn everything there is to know about project management in one day, three days, or a week. It's not a one-week cram course or boot camp that will cost you $2,000 and make your head spin. And it's not the simplified *Sesame Street* class that your boss probably took.

This book isn't an encyclopedia of project management. It contains only the relevant information that you'll need to pass the exam. So don't consider this your *last* book on PM techniques, nor on the other general management techniques.

Finally, this book is not a guarantee — if only that were possible. If you read it carefully, retain what we're explaining, and master the techniques, you should pass the test on your first try. If you don't apply yourself diligently, you might not pass. We can't control whether you study the information in this book seriously. We can't control whether you open it while doing something else, like reading it while thinking about other pressing problems. We can't make you take the practice exams or complete the study plan assignments on the CD. What we can do is present the material that you'll need for the exam in a clear and concise way. That's all we can do — and that's quite a lot, when you think about it.

Who You Are

PMP Certification For Dummies is for aspiring and actual project managers. You'll have experience under your belt working on projects.

- ✔ You have a life to lead that includes priorities other than reading a 1,200-page textbook on project management.
- ✔ You want to pass the PMP or CAPM exam on the first try.
- ✔ You want tips that will help you pass the exam and that you can use in real life on your current (or next) project.

How This Book Is Organized

This book doesn't follow the same structure as the competing books, including the official ones. Instead, it follows the structure of the exam content that the test sponsors have published.

We designed the book so that the contents rigidly follow this list. It's a linear, step-by-step, project life-cycle approach. In some cases, we've reorganized the material so that it fits together in a more logical way. In other cases, we've added material that is on the exam but not covered in other exam-prep books.

As with most *For Dummies* books, you can jump in and out of most chapters. We made the chapters fairly short so that you can read one while waiting for a telephone call or taking a coffee break.

Chapter Structure

Although you might be familiar with some of the other books in the *For Dummies* series, this book has some design features that are specific to the certification titles. Here is a quick overview.

Page one

The first page of most chapters discusses the exam content covered by the chapter, along with a brief description of the subject. Read the first page to find out the main topics in the chapter. You can then skip the chapters if you already know the material.

Quick Assessment

Next is a Quick Assessment test of the exam content covered in the chapter. The purpose of this test is to measure your knowledge. If you get all the questions right, you might want to skip the chapter and move onto the Prep Test at the end of the chapter. The Quick Assessment helps you quickly identify gaps in your knowledge so you can focus your study efforts as efficiently as possible.

Prep Test

Each chapter ends with a Prep Test so that you can determine how well you know the material. It's designed to look and feel like an actual test. Although there is no guarantee that these exact questions will appear on the exam, we include different question formats so that you'll be familiar with them on test day.

Icons Used in This Book

Like the other books in the *For Dummies* series, we use several icons in the margins of the book.

This icon highlights short suggestions, hints, and bits of unusual information.

This icon marks the most common traps and pitfalls, whether in test taking or in your understanding of PM methodology.

This icon is the PM methodology that you need to know.

Memorize this information. It will appear on the test.

That wraps up the introduction. In PM terms, it's the *closeout* of a *phase*. Take a break. Stand up and stretch. Or take a short walk and grab that mug of coffee. You're now ready to begin to prep in earnest for passing the exam.

Part I
PMP Certification Exam and PM Overview

The 5th Wave   By Rich Tennant

"I can tell a lot from your resume. You're well educated, detail oriented and own a really tiny printer."

In this part...

"**C**amera rolling," shouts the camera operator. A few seconds pass, then the sound recordist shouts, "Speed." The second assistant director bellows, "Background action," cueing an army of extras to start roaming through the set—a battlefield where anything can happen. The first assistant director shouts, "Action!" The cast, a team of principal actors and stars who never worked together before, moves through their rehearsed plan (a battle scene). The director beckons to the stunt coordinator, "Lob some bombs. I want big, flaming explosions." The movie project begins....

Wrong! If you've had any experience as a project manager, you know that a movie project—like any other type of project—doesn't begin with people running around, any more than construction of a building begins with the pouring of concrete or writing software begins with coding. Project management (PM) begins with discussions about business needs, which lead to plans on paper— scripts, if you will—schedules, budgets—and only then does the "action" commence.

If you're committed to sitting for the Project Management Professional (PMP) certification exam, we don't need to convince you how important mastering this material is to your career.

Reel one opens on a raging battle. The camera zooms to a closeup on the project manager...

Chapter 1

The PMP Certification Exam

In This Chapter

▶ Examining why project management is important

▶ Getting ready for prime time with PMP certification

▶ Obtaining your PMP credential

▶ Taking a look at the exam

▶ Tracking your study plan as a project

*T*his chapter introduces you to the Project Management Professional (PMP) Certification Exam. Our goal is to enable you to pass the certification exam and be recognized in your organization and in the business world as a certified PMP. This chapter gives you an overview of the exam, introduces you to the organization behind the exam, and discusses the generally accepted principles and methods of modern project management. You discover why project management is important, how project management differs from general management, and how having the project management (PM) skills described in this book can help you pass the test and enhance your career. You find out about a formal methodology for leading a successful project team in the real world — all the while picking up tricks for passing the exam.

As a sample project, you find out how to prepare a study plan that matches the methodology you need to know to pass the exam. We strongly recommend that you develop your own study plan and monitor your progress by using these tools and techniques. Putting theory into practice helps you master the core principles that are covered on the exam.

Although taking a professional certification exam may seem intimidating, we simplify the process for you. We give you a secret road map to the process.

How the PMP Certification Gets You Ready for Prime Time

The PMP certification is proof that you have the ability to manage a project. The exam was designed specifically to measure the knowledge, skills, tools, and techniques that are utilized in the practice of project management. In today's competitive job market, white-collar managers need a way to differentiate themselves.

The recent boom-bust cycle in dot-com companies is a good example. Not so long ago, anyone who could create a simple Gantt chart with Microsoft Project called himself a project manager. These were typically project leads, or senior programmers, for small- to medium-sized development teams. Most of these "project managers" had little practical experience in projects and practically no formal PM methodologies. They're called accidental project managers. When the dot-com bubble burst, their resumes poured into human resources (HR) departments. How could an HR staffer know the difference between a battle-scarred project manager with hard-won PM experience and an accidental project manager with a similar title and no real experience? The answer is that HR recruiters *couldn't* tell the difference. Nor could the actual hiring managers make the distinction. The accidental project managers flooded the IT market, and corporations were swift to take advantage. Employers dropped the rates they were willing to pay for project managers' salaries by 25 to 45 percent.

The best way to distinguish yourself from the growing list of project managers is to become a certified Project Management Professional — the coveted PMP designation. According to recent salary surveys, achieving PMP certification brings an average salary increase of 8 percent across all industries — as high as 14 percent for IT managers. To employers who hope their projects aren't among the 83 percent that fail, PMP certification is now a preferred risk-reduction tool for screening job seekers and making promotion decisions.

Why PMI is the PMP overlord

The profession of project management is becoming a formal discipline. To ensure that project managers have a core level of professionalism, project management has its own rigorous certification exam — much as accountants have their Certified Public Accountant (CPA) exam.

The Project Management Institute (PMI) is the nonprofit organization that develops and administers the Project Management Professional Certification Exam. Just consider PMI as project management's indispensable trade association. PMI is dedicated to the advancement of high standards and methods in the field of project management. PMI not only grants you entrance to the profession by way of its certification, but it can also help you in your long-range career plans.

The PMP is the most widely accepted PM certification in the world. Currently, PMI has 100,000 members worldwide and expects that number to reach 200,000 by 2005. Membership rose about 16 percent last year. Among PMI members, about 50,000 have passed its certification exam. That's about 50 percent of the members, a percentage that varies widely among local chapters. PMPs are a small fraction of all project managers.

PMI's Certification Board Center, a special group within the institute, handles all matters relating to the exam and certification. It has authority over credentialing activities for PMI, the profession, and individuals. The Certification Board Center's mission is for the global PM community, and its programs are the best in the world. In fact, the PMI Certification department is the first professional certification department in the world to obtain ISO 9001 recognition, a corporate quality-assurance program promulgated by the International Standards Organization.

Focusing on practical PM skills

PMI's Certification Board designed the exam to measure the knowledge, skills, tools, and techniques involved in the practice of project management. So everything that you learn for the exam could be applied to one of your future projects. Naturally, you won't use all these skills on every project; you'll use large portions of the methodology on every project.

The best way to prepare for the exam is to use all these methods on a project. That's why we encourage you to create a sample study plan as a project, as described later in this chapter.

Getting a handle on PM jargon

The practice of project management requires knowledge of many disciplines. Each discipline comes with its own jargon. For example, you need to know about the discipline of finance for justifying projects and performing cost/benefit analysis. You need to shine at budgeting and comparing actual costs to budgeted costs. You must develop mastery of technical disciplines such as quality and risk management, as well as softer ones centered on communications management and people skills. How a project moves through its life cycle phases and how each step affects these competencies will become second nature to you. We cover these topics in later chapters. We explain the terms and definitions that you'll have to master for the exam — and for practicing PM in the real world.

From an extensive, enterprise-wide basis, the terms and definitions of multiple disciplines will become part of your basic vocabulary. You need to know these definitions because you'll deal with stakeholders and staff who use them on a daily basis. In fact, much of the core exam material requires you to memorize the terms and definitions of project management. As we explore next, the core study material for the exam contains lots of definitions, lists, and charts that you need to memorize.

Introducing the PMBOK

On the exam and throughout your career as a PMP, you'll hear people refer to the *PMBOK Guide*. The *Guide to the Project Management Body of Knowledge* is the PM bible according to PMI. It includes the generally accepted practices and methods of PM and provides the core study material for the exam. Don't expect this book to be a page-turner. If it were interesting or easily understandable, you wouldn't need this book. The *PMBOK Guide* is full of dry lists and explanations. (Pete reads the book aloud to get his colicky baby back to sleep after night-shift feedings.)

Don't confuse the *PMBOK Guide* — a single book — with the PMBOK itself — everything you always wanted to know *or will ever know* about project management. The PMBOK is an idea, not a thing. It includes all the knowledge ever collected about project management. That body of knowledge includes all books, articles, lectures and speeches, recordings, coffee-shop conversations — anything now or yet to be written or said about project management.

The *PMBOK Guide* is the main source material for the exam. Although it's not the only reference, it is the main one. Like it or not, you'll probably end up reading it three times for the exam; we help you to be selective and effective in your reading. The current *PMBOK Guide 2000* version was updated by several PMI committees with subject-matter experts. If you have the 1996 version, there have been some changes in methodology in the 2000 version. *These changes are on the new exam,* so get the latest *PMBOK Guide* version. Another updated *PMBOK Guide* is expected to be released in 2004.

Finding Out about PMI

In addition to being the sponsor of the exam, PMI is an extremely helpful organization that offers many other services. We urge you to find your local chapter and join. In the next few sections, we explain what PMI is, how you can become involved, and how PMI can help your career.

Those influential people who wrote the test

PMI developed the first PMP certification exam in 1984. The initial exams were handwritten tests, eight hours long. PMI's current exams are four hours of multiple-choice questions, with automated scoring.

After you pass the exam, you have to satisfy continuing education requirements to keep your certification active. Attending local chapter meetings helps you satisfy some of the requirements. So does attending the annual seminars and symposium. These trade conventions are national meetings for the profession. These yearly events have exhibitions; provide opportunities for networking and contacts, and provide world-class seminars from top business leaders, consultants, and scholars on all topics relating to PM.

Getting in contact with PMI

PMI has an online presence for the national organization at www.pmi.org. PMI also has many local chapters that you can join. Or if you're just looking for PM information to pass the exam, attend a meeting. There are more than 180 chapters, 9 student chapters, and approximately 50 international chapters in 45 countries. The United States has 71 percent of the members, Canada has 11 percent, and the International division has 17 percent. To find out more information about a local chapter in your area, check out the chapter location page at www.pmi.org/chapterinfo/.

The U.S. chapter locator page is at www.pmi.org/chapterinfo/acp_us.htm. Grouped by state and city, the chapter contact information tells when the chapter was chartered and lists an officer's name, phone and e-mail contact information, and annual chapter dues.

Studying the right materials

The core material for the exam is in the *PMBOK Guide,* but even if you commit all of it to memory, you won't be assured of passing the test. Project management covers many disciplines, and your study materials for the exam will encompass many of them. Some overlap with general management; others are specific to project management. We summarize those other sources for you, and we make sure you know all the topics the test covers.

The *PMBOK Guide* is an *abridged* overview of all existing material on project management: books, lectures, academic notes and studies, and so on. Because the entire body of knowledge (a notion called the PMBOK) couldn't fit into one book, the guide is not comprehensive; it's a survey or standards manual.

Only 70 percent of exam is derived from the *PMBOK Guide.* In the following chapters, we tell you where to find the other 30 percent and what to concentrate on in your test preparation.

Getting PMP Certified

Before you can take the exam, you have to qualify for it. PMI verifies and qualifies your background experience. You start by submitting an application.

In the next few sections, we detail various exams and background requirements, and help you with the application.

Understanding exam requirements

PMI gives three types of exams, and each has different requirements. PMP certification — the subject of this book — is the senior-level project management exam. CAPM is an entry-level project management exam. CAQ is an additional, industry-specific exam. Before you can take the CAQ, you need to be PMP certified.

The PMP is the major league exam for project managers. There isn't any other PM exam as widely recognized. The exam is a grueling four-hour-long marathon. It starts with an optional 15-minute tutorial, which explains how the exam works; it does not count as part of the four hours. (If you start the tutorial and the rundown clock shows 3:45, immediately let the proctor know and have him or her reset the clock.) The PMP Certification Exam has 200 multiple-choice questions. Each question has four options, and you must select the best one. It might not really be the best one in your opinion or even in your experience, but the best one according to the PMI mindset.

The test is pass or fail. To pass, you must score at least 137. A score of 138 or 200 gets the same passing grade as 137. So, don't sweat the numbers; you'll get no extra credit for a perfect score!

CAPM

The *introductory level* CAPM (Certified Associate in Project Management) exam is aimed at people who do not have enough job experience to answer situational questions. These questions take the form, "What would you do in this situation?" (These experiential questions account for about 40 percent of the *advanced level* PMP exam.) It's an easier test than the PMP, but it covers the same topics. Just about everything you'll read in this book will help you pass the CAPM exam as well as the PMP exam. The major differences are that the CAPM exam has only 150 questions, and it's less situational. It also requires shorter periods for both project experience and training, so the application form is different. To determine if you meet these requirements, see the CAPM Handbook. You can download it from `pmi.org/info/PDC_CAPMHandbookFile.asp`.

CAQ

Don't worry about taking the CAQ exam just yet. Just added in 2002, the Certificate of Added Qualification (CAQ) is an additional exam that you take after you've passed the PMP exam. It ensures PMPs have industry-specific knowledge and skills. There are exams for specializations in IT, automotive, and project management offices. Future exams for other industry segments are planned. There are some different eligibility requirements for taking these new exams.

Applying to take the exam

The next few sections take you through the application process.

PMI membership entitles you to a discounted exam rate of $405 instead of the full $555 rate. Membership costs equal the membership discount for the exam. So join PMI! You can pay PMI for membership and the exam with your credit card online at `secure.pmi.org/add/memberinfo1.asp`. You'll get a member ID number and password for accessing the PMI member's areas.

Go to the PMI certification Web site

You can apply online for the exam at `https://certificationapp.pmi.org`. This is a secure Web page that encrypts all your information. You'll get a CE Number (for Certification Exam) and a password. Write the CE Number and password down and keep them handy. The CE Number permits you to complete the entire application in multiple sessions. You can submit your application in sections by returning to the exact place where you left off. That's a great timesaver for you, especially if you forget something or have to gather additional information.

The Certification Handbook is a PDF file that you can use as a reference for the application process. Download the Certification Handbook at `pmi.org/info/PDC_PMPHandbook.pdf`.

Fill out the application

The application differs slightly depending on your background. There are two sets of educational and experiential requirements called Category 1 (if you have a BA/BS degree) or Category 2 (if you don't have a BA/BS degree). These experiential requirements distinguish the PMP from other certifications.

- **Category 1** requires a baccalaureate degree, as well as a minimum of 4,500 hours of project management experience in the five PM process groups (initiation, planning, execution, control, and closure; see Chapter 3). The project dates must show three years (36 non-overlapping months) of project management experience within six years. You also need 35 hours of PM training.

- **Category 2** is for candidates without a baccalaureate degree. You must have a minimum of 7,500 hours of project management experience, at least five years of PM experience within eight years. You also must indicate at least 60 unique (non-overlapping) months of PM experience.

Both categories require 35 hours of PM education in a classroom setting. There is no time limit on when you take these classes.

Wait for your eligibility letter

After PMI completes your application, you get an eligibility letter in the mail. If you applied online, you also get an e-mailed version. This letter contains your magic PMI ID number that confirms your eligibility to take the exam. You need this number to apply for the exam, and you must show the letter at the exam site. Save this letter! The eligibility letter expires after six months.

Schedule your exam

After you get your eligibility letter, you have to contact Prometric Test Center (the exam contractor) to schedule an exam appointment. Schedule the exam sometime within the six-month window. To verify your identity, the test center requires your PMI ID number. Because you have already paid PMI for taking the exam, you don't have to pay anything at the Prometric Test Center. Everything is covered in the PMI application fee.

The exam is given via computer at Prometric Test Centers throughout the United States and Canada, and in other countries. Prometric doesn't offer the PMP exam at all of its locations. For a list of testing locations, check www. 2test.com. Here is a shortcut to the Test Center Locator page: www.2test. com/tcl/ZipCode.jsp?pts=1026763528353.

We suggest that you use the Prometric Web site because its automated telephone response system is difficult to navigate. But if you want to call, here are the numbers:

 ✔ In the United States and Canada, dial 800-755-EXAM.

 ✔ In all other countries, dial the U.S. country code and then 410-843-8000.

Inspecting the test question structure

Your exam is prepared from 200 questions that are randomly selected from PMI's question database. Each question has four response choices. You select the *best* answer — best according to the PMI methodology. Your answers are all single choices. (The test no longer offers possible answers that are combinations such as "A and B" or "all of the above.")

Some of the questions refer to the same information. Answering one question in a set might help you determine the answer to another question. The group of questions might be in a random order, so you might have to go backward or jump forward. Mark these questions so you can check on them later.

The biggest single reason people miss questions is that they go too fast and don't read the question carefully. Some of the questions are simple definitions of PM terms. About 40 percent of the questions relate to situations (given a set of facts, what would you do?). There are also some questions where you apply your knowledge of commonly used PM formulas.

What percentage of questions relate to each exam section?

The following list shows the breakdown of questions. Planning, Execution, and Control comprise the bulk of the exam. Initiation and Closing have the least number of questions. Plan your study time accordingly!

Initiation	17 questions
Planning	47 questions
Execution	47 questions
Control	46 questions
Closing	14 questions
Professional Responsibilities	29 questions

During each of the phases, you'll repeat steps and functions, and the processes overlap and integrate. You'll see questions on managing *Integration, Scope, Time, Cost, Quality, Human Resources, Communications, Risk,* and *Procurement.*

Criteria for passing the exam

A passing score is 68.5 percent — 137 correct answers. This exam is pass or fail. Scoring 137 is the same passing grade as a perfect 200.

If you score less than passing, you can retake the exam. You can't take the exam more than twice in a six-month period.

What the Exam Measures

We work on breaking down the important things for you as the book proceeds. The next section starts off showing a few things to keep in mind as you think about the scope of the material that you'll have to study.

Creating a study plan

Check out our sample study plan on the CD. You must personalize any study plan to suit your individual skills, experience, and needs, but we give you some general tips throughout the book and on the CD.

The study plan is your *project plan* for taking the certification exam. You are the project manager.

Memorizing key lists

To answer many of the exam questions, you have to know definitions, terms, jargon, formulas, and various lists of processes. Here are five major lists to memorize (we help you master them, starting in Chapter 2):

- ✔ Five project management processes
- ✔ Nine knowledge areas
- ✔ 39 component processes
- ✔ Component process interactions
- ✔ Formulas

Study tips

Throughout this book, we give you some tips on how to master the material. We suggest mnemonics, give you study tips and memorization tips, and point out traps.

Deciphering repeated patterns

PMPs excel at discovering and learning repeated patterns. It's what makes the methodology so useful. The material has lots of repeated patterns that you'll discover in each chapter.

Color-coding process groups as an aid to memory

Relationships among the process groups are broken into *core* and *facilitating* processes. Each of the 39 component processes is either a core or facilitating process.

Consider coding these with different-colored markers. Use more garish colors for the single initiating process and the two closing processes. The bulk of the processes are in the other three — planning, execution, and controlling.

Tracking Your Study Plan by Using PMI Methodology

The exam requires a serious commitment. Most of the people we know from local PMI chapters take an unpaid week off before the exam and cram for the last 40 hours. Additionally, the average study plan calls for at least 180 hours of preparation time. That's about 4½ weeks. So, we're going to set up a study plan for you to customize. Although the study plan contains some accelerated tools to help you, you must use it consistently throughout the book. Remember, it's the same methodology that will be on the exam. The best way to pass the exam is to use the methodology on sample projects.

Your exam is the product of your project

You are now being assigned to a new project. We'll call the project by a catchy name: (insert your name here)'s PMP Exam Prep Project, or your own personal *PEPP*. You are the project manager for the PEPP project and are accountable for achieving a successful outcome. You have all the power necessary to make things happen. The product of your PEPP project is passing the exam. The distinction between the project and the product of the project is fertile exam question material; see Chapter 2 for details.

Project scheduling tools to plan your exam baseline

The sample study plan on the CD uses a few of the included tools to create a project plan. That's a project plan in the *PMBOK Guide* sense. According to the modern PM definition, a *project plan* contains all the information about the project; it's not just the schedule. We'll start with creating a *project charter*, or defining document, from a simple template. Then you'll master how to create a *work breakdown structure* — an organizational hierarchy chart for your project. You find out how to *decompose* tasks and activities by using WBS Chart software. You'll set some key dates by using the Milestones Professional application. Print these milestone charts and keep them at your desk for motivation. We'll use a template for Microsoft Project Schedule to tie all this together and chart your progress.

As you move forward, you'll set up a network diagram. Network diagrams were formerly called PERT charts, so you may be familiar with them. You'll calculate the *critical path*. You can expect some critical path types of questions on the exam.

We show you how to set up and graph the schedule and the budget for the PEPP project.

Project controls on your study progress

After you have a baseline, you'll get to study the material and track your progress. The project controls that you'll master include variances from time and cost baselines. We'll be charting your progress along the way so you can graphically see how to control your exam study plan and manage your time and effort. The Gantt chart tools are a great aid for this.

Measuring your earned value

Earned value analysis (EVA) tells a project manager about the "health" of the project. EV analysis is an elegant method showing how budgets and schedules work in unison. You'll see how your earned value plots out on a graph.

Chapter 2

Exam Basics and Study Tips

• •

In This Chapter

▶ Identifying exam essentials

▶ Tricks and traps

▶ Types of questions

▶ Learning tips in this book

▶ Question breakdown structure

▶ Studying basic materials

• •

*I*n this chapter, we share our strategies for answering the exam questions. Our goal is to improve your chances of passing the exam. We give you insights from successful PMP candidates we've met. Without exception, they say this was the most challenging exam they've ever taken; no other certification exam comes close. In this chapter, we tell you where to concentrate your efforts and why it pays off.

Because the exam covers more than is covered in the *PMBOK Guide,* we advise you on what to study and how to approach it. Not only should you know the definitions like the inputs, tools and techniques, and outputs, but you also need to think like a PM to answer situational questions. Reading the *PMBOK Guide* gives you the definitions of terms from a skills perspective (from the knowledge areas). You can't pass the exam without reviewing the *PMBOK Guide* several times.

Thinking Horizontally and Vertically

Use this book in conjunction with the *PMBOK Guide.* We help you coordinate your studying with its potentially bewildering mass of material. As you read this book and that bulky bible of the PMI, be aware of a fundamental difference in approach.

This book follows the chronological flow of a project, from initiation through closeout. The core function of a project manager is *Integration* — making sure that all required processes, inputs, tools and techniques, and outputs come together at each step of the lifecycle. We stress how a PM handles the integration of all aspects of the project.

The *PMBOK Guide* presents a more complicated view — encompassing the horizontal project flow in time, as well as a vertical dimension — of skills and knowledge you apply to all processes. Don't worry; we cover that vertical dimension, too, but within the context of the process flow. This will help you think more like a PM, dealing with issues as you'd encounter them in an actual project.

Passing the exam is *thinking* like a PMI project manager, being able to handle typical scenarios that a PM may face on the job.

The Secret Scheme of Tricks and Traps

PMI's Certification Board has put a lot of time and effort into the exam. Test design professionals work with PMPs to develop the questions. Draft versions of the questions go through a process to eliminate unintended barriers, unintended clues, or other potential problems. Questions are grouped, tested for validity, and continually measured for effectiveness on the exam.

Knowing the types of questions

Knowing the types of questions you'll see on the exam will save you time. The types of questions correspond to cognitive levels:

- **Recall questions** involve spitting back the material stored in your memory. These are mostly definitions of terms. Recall questions are most of the exam.

  Some recall questions can be tricky. For example, a question may ask you to identify which process has a step or when in the lifecycle a process first starts. So memorize the definitions and the lists in their proper sequences.

- **Application questions** pose a situation that any PMP can be reasonably expected to handle. To answer these questions, use your knowledge of facts and procedures that you know and understand from experience. Many of the sample questions in this book are situational, and we point out their trickier aspects in the answers. Many of the math questions are of this type; these include questions that deal with probability, discounted cash flows, and earned value calculations.

✔ **Analysis questions** require you to demonstrate your understanding of the relationships among facts, principles, methods, and procedures. To answer questions at this higher situational level, break the material into its components. These are the least common questions on the exam.

You must also understand organizational structure and interrelationships. For example, an analysis question may ask you to find the critical path if an activity is late. Or you may be asked, given changed circumstances, whether another path would become the critical path.

Learning Tips

No matter how you cut it, you'll have to spend time simply memorizing information, such as the definition of terms. Memorization is a skill that increases with motivation. You'll find yourself charged up at the beginning of your studying. As you move forward, you'll find the material pretty dry, and you'll lose some of your motivation. About a month or two into your studying, you'll have to find ways of challenging yourself.

Memory aid tricks

Throughout this book and on our Web site (www.projectmania.com), we offer some suggestions on grouping items as *mnemonics,* or shorthand ways of recalling complex information. We give you mnemonics for the nine knowledge areas and some of the 39 process interactions.

Recognizing patterns in questions

Simple test-taking tricks can help you answer more questions in the allotted time. One helpful trick is deciphering repeated *patterns* in the question. The pattern is the form in which a question is posed rather than its content. You have to be observant to uncover the patterns; they're not always obvious.

The sequence of the questions on the test doesn't yield any clues; the 200 questions appear in random order.

Even though the exam creators spend a great deal of time removing unintended barriers and clues, you can apply some patterns to figure out what answer the question might be seeking. We point out these patterns in the answers to the sample questions in this book.

As you read a question, determine what its pattern is or, at least, try to identify some aspect of the pattern. Don't let the suggested answers influence the pattern that you select. Determining the pattern for the question helps you eliminate bad responses, improving your chances for success.

Here are some tips for deciphering repeated patterns:

✔ Determine whether the question is looking for matching the pattern or the exception to the pattern.

✔ Find out if the question is looking for an input, tool and technique, or an output.

✔ Determine what process group the question covers.

✔ Identify what knowledge area the question covers.

Here are the two basic types of patterns:

✔ **Matching:** A question that calls for a matching pattern names a series of items and asks you to pick the item in the responses that's most nearly like the others:

> *Banana* is a match for apple, orange, and grapefruit.

✔ **Exception:** The exception pattern presents you with a list of items and asks you to identify the one that doesn't belong:

> Among apple, brick, orange, and grapefruit, *brick* is the exception.

Another term for an exception pattern is a *mismatch*. Some questions will ask which of the following four terms are inputs to a particular process. You have to know which term is an input to that particular process — only one choice is correct — and which of the remaining three terms don't belong to that process, or are outputs, or are tools and techniques.

Here are some sample test questions for the types of patterns:

✔ Which of the following processes *belongs* to Project Risk Management? *[Match pattern]*

✔ Which of the following processes *does not belong* to Project Risk Management? *[Exception pattern]*

For the preceding risk question, the answer depends on whether the question is seeking the match or the exception. Remember that PMI's question bank probably contains both the *belongs to* and the *doesn't belong to* variations of this question, so you could get either one. Read the question carefully.

Pace yourself when reading the questions. Take special care in reading word problems that contain dates, lists of figures, or dollar amounts. They're not meant to be read fast. If you're not sure of the question or the pattern in the question, read it again. Look for key words and phrases in the question, such as:

- ✔ Best or worst
- ✔ First or last
- ✔ Belongs to or does not belong
- ✔ Must or except for
- ✔ Most effective or least effective
- ✔ First or last
- ✔ Greatest or least
- ✔ Most helpful or least helpful
- ✔ Not including
- ✔ Key activity
- ✔ Preferred response

Becoming test-wise

Identifying patterns in questions, as described in the preceding section, will improve your score on the exam. It can also help you eliminate incorrect choices. For example, if you know the question pattern is looking for an output as the answer, you can eliminate all choices that are in tools and techniques, inputs, or process groups. In the fruit example in the preceding section, the mismatch was the brick.

Red herrings

Be on the lookout for red herrings, or extraneous details, in questions. Extra details are put there to throw you off track. You need to be able to translate a word problem into the correct pattern and then determine what information is relevant. Often in the earned value and contract cost/profit questions, you have to sort out bits of information. If you know the right pattern and formula, you can focus on what's relevant and forget about the rest. Note that sometimes the part that is not relevant in one question might be vital to another group or give you a clue in solving a series of questions.

Question sets

Although the order of exam questions is random, sometimes questions occur in related pairs, sets, or groups. For example, a set of questions might relate to a particular diagram. Within a set, you'll likely find extraneous details in one question that are relevant to another question.

A set of questions that refers to the same diagram, formula, or word problem is a *scenario*. The random order of questions disperses the scenario throughout the test; two questions in the same scenario might be separated by 50 questions. Unless you're looking for a pattern, you might forget about it, along with those useful red herrings. As if to further aggravate you, a later question in the set might give you the information you need to solve a previous question. So don't be afraid to mark questions and go back through your answers.

Although the exam is computer-based, you'll receive a few sheets of scratch paper. For questions that belong to the same set, make notes on your scratch paper; you may find the information useful for answering other questions. For example, if you see a network diagram on the test, probably more than one question refers to it. Skim the questions to see how many of them refer to the same diagram. Required calculations might include the early start date of a particular task, the critical path, and the float for a particular task. You might be able to easily answer the early start date if it was the first question in the set, in which case the rest of the tasks in the network would be irrelevant. Yet, those other tasks in the network would be vital to determining the critical path. If you've already completed the forward and backward pass in the network to find the critical path, you have the basis for solving the float. Checking the answer on a scratch sheet will save time.

Another example is an EV question set in which you have to estimate the EAC. You might have previously answered other questions in that scenario that have relevant data. For example, one question might tell you how much work was completed and another how much work remains. By combining data from both questions, you can solve the last question in the set.

You can use any of these test-taking techniques by itself or in combination with others. Any of these that help you to eliminate an incorrect answer, find the right answer, or logically choose between two close choices is well worth the time that you'll put in to applying them in practice sessions.

This book contains Quick Assessment questions at the beginning of each chapter. In the margins beside the questions, you'll see section headings, which indicate where you can find the answers for the questions. These section headings are pattern indicators.

The Vocabulary of Project Management

Know the terms and their definitions. This is the core of the exam. You need to memorize and know more than 500 project management terms that describe the methodology.

You might think that questions involving definitions would be pretty straight-forward. Wrong! The questions drill down to finer levels of detail to determine whether you understand what the definitions mean. You're not only expected to know the definitions of many terms but also must be able to make subtle distinctions between them. We've seen distinctions so arcane that many senior managers, like the ones who might hire you or manage you, don't understand them. We've explained some of those nuances to senior managers. This is one type of question for which experience isn't necessarily the best teacher.

The *PMBOK Guide* contains many lists of terms that make up the process steps needed to run a successful project. We explain the terms, give you insights on what's important in the definitions, as well as make distinctions that can represent shades of meaning. We show you the areas and concepts that PMI stresses throughout the methodology. They are repeated so often that we'll identify these for you as *mantras* through the chapters. Familiarize yourself with these mantras, which give you further insight into the PMI mindset and the "approved" methodology.

Always answer the questions from PMI's perspective, even if you know a better answer.

Splitting hairs

We've spoken with many PMs who have years of experience practicing their craft. You'd think it would be easy for them to pass the certification exam. Yet, it isn't easy for anyone, and passing isn't a sure bet. Why shouldn't a project management practitioner with over ten years of experience pass the test without even cracking a book?

Some PMs cite conflicting methods, terms, and hair-splitting differences between the *PMBOK Guide* and the methodologies promoted by their companies, by PM gurus, and by other experts. We show you some of these hair-splitting distinctions — not to impress you with how clever we are, but to help you pick the best choice from several apparently correct answers — and how you how to avoid the traps. Not appreciating those distinctions is the main reason seasoned PMs can fail the test, despite their experience.

The Breakdown of Exam Questions

The actual number of exam questions in each process grouping can be summarized like this:

✔ Initiating the Project: 16 questions

- Determine Project Goals: 2 questions

- Determine Deliverables: 2 questions

- Determine Process Outputs: 1 question

- Document Project Constraints: 1 question

- Document Assumptions: 2 questions

- Define Project Strategy: 1 question

- Identify Performance Requirements: 2 questions

- Determine Resource Requirements: 2 questions

- Define Project Budget: 1 question

- Provide Comprehensive Information: 2 questions

✔ Planning the Project: 47 questions

- Refine Project Requirements: 8 questions

- Create WBS: 7 questions

- Develop Resource Management Plan: 6 questions

- Refine Time and Cost Estimates: 6 questions

- Establish Project controls: 6 questions

- Develop Project Plan: 7 questions

- Obtain Plan Approval: 7 questions

✔ Executing the Project: 48 questions

- Commit Project Resources: 10 questions

- Implement Project Plan: 9 questions

- Manage Project Progress: 11 questions

- Communicate Project Progress: 9 questions

- Implement Quality Assurance Procedures: 9 questions

✔ Controlling the Project: 45 questions

- Measure Project Performance: 7 questions

- Refine Control Limits: 4 questions

- Take Corrective Action: 7 questions

- Evaluate Effectiveness of Corrective Action: 5 questions

- Ensure Plan Compliance: 7 questions

- Reassess Control Plans: 4 questions

- Respond to Risk Event Triggers: 6 questions

- Monitor Project Activity: 5 questions

✔ Closing the Project: 14 questions

- Obtain Acceptance of Deliverables: 4 questions

- Document Lessons Learned: 2 questions

- Facilitate Closure: 3 questions

- Preserve Product Records and Tools: 3 questions

- Release Project Resources: 2 questions

✔ Professional Responsibility: 29 questions

- Ensure Professionalism and Integrity: 8 questions

- Contribute to Knowledge Base: 3 questions

- Enhance Individual Competence: 5 questions

- Balance Stakeholder Interests: 7 questions

- Interact with Team and Stakeholders: 6 questions

Anticipating the Exam

People generally tell us that the PMP exam is the toughest exam they have taken. Their feedback and general tips have been instrumental in creating advice for your exam prep. The exam is not that hard intellectually, but you need to focus all your concentration and effort on it. Passing is largely a measure of your commitment and discipline. We point out what's important in the elephant-sized *PMBOK Guide,* which is the source of most questions. Although memorizing the five process groups, nine knowledge areas, 39 component processes, 186 inputs, 137 tools and techniques, and 113 outputs is important, it's not enough. You have to *think* like PMI's idealized PM. Most questions are pretty straightforward, but you need to know what information to eliminate when you answer.

Budgeting your time is not only important during the exam but also during your preparation. Knowing what to study isn't that obvious. Project management is an emerging professional discipline with strict certification requirements.

As the PMI defines it, the PMBOK is literally every book ever written on every project management topic, and then some. The *PMBOK Guide* is a summary (albeit lengthy) of that material. If you were to study every book PMI recommends for the exam, you'd have a very long and costly reading list. So, for many, the initial hurdle is to figure out what to study. Throughout the chapters, we cover the core concepts on the exam. And we often include cross-references to specific pages in the *PMBOK Guide*. However, many of the concepts we cover aren't found there. Thirty to 40 percent of the exam relates to other sources. We summarize that content here, as well. And on our Web site (www.projectmania.com), we have lots of resources for project management theory, principles, techniques, and procedures. And many more prep questions and answers.

As a professional, you'll already have a handle on at least part of the material. Be alert to your weaknesses and knowledge gaps. For example, some of the terms and definitions in your industry or company may be different from those in the *PMBOK Guide*. Knowing where to concentrate your efforts is the secret to passing the exam with minimal pain.

After you have planned where you need to concentrate your studying, execute your study plan as meticulously as you would work on any other project. You'll get there. Make studying part of your daily routine. The average person spends four to five weeks studying over three to five months.

On our Web site, a downloadable wall chart will help you memorize all the component process interactions. It shows the inputs, tools and techniques, and outputs to the 39 component processes. It's grouped by knowledge area. We recommend that you print several copies of this chart so you can make notes on it. With these copies in hand, you can study the material in different ways. Try color-coding each of the 39 component processes and grouping them by their five process groups — this yields a 6- to 8-point return on your exam score. Indicate whether the 39 component processes are core or facilitating processes — this is a short exercise yielding about 3- to 5-point return. Link the outputs of one process to the inputs of another process. Knowing the process can yield up to a 10-point return.

Keep your study material handy wherever you go. When you have a few minutes, read the definitions and skim the chapters of this book. Try making your study session a quiz to challenge yourself. For example, read the term and repeat the definition to yourself — before actually reading the definition. Vary your starting point; open the book at the end one day and in the middle another — instead of always starting from the beginning. Keep your quiz scores handy. Don't worry about making low scores, especially in the beginning. Use them as a guide to show you where you need to improve.

Chapter 3

Project Management Basics

In This Chapter

▶ Speaking the jargon

▶ Getting the PM context

▶ Distinguishing the five process management groups

▶ Distinguishing nine knowledge areas

▶ Structuring the 39 component processes

▶ Understanding process interactions

This chapter is your introduction to the project management methodology. We survey critical areas of study, pointing out where to pay particular attention and put extra effort. It's also a guide to the methodology as it's explained in further detail in the rest of the book. We give insight into what's important, why it's important, and how to use it.

This chapter explores the repeatable processes used in all projects. We focus on how PMI methodology addresses the principles, practices, and procedures for performing project management. We break down the components of PMI's methodology to discover some fundamental groupings for exam questions.

Benefiting from PM Methodology

Projects benefit from following a formal methodology. The dictionary defines *methodology* as a body of practices, procedures, and rules used by those who work in a discipline or engage in an inquiry. Following a formal methodology helps you stay in control — and keep your sanity.

Project Management Context

Projects and project management operate in an environment broader than that of the project itself. That broader environment is the *context* of project management. The next few sections examine it.

Organizational culture and structure

Organizations are typically ongoing businesses with distinct cultures, values, styles, and norms. The formal business attire on Wall Street represents a distinct cultural norm, unlike that of the T-shirts and jeans culture in dot-com companies.

Here is a rundown of the different types of organizations:

- ✔ **Functional organization:** The hierarchy in which each employee has one clear superior.

- ✔ **Projectized organization:** Most of organization's resources are involved in project work. Team members report to a project manager, who is independent and has a great deal of authority.

- ✔ **Matrix organization:** A blend of both functional and projectized organizations.

General management skills

General management covers the broad range of functions that keep an organization running. These functions include

- ✔ Finance and accounting, marketing and sales, research and development, operations, human resources, manufacturing, and distribution

- ✔ Planning — strategic, operational, and tactical

- ✔ Organizational structure, organizational behavior, and personnel

- ✔ Personal disciplines — time management, stress management, and communications

- ✔ Leadership (as opposed to management), influencing the organization, negotiating, and problem solving

These functions and their skills require influence and interact with project management.

Social, economic, and environmental influences

Projects often must accommodate social, economic, and environmental influences, standards, regulations, and compliance issues. We have to account for internationalization and cultural differences. The International Standards Organization (ISO) makes these distinctions:

✔ A *standard* is a "document approved by a recognized body that provides, for common and repeated use, rules, guidelines, or characteristics for products, processes, or services with which compliance is not mandatory."

Compliance with standards is not mandatory.

✔ A *regulation* is a "document, which lays down products, processes, or service characteristics, including the applicable administrative provisions, with which compliance is mandatory."

Compliance with regulations is mandatory.

Setting Your Sights on PM

You will need to memorize lots of terms for the exam. This gives project managers a common vocabulary.

Here are the three most basic terms you need to know for the exam:

✔ A **project** is a temporary endeavor undertaken to create a unique product, service, or result.

✔ **Programs** are groups of related projects managed in a coordinated way to obtain benefits not available from managing them individually.

✔ **Project management** is the application of knowledge, skills, tools, and techniques to project activities to meet project requirements in order to meet or exceed stakeholders' needs and expectations from a project.

Taking a closer look at projects

The key points to remember about projects are that they are both *temporary* and *unique*.

Temporary

The word *temporary* separates project work from ongoing operations because a project has specific start and end dates. Ongoing operations have a start date but not an end date; they sustain the business. Here are a few examples:

✔ A newspaper is an ongoing operation. The Sunday edition of the paper is a project.

✔ A TV series is an ongoing operation. A single episode is a project.

✔ Producing and distributing a movie is a project.

✔ Software development is a project. Keeping that software running is a long-term effort that sustains the business in its ongoing operations.

A program-oriented approach

An example of a program that Pete faced recently was at a Hollywood movie studio that creates cartoons. The company had a standards group in the IT department responsible for ensuring that all software applications used the same types of computers and programming tools. All the divisions were to be informed about volume discounts on purchases, and management encouraged them to leverage programmers' application-development knowledge to reduce costs for new software. The IT group managed each division as a separate project. Each division claimed unique requirements and maintained separate standards.

A program-oriented approach would have shown better results. The IT department should have managed all the projects in a coordinated way to ensure that the benefits of a comprehensive standards program exceeded the boundaries of a single division. That's the definition of a program. The VP of the department didn't know the distinction between a project and program. As a result, she listed the manager's title as project manager when it should have been program manager. The program could have been more successful if she had understood the distinction.

Being temporary does not imply that the project is short. Many projects, such as building a skyscraper, last for years.

A project reaches the end when one of the following events has occurred:

- ✔ The project's objectives and goals have been *reached.*
- ✔ The project's objectives and goals *cannot be reached,* so the project is cancelled.
- ✔ The *need* for the project no longer exists, so the project is cancelled.

Unique

When applied to projects, the word *unique* means that — unlike the sameness of ongoing, repetitive work — a project sets out to do something new and different. The purpose of a project is to bring about some type of change.

In each TV episode, the story must change to hold your interest and keep you watching. The characters and location might stay the same, but each episode must be unique in some way. (Nope, TV reruns don't qualify as projects.)

Defining the org chart

A team usually handles the project work, and project teams can range from one person to thousands. The organizational (org) chart shows who will do what work and defines reporting relationships. Org charts usually don't show all the stakeholders in a project — just the members of the project team.

A *stakeholder* is anyone involved in the project and whose interests may be affected by the project. This includes all team members and project managers, company operational executives to which the program manager reports, and internal and external clients.

On the organizational chart hierarchy, many project managers will often report to a single program manager. Over the years, we've seen many defense contractors on complex development projects. As an example of organizational structure, we take a look at the PM organization for the FX Fighter project.

The FX Program Manager is responsible for designing, building, and testing the new FX aircraft from beginning to end. After the program manager turns over the completed design to production, the project is completed. The plane then moves into an ongoing operations phase, which is generally a longer period of time than the development project. The program manager is likely to have lots of experience. He has a large staff on this project, including the following project managers.

- ✔ **FX Avionics Senior Project Manager:** Responsible for any and all electronic systems throughout the design, build, and test phases. This includes radios, radars, receivers, computers, offensive electronics (called "jammers"), defensive avionics (including flare and chaff dispensers, as well as electronic ghost image generators), instrument-landing systems, electronic flight displays and instruments, and so on. The FX Avionics Senior Project Manager is responsible for avionics, navigation, and control systems.

  She is likely to have a PMP certification and lots of experience. She would have under her an Avionics Project Manager for cockpit displays, a project manager for weapons, a project manager for defensive electronic warfare, a project manager for offensive electronic warfare, and so on. Each subgroup might consist of six to eight engineers as team members. Each team, in turn, might have an engineer serving as team lead. The team lead would most likely be an engineering manager. In some cases, he could be a CAPM.

- ✔ **FX Flight Controls Project Manager:** Responsible for the design and integration of all electronic, hydraulic, and pneumatic devices that drive the flying surfaces (such as ailerons, rudder, and elevators). His team ensures that no spurious signals enter the flight-control systems and that the plane is jam-proof from outside signals.

- ✔ **FX Weapons System Project Manager:** Responsible for the integration of all weapons into the FX system: guns, bombs, rockets, mines, and whatever is envisioned for the future. All weapons must be independent from all other systems to be carried safely and employed accurately.

Understanding progressive elaboration

Progressive elaboration combines the concepts of *temporary* and *unique*. Because the product of the project is unique, you will know more about the project and its requirements as you move forward in your project work. Early in the project, these descriptions are broadly defined, but you must make them more explicit as the work continues. If you don't or can't, something's wrong.

Many of the processes that we show you are *iterative;* they are *repeatable* steps. They repeat as you know more about the project and repeat again as you advance to other phases. With each iteration, your notions about the project and its product become more detailed. That's progressive elaboration. It's another reason why you have to update your documentation, because it keeps changing.

Most PM definitions hinge on whether an issue or resource is project-related. To fall within the discipline of project management, all work activities and requirements must relate to project work — it is not operational in nature or otherwise extra to the project. If something is not related to the project exclusively, it is *out of scope,* unauthorized, and should not be permitted.

Understanding PM Models

All projects are comprised of a series of processes. Taken together, these processes create a model, or mental picture, for PM methodology.

What is a process?

A *process* is a series of actions, changes, or functions that bring about a result. A process can also be a series of operations performed in the making or treatment of a product. Processes are iterative; their steps are repeatable. Processes are also *integrative;* many processes can work together, in coordination.

The following processes overlap and interact throughout a project:

   ✔ **Project management processes:** Describe, organize, and complete the work of the project. Project management processes involve the business area. The interaction of these processes is at the core of PM methodology. It includes 39 component processes that you need to master.

✔ **Product-oriented processes:** Specify and create the product or service. Product-oriented processes involve the technical area and are more likely to involve a project's life cycle. For example, product-oriented processes typically include a design phase, a development phase, and a test phase.

Diving into the matrix

The framework for the PM methodology is based on a matrix with two dimensions. The first dimension of the model is time — the way project work flows from its start date through to its end date. This section explores some basics along this time dimension.

Projects start and close. Because of the unique nature of projects, there is a certain degree of risk. The risk is that the desired result might not be the outcome you'd hoped to see. (In fact, you might say that PM is a management technique to reduce risk.) Breaking projects into smaller steps, or phases, helps reduce that risk. Taken together, these phases comprise a *project life cycle.*

At the end of each phase, there are some results, or *deliverables.* A deliverable is a tangible, verifiable work product. Some examples of deliverables are a movie script, a working prototype, an analysis, a software application or database, a blueprint, a design, linear feet of poured concrete, and a feasibility study.

✔ **Tangible** describes something that's provable or written down. A verbal report or any idea that's not expressed in writing doesn't satisfy the definition. A result needs to be documented to be tangible.

✔ **Verifiable** means that there is some form of inspection as part of the controlling processes. Generally, inspections come at the end of each *work package,* or unit of work, and at the end of each phase. Inspections at the ends of phases are generally referred to as phase (or stage) gates, phase exits, or kill points. These milestone events require an inspection and approval before the project is handed off to the next phase. If approval is withheld, the project is canceled, hence the term *kill point.* Examples of project phases are feasibility, requirements, design, build, development, test, startup, and turnover.

Sometimes you'll begin a subsequent phase prior to approval of the previous phase. This is called *fast tracking.*

Phases divide the project into segments as a way of providing better control. This segmentation also helps align appropriate links to ongoing operations — providing *ramp-up* and *ramp-down* periods. During a ramping up, costs and staff start out at a low level. They rise higher toward the middle of a phase and then drop off, or ramp down, when the phase or the project closes.

The chance of project success is lowest at the start of the project and gets progressively higher as the project continues. Risk is highest at the start of the project and gets progressively lower as the project continues.

The costs of changes and error correction increase as the project continues. For example, the cost of changing an application design document is minimal compared with the cost of making that change after thousands of hours have been invested in coding. The cost of making a change in an engineering blueprint is millions less than tearing down and reconstructing a bridge.

Distinguishing the Five Process Management Groups

This section shows how processes overlap and interact throughout the project. You absolutely must know this material for the exam. You will also use it as a reference for other chapters in this book. Figure 3-1 shows these relationships.

Project Management Processes

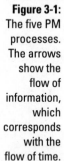

Figure 3-1:
The five PM processes. The arrows show the flow of information, which corresponds with the flow of time.

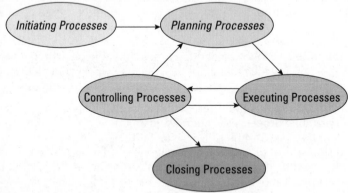

Distinguishing the Nine Knowledge Areas

The specialized knowledge and practices of project management are organized into nine distinct business skills, called the nine knowledge areas (see Figure 3-2).

Remembering the five PM processes

We have a great memory trick to help you remember the five PM processes. Make a fist with your hand. Because you open your fist by using your thumb first, the thumb is an aid to opening or initiating the project. The pinky is the last finger to close on a fist, so it is an aid to closing the project. If you think about what it means to wear a wedding ring on your fourth finger, you'll never forget controlling a project. The index finger relates to planning because it's the first finger to close in making a fist. The middle finger relates to executing; you can probably think of several reasons it's the strongest finger, but a useful reason is that it's the last finger after you've accounted for the others.

- Thumb — Opening
- Index — Planning
- Middle — Executing
- Ring — Controlling
- Pinky — Closing

These skills are the second dimension of the matrix. This dimension has nothing to do with time. You can draw on these skills at any step of a project. They are fundamental business skills that are particularly useful on projects. You'll be using these nine knowledge areas all the time, and you should memorize them for the exam. Understanding these knowledge areas will enable you to appreciate how projects and businesses operate, making you a more sophisticated manager.

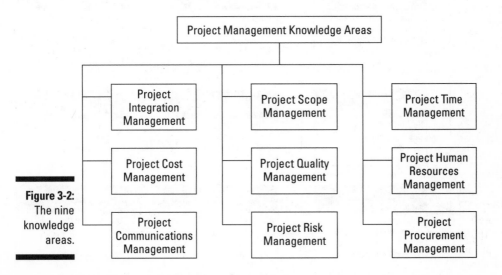

Figure 3-2:
The nine knowledge areas.

Correlating the Processes, Knowledge Areas, and Exam Parts

The nine knowledge areas break down into 39 component processes, as shown in Figure 3-3. Think of these process interactions as containers — small building blocks making up larger blocks. (For those of you in IT, it's the object-oriented principle of encapsulation.) These terms are explained and applied elsewhere in this book.

Each of the 39 component processes fits across the time dimension, mapping inside the five process groups, as shown in Figure 3-4. Each is either a core or facilitating process:

- ✔ **Core processes** have understandable dependencies that must be performed in the same order on all projects.

- ✔ **Facilitating processes** depend on the nature of the project. They are performed intermittently as needed, but they are not optional.

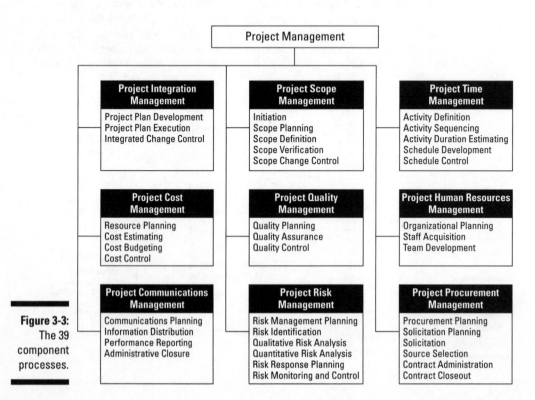

Figure 3-3: The 39 component processes.

Project Management

Project Integration Management	Project Scope Management	Project Time Management
Project Plan Development	Initiation	Activity Definition
Project Plan Execution	Scope Planning	Activity Sequencing
Integrated Change Control	Scope Definition	Activity Duration Estimating
	Scope Verification	Schedule Development
	Scope Change Control	Schedule Control

Project Cost Management	Project Quality Management	Project Human Resources Management
Resource Planning	Quality Planning	Organizational Planning
Cost Estimating	Quality Assurance	Staff Acquisition
Cost Budgeting	Quality Control	Team Development
Cost Control		

Project Communications Management	Project Risk Management	Project Procurement Management
Communications Planning	Risk Management Planning	Procurement Planning
Information Distribution	Risk Identification	Solicitation Planning
Performance Reporting	Qualitative Risk Analysis	Solicitation
Administrative Closure	Quantitative Risk Analysis	Source Selection
	Risk Response Planning	Contract Administration
	Risk Monitoring and Control	Contract Closeout

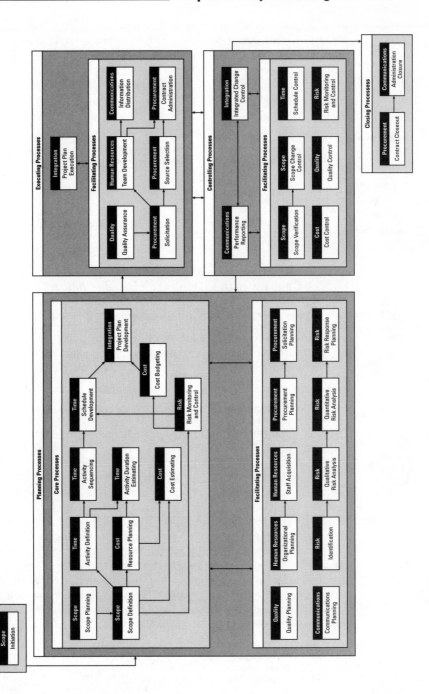

Figure 3-4:
The core and facilitating processes combined.

It's important to master the way the knowledge areas map to the process groups. Every skill in the knowledge areas interacts and is defined by various internal processes. Each of the component processes is defined by the same three groupings called the component process interactions: inputs, tools and techniques, and outputs. Figure 3-5 is an example of these relationships.

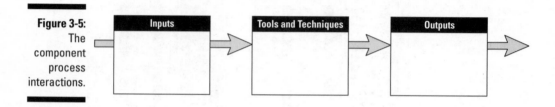

Figure 3-5:
The component process interactions.

All component processes have at least one interaction; none are empty. Figure 3-6 illustrates this. Think of *tools and techniques* as a single grouping.

✔ **Inputs** are documents, or documentable items, that will be acted upon.

✔ **Tools and techniques** are mechanisms applied to inputs to create outputs. A tool is a mechanism or device used to perform or facilitate some work. This is a group, so you might have only one item.

✔ **Outputs** are documents, or documentable items, that result from a process.

Think of the inputs and outputs as the *nouns* of project management because they are things — *documents* or *items*. Think of techniques as the *verbs* of project management because you have to take some action on these items. (This includes gerunds, the *-ing* form of a verb when it is used as a noun.) For example, a performance report is a noun, a document, so it's an input item (to the Schedule Control process) or an output item (of the Performance Reporting process). Plans, reports, change requests, corrective action, and lessons learned are other PM nouns or items, so they're inputs or outputs. Performance report*ing* and statistical sampl*ing* are verbs — techniques or mechanisms — so they belong in the tools and techniques grouping. This simple distinction only covers techniques as verbs; tools are nouns. Some tool examples are systems, skills, expert judgment, knowledge, analysis, audit, and inspection. These tools, systems, and skills are actions that you take or processes that accomplish something.

	Initiating	Planning	Executing	Controlling	Closing
Project Integration Management		Project Plan Development	Project Plan Execution	Integrated Change Control	
Project Scope Management	Initiation	Scope Planning Scope Definition		Scope Verification Scope Change Control	
Project Time Management		Activity Definition Activity Sequencing Activity Duration Estimating Schedule Development		Schedule Control	
Project Cost Management		Resource Planning Cost Estimating Cost Budgeting		Cost Control	
Project Quality Management		Quality Planning	Quality Assurance	Quality Control	
Project Human Resources Management		Organizational Planning Staff Acquisition	Team Development		
Project Communications Management		Communications Planning	Information Distribution	Performance Reporting	Contract Administration
Project Risk Management		Risk Management Planning Risk Identification Qualitative Risk Analysis Quantitative Risk Analysis Risk Response Planning		Risk Monitoring and Control	
Project Procurement Management		Procurement Planning Solicitation Planning	Solicitation Source Selection Contract Administration		Contract Closeout

Figure 3-6:
The matrix.

Chapter 4

Professional Responsibility

● ●

Exam Objectives

▶ Enhancing individual competence

▶ Establishing professional communications

▶ Ensuring integrity and professionalism

▶ Following standards and regulations

▶ Following the *Professional Code of Conduct*

▶ Respecting intellectual property

▶ Not compromising professional judgment

● ●

The Professional Responsibility area of the exam contains approximately 29 questions. Of the six domains, this area ranks as the fourth most important and contains approximately 14.5 percent of the total exam questions. It's tougher than other areas because almost all the questions are situational.

Quick Assessment

Professional
Code of
Conduct

1 The PMP *Professional Code of Conduct* includes two major areas: _____ and _____.

2 Profession Responsibilities are broken into three categories: _____, _____, and _____.

3 By overstating your experience on the PMP application, which area have you violated?

Balancing
Stakeholders'
Interests

4 During your initial planning sessions on a new project, the project sponsor (who has hired you) wants some additional functions and features that are clearly outside the project charter. How should the project manager best handle the situation?

5 During your final customer acceptance session, the customer refuses to accept your product and wants additional functions and features that are clearly outside the original contract. Since the project is under budget, the customer claims the additional work should be covered under the contract. How can the project manager best handle the situation?

6 As senior project manager on an internal project, you discover that an Engineering project manager's schedule estimates for his group will overextend the schedule for the entire team. This Engineering team's critical path work is also crucial technically to delivering the new product. You are afraid engineering is padding the estimates. The Engineering project manager claims he made his schedule on the basis of running Monte Carlo simulations. He claims he was following the generally approved method for developing schedule estimates. What can you do?

Responsibility
to Customers
and to the
Public

7 The customer's representative invites you out to dinner. You're ahead of schedule and right on the estimated $5-million budget. The representative confides that his company will have difficulty paying for your project's contract. He believes that the company might be forced into seeking bankruptcy protection from the courts. This information is confidential, so you have an obligation to your customer to keep it confidential. However, your consulting company has been contracted to handle this work, and your boss might be stuck with a financial loss. How do you handle this situation?

Answers

1 Responsibilities to the Profession and Responsibilities to Customers and the Public. See "Professional Code of Conduct."

2 Compliance, Professional Practices, and Professional Advancement Project Plan. See "Professional Code of Conduct."

3 Compliance with all organizational rules and policies. See "Compliance with all organizational rules and policies."

4 The project manager has a mission to ensure that he properly defines and completes the work of the project. Gold-plating additional functions and features outside the scope must not become requirements. This question tests your understanding of relationships among facts, methods, and principles.

5 The project manager has a clear mission to be truthful, accurate, and technically correct with regard to project scope and other requirements. You must properly define and complete all the work of the project and only the work of the project. The project manager must request that the customer submit a formal change request and pass it through the change control process. This question requires that you show your understanding of relationships among facts, methods, and principles.

6 Withhold judgments until you perform additional verification tests on his results. You also have to perform Quality Control (QC) on the performance of project-related activities. QC's main concern lies in determining the correctness of work results. The results from a Monte Carlo simulation depend on which distribution you select. You'll have to determine if the results are objective or if the Engineering project manager knows how to fudge results. If you suspect that the Engineering project manager is padding his estimates, you'd better be able to develop a more realistic approximation and prove its accuracy. This question tests your understanding of relationships among facts, methods, and principles.

7 Your professional responsibilities obligate you to maintain and respect the confidentiality of this information. However, the partner-in-charge of your consulting firm will fire you if you intentionally withhold information. Ask your partner-in-charge for a update meeting, inform her of the rumors, and suggest that she meet discreetly with the customer's top management to assess the situation. When presented with complex dilemmas, most project managers realize that a wide "gray area" exists in applying ethical principles.

Professional Responsibility

Professional Responsibility is a new area for the *PMBOK Guide* 2000 edition. It represents an all-encompassing domain that covers everything you do as a project manager. Professional Responsibility covers all aspects of how you act and communicate, it defines professional and ethical constraints, and it obligates you to follow professional practices in dealing with customers, sponsors, stakeholders, project team members, as well as other members the profession. Serving as an ethical guideline to ensure a consistent level of professionalism and integrity for all PMPs, the Professional Responsibility standard goes beyond a "do the right thing" attitude and even obligates you to avoid such things as:

- ✔ Any chance of improprieties
- ✔ Looking the other way at improprieties and violations
- ✔ Making do with unrealistic constraints imposed by management

The major result of the Professional Responsibility domain and the Code of Conduct is very simple — it minimizes the risk of any PMP being accused of an inappropriate activity — or even the appearance of inappropriate activity. The secondary result is that it maximizes the project manager's responsibility to make the project work in spite of obstacles such as a contrary customer or bull-headed Minotaur of a sponsor. It implies that if you don't have the authority to get something done, you must figure out a way to get it.

While Professional Responsibility covers approximately 15 percent of the exam, it isn't mentioned in the *PMBOK Guide.* Two separate documents, *PMP Code of Professional Conduct* and *Member Code of Ethics,* cover the main portions of the domain.

To pass the exam and to succeed as a PMP, know the key points of this highly sensitive area. You must also learn to trust your own experience and judgment. As you prepare for the exam, place your emphasis on memorizing and understanding the *Professional Code of Conduct.* The code has two main parts: "Responsibilities to the Profession" and "Responsibilities to Customers and the Public."

These two areas of responsibility are provided as much to protect you and ensure your success as to constrain your actions. All PMPs agree that the addition of this "do the right thing" attitude to our duties has significant implications for how we deal with customers, sponsors, stakeholders, and the public. It's another sign that the profession is maturing.

The changes in the financial scene force us to view this Professional Responsibility and ethics domain in a new light and with increased sensitivity. In this post-Enron era, government authorities are vigorously prosecuting individuals who, at the directives of their bosses, deliberately falsified accounting records and other reports. The companies responsible have been punished financially by Wall Street with billion-dollar stock devaluations. New legislation such as the Corporate Reform Bill will further encourage stockholders to press for organizational governance reforms. PMPs and our projects face greater scrutiny. This fishbowl atmosphere is especially true for projects involving government contracts, regulated industries, and substantial investments, and especially those projects impacting an organization's bottom line. Being a project manager has never been so challenging.

In addition to dealing with increased regulations, we project managers have to deal with the realities of business pressures and organizational behavior. Among the business pressures we'll still face is the triple constraint: Sponsors and customers want their products faster, cheaper, and with greater quality. We'll never escape the fact that our projects are expected to produce future cash flows. As the concept of managing even the organization's routine operations by projects increases, you must align your projects with the organization's strategic goals, taking into account where and how your projects and your products fit into the strategic organizational picture and then communicating this vision to stakeholders. It's a tough juggling act — made even more difficult because many organizations still don't understand how project management fits into their environment. This misfit occurs because project management

- ✔ Isn't a job. It's an organizational function or role that's best handled by an experienced professional.
- ✔ Rarely is handled well by a functional manager who has no project management training and who is attempting to perform double-duty responsibilities.
- ✔ Rarely is handled well when a project manager wears two hats, acting as both a project manager and a functional team member.
- ✔ Usually produces results that are intangible.
- ✔ Rarely is depicted as a separate product of your project.

As an organization witnesses the results of successful, professional project management, that organization will rely even more on its project manager.

Professional Code of Conduct

As part of your acceptance of your PMP, you agree to adhere to PMI's *Professional Code of Conduct.*

The code is pretty simple; it's only two pages long. It's broken into two major areas:

✔ Responsibilities to the Profession

✔ Responsibilities to Customers and the Public

Responsibilities to the Profession

Compliance, Professional Practices, and Professional Advancement Project Plan Profession Responsibilities fall into three categories:

✔ **Compliance:** Following PMI's rules and policies, as well as disclosing conflicts of interest

✔ **Professional practices:** Addresses truthfulness in advertising and representing your experience, as well as complying with laws, regulations, and ethical standards

✔ **Professional advancement:** Includes recognizing the intellectual property of others, supporting the *Professional Code of Conduct,* and distributing the code

Compliance with all organizational rules and policies

This area really concerns PMI as an organization to which you have responsibilities. The compliance section discusses your obligations in all dealings with PMI.

First, you must provide accurate and truthful information for PMP certification, including the

✔ Application

✔ Examination

✔ Fulfillment of continuing education and certification requirements

The PMI takes compliance seriously, as demonstrated in the following examples. If you misrepresent your experience hours, you are in violation and could find your PMP certification revoked because the PMI regularly audits the applications. The organization is serious about the exam, too. You can't remove answer sheets, test questions, or even scratch paper from the exam room. After you pass the exam, you are sent a warning letter indicating your obligation not to divulge specific exam questions to others — not to trainers, teachers, or other candidates.

You have a policing obligation to report violations of the code of conduct by other PMPs. You need to have "a reasonable and clear factual basis" for reporting possible violations. If you know of a possible violation and don't report it, you might face a code violation yourself. You could also be subject to disciplinary action by the ethics committee and could find your PMP certification revoked.

As well as having an obligation to report a possible violation, you must also cooperate with PMI during any investigation into another PMP's alleged ethics violation. The example usually given is that you must actively cooperate if you know another PMP misrepresented his experience on the application. If you don't cooperate with PMI during an investigation, you'd face a code violation yourself and could find your PMP certification revoked. Don't jeopardize your career by stonewalling the PMI.

The last compliance area concerns your obligations to customers, owners, or contractors. You must reveal any significant circumstances that could be construed as a conflict of interest or might give the appearance of any impropriety. We are in an era of "full disclosure." The best policy is to behave as though there are no secrets; be truthful and "upfront" about everything. The conflict of interest area is more fully explained in the next section of the code, "Responsibilities to Customers and the Public." Take the hint that, because PMI covers it twice, it's doubly important.

Professional practice

You are obligated to provide accurate, truthful advertising and representations concerning your qualifications, your experience, and your performance of services on previous projects. For example, Pete interviewed with a CTO who claimed a great deal of PM expertise by saying that every software project he had ever worked on had been a complete success. However, Pete knew the statistics that only 15 percent of all IT projects are successful, so he figured (with an 85 percent probability) that this was just a boastful exaggeration. If the CTO had been a PMP, his misrepresentation would have been a violation of the code. In fact, Pete later learned during the project that the only thing the CTO really knew about PM was to buy a CD with nice-looking project templates. During your next interview, if you're asked whether every single project you worked on was an unqualified success, provide an accurate and truthful account of your experience. Not every project is going to be successful in all areas; all projects involve some compromises. Be truthful about what was successful, what was unsuccessful, and what you learned so that the next project will be even more successful.

Wherever you function as project manager, you're obligated to comply with the laws, regulations, and ethical standards governing professional practice. This mandate implies that you shouldn't conduct business in a country that violates fundamental rights, such as a government that encourages discrimination.

Advancement of the profession

This section of the code reiterates that, as a PMP, you agree to recognize and respect the intellectual property of others. On all professional work and research, you must act in an accurate, truthful, and complete manner. And you agree to support and disseminate the *Professional Code of Conduct* to others.

Contributing to the Project Management Knowledge Base represents approximately three questions on the exam. This responsibility also encompasses assisting future projects by completing your lessons learned and growing Best Practices in the organization. Several other topics have crept into this area. It's your professional responsibility to ensure that the performing organization's policies are followed during the project. When you're working on a federal government contract, you must follow its strict standards.

Rarely is a project perfect. Mistakes and disagreements happen. If a project team member makes a mistake, allow him to fix the problem. If the error is more than a project-related issue — a serious Human Resources issue such as theft, harassment, or discrimination, for example — confer with the project team member's manager and the HR department. All stakeholders, everyone on the team, must work through conflicts that arise from having a different perspective on the product or on the project. You probably will have disagreements with the functional manager over staff resources, for example, or team members will have disagreements. Facilitate and resolve all disagreements. Only if you face an impasse should you take an issue to your sponsor.

Responsibilities to Customers and the Public

Responsibilities to customers and to the public fall into two categories:

- Qualifications, experience, and performance of services
- Conflict of interest and prohibited conduct

Interacting with the project team and stakeholders in a professional and cooperative manner represents approximately six questions, and balancing stakeholder interests represents approximately seven. These areas are tricky and require skillful approaches. Enhancing individual competence contains approximately five questions, and ensuring professionalism and integrity contains approximately eight.

Balancing stakeholders' interests

Project managers often have to balance the needs of conflicting customers when defining a project's scope. You probably will encounter many variants of this balancing act. For example, telling a customer or a sponsor — in many cases is your boss — that he is gold plating the requirements with unnecessary features can be difficult. Diplomatically saying "No" to such requests is an acquired skill. Here's another scenario: As the project manager, you're placed in the middle of two conflicting groups and have to sort out the real requirements of a project.

Conflict is a common dilemma in systems development projects for which accountants want tight controls, but operational managers want unlimited freedom. Project management is supposed to be a discipline in which non-adversarial facilitating is the norm, not the exception, but we've seen scope-definition sessions digress into shouting matches in which other unresolved issues surface. Remember that many project environments are turbulent. The nature of projects stimulates changes. You have to work hard to control the project and the changes it brings.

Every project has to satisfy several groups: the customer, the performing organization, the sponsor, the project team, and you as project manager. It's a truism that when your customer expectations are met or exceeded, the customers are satisfied; but when their expectations aren't met, they're dissatisfied. And they are dissatisfied even when their expectations are totally unrealistic. Haven't you ever had a customer ask for the moon on a string? This expectation factor can affect the perception of how successful your project really is, and you must manage those expectations, however unrealistic they might be.

Ensuring integrity and professionalism

In a National Business Ethics Survey, the Ethics Resource Center concluded that companies are particularly prone to risks of unlawful or unethical behavior when they undergo transitions due to mergers, acquisitions, or restructuring. Since restructuring is commonplace in today's business climate, you need to be aware of the risks. In addition, because projects are temporary by nature, project managers often face similar transition risks at the end of every project. Unfortunately, all too often tools, machinery, and supplies are missing at the end of your project. And you might be accountable for them. Consider what you're up against: KPMG's 2000 Organizational Integrity Survey study observed that 76 percent of employees have witnessed unlawful or unethical conduct.

Let's be truthful and pragmatic. Given today's accelerated pace of business, you probably will be pressured into managing an unrealistic project schedule, to accelerate the schedule (especially toward the end of the project), to increase scope, or to unrealistically decrease the costs. When you face such situations, you're expected to confront your sponsor with the facts backing up your position. You must state that the proposed schedule or budget is unrealistic (or make whatever other truthful disclosure the situation calls for). Yet disclosure is not enough; you must provide a viable solution — a more realistic schedule or budget. You're obligated to prove your case. You're expected to follow the *PMBOK Guide* methodology — defined as Best Practices — as you proceed. Why? These methods provide the most reliable PM controls we have.

This new ethical mindset requires a radical departure from traditional project management. Project managers will have to think more broadly about what the project outcome and success really mean. You are obligated to document unambiguous requirements, plans, decisions, and outcomes — whether successful or unsuccessful. You must ensure the team objectively derives cost, schedule, and technical deliverables. To get specifics in writing, you'll have to confront a particular stakeholder and force the issue. And, throughout the project, you must quality control the PM processes.

Following standards and regulations

This section of the code obligates you to comply with laws, regulations, and ethical standards governing professional practice wherever and whenever you provide project management.

Conflicts of interest

One of the cornerstones of the code is that you have to do everything in your power to avoid a conflict of interest — or anything that might give even the appearance of a conflict of interest. On learning of a possible conflict, the code of conduct requires you to investigate whether the legitimate interests of your customer might be compromised. You must act if you find something has been compromised on your project.

Certainly, you can't accept a gift or favor from a vendor or customer if it might influence your decision-making. Remember the "favor bank" works both ways. Everyone knows the importance of doing favors, such as making referrals, giving references, sharing information, and giving favorable terms or discounts. We all know that jobs, power, or even promotions often come from returned favors. In consulting, *who* you know is the all-important factor. Referrals and personal references are vital. Giving a favor, especially something expensive, is almost always presumed to be a bribe. You'd better know what your company policy is on accepting gifts. Generally, you can't accept a gift over a certain dollar amount. The assumption is that you can't make an objective business decision about the giver if you accept his gift. Salesmen have used the system of *quid pro quo* forever, and they know it works. But the PMP code says that if you get tickets to the Super Bowl, you'll have to give them back. You have to protect both your company's interests and your professional reputation.

Respecting cultural differences

The world grows ever smaller. We're increasingly international and multicultural. We must be more flexible in interpersonal skills when dealing with cultural diversity. Project managers are responsible for Equal Employment Opportunity (EEO) guidelines and other HR policies. The competencies to deal with cross-cultural differences haven't been taught in our schools. Suddenly, there are new ways to look at things. Here's an example: Do you realize that 30 percent of all French workers won't show their emotions when they're upset at work, and the percentage increases to 50 percent for Canadians and 75 percent for Japanese? Here's another example: A programmer from Bombay disagrees by nodding his head, agrees by shaking his head, and doesn't consider Christmas a holiday. You may have a rude awaking if you use a baseball analogy when alerting the team to expect task handoffs and then realize that none of your international team has ever played baseball. Respect, empathy, and understanding go a long way.

Prep Test

1 Your team needs to use various software programs to complete a portion of the project involving new application development. You call the IT manager and request that he install the software the team needs. He informs you that the company has only a single subscription license to all the software you need. He doesn't have enough individual user licenses for all your team members and asks that you use your project budget to pay for the software. Your budget is already tight without this cost factored into it, so the IT manager offers to install the software on all computers from this single copy. This solution would help the project budget. What is the preferred approach?

  A ○ Have the IT manager install the software on all systems.

  B ○ Meet with your team and ask for recommendations.

  C ○ Meet with your sponsor.

  D ○ Cut another area in the budget.

2 As a project manager of an IT project, you are pushing for a milestone acceptance from your sponsor and client. Your recommendation is to purchase a costly software package for the next phase of this project. The sponsor and client aren't all that savvy technically and quite possibly will accept your findings without any discussion. You know that getting them to sign off on your recommendation will be easier if you don't present the software package another division has already chosen and implemented. What is the preferred course of action?

  A ○ Inform them of alternatives in the other division and stress their problems.

  B ○ Fully disclose a complete analysis of the technical merits of each package.

  C ○ Let them make the decision on which software package your team installs.

  D ○ Because they don't understand the technical merits of either package, don't muddy the issues.

3 The divisional controller hires you as a project manager on an important multi-year, multimillion-dollar project. He will be your project sponsor. He claims that he was burned when the last project went over budget, and he vows that he won't let that happen again. Your team and you start your initial planning and develop schedule and budget estimates for the project. The divisional controller informs you that he is planning for rigorous budgetary checks at every major milestone. He rejects your budget and demands that you increase your budget estimates. He states he wants a "pessimistic" budget estimate so that you don't go over the budget. You are sure that complying with his request would seriously overstate the budget. What should you do first?

A ○ Refuse the request and report the sponsor to his boss.

B ○ Insist that the original budget is correct, and his request amounts to budget tampering.

C ○ Completely rewrite the budget and include the pessimistic budget estimate.

D ○ Seek to understand what's motivating the controller's instructions before acting.

4 Your sponsor, the divisional controller, has rigorously grilled you at every major milestone, checking your budget against actual costs. As you prepare for a milestone review next week, you are surprised to find a large variance in the hardware budget. This variance puts your project significantly over the budget. You don't have time to fully investigate the reasons for the variance, but you expect it is an accounting mistake. What is the preferred method for handling this situation?

A ○ Just report the facts at the milestone review meeting.

B ○ Immediately inform the sponsor of the variance.

C ○ Uncover the reasons for the variance before taking any action.

D ○ Delay covering the overages in hardware costs during this milestone meeting.

5 The divisional controller likes the way you completed his last project, so he invites you to sit in on a meeting for a new project in hopes that you'll remain with the company and tame this project. In the first meeting to discuss requirements, you discover that the joint customers of the new software development project — Operations Department and Accounting Department — are deadlocked. Operations wants the software to be totally flexible so they can run their department effectively. Accounting wants to control what they perceive as a fly-by-the-seat-of-the-pants Operations department. The situation deteriorates into a shouting match. What is the preferred method for handling this situation?

A ○ Thank the controller, walk out of the meeting, and take another job. This project isn't worth the hassle. Life is too short.

B ○ Immediately inform the customers that you will be facilitating the meeting from now on and demand that everyone be treated with respect.

C ○ Uncover the reasons for the conflict and implement conflict resolution techniques.

D ○ Thank the controller during this meeting for making you project manager and for providing you with the authority as project manager to manage the departmental, operational, and organizational changes that will occur during this project.

6 The divisional controller is your project sponsor. He is the senior manager of the Accounting Department. He loans you a member of his staff to serve as project controller. This project controller has been extremely effective in his job for about a year, and you find him very helpful in satisfying his boss's every whim. He handles the project finances, gives you up-to-date actual costs, and pays suppliers as needed. You wish the other members of your team were as meticulously accurate in their work. During the project, the project controller is unexpectedly absent for several days. At a local PMI dinner meeting, a PMP you know from the project controller's previous employer tells you that your project controller has just pled *no contest* to a charge of financial fraud. At his previous company, the project controller was employed in the Accounting Department in a similar position. He submitted, authorized, and paid falsified invoices to another person in the company. They split the embezzled funds. This fraud wasn't uncovered until the person had been working in your company for a year. What is the preferred method for handling this situation?

A ○ Immediately inform the divisional controller of the situation and request an investigation.

B ○ The project controller has not done anything wrong on your project, so what do you care?

C ○ Inform Human Resources and ask them to handle the situation.

D ○ Confront the project controller and ask what's going on.

7 As a project manager in a consulting firm, your boss rewrites major portions of your project documentation. You disagree with his analysis. What is the preferred method for handling this situation?

A ○ Insist that both your names appear on the project documentation.

B ○ Ask your boss to remove your name from the project documentation.

C ○ Ask your boss to explain his analysis.

D ○ E-mail your boss, requesting details of the changes and an explanation for the changes.

Answers

1 **C.** In this case, meet with your sponsor and ask whether he can find other budget options for the required software. Don't violate copyright laws! You'll find yourself and the company in a great deal of trouble. Recognize and respect the software vendor's intellectual property and copyrights. *See "Responsibilities to Customers and the Public."*

2 **C.** In this case, let them make the decision. After all, it's their budget and their decision to make. When you ask for their decision, if they are smart, they will ask you for a complete analysis of the technical, operational, and financial merits of each package, as well as a recommendation. Provide an unbiased and objective case. Withholding such pertinent information from superiors is a clear code violation. *See "Responsibilities to Customers and the Public."*

3 **D.** The best choice for everyone is for you to understand the situation before taking any action. You might meet with the controller to find out the background of the last project and historical information on other projects. Perhaps the controller knows some privileged information that you don't. Allocating more than the original budget estimate may very well be inaccurate. In a sense, the sponsor is questioning both your competence and integrity as a project manager. You have the option of following choice B, insisting the original budget is correct. However, A, refusing the request outright and disobeying would be grounds for immediate termination. In almost all organizations, when you go over the head of your immediate superior, you could face termination. If you take this action, you're asking for trouble. In effect, you're asking the sponsor's boss to make a judgment call to either fire the controller or the project manager. C, completely rewriting the budget in compliance, is also a violation. You can't tamper with the budget just because a customer or sponsor requests it. You must have a compelling business justification for altering a budget. If you still believe the budget is correct and the sponsor makes a case for increasing it, make up the difference in a contingency account to cover risks. The key word in this question is what should you do *first? See "Responsibilities to Customers and the Public."*

4 **C.** The best choice is for you is to understand the situation before taking any action. By all means avoid "stakeholder panic," which would be the only result of choice B. You might meet with the hardware project lead to learn the background of the situation. If you take the action in A, you're asking for trouble. In effect, you're doing nothing and risk surprising a sponsor who is already nervous about budget issues. As the controller, he has every right to protect the budget and demand you be proactive. D is clearly a violation. You can't tamper with the budget just because you have bad news. If this overage is a true unforeseen risk, just be thankful that the controller created a contingency reserve account to cover it. The key word in this question is *preferred. See "Responsibilities to Customers and the Public."*

5 **D.** These are all valid options, but if you've "been there and done that,"' you know only one choice is *preferred*. The best choice is for you is to take control of the chaotic situation and provide order. Then you can try to understand the situation before taking any further action. By all means avoid conflict and insist on civility at the very least. But this would be the only result of choice B; it doesn't get you anywhere else. If you take the action in A, you haven't violated anything in the code of conduct. You're not asking for trouble. In effect, removing yourself from the project is a risk-adverse way of dealing with the dilemma. At this point, you are not obligated to the project. For many of us with families and mortgages to cover in a tight job market, walking out is not an option. We need the job. C is a good option; it just doesn't go far enough. It doesn't indicate whether you accept the position and it doesn't resolve the issues. D is clearly forcing the customers to recognize your authority and see that changes are coming. You might not know what those changes are just yet, and that's where you'd used choice C as a jumping-off point. The key word in this question is *preferred. See "Responsibilities to Customers and the Public."*

6 **A.** If this answer seems too far out or doesn't seem like a real-world situation to you, let's assure you that it happened at a major Hollywood studio. The *preferred* choice the project manager took was to inform the divisional controller. This unusual situation presented some difficulty for the current company. The project controller couldn't be trusted to handle the accounting functions. HR couldn't terminate him for lying on his job application about prior convictions, since the conviction occurred after the application was made. The situation became even more difficult because the employee was a member of a protected category. B is a clear violation of the PMP code. Resolving the issue is the responsibility of the employee's boss, who would have to request help from HR, so that eliminates C. Clearly, the worst choice is D; do not directly confront the project controller. That's not your role, and it wouldn't solve anything.

7 **D.** The best approach in this situation is to have complete information as to the specific changes and who authored the changes. Differences of opinion happen all the time; they should be recorded, even if the conclusion remains the same. Always keep e-mails or copies of original documents as an audit trail and for lessons learned.

Part II
Initiating the Project

The 5th Wave   By Rich Tennant

In this part...

Reel one: Fade in on planning for a movie, which begins with the script as the product's concept. After the script gets the "green light" as a formal initiation, the real work begins. The executive producer knows the project he is sponsoring has a big production phase. So, he'll split the duties for managing the project. The Unit Production Manager (UPM) and the First Assistant Director (AD) divide the work between them. The producer knows having smooth working relations between these two PMs can make or break the project.

Even in the glitter and glamour of Hollywood, PM is hard work.

Chapter 5

Determining Goals, Deliverables, Scope, and Initiation Processes

• •

Exam Objectives

▶ Conceiving projects

▶ Shaping project goals

▶ Organizing the project plan

▶ Determining project selection criteria and methods

▶ Understanding scope, requirements, and expectations

▶ Determining deliverables

▶ Developing and drafting a charter

• •

This chapter kicks off project initiation processes. Initiation is the beginning phase for a project. You discover how to build a business case for the project, perform analysis to determine its nature and scope, and take the planning steps that make it possible for the organization to recognize the project. This step answers key questions that you will use throughout the project. What are we going to do? How are we going to do it? Why are we going to do it?

Establishing project scope is very difficult, yet vital to success. The key to any project is to discover its real goals. Understanding the boundaries of the project — what's in scope and what's outside — is important for everyone involved.

In this chapter, you'll draft a sample project charter by filling in a template on the CD. This is your project charter for passing the exam. It will be easy to complete because all the required resources are already under your control. Print out your personal project charter and use it periodically to motivate and guide your study effort.

The best organizations recognize that projects don't fail at the end. They fail at the beginning. We discuss the importance of that distinction in this chapter.

Quick Assessment

1 _____ is the process of formally authorizing a new project or that an existing project should continue on to the next phase.

2 Project selection criteria are _____ to the Initiation process.

3 Project selection methods are ____ to the Initiation process.

4 _____, _____, _____, and _____ are the inputs to the Initiation process.

5 Mathematical models using linear, dynamic, integer, and multi-objective programming algorithms are called _____.

6 The project selection method that uses general techniques such as decision trees, forced choice, and specialized techniques such as an analytic hierarchy process and logical framework analysis is called a _____.

7 _____ describes the processes required to coordinate various elements of the project.

8 The first process in Project Scope Management is the _____ process.

9 _____ and _____ are the tools and techniques for Scope Initiation.

10 The _____ documents the characteristics required to ensure that the project will satisfy the needs for which it was undertaken.

Answers

1 Initiation. Project Initiation is a scope skill or knowledge area. This pattern requires you to know the definition of the process. See "Identifying the Need."

2 Inputs. This pattern requires you to know the definition and inputs of the process. See "Project Selection Criteria and Methods."

3 Tools and techniques. This pattern requires you to know the definition of the process and tools and techniques. See "Project Selection Criteria and Methods."

4 Project selection criteria, product description, strategic plan, and historical information. This is an input pattern. See "Project Selection Criteria and Methods."

5 Constrained optimization methods. This pattern requires you to know the definition of the term. See "Project Selection Criteria and Methods."

6 Decision model. This pattern requires you to know the definition of the method. See "Project Selection Criteria and Methods."

7 Project Integration Management. This pattern requires you to know the definition of the process. See "Determining and Defining Project Scope."

8 Initiation. This pattern asks you to know the order of the processes in Project Scope Management. See "Determining and Defining Project Scope."

9 Project selection methods, expert judgment. This is the tool and technique pattern. See "Determining and Defining Project Scope."

10 Product description. This pattern requires you to know the definition. See "Determining and Defining Project Scope."

Conceiving Projects

Before the official project start, you may have a preliminary discovery phase or conception phase. That preliminary work might include a feasibility analysis, preliminary plan, project proposal, project business plan, or some other kind of analysis. This is where the project management office (PMO) takes a leadership role. The PMO shepherds the project through these processes. You can also begin with a "blue-sky" or conceptual thinking approach to initial project planning, which can be as informal as getting an idea in the shower.

Another useful technique is *needs analysis.* This is the process of identifying, articulating, and documenting the various needs of the customers, sponsors, and stakeholders to ensure that the product of the project will satisfy all their needs. Needs are usually documented in technical and functional requirements. Don't those sound a whole lot like benefits measurement methods to you? Needs analysis would be categorized as an Initiation process under project selection methods.

There is no special planning phase. Planning *processes* involve ongoing and iterative skills that you apply in each project phase.

Performing a Feasibility Study or Analysis

In the earliest conceptual or discovery phases, the sponsor's main concern is, "Should I undertake this project?" One way to alleviate concerns and reduce the risk of improperly selecting a project is to perform a project *feasibility study* or *analysis.* (The terms are fairly interchangeable.)

What is a feasibility study?

A *feasibility study* examines possible options and potential issues, and forms the basis for a solid project business case document. A feasibility analysis can determine whether the project should be performed. It examines cost and technical data, evaluates issues that influence success, and ranks the advantages and disadvantages of each option. Often, it includes a cost/ benefit analysis. Feasibility studies result in a *feasibility report,* a technical document that determines whether the project is capable of achieving a financial return sufficient to justify capital expenditures and resources. All reports discuss the degree of reliability of the estimates and provide some conclusions or recommendations.

The feasibility study demonstrates that the client's requirement can be achieved. It identifies and evaluates the available options to determine a preferred solution. The outcome of feasibility analysis determines how to manage the larger project. If the analysis is completed during project initiation, one of outputs may be the preliminary project business case document. The business case should provide enough information to enable the authorizing executives to reach a decision. If feasibility analysis is completed after the business case has been made, the analysis can help refine the business case. Feasibility analysis narrows and assesses options and offers solutions to issues.

Feasibility studies generally involve *technical practicality, market potential, potential economic justification,* and *financial projections.* When used to determine which of several projects should be selected, the studies use such economic techniques as the time value of money to assess projects on an equivalent scale. (Chapter 10 covers the main formulas for the time value of money.) Many industries have different standards and requirements for issuing contracts for feasibility studies.

Conducting a project feasibility study

The first step in conducting a feasibility study is to gather an experienced manager and team. Team composition depends on the nature of the project. The composition should include a range of specialists who are qualified to examine all possible options. They should review each option thoroughly. If a business case document exists, it helps the team understand the scope of the work involved, and any constraints, such as time, cost, and quality.

The project manager creates a work plan for the study. The simplified work plan should outline the study's *delivery schedule, interim milestones,* and the *final report.* Always allow adequate time to request and collect data, as well to interpret the results. Identify and rank the available options according to the sponsor's *goals, project constraints,* and other *external issues.* The resulting document helps define the future direction of the project. All of these documented findings will be used in later phases, such as Scope Planning.

Organizing Project Plan Materials

A large part of a project manager's job is planning. Planning requires organizational and communication skills. At the beginning of a project, you have incomplete knowledge. It is impossible to give precise answers and create detailed project plans. Requirements emerge and evolve as the project scope takes shape. These PM processes overlap and interact with each other.

Your planning will be captured in various documents that serve as inputs to the project plan. Especially important at the inception stage is to document areas where conflicts often arise: *administrative procedures and organizational policies, project priorities,* and *schedules.* All of this material must be arranged to create a clear picture of the project. The project plan pulls all the information together in one place. Later, it serves as a road map to guide the project through all its phases. Start by answering the two most basic questions of the project and begin your planning process.

Can the project deliver the results?

No matter how small or large the project, you need to define its *boundaries,* or *scope.* You must consider if your team can realistically achieve the entire scope. The cost of delivering all wish-list items might be prohibitive. Or the deadline constraints make the project's already unrealistic goals impossible to achieve. If the project is defined to be impracticable, poorly scoped, and improperly linked with organizational objectives, it will not be completed successfully. A project should be achievable within a relatively fixed timeframe and within your resource constraints.

Should the company undertake this project?

Project managers and sponsors must engage in conceptual thinking to determine if the results will be worthwhile. The project manager must start to plan the project with the end result in mind. The process of preparing a plan involves answering questions. What actions do you take to reach the project's objective? How will it be done? Who will do it? How long will it take?

This discovery process is more complicated than scheduling activities on a timeline. Although scheduling and charting progress was once considered the core discipline of traditional project management, project managers are no longer scheduling engineers. You are expected to align the project with the strategic business plan of the organization. Inevitably, project managers discover that constituents have different priorities. It's difficult to know the project's true requirements, goals, and objectives. The project manager often needs to sort through conflicting opinions by creating a consensus among stakeholders. A *project mission statement* does that.

The project mission statement summarizes the goals and purposes of the project, identifies the client, and outlines the general approach to follow.

Identifying the Need

All projects are based on management's recognition of a problem, business requirement, or an unfulfilled need. Management may present you with a clearly defined problem summarized in a project mission statement or with a vague concept that requires further discovery. The key to this phase is to figure out exactly what the objectives and goals of the project encompass. The official start of this journey is called the *Initiation*.

Initiation is the process of formally authorizing a new project or that an existing project should continue on to the next phase.

As the first of the all-important five process groups, the Initiation process marks the beginning of management's commitment to execute a project. That commitment is a formal recognition to *start* a new project, *continue* into the next phase, or *begin* a new phase of the product development process. Initiation is fundamental to project management.

Initiation

✔ Scope Initiation has four inputs, two tools and techniques and, four outputs. Be able to re-create this table for the test.

✔ Three (of the four) outputs of the Scope Initiation process (the project charter, assumptions, and constraints) become inputs to the Scope Planning process.

✔ Draw a line that connects the outputs of one process and the inputs of the next process. Linking these interactions will help you remember both processes.

✔ Scope Initiation is a *core* process of Initiation. (It's the only process in Initiation.)

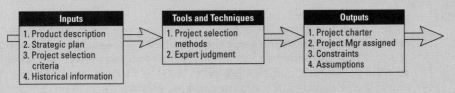

Inputs	Tools and Techniques	Outputs
1. Product description 2. Strategic plan 3. Project selection criteria 4. Historical information	1. Project selection methods 2. Expert judgment	1. Project charter 2. Project Mgr assigned 3. Constraints 4. Assumptions

The four inputs to Initiation are

✔ **Product description:** Documents the characteristics of the product or service that the project was undertaken to solve. It also documents the business need that created the project.

✔ **Strategic plan:** Describes the organization's mission, vision, and goals for the future — all of which the project supports. Everything in project management supports the strategic business plan of the organization.

✔ **Project selection criteria:** Defined in terms of the product, this covers the full range of management concerns.

✔ **Historical information:** Results of previous decisions and performance.

- Relevant lessons learned from past projects

- The history with a particular customer

- The history with similar projects

Project Selection Criteria and Methods

According to modern management experts, project Initiation is strictly a business decision. All projects should support the strategic plan of the organization. The current buzzword is *alignment,* as in aligning the project (or portfolio of projects) with business goals. That's why the strategic plan and historical information are inputs to the Initiation process. They provide the background or business context for project selection.

Project selection criteria are always tied to the ongoing business. The criteria are typically defined in terms of specific benefits of the product to the business. Later in this chapter, we revisit these benefits and explain how to measure them.

All projects must support the strategic objectives of the performing organization.

Project selection *criteria* are inputs to initiation. Project selection *methods* are the tools and techniques of initiation. They are the techniques, practices, or procedures for selecting a project that best supports the organization's objectives. Applying complex project selection criteria in a sophisticated model is often treated as a separate project phase. Project selection methods generally fall into two broad categories.

✔ **Benefit measurement methods:** Comparative approaches, scoring models, and benefit-contribution and economic models

✔ **Constrained optimization methods:** Mathematical models using linear, dynamic, integer, and multi-objective programming algorithms

Every company has its own project selection criteria and methods. The criteria are typically picked by the merits of the product or service that the project is designed to create. Some companies pick their projects by decision models (such as rank ordering) and calculation methods (such as probabilistic weighting systems). Some economic models use established methods of financial analysis as the criteria: return on investment (ROI), payback, cost-benefit analysis, or internal rate of return (IRR). All methods are categorized as *decision models* because they result in a decision. They include general techniques such as decision trees and forced choice, and specialized techniques such as analytic hierarchy process and logical framework analysis.

The other tool and technique is *expert judgment.* Subject experts with specialized knowledge or training assess the inputs to this process. Results of this analysis are a documented opinion or recommendation.

Describing a Product or Service

Everything you do on the project relies on an accurate product description. The *product description* is a document that evolves throughout the project. It is generally less detailed in the early phases. Details are added as work progresses and you discover more about the product. Your description of the product is vital because all project estimates and future decisions will be based on how well the team understands the product.

You may get tricky exam questions about the product description. Memorize the following two sentences to answer these types of questions:

> ✔ The product description documents the characteristics of the product or service that the project was undertaken to create.

> ✔ The product description documents the relationship of the product or service and the business need.

A question may list both parts of the definition as choices — either A or B. Either is part of the correct answer, but they are only half right. Because neither is correct alone, look for a third choice that combines A and B.

Dividing the Project into Manageable Components

Dividing project work into manageable components is basic to project management. Big projects requiring many people and lots of resources and months or years to complete can't be achieved unless you can break them down into incremental steps that can be performed readily.

Projects fail because of poor requirements definitions, too many requirements changes, increased scope, lack of control over changes, and unplanned rework. Obvious answers to these troubling issues are to spend more effort in planning and to divide work into smaller, more manageable components. This type of planning can prevent the changes to requirements and scope that cause so much unplanned rework. The next few sections explore how the PM methodology breaks down project work into its components.

Introducing the knowledge area processes

The knowledge areas are the skill sets that project managers use on a daily basis. Each of these knowledge areas contributes to the planning process. The project plan is a composite of the subplans from each of the areas described in this section. In our descriptions, we've simplified the PMI wording to make your studying easier. On the test, each knowledge area is preceded with the word *Project* to denote that the skill has a project basis. And each is followed by the word *Management*. So, in our definitions, we simplify *Project Integration Management* to just *Integration*.

✔ **Integration:** Properly coordinate various elements of the project. Project Plan Development is the first process. In this process, you collect all the outputs from the other processes described in the following list and compile them into the project plan.

The outputs of all the following processes become subsidiary plans of the project plan:

✔ **Scope:** Identify all the work required to complete the project successfully. The output is the scope management plan.

✔ **Time:** Ensure the project is completed on time. The output is the schedule management plan.

✔ **Cost:** Ensure the project is completed within budget. The output is the cost management plan.

✔ **Quality:** Ensure the project satisfies customer requirements. The output is the quality management plan.

✔ **Human Resources:** Make effective use of the people involved with the project. The output is the HR management plan.

✔ **Communications:** Ensure timely development, collection, dissemination, storage, and disposition of project information. The output is the communications management plan.

✔ **Risk:** Identify, evaluate, and respond to project risks. Emphasis is on maximizing the results of positive events (opportunities) and minimizing the consequences of adverse events (risks). The output is the risk management plan.

✔ **Procurement:** Acquire goods and services from outside the organization. The output is the procurement management plan.

The nine knowledge areas are easier to remember if you break them down into a 3 x 3 matrix. The following mnemonics might help: Rapper Ice-T seeks the HR department to take a CPR class.

Ice T	*IST* for Integration, Scope, and Time
Seek HR	*CQ HR* for Cost, Quality, and Human Resources
CPR	*CPR* for Communication, Procurement, and Risk

Interlinking life-cycle processes

You repeat the life-cycle processes for each project phase, as shown in Figure 5-1. Closing one phase can provide an input to the next phase. In this way, the Definition, Initiation, and Planning phases each refine the project scope.

Overlap of process groups

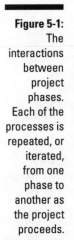

Figure 5-1: The interactions between project phases. Each of the processes is repeated, or iterated, from one phase to another as the project proceeds.

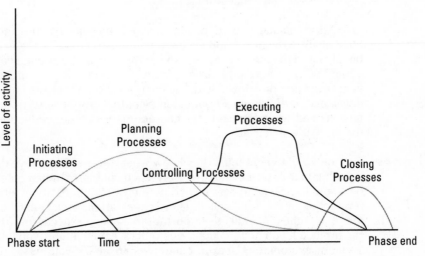

As a project manager, you should repeat the Initiation process at the start of each phase. This keeps the team focused on the business need that is driving the project. New iterations of the Initiation process should also disclose whether the project should be terminated if the business need no longer exists or if the project cannot satisfy that original need. Although the figure shows discrete processes and discrete phases, a project will have many overlaps. Exam questions on this area involve customer buy-in or acceptance of your deliverables. Involving stakeholders in all the project phases improves the probability of satisfying customer requirements and ensures customer buy-in.

Determining and Defining Project Scope

Project managers must manage the uncertainty that goes along with the unique characteristics of a project. At the beginning of a phase, most of the uncertainty stems from not yet knowing the specifics of the product or service that you've committed to produce. In progressively elaborating product specifics, the project defines them and reduces the uncertainty about them.

Identifying requirements and expectations

This section takes a look at how project managers identify requirements, wants, needs, and expectations.

Projects are managed with the aim of satisfying some business needs. You must analyze the needs and wants of your customers. Are the needs really beneficial to the business? Is satisfying them realistically achievable? If so, you make these needs requirements for the project. Requirements are negotiated and prioritized with the customer. Requirements are what's *demanded* or *obligatory.* Requirements are the specific objectives that must be achieved, as embodied in the characteristics of the product or service the project will deliver.

Generally, customers think they know what they need but have difficulty defining their requirements precisely. Each customer has an opinion of the best solution. Stakeholders have different expectations about what the product or service will be like. These expectations aren't specifications and aren't documented. Still, it's important to manage expectations throughout the project. If you don't manage customers' expectations, you'll have unhappy customers. Unhappy customers are an indication that the project wasn't as successful as it could be, even if it met technical requirements.

Early in the project, the project manager creates some preliminary plans. These requirements can change over time, and you should make stakeholders aware of the extent to which the requirements can change.

Organizational policies and influences

Organizational policies are inputs to Project Plan Development that can affect the scope of the project. These include the organization's formal and informal policies. In PMI terminology, an organization is loosely defined as a generic group. An organizational policy could mean a corporate, divisional, departmental, or group policy. Any or all groups within or related to a larger organization might have their own policies to follow, like these:

- ✔ **Quality management:** Process audits or continuous-improvement targets
- ✔ **Information technology:** Platform or operating system, service-level agreements, application selection, application development, data formats, or data-sharing policies
- ✔ **Human resources:** Equal Employment Opportunity guidelines, personnel hiring and firing guidelines, employee performance reviews, seniority, overtime, or travel policies
- ✔ **Financial controls:** Time reporting, accounting codes, level of authorities reviews for expenditures and disbursements
- ✔ **Procurement:** Sourcing from multiple vendor bids or least-cost sourcing

When planning for resources, organizational guidelines for staff, equipment, and purchasing may influence your choices. For example, the organization may try to give the bid to minority-owned businesses.

The basis of future decisions

Everything that helps define scope also provides the basis for making future decisions. Requirements, wants, needs, expectations, assumptions, and constraints identified by the planning process must be in the project record.

Here are two mantras of the PMI methodology:

- ✔ All outputs become the basis of all future decisions. Become familiar with the workflow concept of outputs being used as inputs to define other processes. You'll use this workflow information often.
- ✔ Processes are never used in isolation; they overlap or integrate. Process outputs are the inputs to other processes.

Assumptions or constraints can arise from previous documents, such as a project proposal, an information systems plan, or other existing strategic business documents. As you identify assumptions, include any requirements for special skills or any dependencies with other projects.

Developing a Project Charter

The project charter is a document that formally recognizes the existence of a project. It describes the product to be delivered and addresses the business need of the project. It should be issued *externally* from the project and at a management level high enough to support the needs of the project. For example, the sponsoring executive should have authority to solve problems like jurisdictional or boundary disputes. Ideally, the charter should be signed by *senior management, sponsor,* and *customer.*

Your charter should describe the objectives that the project will deliver. Objectives should be SMART: *S*pecific, *M*easurable, *A*chievable, *R*ealistic, and *T*ime-specific. Qualify specific items you'll deliver. List one or more deliverables per objective. These become your performance criteria and must be measurable. If the statement doesn't imply the creation of a deliverable, it may be a goal instead of an objective. If the statement describes the features and functions of the product, it may be a requirements statement.

Drafting the Project Charter/Letter of Engagement

The project charter is a document that formally recognizes the existence of a project. The project charter should define

- ✔ Objectives
- ✔ The end result
- ✔ The customer
- ✔ Delivery dates
- ✔ Costs

A few equivalent terms all refer to written confirmation of what you'll produce and the terms by which you'll perform the work. The exam generally doesn't split hairs between a *project charter, statement of work (SOW), project abstract, business requirements document,* or *letter of engagement.* The charter can include many different documents. Just be familiar with the terms and the concepts behind them.

A letter of engagement, letter of intent, letter of agreement, or letter contract allows contractors to mobilize or to start work after a requirement has been identified. These documents are a preliminary binding authorization to start an activity within its terms and conditions before actual pricing determinations can be made and pending the signing of formal contracts. The following lab creates a project charter. Find the Microsoft Word template on the CD and fill it in for your sample project. This creates a personalized project charter for your new project: *Pass the PMP Exam Project.*

Lab 5-1   Building a Project Charter

1. On the CD, select the `Project Charter Template.doc` file.

2. Double-click the filename to open the file in Microsoft Word.

3. Fill in the blue-formatted template notes. This is your project. You are the project manager. The product of the project is for you to pass the PMP exam.

4. Print out your PEPP Project Charter document.

5. On page 10 of the charter, sign as project manager. Get some people who care about your success to sign as customer and project sponsor.

6. Keep your PEPP Project Charter document in a folder or binder.

7. Whenever a distraction arises, cite this charter. It gives you permission and authority to act, to use resources, and to enlist the support of others.

Prep Test

1 **The major processes in Project Integration Management are:**

- **A** ○ Inputs, tools and techniques, outputs
- **B** ○ Project Plan Development, Project Plan Execution, Overall Change Control
- **C** ○ Project Plan Development, Project Plan Execution, Integrated Change Control
- **D** ○ Stakeholder skills and knowledge, project planning methodology, and project management information systems (PMIS)

2 **The _____ is a document, or collection of documents, which should be expected to change over time as more information becomes available about the project.**

- **A** ○ Project charter
- **B** ○ Project plan
- **C** ○ Scope statement
- **D** ○ Product description document

3 **The product description documents _____.**

- **A** ○ The characteristics of the product or service that the project was undertaken to create
- **B** ○ The relationship of the product or service that the project was created for with a perceived business need
- **C** ○ The product of the project
- **D** ○ The characteristics of the product or service that the project was undertaken to create and the relationship of the product or service that the project was created for with a perceived business need

4 **The project charter documents _____.**

- **A** ○ The project manager's authority
- **B** ○ The business purpose of the project
- **C** ○ The product of the project
- **D** ○ The project manager's authority, the product, and the business need

5 **The project plan is _____.**

- **A** ○ Created using inputs, tools and techniques, and outputs from all processes
- **B** ○ Used to guide project execution, document project planning assumptions, facilitate communication among stakeholders
- **C** ○ A schedule, created in a tool like Microsoft Project
- **D** ○ Created by the performing organization's policies and standards using stakeholders' skills and knowledge

6 The technical and business requirements of customers, sponsors, and stakeholders to ensure that the product is what was intended are in the _____.

A ○ Design document

B ○ Scope statement

C ○ Feasibility analysis

D ○ Needs analysis

7 A _____ is a formal technical report that determines if the project is capable of a financial return sufficient to justify the capital expenditures and managerial resources.

A ○ Cost-benefit analysis

B ○ Scope statement

C ○ Feasibility analysis

D ○ Needs analysis

8 Comparative approaches, scoring models, benefit contribution, and economic models are all part of:

A ○ Constrained optimization methods for selecting a project

B ○ Benefit measurement methods for selecting a project

C ○ Project selection tools and techniques

D ○ Project selection criteria

9 Project selection criteria cover such management concerns as:

A ○ Market share

B ○ Return on investment

C ○ Public perceptions

D ○ Market share, ROI, and public perceptions

Answers

1 **C.** The term *major processes* eliminates A; inputs, tools and techniques, and outputs are the interactions among processes. Eliminate D because they are tools and techniques. That leaves choices B and C. A change in terminology, Overall Change Control was updated to become Integrated Change Control. This pattern asks you to list all the integration processes.

2 **B.** This is a definition-pattern question. The project charter document should not change during the course of the project unless there are drastic scope changes. The scope statement and product description change throughout the project, so they are both good answers. However, they are not the best answers. The scope statement is an output of Scope Planning, a Planning process. The definition of product description is close; it will have less detail in the early phases and more detail in later ones as the product characteristics are progressively elaborated. *See the* PMBOK Guide, *p. 44.*

3 **D.** The question uses a best-choice pattern. You might have a question that lists both parts of a definition as an either-or choice — either A or B alone. Either of these could be the correct answer, but neither is correct by itself. Choice D combines answers A and B, so it's more complete.

4 **D.** This is a tricky multiple-part, best-choice pattern. Each individual answer — A, B, or C — is a correct statement, but the best answer is D, which combines them.

5 **B.** This is the project plan definition from the *PMBOK Guide,* p. 44. This pattern requires you to know the definition of the process.

6 **D.** This pattern requires you to know the definition of the process. *See* "Conceiving Projects."

7 **C.** Cost-benefit analysis seems to fit, but it is a tool and technique used during later planning phases to elaborate progressively feasibility. This pattern asks for the definition of the process.

8 **B.** This is the most specific, correct, and best answer. Notice the word *benefit* in the question. Although answer C also seems correct, it is too general. If C were *project selection methods* rather than *project selection tools and techniques,* it would be a better choice. This pattern requires you to know the examples that explain the definition. Methods and models are generally tools and techniques, which eliminates D, an input. *See the* PMBOK Guide, *p. 54.*

9 **D.** This is the most specific, correct, and best answer. This pattern requires that you know the list of methods that explain the definition. *See the* PMBOK Guide, *p. 54.*

Chapter 6

Identifying Boundaries

● ●

Exam Objectives

▶ Managing expectations

▶ Identifying stakeholders

▶ Measuring project benefits

▶ Setting milestones

▶ Setting quality standards

▶ Coping with organizational structures

● ●

*T*his chapter paints a bull's-eye on your project. Starting with the project's end results is the best route to understanding the project's scope.

The first order of business is to identify your customer and sponsor definitions of a successful project. You'll see how to make the definition of success measurable and quantifiable. By being able to define what makes your project successful, you learn how to

✔ Manage expectations for customers and sponsors

✔ Set the appropriate criteria for project acceptance

✔ Determine how the project should be measured

You'll also learn

✔ Key milestones: set, track, and control

✔ Quality standards you must satisfy

This chapter defines the project in the context of the organization.

Quick Assessment

1   Successful completion of product scope is measured against _____.

2   Successful completion of project scope is measured against _____.

3   _____ define how you will deliver the product's results.

4   Requirements involve a negotiation, wants and needs, and _____.

5   Product measurement criteria include durability, conformance, and performance, but not _____ events, which mark the completion of a major deliverable.

6   Quality management processes required to ensure that the project satisfies the needs it was undertaken to meet include _____.

7   The cost of quality includes _____.

8   Quality is defined as the totality of features and characteristics that satisfy _____.

9   In a matrix organizational structure, the _____ and _____ share responsibility for the project.

10   An organization grouped by engineering, IT, accounting, finance, marketing, sales, purchasing, HR, and design is a(n) _____ organization.

Answers

1 Requirements. This pattern asks for you to know the definition. It's the simplest type of question. See "Measuring Project Benefits."

2 The project plan. This pattern asks for you to know the definition. It's the simplest type of question. It's a variant of Question 1. You may see these kinds of variations on the exam separated by many questions, and it might seem confusing. Mark the second one, and when you're reviewing the questions at the end, you can jump easily to each one. That'll make it easy for you to make the distinction. See "Measuring Project Benefits."

3 Requirements. This pattern asks for you to know the definition. It's the simplest type of question. See "Measuring Project Benefits."

4 Measurability. This pattern asks for you to know the definition. It's the simplest type of question. It's a variant of Question 3. You may see these kinds of variations on the exam separated by many questions, and it might seem confusing. Mark the second one, and when you're reviewing the questions at the end, you can jump easily to each one. That'll make it easy for you to make the distinction. See "Measuring Project Benefits."

5 Milestone. Milestones are project measurements; the rest are product measurements. This pattern asks for you to know the definition. It's the simplest type of question. This pattern introduces some irrelevant information in the first half of the question. See "Setting Milestones."

6 Quality Planning, Quality Assurance, and Quality Control. This pattern asks for you to complete all process in the knowledge area. See "Setting Quality Standards."

7 Prevention costs, appraisal costs, failure costs (internal and external). This pattern asks for you to complete the definition for a tool and technique of Quality Planning. Our trick in remembering the definition is to think of this as *defining the cost of quality*. *Defining* fits our verb pattern for identifying tools and techniques. See "Setting Quality Standards" and Chapter 10.

8 Stated or implied needs, conformance to requirements or specifications, and fitness for use. This pattern asks for you to complete the definition. This is the simplest pattern. See "Setting Quality Standards."

9 Project manager, functional manager. This question pattern tests your ability to demonstrate an understanding of the relationships among facts, principles, and methods. See "Coping with an Organization's Structure."

10 Functional. This question pattern tests your ability to demonstrate an understanding of the relationships among facts, principles, and methods. See "Coping with an Organization's Structure."

Managing Expectations

The success of your project requires setting, managing, and meeting or exceeding customer expectations. If you meet or exceed their expectations, your customers will be satisfied and happy. Happy customers are a key element in determining the success of your project.

We've seen situational exam questions with the scenario of an unsatisfied customer. The question asks:

> What could the project manager have done to prevent the situation?

Or two variants:

> What can you do to prevent a customer from becoming unsatisfied?
>
> How can you change an unsatisfied customer to a satisfied one?

The correct response is for the project manager to begin by setting customer expectations. You set expectations by clearly defining the scope of the project — that's before the customer has the chance to become unsatisfied. Documenting requirements and having the customer sign off on those requirements round out the answer. The key to understanding unsatisfied customer questions is to recognize how the processes in the given scenario relate to each other (process interactions) and to their results (process outputs). Because each scenario is different, the processes involved vary. Sometimes, it's a scope scenario. But it could involve time, cost, or quality scenarios. Think of a linear process — going forward along the project timeline from the beginning. Determine where the customer became unhappy: at what process interaction or output. Then think about the process steps going backwards from the end result (or output) to the intermediate results. When you get into this mindset, you'll be able to visualize how to re-create the steps of any process, as well as how to correct or prevent a missed step.

Identifying Project Stakeholders

A *stakeholder* is anyone who has a clear stake in the project's success. For example, any individual or organization actively involved in the project — and whose interests may be positively or negatively affected by the project's success or failure — counts as a stakeholder. Stakeholders can be internal or external to the performing organization, and all their expectations must be managed. Each stakeholder risks something of value in the project's outcome.

The most important stakeholder is the customer. Internal stakeholders include internal customers, departments, management, employees, and administrators. External stakeholders include customers, suppliers, investors, community groups, and government agencies. Naturally, stakeholders have their own agendas, goals, and priorities. *Stakeholder management* is the process of aligning stakeholders with each other and the team.

In a typical project, key stakeholders are the people in the following roles:

- ✔ **Steering committee:** A group of high-level executives from functional company areas (and customer representatives) who provide guidance and overall strategic direction. By contributing their functional expertise, they add strategic input to the project. They can also enlist cooperation from their functional groups, making it possible for a larger part of the organization to have a stake in the project's success.

- ✔ **Project champion:** A senior executive who promotes and defends your project within the larger parent organization.

- ✔ **Sponsor:** The one who provides financial resources and direction. This person must have the management authority to settle any disputes between project staff and functional staff.

- ✔ **Performing organization:** The company or group doing the work.

- ✔ **Project organization:** A group that serves the project and participants. It includes the structure, roles, and responsibilities of the project team, as well as its interfaces to the outside.

  The project organization is not the same thing as a project*ized* organization. The project organization refers to the project team itself. Project*ized* refers to a specific model where organizations are structured by projects rather than by functional departments. The project doesn't belong to any department, but to the entire organization. See "Projectized organization," later in this chapter.

- ✔ **Project manager:** The person who manages the project daily.

- ✔ **Customer:** The buyer expected to use the product or service that the project creates. In practice, it's anyone who participates in focus groups or has bought the company's (or competitors') products.

- ✔ **Project team member:** Anyone performing work on the project, especially someone who manages (or reports directly to) the project organization; team leaders are the heads of individual groups within the project team. In addition to people loaned from other departments or from resource pools, the team also includes all contractors and consultants.

- ✔ **Individual contributor:** Anyone working on the project without a management role but sharing accountability for achieving results.

- ✔ **Functional manager:** Handles the business and technical management of a functional group — in particular their performance review.

- ✔ **Project accountant:** Provides cost and budget information for the project. Usually this is a member of the accounting department (often on the controller's staff) who can ensure that invoices for project work get paid on time and can provide data for your earned value measurements.

- ✔ **Project influencer:** Is positively or negatively impacted because of the result of the project or potential changes from the project.

- ✔ **Information sources:** Individuals who provide helpful information. They may have special knowledge of the project as a result of their roles in similar projects, or they might be customers of similar products. They may be experts in law or human resources, or in an industry association.

You must ensure that diverse individuals function as a team. You have to coach, lead, and ensure the team's commitment to a common mission for which they are mutually accountable. With functional managers, you'll resolve conflicts between team members; each may have different time priorities, individual objectives and goals, and available resources. Also with functional managers, you'll resolve resource conflicts and negotiate compromises.

Expectations of Managers and Sponsors

The responsibility assignment matrix (RAM) is a chart that identifies specific roles and responsibilities for project stakeholders. For the moment, however, a short list can help define the most important responsibilities — for both departments and individual competencies; see Chapter 9.

- ✔ The project manager is accountable for project performance.

- ✔ The sponsor has ultimate accountability and responsibility for the project. The sponsor provides resources (both financial and human) and direction. His senior management rank gives him the authority to settle any disputes between project staff and functional staff. Customarily, the sponsor also champions the project to senior management.

- ✔ Success requires the participation of *all* team members, but management is responsible for providing resources needed for success.

- ✔ Management is responsible for the quality of the finished product.

What makes a good sponsor?

Your project has a better chance for success if your sponsor has certain characteristics, including a sense of responsibility to the project and the team. The short list of desirable qualities for a sponsor looks like this:

✔ Has a vested interest in ensuring the project is successful.

✔ Has enough rank and political power inside the organization to coordinate resources and settle boundary disputes between the project team and other groups.

✔ Selects the project manager. Together they should select the team to ensure balance. In team selection, the project manager should take the primary role, and the sponsor should assist.

✔ Can have frequent meetings with the project manager and team leaders, especially true at the outset of the project. The sponsor should meet only occasionally with the entire team — and should never meet with individual team members for informal discussions.

✔ Has the authority and resources to ensure adequate team training.

✔ Is informed enough never to be caught by surprise as the project evolves. If the sponsor is surprised during a status update, it's a bad sign.

✔ Never allows conflicts within the team to pass the point of no return. If a team is dysfunctional, the sponsor should resolve disagreements.

Sponsors, being human, aren't perfect. You're likely to run across as many dysfunctional sponsors as dysfunctional project teams (even at the senior-management level). You have a professional responsibility to prevent them from dooming your project. Work it out at lower management levels.

Working with sponsors

The sponsor's role is vastly misunderstood. Little training exists that prepares managers for sponsoring projects. Early in the race, the project manager should negotiate ground rules. (Some ground rules include key outputs of the knowledge areas and the subsidiary project plans.) So how do you work with sponsors?

One exam question pattern is when to ask the sponsor for help and when to handle problems yourself. During the initiation and planning processes, all kinds of conflicts can erupt between project manager and functional manager over resources, priorities, and schedules. Negotiate these with the functional manager. Ask for the sponsor's help *only* after you have reached a stalemate. A sponsor who champions your project and trusts you to make the calls is an invaluable asset. A sponsor who calls project team staff into her office demanding updates because she doesn't trust you is a project liability.

We've seen many exam questions that place the sponsor, functional managers, and customers in particular situations. This question format sets up a tricky situation to see which choice you might take, or steps you could take, to prevent the trouble from happening or recurring. The questions are usually set up as dilemmas, conflicts, or impasses. You'll need experience and sound practical judgment to answer them. The key to these questions is in identifying the roles and responsibilities of the functional manager, project manager, and sponsor.

Understand that project managers and sponsors are caught in some basic conflicts and paradoxes due to their respective roles. The project manager's basic role is to reduce the sponsor's risk (of the project failing). You'd think that would mean the sponsor really needs the project manager and must trust him implicitly. But, here's a paradox. Realizing that the project manager can only estimate project costs, the sponsor must hold some of his funds in two specialized financial accounts — management reserves and contingency reserves. (Management reserve accounts cover the uncertainties in the estimates of schedules and costs. Contingency reserve accounts provide for unforeseen events, errors, oversights, and unplanned work.) The sponsor will always be looking for ways to free up these funds to use as working capital elsewhere. He'll pressure you to complete the project as fast and as cheaply as possible. However, you'll want to keep the funds in reserve as long as possible for that all-too-likely "just-in-case" scenario. This paradox can escalate into trouble, especially toward the project's end if you are over budget or behind schedule. The sponsor may terminate the project early, even if more work remains. Or he might threaten early termination as a motivator to squeeze more work out of the team. You're caught in the middle, between your team and sponsor.

A favorite exam topic involves conflicts when sponsors or customers try to add nonessential features that expand the project scope. Feature *gold plating* can be motivated by a longstanding, unanswered wish list. The sponsor might think the next chance to satisfy these long wished-for features will be after he retires, so he'll add unnecessary items to the projects' scope. He'll insist that his wish list of gold-plated features is absolutely vital to the project objectives. He'll swear the features align with the latest metric of success. Or the laundry list of features can be motivated by political favors or a lack of prioritization. The project manager's role is to understand the true scope and risks of the project, which may be hidden. The project manager also must stop the scope creep from causing project delays. It's like the old blues song says, "troubles ahead and troubles behind." What's a project manager to do?

Negotiate decision-making authority and document it. In a traditional top-down approach, all-wise sponsors set the project's direction and vision. They deploy resources toward that vision. They have the answers and make the decisions. Some sponsors expect the project manager to explain how organizational conflicts impact the project. They'll use a bottom-up approach — even asking for decisions at the project level. Other times, the sponsor's advice and counsel come in handy. Either way, the sponsor probably wants to make these executive decisions — but perhaps a group decision is a better way to go. Getting consensus (or *buy-in*) from all stakeholders is an effective way to enlist support for the project and ensure that customers accept the end results.

As a project manager, you and your project team must anticipate executives' questions and be prepared with well thought-out answers or solutions. The project managers and executives must excel in asking the proper questions. Only then will they discover the optimal solution. It's a joint top-down and bottom-up approach: Both sponsor and project manager must share the vision. Having won the support of the sponsor, the project manager must lead the project's decision-making process. Because project managers drive decisions, they must push back on poor decisions — whether made at the team or at the executive level. Here's the definition of a bad decision, for situational questions: It's bad if it increases the probability of project failure or decreases the probability of success. A good decision increases the probability of success or decreases the probability of failure. (Pretty much says it all, doesn't it?) Good business decisions have to be based on good assumptions and appropriate models, as well as clean and accurate data. As a project manager, insist on sound decision-making — and then document those decisions.

Be prepared to answer tough situational exam questions that reflect your experience in dealing with sponsors. When you face these questions, evaluate them in light of providing solutions. That's a mantra of the methodology.

Measuring Project Benefits

Determining how to measure the benefits a project will deliver is difficult for a variety of reasons. Yet, it's among the most important scope issues for conceptual planning that you must manage. It is your professional responsibility to resolve any and all conflicts among your stakeholders — especially the customers and the sponsor. In this case, you must drive them to make firm decisions. Most of the time, they will hold higher ranking positions in the organization than you. But even if you feel outranked, you must keep them focused on the project's strategic benefits for the organization. Keep in mind that the customer and sponsor must commit to exactly what they want. Without a consensus of the project's final results, you can't stop scope creep or define success. This consensus between the stakeholders and project team sets the project's scope.

To define the scope of the project and its product, you must uncover the stakeholders' real wants, needs, and expectations. There may be gaps in what they say or between what they say and their real wants. You and the project team must uncover these hidden needs. When you've uncovered the true needs, build them into requirements. Requirements define the characteristics of the product. They should include objective measurements about how you deliver the product's results. Work with the customers and sponsor to define those results in objective and measurable terms. Determining how stakeholders gauge success is hard work, and you have to dig. Generally, customers and sponsors don't know how to define or measure success objectively; you can control project scope by helping them arrive at their own answers. You and the team will make thousands of decisions during the project. Make sure those decisions are focused on a clear, measurable result.

Setting acceptance criteria

After you get the customer and sponsor to commit to the end results of the project, you can start defining the terms for acceptance. Some distinctions you must know include

- **Product scope:** All the features and functions to include in a product or service.

  Successful completion of product scope is measured against the *requirements* you have defined.

- **Project scope:** All the work to deliver a product with the specified features and functions.

  Successful completion of project scope is measured against the *project plan* — how well the team has attained its stated goals.

For the customer to accept the product, you will have to identify the features and functions of the product that will be defined in the project requirements. That's one reason why requirements are so critical. If you miss a requirement, the risk is that the customers won't accept the product. For customers and the sponsor to accept the project, all the work to deliver a product must be completed according to the project plan.

Determining project metrics

Among the outputs of scope planning is the scope statement. The scope statement describes the *product deliverables* and the *project objectives*.

- **Product deliverables:** A list of features that the product or service will have. Delivering these features makes the project successful.

- **Project objectives:** Quantifiable criteria (metrics) to meet for the project to be considered successful. These criteria must include performance metrics for judging project success, such as cost, schedule, and quality. During the preliminary phases of a project, metrics may be broadly defined, or you might know some in detail. Metrics become more precise as the project progresses, a concept called *progressive elaboration*.

Product deliverables and project objectives are both *outputs* of Scope Planning, and are *inputs* to Scope Verification (as well as others). Scope Verification results in the formal acceptance of the product.

As an aid to remembering the steps involved, work the processes backward from the results or outputs. What's the easiest way to obtain the customer's formal acceptance of the project? Then plan to ensure that acceptance.

Metrics you might consider tracking include these crucial concepts:

- ✔ **Performance:** Basic operating characteristics

- ✔ **Features:** The basic characteristics and functions that affect the marketability of a product

- ✔ **Reliability:** The probability of how the system operates over a period of time

- ✔ **Conformance:** The degree of compliance with established requirements. This term also relates to quality

- ✔ **Durability:** The useful product life span before replacement is needed

- ✔ **Serviceability:** The ease of repairs, updates, and maintenance

- ✔ **Aesthetics:** Product qualities about the look, feel, sound, smell, or taste

The actual metrics you'll use vary by industry, product definition, and project needs. See Chapter 11.

Setting Milestones

During the conceptual phases of the project, your major scheduling activity involves two indispensable factors for measuring the project's progress:

- ✔ Defining the milestones for each major deliverable (or result)

- ✔ Sequencing milestones (with their deliverables) in a logical order

Milestones or *milestone events* mark the completion of a major deliverable or set of related deliverables. Milestones are results of work and therefore output-driven, not task-driven or date-driven. The definition of milestones contains no time or calendar references because they are not based on calendars. You don't reach a milestone just because you arrive at a date. Rather, milestones provide checkpoints to validate project progress and revalidate the completed tasks. In many cases, milestones call for decisions to be made based on the results. The decision could be an acceptance or rejection of the deliverable (for example, sending it back for rework). Milestones generally occur when some significant or highly visible result appears — such as delivery of a key document, essential equipment, or a phase-end review.

We cover how to set some estimated dates for reaching each milestone in Part III when we explore activity sequencing. For now, just remember that by definition, a milestone has a duration of zero and requires no effort. The results are already attained, so no work is associated with a milestone. It signifies completion of work, but a milestone is not the work itself. Reaching a milestone gives management some factual evidence of the team's progress.

Establishing clear milestones at intermediate points in your schedule has these immediate benefits:

- Gives the project a sense of direction
- Prioritizes and focuses time
- Lets you measure progress

Setting Quality Standards

Project initiation discussions always involve managing quality. Quality management means managing both the project and the product. Ideally, it improves the project management no less than the product. It involves satisfying two objectives:

- Drive a consensus definition on what constitutes quality
- Figure out how to meet the requirements

In addition to your organization's internal standards, your product may have to meet outside constraints on quality as well. Some examples include

- Organizational guidelines
- Standards set by professional organizations
- Government regulations

Although quality can seem hard to define, some key concepts will probably help you to recognize it consistently when you see it:

- **Quality:** The totality of features and characteristics that satisfy stated or implied needs, fitness for use, and conformance to requirements or specifications. Memorize the "needs" phrase; it's an ISO standard.

- **Quality Planning:** Identifies which quality standards are relevant to the project and determines how to satisfy them.

- ✔ **Quality management:** Covers the processes required to ensure that the project satisfies the needs it was undertaken to meet.

- ✔ **Cost of quality:** All costs associated with ensuring quality. These include quality planning and quality control.

  - • **Prevention costs:** Includes training, surveys, and the implementation of quality-management systems.

  - • **Appraisal costs:** Includes inspection and testing.

  - • **Failure costs:** Includes internal and external costs. *Internal costs:* rework, rejects, and scrap. *External costs:* warranties, returns, recalls, and handling customer complaints.

- ✔ **Customer satisfaction:** Involves identifying, managing, and influencing needs so customer expectations are met or exceeded. Management doesn't define quality; the customer defines quality.

- ✔ **Prevention over inspection:** The idea that the cost of avoiding mistakes is much less than the cost of correcting them. Inspection is the cost of nonconformance or poor quality.

- ✔ **Management responsibility:** The acknowledgment that although quality management requires the involvement of all project team members, quality itself is the responsibility of management.

Coping with an Organization's Structure

Projects don't exist in isolation. They're part of a larger organization in which the project is formulated, evaluated, and realized. An organization can be characterized by different models — each has strengths and weaknesses. Such external factors directly impact your project. Each model also impacts the project manager's role, which can vary because of:

- ✔ Level of authority

- ✔ Communication methods

- ✔ Staff management techniques

- ✔ Internal politicking

Exam questions include various types of organizational structures, models, and project cultures. Memorize Table 6-1 for the exam. Different structures place constraints on the availability of resources or on how you are permitted to use the resources.

Table 6-1 describes the project manager's authority in different types of organizations.

Table 6-1	Organizational Structures
Organizational Type	*Project Manager Authority*
Functional	None
Project expediter	Low
Project coordinator	Low
Weak matrix	Low to medium
Strong matrix	Medium to high
Projectized	High

Functional organization

Most organizations are aligned on a traditional hierarchy. The focus is on an organizational model topped by hierarchies of managers, bureaucratic procedures, and interdepartmental politics. Staffs are assembled into departments, grouped by function and by expertise. Functional departments include engineering, IT, HR, accounting, finance, marketing, and purchasing.

In this hierarchical model, each employee has only one boss — the *functional manager*. The staff's first priority is to its own department. Departmental objectives determine how they spend their time, their line of reporting, and responsibilities for performance appraisals. Their loyalties to their departments may hamper the project completion. Often, technical and subject-matter experts get project assignments in addition to their primary departmental jobs. Such departmental priorities can put vital processes (such as resource allocation and prioritization) outside the project manager's control. If team members and stakeholders are drawn from multiple functional departments, managing across those boundaries may be difficult. Significant barriers exist to *horizontal* information flow (across the organization, from one vertically integrated department to another).

Matrix organization

The matrix organization structure has the project manager and the functional manager sharing project responsibilities. This is a *multiple-command* system where both project manager and functional manager assign priorities and direct the project. The project has a team leader in each functional department. Product or project results are passed from team to team. In this model, the functional department staffs are temporarily assigned to the project. At the end of the project, they return to their functional groups. As a project manager, you have to work closely with the functional manager to minimize the negative effects of dual reporting and the potential for conflicts.

Advantages of matrix organizations:

- ✔ Visible objectives
- ✔ Enhanced utilization of resources
- ✔ Enhanced coordination
- ✔ Enhanced information flow
- ✔ Retention of staff and knowledge after project

Disadvantages of matrix organizations:

- ✔ Multiple bosses
- ✔ Complex structure to control
- ✔ Differing priorities of project manager and functional manager
- ✔ Effort duplicated
- ✔ Conflicts

Projectized organization

Projectized organization models use project management as a tool for accomplishing work and changing the organization itself. The project doesn't belong to any single department but rather to the entire organization. Thus the project manager isn't stealing staff from the functional managers (or from their "real" jobs in a functional department). In this model, the project team is a separate organizational entity. It has its own budget, staff, and performance criteria.

- ✔ The project manager selects people for the project from a resource pool — and then "owns" them for a contracted period. Team members from different areas are "loaned" to the project. They *co-locate,* or share office space.
- ✔ The project manager evaluates the project team in a reward system, which affects each individual's compensation and promotions.

Although such an organization might sound perfect for a project manager, it does have some drawbacks. Typically, functional managers are threatened as staff leaves the functional area to rejoin a resource pool. At the project's conclusion, often the staff doesn't know their next assignment. Out of a desire for job security, they might make extra work for themselves. The result is the project manager might retain staff longer and increase costs. Consulting firms are good examples of purely projectized organizations, and the difficulties just cited are typical of their internal politics.

Prep Test

1 **Who is accountable for the success of the project?**

A ○ The project team

B ○ The sponsor

C ○ The project manager

D ○ The customer

2 **Who is accountable for the ultimate success of the project?**

A ○ The project team

B ○ The sponsor

C ○ The project manager

D ○ The customer

3 **Who is responsible for quality?**

A ○ The project team

B ○ The sponsor

C ○ The project manager

D ○ Corporate management

4 **As a new project manager, you find that your customer has refused to accept past projects. What can you do to ensure the customer will accept the product?**

A ○ Set customer expectations.

B ○ Have the customer sign off on milestones.

C ○ Involve the customer in requirements.

D ○ Set customer expectations and involve the customer in requirements.

5 **Which is not the responsibility of the sponsor?**

A ○ Providing resources

B ○ The project plan

C ○ Selecting the project manager

D ○ Issuing the project charter

Answers

1 **C.** This pattern requires you to complete a definition. It tests your ability to demonstrate your understanding of the relationships among facts, principles, and methods.

2 **B.** This pattern requires you to complete a definition. It tests your ability to demonstrate your understanding of the relationships among facts, principles, and methods.

3 **D.** This pattern requires you to complete a definition. It tests your ability to demonstrate your understanding of the relationships among facts, principles, and methods. *See "Setting Quality Standards."*

4 **D.** D is a combination of A and C together; it makes the best answer. Doing both ensures that the customer is satisfied and (presumably) happy to sign the acceptance document. B isn't correct by itself because it's an incomplete answer; it's a hard decision because B is a correct *PMBOK Guide* answer. There are two patterns. The first pattern is *the single most important thing a project manager should do is ___.* The second pattern is the steps that make up the process output, which is customer acceptance. To identify those steps, you may have to work through the methodology backwards. So you must know the tools and techniques, and inputs.

5 **B.** The project plan is the responsibility of the project manager. All other answers given are the responsibility of the sponsor. This is an exception pattern — what's not included in the group.

Chapter 7

Opening the Project

· ·

Exam Objectives

▶ Documenting project authorization

▶ Publishing the project charter

▶ Appointing the project manager

▶ Establishing constraints and assumptions

▶ Keeping project records

· ·

*I*n this chapter, you find out about the results of Initiation, which emphasizes the process of developing and producing the initial project plan documentation. Documentation involves

✔ The physical records or results the project team generates

✔ The planning, executing, controlling, and closing of all project activities required to keep stakeholders informed

A large part of managing projects involves documenting and communicating what you do as the project manager, what the team does, and what the final product or service of the project is supposed to accomplish. Documentation ties together everything that the team achieves during the project.

The process of "getting it in writing" involves all the life-cycle phases of the project and must be repeated at each step. These communications *skills* tie together the work of the project in all the knowledge areas. As a result of these interactions between the project processes, trade-offs of project objectives may be necessary. These trade-off decisions need to be documented in the project plan as the project team advances and makes future decisions. Documentation ties together the results of the product or service the project team sets out to deliver. Creating the documentation implies communicating all this information to appropriate stakeholders.

Documentation provides a permanent record of the transition from the initiation processes into the planning process and other processes you'll master next.

Quick Assessment

Authorizing the Project

1 A project manager is authorized to perform work by the _____.

2 The project charter gives the project manager _____ authority.

Documenting Constraints and Assumptions

3 Schedule constraints can be caused by _____, _____, and _____.

4 Factors that, for planning purposes, will be considered to be true, real, or certain are called _____.

5 _____ generally involve risks.

6 External circumstances or events that must occur for the project to be successful are _____.

7 External circumstances or events that must not occur for the project to be successful are _____.

Maintaining Project Records

8 Laws and regulations, organization structure (or decision-making authority), and predefined budgets are examples of _____.

9 Essential inputs to all planning processes include: process audits, lessons learned, and _____ from previous projects.

10 Items required for documenting the project include: constraints, assumptions, subsidiary project plans, lessons learned, project records, historical information, and _____.

Answers

1 Project charter. This pattern asks for the definition of the process. It tests your ability to demonstrate your understanding of the relationships among facts, principles, and methods. See "Authorizing the Project."

2 Formal or legitimate authority. This pattern asks for definition specifics of the project charter. It's a different level of detail than Question 1, although both are about the project charter. It tests your ability to demonstrate your understanding of the relationships among facts, principles, and methods. The different types of authority or power aren't even mentioned in the *PMBOK Guide.* See "Documenting constraints and assumptions."

3 Task predecessors, resource availability, target dates. It tests your ability to demonstrate your understanding of the relationships among facts, principles, and methods. See "Documenting constraints and assumptions."

4 Assumptions. This pattern asks for the definition. You may see multiple variants of questions like these, so you must know these definitions cold. This is an especially tricky pattern because you might guess one was constraints and the other assumptions. See "Documenting constraints and assumptions."

5 Assumptions. This pattern requires you to complete the definition. Know these types of definitions cold. See "Documenting constraints and assumptions."

6 Assumptions. This pattern requires you to complete the definition. Questions 5 and 6 are related variants. See "Documenting constraints and assumptions."

7 Risks. This pattern asks for examples. It tests your ability to demonstrate your understanding of the relationships among facts, principles, and methods. See "Documenting constraints and assumptions."

8 Constraints. See "Documenting constraints and assumptions."

9 Historical information. This is an input pattern. See "Maintaining Project Records."

10 Supporting details. This pattern asks for examples of documentable items. They're a variety of inputs and outputs. Our learning tip in Chapter 2 is to call them the nouns of project management. It tests your ability to demonstrate your understanding of the relationships among facts, principles, and methods. See "Maintaining Project Records."

Authorizing the Project

The process of initiating projects starts long before you get the official approval. Before you get approval, you must accumulate all the necessary information to ask management for official permission to start the project.

Kicking off the project

The *project charter* sets the ground rules. It deserves a special place as one of the most important documents on your project. It formally authorizes the project, and it is a key output, or deliverable, of the Project Scope Initiation process. The project charter guides the team through all the planning and implementation decisions during the life of the project. Review Chapters 5 and 6 for information on drafting the charter and do the Lab exercise to create a sample project charter on the CD.

How do you get authority (or power) to manage the project? The types of authority or power aren't mentioned in the *PMBOK Guide.* For the exam, remember these important concepts:

- ✔ **Formal (legitimate) authority** in the charter gives the project manager the authority to act in the name of the sponsoring executive or on behalf of the organization. (The charter's authorizer is usually an executive at a high enough level in the organization to assess the needs of the project, but is not actually involved in the project.)

- ✔ **Referent authority** refers to the ability to influence others through charisma, personality, and charm, or a higher-level manager.

- ✔ **Coercive authority** refers to motivating staff by punishment and is predicated on fear (of losing status, positions, bonuses, or jobs).

- ✔ **Reward authority** refers to positive reinforcement and the ability to award something of value.

- ✔ **Expert authority** is earned if the team respects your skills as a project manager (or as a subject-matter expert).

Along with the project charter, you need to document other initiating outputs such as assumptions and constraints and share the information with the stakeholders. What's involved in creating a project charter varies among organizations, which may have different standards and formats for completeness. The main points to initiating a project should provide a high-level view of the following:

- ✔ The purpose of launching the project
- ✔ Deliverables (often called *objectives*)

✔ Roles and responsibilities

✔ Issues and risks

✔ The product or service

✔ Scope

✔ Project organization

✔ Other organizations affected by the work

✔ Estimated effort, cost, and duration

✔ Assumptions

✔ Constraints

If you haven't yet written a sample project charter, do it now. We've provided a template on the CD. It's important for your success not only to have a charter to authorize your study, but also to remember the steps involved in creating it.

Publishing the project charter

The project charter provides the authorization to proceed with the project and perform work. After you get the approval, the project charter becomes the official document you need to obtain resources from the organization. Other functional managers may verify your authorization before they agree to perform any work for you or to assign their resources to your project. After you publish the charter, you issue many other documents, and the hard work of the project really begins.

Selecting the project manager

The selection of the project manager is one of the *outputs* of the Scope Initiation process. It establishes clear management authority for the project. In the project charter, the project manager is named and given authority to apply resources to project activities. In many cases when the charter is drafted, the project manager is a vacant position on the project org chart. Maybe the project manager hasn't been hired yet, or he needs to wrap up another project, or senior management can't determine the right manager for the position. The project manager should be named as early as possible and certainly before the start of project plan execution. The criterion for selecting the project manager is a much-debated topic in general management. Because the selection criteria are out of scope for the exam, don't worry about them.

Documenting constraints and assumptions

Constraints and *assumptions* describe the project's scope. They are often used to manage the expectations of all stakeholders.

Constraints

Constraints are factors that limit the team's options. A project can be constrained in many ways. Schedule constraints affect when a task can start or finish. Causes of schedule constraints are predefined budgets, task predecessors, resource availability, duration, or target dates. Laws and regulations, as well as organizational structure (or decision-making authority), also provide constraints. As background for situational questions on the exam, here are some constraints you need to remember:

✔ **Budget constraints:** Budget constraints are financial limitations placed on the project either internally by the project management team or externally by management or the customer. Lots of contracts and contract types are aimed at ensuring that project costs are within budget.

  • One Hollywood producer sets such tight budget restrictions that he has been known to remove all production filming equipment immediately after the original budget figure has been spent. It doesn't matter if the filming is complete; he'll edit the picture with whatever has been shot.

✔ **Target-date constraints:** Management routinely sets the target dates of product development projects without the benefit of performing a work breakdown or scheduling. Contractual penalties for late delivery provide a severe target-date constraint with great financial risks to the performing organization.

  • The end-of-year target-date constraint required software modifications for Y2K projects to be completed in time for testing and full deployment.

  • Marketing plans hinge on being able to announce the new product at a trade show to take advantage of publicity aimed at a particular audience.

  • When a portion of the Santa Monica Freeway collapsed after the 1994 Northridge earthquake, the California Department of Transportation's restoration project imposed contractual penalties if the contractor didn't complete the job on time.

✔ **Resource-availability constraint:** Resources (people, materials, or equipment) might not be available when you need them and constrain your options. Delays in delivery of components or in performance by subcontractors are major sources of resource constraints.

- A senior staffer who could accomplish the assigned project tasks is working on another project and is not available for your project. A junior staffer is available, but he will take twice as long to complete the work or isn't qualified to perform it. Movie producers find themselves with this kind of resource availability constraint if their box-office star sustains an injury, and Mel, Sly, and Arnold are busy working on other pictures. Imagine a crew of 300 people waiting for the star to arrive.

✔ **Duration constraint:** The length of the project or task may limit the team's options. Also, time availability to perform specific tasks may be limited by access restrictions. Activity durations may not be driven by work content but constrained by paint drying or concrete curing, for example.

- A movie's production crew has to plan its shooting schedule around the resource availability of an external demolition project. A building explodes just as the hero drives up. The duration constraint is that the movie crew is limited by the explosion and the collapse of the building. They get one chance to get it right. Road construction crews often work under a duration constraint when closing down roads for short periods of time or when working nights.

✔ **Task-predecessor constraint:** When two tasks are scheduled in sequence, often the second task cannot start until the first task (the predecessor task) has been completed.

- Repairing a wall could involve a time delay that constrains activities. The length of time plaster takes to dry constrains the start time for painting.

Assumptions

Assumptions are external circumstances or events that must occur for the project to be successful, and they involve some risk. The risk is that the assumptions aren't accurate or that they will change. So, they are progressively elaborated through the project. By contrast, *risks* are external circumstances or events that must *not* occur. Because assumptions are part of all planning processes, they affect everything you do. Identifying an assumption increases its visibility and sets expectations. That's why it's important to identify assumptions, document them, and later validate them.

Assumptions are factors that are true, real, or certain. They generally have a degree of risk. Here are some typical examples:

✔ Budgets and resources will be available when needed.

✔ The new Y2K software fixes will be available for testing and implementation before December 31, 1999.

✔ Work calendars include only regular hours without any overtime.

✔ No newer technologies will be introduced mid-project.

Maintaining Project Records

Documenting all planning activities, results, and supporting details is an important part of the project management methodology. The process of "getting it in writing" involves all project life-cycle phases and must be repeated at each step. The inputs and outputs of every process are documents or documentable items, which you add to the project records. Lessons learned and historical information from previous projects are essential inputs to planning processes.

Project records, subsidiary plans, project details, supporting details, lessons learned, historical information, technical documents, standards, constraints, and assumptions are either *inputs* or *outputs* — they're documents or documentable items, which we call our *nouns*. They are never tools and techniques, which we call *verbs*.

Gathering the information to be documented will test your communication skills. You must be like a reporter uncovering a story and a diplomat trying to reconcile competing interests. For example, as project processes interact, tradeoffs of project objectives may be necessary. Trade-off decisions need to be documented to demonstrate to management and to customers how the objectives evolved. Otherwise, you'll have no way of justifying the product or service you deliver. Ultimately, documentation is your best proof to customers that the project gave them what they requested.

Good communication among the stakeholders helps you mold individual viewpoints and different needs, expectations, and interests into team-oriented commitment. For project success, all stakeholders must share a common understanding of what the project is supposed to accomplish. Scope statement documentation is one of the project manager's tools and techniques that literally places everyone on the same page! The more stakeholders know about the project, the better the team can manage it, and the easier it will be for the team to visualize and produce the desired results.

Customer satisfaction involves setting clear requirements and expectations and then managing them. Often, this is a journey of discovery. Customers may not know or be able to articulate what they want. The project team will have to uncover its requirements by conducting interviews, asking questions, and challenging assumptions. The investigation doesn't end until conclusions are documented in a form that can be presented to customers for review, approval, and signoff.

A defining principle of project management methodology is *progressive elaboration* — the refinement and detailing of a product or service in steps. You don't know everything at the outset, but the orderly process of the project gradually builds a clearer picture of the deliverables. You need formal documentation at every step to keep those competing needs from expanding beyond the project's scope. You can't hit a moving target! You have to remember what decisions you made along the way and why you made them. Finally, you can't allow an armchair quarterback to claim at the end of the project, "But that's not what I asked for!"

Bottom line, you'll have a better chance of being perceived as successful if you put important decisions and plans in writing and share that documentation with all stakeholders.

Prep Test

1 Factors that, for planning purposes, will be considered to be true, real, or certain are called:

A ○ Hypotheses

B ○ Constraints

C ○ Assumptions

D ○ Project environment

2 Assumptions generally involve:

A ○ A certain degree of risk

B ○ Input from the project sponsor

C ○ Factors that are true, real, and certain

D ○ Input from the project sponsor and factors that are true, real, and certain

3 Identifying external factors that must happen for the project to be successful involve:

A ○ Constraints

B ○ Assumptions

C ○ Project assumption analysis

D ○ Risks

4 The project charter documents:

A ○ The project manager's authority

B ○ The business purpose of the project

C ○ The product of the project

D ○ The project manager's authority, the business purpose of the project, and the product of the project

5 Outputs from Project Plan Development are:

A ○ Project plan

B ○ Constraints

C ○ Assumptions

D ○ Project plan, constraints, and assumptions

6 Organized storage and maintenance of correspondence, memos, reports, and other documents describing the project are called:

A ○ A project management information system (PMIS)

B ○ Project records

C ○ Archives

D ○ Supporting details

7 **The outputs of Initiation include:**

A ○ Issuing the project charter

B ○ Assumptions

C ○ Project manager identified and assigned

D ○ Project charter, assumptions, and project manager identified
and assigned

8 **Which of the following is a document, or collection of documents, which
should be expected to change over time as more information becomes available about the project?**

A ○ Project charter

B ○ Project plan

C ○ Scope statement

D ○ Product description document

9 **Schedule constraints can be caused by:**

A ○ Task predecessors

B ○ Resource availability

C ○ Target dates

D ○ Imposed deadlines, resource constraints, and task dependencies

10 **Which of the following are meetings held to assess project status or progress?**

A ○ Performance reviews

B ○ Status reviews

C ○ Weekly status meetings

D ○ Phase review progress meetings

Answers

1 **C.** Assumptions. This pattern asks you to complete the definition. It's the simplest type of question. Know these definitions cold. *See "Documenting constraints and assumptions" and the* PMBOK Guide, *p. 43.*

2 **A.** A certain degree of risk. This pattern asks you to complete the definition. Although all answers could be correct, you must identify the best answer. C is the first part of the *PMBOK Guide* definition, and B is perfectly reasonable, especially if you are new to the project or organization. A completes the key phrase "generally involve," which makes it the best choice. *See "Documenting constraints and assumptions" and the* PMBOK Guide, *p. 43.*

3 **B.** Assumptions. This pattern asks you to distinguish between terms that are closely related. *See "Documenting constraints and assumptions."*

4 **D.** The project manager's authority, the business purpose of the project, and the product of the project. Each individual answer — A, B, or C — is a correct statement, but the best answer is D, which combines them. This pattern asks for the definition. *See "Authorizing the Project."*

5 **D.** Project plan, constraints, and assumptions. Project Plan Development outputs are project plan and supporting details. Here's the trick: Supporting details can include constraints and assumptions that weren't previously known. This output pattern drills down to a fine level of detail. *See the* PMBOK Guide, *p. 45.*

6 **B.** Project records. This pattern asks you to distinguish between terms that are closely related. Compare just how closely related project records and archives are. *See the* PMBOK Guide, *pp. 122, 125.*

7 **D.** Project charter, assumptions, and project manager identified and assigned. This is an output pattern. Know these outputs for the exam. *See the* PMBOK Guide, *p. 54.*

8 **B.** Project plan. The project charter should not change during the course of the project unless there are drastic scope changes. The scope statement and product description will change over the course of the project, so C and D are both good answers. The scope statement is an output of Scope Planning, not Initiation. The definition of product description is close; it will generally have less detail in the early phases and more detail in later ones as the product characteristics are progressively elaborated. But it's an input to Initiation. This is an output pattern. *See the* PMBOK Guide, *pp. 53–55.*

9 **D.** Imposed deadlines, resource constraints, and task dependencies. These can cause schedule constraints. This pattern asks for examples. It tests your ability to demonstrate your understanding of the relationships among facts, principles, and methods. *See "Documenting constraints and assumptions."*

10 **A.** Performance reviews. B is an easy answer, but status is contained in performance reporting. This is the definition pattern. *See the* PMBOK Guide, *p. 123.*

Part III
Planning the Project

The 5th Wave By Rich Tennant

"This isn't a quantitative or a qualitative estimate of the job. This is a wish-upon-a-star estimate of the project."

In this part...

1n reel two of *PMP, The Movie,* the behind the scenes peek at making a movie must confront reality. The cost and schedule estimates the team made during the initial, conceptual phases need refinement. During the conceptual phase, a production accountant flipped to the last page of the script and gave a heuristic estimate: "The script is 120 pages. On his last film, the director you're using shot a page and a half a day. So you can expect a four-month shooting schedule. And you'll need two months for preparation and three for editing. With a four-month shoot, if it's an 'A' picture, it'll come in at $75 million. You start adding in special effects and stars, and production costs will run higher. If it's a 'B' picture, it'll come in at $30 mil." Those ballpark estimates stuck in the mind of the studio's senior managers who authorized the project.

Reel three opens before filming begins. Our hidden spycam camera zooms to a close-up on the producer, UPM, and AD. They are "planning the plan." They need to develop their project plan, refine time and cost estimates, and plan for inevitable future changes. The AD will decompose the script into a work breakdown structure, determine resource constraints, develop a resource matrix, and get estimates as he meets with functional department mangers: Director, Designer, Director of Photography, Wardrobe, Property Master, and a dozen more managers. With those estimates, the AD will finalize a shooting schedule. From those detailed estimates and the schedule, the UPM will develop a detailed budget. He'll haggle with various studio managers and beg for funding that accurately reflects what the production will actually cost.

Chapter 8

Refining the Project

• •

Exam Objectives

▶ Developing the project plan

▶ Refining project requirements

▶ Planning and defining scope

▶ Using estimating formulas for the time value of money and discounted cash flow

• •

*P*roject Plan Development involves taking the results of other planning processes and putting them into a consistent, coherent document. Because planning accounts for more questions on the exam than any other topic (47 out of 200), concentrate your study effort on this important area.

Planning is the *key* project management process. Some managers don't trust planning processes because they don't use their plans to facilitate execution. Project plans guide execution. Every knowledge area includes planning.

We can't overstate the importance of good Project Scope Management. The 1995 CHAOS Report cited a clear project mission, a clear statement of requirements, and proper planning as vital elements for project success. The study also showed that lack of proper project definition and scope is the main reason projects fail.

Quick Assessment

Project Integration Management

1 Tools and techniques for project plan development include _____, _____, _____, and _____.

2 The _____ is a formal, approved document used to manage and control project execution.

3 The _____ is a document or collection of documents that should be expected to change over time as more information becomes available about the project.

Project Planning

4 _____ are the differences between the project plan and the project performance measurement baselines.

5 _____ is the difference between project and product scope.

6 _____ is how you measure the project and product scope.

TVM/DCF

7 You win a $1 million lottery prize. How much cash do you really get? The state will pay you $50,000 a year for 20 years. If the discount rate is 10 percent, _____ is the present value of the lotto.

8 _____ is the present value of $10,000 in 5 years at a discount rate of 10 percent.

9 _____ is the future value in five years of $10,000 today at a discount rate of 10 percent.

10 _____ get to see the project plan.

Answers

1 Project planning methodology, stakeholder skills and knowledge, project management information system (PMIS), and earned value management (EVM). This is the tool and technique pattern. See "Project Plan Development."

2 Project plan. This pattern asks for you to know the definition. It's the simplest type of question. See "Project Plan Development."

3 Project plan. This pattern asks for you to know the definition. It's the simplest type of question. See "Project Plan Development."

4 You should expect the project plan document(s) to change over time as more information becomes available about the project. The performance measurement baselines represent a management control that will generally change only intermittently and then generally only in response to an approved scope change. This pattern asks for definitions and for you to distinguish between terms that are closely related. See "Planning and Defining Scope."

5 Product scope refers to the features and functions of the product delivered by the project, whereas project scope refers to the work required to deliver the product. This pattern asks you to distinguish between terms that are closely related. See "Planning and Defining Scope."

6 Completion of the project scope is measured against the project plan, whereas product scope is measured against the requirements. This pattern asks you to distinguish between terms that are closely related. See "Planning and Defining Scope."

7 $616,889. That's about half of what the lottery stated it would give you. See the present value formulas in "Discounting cash flow."

8 $6,209. $PV = (FV)^n \div (1 + i)^n$. $PV = \$10,000 \div (1 + 0.10)^5 = \$6,209$. See the present value formulas in "Discounting cash flow."

9 $16,105. $FV = P (1 + i)^n$. $(FV)^5 = \$10,000 (1 + 0.10)^5 = \$16,105$. See the future value formulas in "Discounting cash flow."

10 Stakeholders as defined in the communications management plan. This definition pattern tests your ability to demonstrate your understanding of the relationship among facts, principles, and methods. See "Project Plan Development."

Project Integration Management

Integration is defined as the processes required to coordinate various elements of the project. It involves making trade-off decisions among competing objectives and alternatives. Although the other processes may overlap and integrate, the chief function of Integration processes is to combine and harmonize the results of all other processes. The exam covers three processes:

- **Project Plan Development:** The process of taking the results of other planning processes and organizing them into a consistent, coherent document. This plan guides execution and control. The plan includes the following:

  - Project charter
  - Project management approach or strategy
  - Scope statement
  - Work breakdown structure (WBS)
  - Cost estimates
  - Schedule
  - Major milestones and their target dates
  - Performance measurement baselines
  - Key skills or required staff
  - Key risks
  - Open and pending issues

- **Project Plan Execution:** The process of carrying out the project plan by performing activities identified in the plan.

- **Integrated Change Control:** The process of coordinating changes across the entire project. In the 1996 *PMBOK Guide,* the term was *Overall Change Control.* The new term emphasizes the integrative aspect of all processes.

Project Plan Development

These are the five inputs to Project Plan Development:

✔ **Other planning outputs:** Documented outputs of the planning processes in the other knowledge areas.

✔ **Historical information:** Includes lessons learned from past projects and similar projects, and the particular customer's history. You should consult this data during the other project planning processes.

✔ **Organizational policies:** Defined in terms of the product and cover the full range of management concerns. (See Chapter 5 for details.)

✔ **Constraints:** Factors that limit the team's options.

✔ **Assumptions:** Factors that, for planning purposes, will be considered true, real, or certain.

Here are the four tools and techniques to Project Plan Development:

✔ **Project planning methodology:** Documents the characteristics of the product or service that the project was undertaken to solve. It also documents the relationship to a business need that created the project. It's really any structured approach used to guide the project team during the development of the project plan.

✔ **Stakeholder skills and knowledge:** People using the product or service may have particularly valuable insights in developing the project plan.

✔ **Project management information system (PMIS):** Includes the systems, activities, and data that permit information to flow in a project. It also includes the tools and techniques used to gather, integrate, and disseminate the outputs of all project management processes.

✔ **Earned value management (EVM):** A distinction for the exam is that EVM is an integrated approach combining scope of work, schedule, and costs. EVM uses the values from earned value (EV) analysis to manage the project and to determine project status. Early detection of variances to the plan enables decision making while there is adequate time to take corrective actions. Earned value analysis is taking the actual and estimated costs and calculating the three values (EV, PV, and AC or older terms BCWP, BCWS, and ACWP; see Chapter 9 for details) as well as all the other ratios (such as CPI and SPI). U.S. government contracts require EVM.

The two outputs of Project Plan Development are as follows:

- **Project plan:** The project plan documents planning assumptions, decisions, and baselines for scope, cost, and schedule. As a formal, approved, and composite document, it contains subsidiary plans from the knowledge areas. It is used to guide execution and control of the project, and to facilitate communication among stakeholders. The plan is a document (or collection of documents that integrates all parts of the project) that will change over time as more information becomes known about the project. It establishes performance measurement baselines as a management control. The baseline will change intermittently, but later in the project, it should only change due to approved scope changes. Distribute the plan documents to everyone defined in the communications management plan.

- **Supporting detail:** Includes the results of previous project decisions and performance, as well as relevant lessons learned from past projects, and the history with a particular customer and with similar projects. You may develop additional information from other planning processes such as technical documentation — requirements, specifications, or designs, for example. These outputs, which are not included directly in the plan, provide important reference material. This is a vague term, so review what's included. For example, you may be surprised to find out that constraints and assumptions that weren't previously known are included.

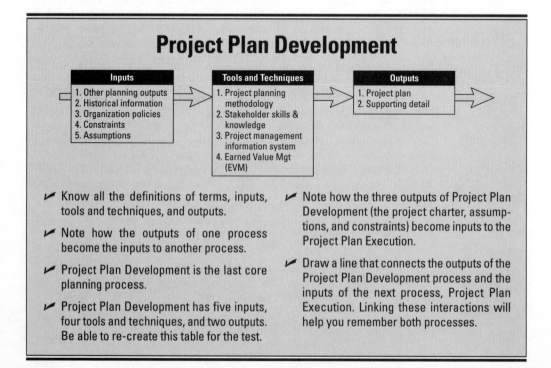

Project Plan Development

Inputs	Tools and Techniques	Outputs
1. Other planning outputs 2. Historical information 3. Organization policies 4. Constraints 5. Assumptions	1. Project planning methodology 2. Stakeholder skills & knowledge 3. Project management information system 4. Earned Value Mgt (EVM)	1. Project plan 2. Supporting detail

- Know all the definitions of terms, inputs, tools and techniques, and outputs.

- Note how the outputs of one process become the inputs to another process.

- Project Plan Development is the last core planning process.

- Project Plan Development has five inputs, four tools and techniques, and two outputs. Be able to re-create this table for the test.

- Note how the three outputs of Project Plan Development (the project charter, assumptions, and constraints) become inputs to the Project Plan Execution.

- Draw a line that connects the outputs of the Project Plan Development process and the inputs of the next process, Project Plan Execution. Linking these interactions will help you remember both processes.

Integration

Integration has three main processes: Project Plan Development, Project Plan Execution, and Integrated Change Control. Try this mnemonic: a *DECk* of cards. Creating a project plan is like shuffling a deck of cards because you use the outputs of all the other processes.	Integration	Stack the *DECk* in your favor.
	Integration	Development, Execution, Change Control
	PM processes	Planning, Execution, and Control

Establishing a PMIS

During the life of the project, you need to collect information. A project management information system (PMIS) includes the systems, activities, and data that permit information to flow in a project. A PMIS also uses tools and techniques to collect, integrate, and distribute the results of all project management processes. In this specific context, *system* refers to a method of doing things and doesn't necessarily indicate automation or computerization. PMIS ranges from manual and paper-intensive systems, to those completely computer-automated. The *PMBOK Guide* definition of PMIS shows up for the first time in the Project Plan Development process as a tool and technique. Did you just see the PMIS missing from every Initiation process? The *PMBOK Guide* covers it by saying it supports all aspects of the project from initiation through closing. PMIS is an area where your organization's project management office (PMO) may have some standards — even during conceptual or development phases.

Unless you are working on a military project, your project generally won't have any secret information.

Growing the Project Plan

All planning processes are about defining and refining objectives. The goal is to select the best alternative course of action to accomplish the business need the project was created to solve. For example, project scope management processes capture all the work, and only the work, needed to produce the product of the project. When you deal with scope issues, you have to refine what is in scope and deliver that work. Also, you must identify what's not in scope so you don't waste time and resources producing the wrong things.

Using rolling wave planning

Project plans are developed in incremental steps by an iterative process. Initially, you don't know much about the project, and your task is growing the knowledge base of what the project is all about. Project planning's main purpose is providing focus, organization, and preserving options. Your understanding of the results of the project and how the customer will use the product will become more detailed as the project progresses. Growing your knowledge is called *rolling wave planning.* This is a method of progressively detailing the project plan. It's important to keep updating product information and project data in your documentation.

The concepts of iterative planning, refinement, and progressive elaboration are mantras of the PMI. Evaluate exam questions in this light.

Here are some points to remember about refining your plans:

✔ All plans are only estimates; some estimates are better than others. The rolling wave method enables you to refine these estimates as you discover more about the project. You get the opportunity to refine the plan at the start of each phase.

✔ Forget the road directly in front of you and focus on the results. How will you finish the project? Remember physicist Heisenberg's principle: The observer can't help affecting the results of the observation. Become aware of your own biases and don't let them interfere.

✔ Consider relevant trade-offs of quality, time, and cost.

✔ Don't spend all your time planning!

✔ No plan is perfect. If you ever find someone who makes perfect estimates and creates the perfect project plan, have him or her pick some lottery numbers for us.

Developing the project plan

Lots of things go into developing a project plan. During Project Plan Development, you take the results of all planning processes and place them into a consistent, coherent document — the project plan.

Lots of planning processes, which produce lots of outputs, must be organized into the plan. Each of the nine knowledge areas has a planning process. Eight knowledge areas create their own subsidiary project plan that will be added as a section of the project plan (which is the ninth). In some organizations, this combined document is called the integrated project plan. When you are working on the schedule, it's only one part of the project plan. Be aware that most people refer to the project *schedule* as the project plan. They are wrong; know this distinction for the exam. For example, a quality management plan is also part of the project plan. Cost, human resources, quality, procurement, and risk are examples of the many types of subsidiary project plan inputs to project planning.

The project plan is not a static document. It's not wallpaper. The activities of the project will produce various results. As work progresses, you'll make additional measurements and refine estimates. You'll discover additional functions and hidden requirements by using rolling wave planning methods. You'll make assumptions, as well as identify and monitor risks. The project plan must reflect all these changes. Actual data continually replaces estimated data. As you monitor the project and compare estimated to actual results, you'll see the validity of your earlier assumptions and risk assessments. Do they still need to be tracked? Perhaps you've passed the time when you have to worry about a particular risk and can drop it from your watch list. Perhaps a planning assumption is no longer true because a new technology appeared. Check assumptions and risks periodically.

Planning and Defining Scope

Planning and defining scope are the project manager's most important planning processes. *Scope* refers to the boundaries of the project. It defines the road map for creating the product or service of the project. It also refers to various project management processes used to create the scope. If you do a poor job of planning and defining the scope, managing the scope will be a problem throughout the project. Project scope management includes the processes involved in defining and controlling what is, or is not, included in the project. Everyone on the project and all stakeholders must share a common vision of the project and product.

Here are the two approaches to planning:

- **Top-down approach:** Start with the largest items, or most-generalized descriptions, of the project and break them down to the finest level of detail.

- **Bottom-up approach:** Start with the detailed tasks and roll them up to higher levels of detail.

In a situational question, the exam might ask how team exercises can help determine and refine product definitions. Here is a team exercise. Include some key customers and your sponsor in a meeting with the team. Draw a large circle on a whiteboard. Everything inside the circle is in scope. Everything outside the circle is out of scope. Write down those characteristics or functionalities that you intend to deliver inside the circle. Ask the group to suggest other product specifics. As a group, decide whether to write them inside the circle (within the scope of the project) or outside (out of scope). Transcribe the resulting diagram and include it in your project documentation.

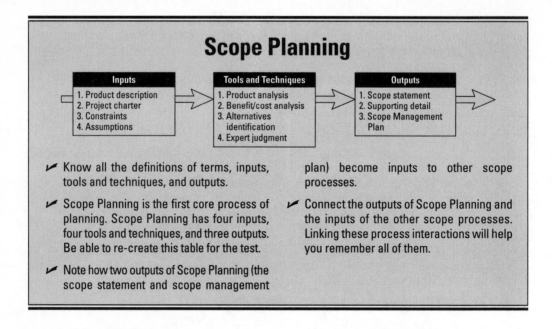

Scope Planning

Inputs	Tools and Techniques	Outputs
1. Product description	1. Product analysis	1. Scope statement
2. Project charter	2. Benefit/cost analysis	2. Supporting detail
3. Constraints	3. Alternatives identification	3. Scope Management Plan
4. Assumptions	4. Expert judgment	

✔ Know all the definitions of terms, inputs, tools and techniques, and outputs.

✔ Scope Planning is the first core process of planning. Scope Planning has four inputs, four tools and techniques, and three outputs. Be able to re-create this table for the test.

✔ Note how two outputs of Scope Planning (the scope statement and scope management plan) become inputs to other scope processes.

✔ Connect the outputs of Scope Planning and the inputs of the other scope processes. Linking these process interactions will help you remember all of them.

Scope planning results in a written *scope statement* that includes:

✔ Project justification, major deliverables, and project objectives

✔ Project strategy — how you'll develop and manage the project

✔ Measurable criteria that determine if the project or phase has been completed successfully

Scope planning provides the inputs to how you'll measure your team's success. It's foolish to start a project before the sponsor determines how to measure its success. You might put a lot of effort into delivering the wrong features.

Identifying and refining scope is a major part of project planning. The notions that progressive elaboration is a planning method and that the scope needs to be re-verified at each phase are PMI mantras.

Here are some key terms on scope that you need to know for the exam:

✔ **Project scope management:** Includes the processes required to ensure that the project includes all the work required, and only the work required, to complete the project successfully.

✔ **Product scope:** Describes the features and functions in the product to be delivered. These are qualities or characteristics of the product or service. If a feature is in scope, you must deliver it.

✔ **Project scope:** Describes the work required to deliver the product with the specified features and functions.

In the next few sections, you find out how to determine the project's scope.

Successful completion of *product* scope is measured against the requirements; *project* scope is measured against the project plan.

Creating the Scope Management Plan

You develop the scope management plan and the scope statement during the scope-planning process. This is a high-level process to manage the scope of the project and guide how to handle scope changes. It usually includes an assessment of how stable the project scope is and tells how to identify and organize scope changes.

This limerick might help you to remember the scope processes:

> There once was a PM from Van Nuys,
>
> Who saw an initiation in front of his eyes.
>
> The stakeholders argued planning and definition
>
> Before the court of Judge Verification.
>
> The PM saw just what scope change control buys.

Planning the scope

Scope Planning is the process of writing a scope statement, which will be used as the basis for future project decisions. The statement includes project justification, the major deliverables, the project objectives, and the criteria used to determine if the project or phase has been successfully completed.

These are the four inputs to Scope Planning:

- ✔ **Product description:** Documents the characteristics of the product or service that the project will create. It's less detailed in the early phases.
- ✔ **Project charter:** The document that formally recognizes the existence of a project. It's issued by a manager external to the project and at a level appropriate to the needs of the project.
- ✔ **Constraints:** Factors that limit the project management team's options.
- ✔ **Assumptions:** Factors that, for planning purposes, will be considered to be true, real, or certain.

Here are the four tools and techniques to Scope Planning:

- **Product analysis:** Involves developing a better understanding of the product of the project. It includes techniques such as systems engineering, value engineering, value analysis, function analysis, and quality function deployment. It stresses reducing costs, maintaining quality, and ensuring structured approaches to developing the product.

  - **Systems engineering:** An interdisciplinary, systematic, and structured approach to developing a quality product. It focuses on identifying customer needs and required functionality, documenting requirements, and validating authorized tasks that satisfy the control-gate requirements. (A *control gate* is a requirement that must be met before work can continue to the next phase.)

  - **Value engineering:** A structured approach to optimizing project value through examination of the project's design. This technique analyzes qualitative and quantitative costs, as well as the benefits of component parts of a proposed system. It provides functionality at the lowest life-cycle cost that is consistent with required performance, reliability, quality, and safety.

  - **Value analysis:** A cost-reduction tool for handling the scope of work. It considers whether a function of a design or item is necessary. Can the functions be provided at a lower cost without degrading performance or quality?

  - **Function analysis:** A graphical representation of system functions in a logical diagram, called a *behavior diagram.*

  - **Quality function deployment:** Provides better product definition and product development. The main features are capturing customer requirements, ensuring cross-functional teamwork, and linking the main phases of product development.

- **Benefit/cost analysis:** Estimating tangible and intangible costs (outlays) and benefits (returns) of various alternatives and using financial measures to assess the relative desirability of the alternatives.

- **Alternatives identification:** Any technique used to generate different approaches to the project (such as brainstorming or lateral thinking).

- **Expert judgment:** May be provided by any group or individual with specialized knowledge or training.

The three outputs to Scope Planning are as follows:

- **Scope statement:** Provides a documented basis for making future project decisions and for confirming or developing common understanding of project scope among stakeholders. When known, identify all exclusions. Any item not specified is assumed to be out of scope, by default. The reason the scope statement might exclude specific items that will *not* be done is to help you manage customer and sponsor expectations. As the project progresses, the scope statement may need to be revised or refined to reflect scope changes. The scope statement is an agreement made between the client and project manager, whereas the statement of work (SOW) is an agreement made between the project manager and seller. Major sections of the scope statement include

- **Project justification:** Describes the business need, the reason this project was undertaken. It provides a basis for evaluating future trade-offs.

- **Project product:** A brief product description.

- **Project deliverables:** List summary level subprojects whose full and satisfactory delivery marks completion of the project.

- **Project objectives:** Quantifiable criteria that must be met for the project to be considered successful. This section must include measures of cost, schedule, and quality.

    Some organizations call project objectives the deliverables, whereas others call critical success factors the project objectives.

✔ **Supporting details:** This output should be documented and organized as needed to facilitate use by other PM processes. This output should include all identified assumptions and constraints. The performance specifications, which describe the product's needs, are an important component. These specs define the expected performance of a deliverable. They are the sum total of the benefits that make up the product. They are described by features, characteristics, process conditions, and constraints.

✔ **Scope management plan:** Describes how the project scope will be managed and how scope changes will be integrated into the project. It must also include an assessment of the expected stability of the project scope. A scope management plan may be *formal* or *informal*, highly detailed or broadly framed, based on the needs of the project. It is a *subsidiary element* of the overall project plan.

Writing the scope statement

Before drafting the scope statement, you should have a clear understanding of the project. The scope statement describes the project deliverables and objectives. It provides a basis for a common understanding of project scope among the stakeholders. Talk with them and find out their needs. Make sure that you share the sponsor's vision. You might even get lucky; the information you're seeking might be available in one of the preliminary documents that have already been approved by the sponsor. But if a ready-made scope statement is not available, you must create one.

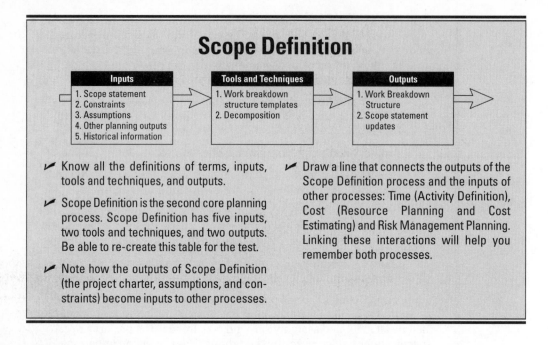

Scope Definition

Inputs	Tools and Techniques	Outputs
1. Scope statement 2. Constraints 3. Assumptions 4. Other planning outputs 5. Historical information	1. Work breakdown structure templates 2. Decomposition	1. Work Breakdown Structure 2. Scope statement updates

✔ Know all the definitions of terms, inputs, tools and techniques, and outputs.

✔ Scope Definition is the second core planning process. Scope Definition has five inputs, two tools and techniques, and two outputs. Be able to re-create this table for the test.

✔ Note how the outputs of Scope Definition (the project charter, assumptions, and constraints) become inputs to other processes.

✔ Draw a line that connects the outputs of the Scope Definition process and the inputs of other processes: Time (Activity Definition), Cost (Resource Planning and Cost Estimating) and Risk Management Planning. Linking these interactions will help you remember both processes.

A scope statement develops and confirms a common understanding of the project scope. Because this is important exam material, the following list expands on what the scope statement should include:

✔ A project justification

✔ The business need that the project addresses

✔ A description of the project's end products or services

✔ A summary of all project deliverables and objectives, the quantifiable goals that determine project success

✔ All assumptions, constraints, and work specifically excluded

Both the sponsor and customer should approve the scope statement. Make sure that the version of the scope statement you give to the customer doesn't expose confidential information such as internal budgets or costs.

Beginning with this rolling wave planning process, you'll use the outputs from the deliverables and objectives in the scope statement to set the performance measurement baseline against which you'll measure later progress. In the project plan, you elaborate on the baselines for technical scope, costs, and schedule. Performance measurement techniques provide the methods used to estimate earned value. You'll use appropriate measurements for different work packages because of the type of work or the task's duration. Performance measurement techniques are also discussed in the tools and techniques section of the Integrated Change Control, Scope Change Control, and Cost Control processes.

Defining the scope

Scope Definition divides major project deliverables into manageable components. It improves the accuracy of cost, time, and resource estimates. It provides a baseline and assigns responsibility. A scope baseline is the original plan, plus or minus approved changes.

These are the five inputs to Scope Definition:

- ✔ **Scope statement:** See the earlier section, "Writing the scope statement."

- ✔ **Constraints:** Factors that limit your options.

- ✔ **Assumptions:** Factors that are considered to be true, real, or certain.

- ✔ **Other planning outputs:** Outputs from processes in other knowledge areas should be reviewed for possible impact on project scope definition.

- ✔ **Historical information:** Information from similar or previous projects.

Here are the two tools and techniques to Scope Definition:

- ✔ **Work breakdown structure templates:** Use templates from a previous project for a new project. We explore the work breakdown structure in Chapter 9.

- ✔ **Decomposition:** Subdividing the major project deliverables into smaller, more manageable components. Decomposition is defined in terms of how you'll manage the project. We explore this technique in Chapter 9.

The two outputs to Scope Definition are as follows:

- ✔ **Work breakdown structure (WBS):** A fundamental project document that has a great emphasis in PM methodology. It provides the basis for planning and managing the project. It's a deliverable-oriented grouping of project elements that organizes and defines the total scope of the project. Work not contained in the WBS is outside the scope of the project. We cover the WBS in detail in Chapter 9.

- ✔ **Scope statement updates:** Refinements of the scope statement. It involves the rolling wave planning method.

Understanding Formulas for the Time Value of Money

The exam has a group of questions on measuring profitability that use the concept of the *time value of money* (TVM) and *discounted cash flow* (DCF). This section shows you some shortcuts to using these formulas on the exam. If these profitability questions appear on your exam, just remember the formulas, plug in the numbers, and do the math. Before we get to the formulas, here are two concepts you need to know:

- **Opportunity cost:** The cost of choosing one alternative. This forgoes the potential benefits of another alternative; it's the value of lost opportunity. Think of this as having a *future dimension*.

- **Sunk cost:** The cost already expended. Your decisions about continuing investments should ignore every sunken cost. Think of this as having a *past dimension*, as in "don't cry over spilled milk."

These calculations are used most frequently in the project selection process to determine which of several alternatives to fund. If you have two projects that cost the same amount, how do you determine which to fund? TVM and DCF come to the rescue. These techniques are used in both scope and quality planning (benefit/cost analysis). The next few sections refer to the examples in Table 8-1.

Table 8-1	TVM Examples		
	Project A	*Project B*	*Project C*
Discount Rate	10%	10%	10%
Initial Investment	$27,500	$27,500	$35,000
Cash Inflows			
Year 1	$10,000	$14,000	$18,000
Year 2	$10,000	$12,000	$10,000
Year 3	$10,000	$13,000	$12,000
Year 4	$10,000	$8,000	$8,000
Year 5	$10,000	$3,000	$4,000

Benefit/cost ratio

The benefit/cost ratio is

```
Expected Revenues ÷ Expected Costs
```

You measure the benefits, or the paybacks, to the total costs of the project. It's not just the profits. The higher the ratio, the better. If the ratio is greater than 1, the benefits outweigh the costs.

Project A

For Project A in Table 8-1, the cash inflows from years 1 through 5 total $50,000. That's the expected revenue. The expected cost is the initial investment (the project costs), which is $27,500. Apply the formula:

```
$50,000 ÷ $27,500 = 1.81
```

Because the result (1.81) is greater than 1, the benefits of doing this project outweigh the costs.

Project B

For Project B, the cash inflows from years 1 through 5 total $50,000. This project has the same expected revenue and the same expected cost as Project A. Therefore, the Benefit/Cost ratio is the same: 1.81.

Project C

For Project C, the cash inflows from years 1 through 5 total $52,000. The expected cost is the initial investment (the project costs), which is $35,000. Apply the formula:

```
$52,000 ÷ $35,000 = 1.48
```

The benefits outweigh the costs, but to a lesser extent than Projects B and C.

Payback analysis

The simplest method of looking at multiple alternatives is *payback analysis*. This technique evaluates the length of time before the payback occurs. *Payback* is earning back the money that you'll spend. The payback period is the amount of time it takes to recoup the dollars invested in a project. Shorter payback periods are desired. Payback analysis has two weaknesses:

- ✔ It doesn't account for the time value of money.
- ✔ It doesn't consider any value in the magnitude of benefits after payback.

The formula for payback analysis is

```
Costs ÷ Annual Cash Inflow = Payback Period
```

Refer to Table 8-1 and apply payback analysis to those projects.

Project A

The payback period for Project A is the initial investment (the project costs), which is $27,500. The annual cash inflow is $10,000 for five years. Apply the formula:

```
$27,500 ÷ $10,000 = 2.75 years
```

Watch for questions that ask you to convert the 0.75 decimal value from years to months. In that case, the answer is 2 + 0.75 ÷ 12; 2 years and 9 months.

When you have uneven annual cash inflows, add the expected cash flows for each succeeding year until you arrive at the total cost of the project.

Project B

Calculating the payback period of Project B is slightly more complicated because of the uneven annual cash inflow. In this case, you add the annual cash inflows until you go over the project's cost limit of $27,500. In the case of these cash inflows, you go over the limit in year 3 (14,000 + 12,000 + 13,000 = 39,000). Therefore, the payback is somewhere in year 2.

The first two years total $26,000. Assume that the $13,000 cash flow in year 3 is disbursed evenly throughout all 12 months of the year; that equates to a cash inflow of $1,083 per month. You only have to reach $1,500 for payback, so it takes 1.4 months ($1,500 ÷ $1,083). The payback period of project B is 2 years and 1.4 months.

On the exam, watch for questions that require you to convert the months back to years or the decimal fractions of years to months.

Project C

The payback period of Project C is the project cost: $35,000. Cash inflows during the first three years exceed costs: 18,000 + 10,000 + 12,000 = 40,000. Therefore, payback is between years 2 and 3. This is an easy calculation because $12,000 equally disbursed over a year is $1,000 per month. Complete the calculation:

```
35,000 - 28,000 = 7,000
```

The payback period is 2 years and 7 months.

As positive cash flow increases, payback periods decrease.

Discounting cash flow

Focusing solely on the total cash outflow ignores the *time value* of the cash flows: A dollar received today is worth more than a dollar in the future because of the opportunity to earn interest. Money today is worth more because of the cost of interest on borrowed capital (such as your mortgage).

Future value

The *future value* (FV) is the value at some future time (a number of years) of a present amount of money (or a series of payments) at a known interest rate.

```
Future Value (FV) = PV (1 + r)ⁿ
FV = Principal + (Principal × Interest)
```

where

```
PV = present value
n = the number of periods
r = the discount rate (or interest rate)
```

Alternatively, you can solve it as:

```
Future Value = amount × 1 ÷ PV
```

The future value of $100 for one year at 10 percent is

```
$100 × 10% = $110
```

The FV of $1,000 for one year at 10 percent is

```
$100 × 10% = $110
```

The FV of $100 for two years at 10 percent is

```
$110 × 10% = $11 (in interest)
```

Figure 8-1 shows the timeline.

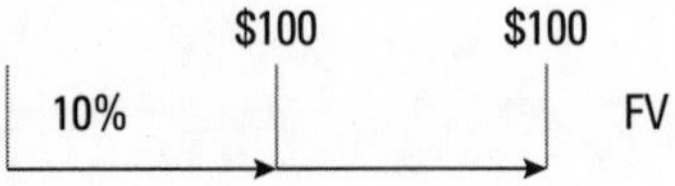

Figure 8-1:
The FV timeline.

$100 $100

10%   FV

The future value of $100 for two years at 10 percent is $121 (that's $11 interest plus the $110).

Present value

The present value (PV) is the total amount that a series of future payments is worth today by using a specified rate of return. Figure 8-2 shows a typical timeline.

```
Present Value = FV ÷ (1 + i)ⁿ
```

where

```
FV = Future Value
n  = number of periods
i  = discount rate (or interest rate)
```

If the interest rate is 10%, the present value of $100 one year from now is

```
$100 ÷ 1.10 = $91
```

The present value of a future payment of $110 a year from now at 10 percent is

```
$110 ÷ 1.10 = $100
```

Figure 8-2:
The PV timeline.

PV   10%

$100 $100

Net present value

The net present value (NPV) is a variation of present value. Figure 8-3 shows the timeline. If you've mastered PV, NPV is simple. NPV analysis discounts all expected future cash inflows and outflows to the present. To calculate the NPV, calculate the present value of future payments and then subtract investments. If the result is positive, the investment should be considered. If it's negative, forget it.

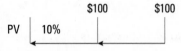

$$\text{Net Present Value} = CF_0 + CF_1 \div (1 + r)^1 + CF_2 \div (1 + r)^2 + CF_3 \div (1 + r)^3 + CF_n \div (1 + r)^n$$

where

CF_x = cash flow in period x
n = the number of periods
r = the discount rate

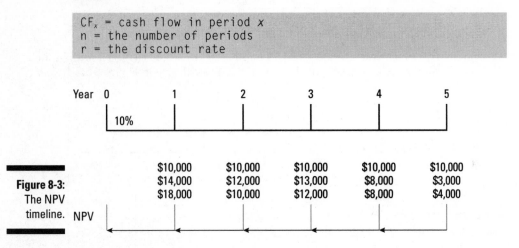

Figure 8-3:
The NPV
timeline.

Assuming that the cost of capital (or discount rate) is 7.5%, what is the net present value of the cash flows in Table 8-1 for Projects A, B, and C? Just plug in the discount rate, r, and solve the equation. The discount rate is 10 percent, and the periods range from one to five years. Be sure to include the initial cost as an outflow — that's a negative number. Plug in the values:

$$\text{Project A} = -27{,}500 + 10{,}000 \div (1 + 0.1)^1 + 10{,}000 \div (1 + 0.1)^2 + 10{,}000 \div (1 + 0.1)^3 + 10{,}000 \div (1 + 0.1)^4 + 10{,}000 \div (1 + 0.1)^5$$

This gives you –27,500 + 9,090 + 8,264 + 7,513 + 6,830 + 6209 + 10,407. Adding the numbers for the NPV, the total is $10,407, as shown in Figure 8-4.

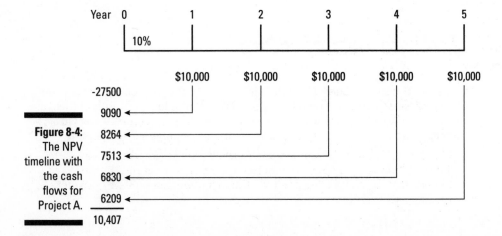

Figure 8-4:
The NPV
timeline with
the cash
flows for
Project A.

```
Project B = -27,500 + 14,000 ÷ (1 + 0.1)¹ + 12,000 ÷ (1 +
            0.1)² + 13,000 ÷ (1 + 0.1)³ + 8,000 ÷ (1 + 0.1)⁴ +
            3,000 ÷ (1 + 0.1)⁵
```

This gives you –27,500 + 12,727 + 9,917 + 9,767 + 5,464 + 1,862. Adding the
numbers for the NPV, the total is $12,238, as shown in Figure 8-5.

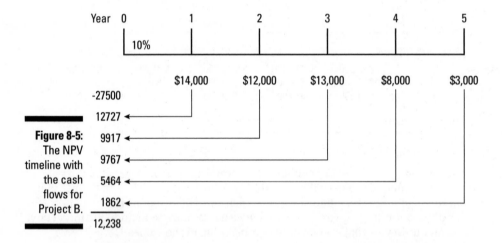

Figure 8-5:
The NPV
timeline with
the cash
flows for
Project B.

```
Project C = -35,000 + 18,000 ÷ (1 + 0.1)¹ + 10,000 ÷ (1 +
            0.1)² + 12,000 ÷ (1 + 0.1)³ + 8,000 ÷ (1 + 0.1)⁴ +
            4,000 ÷ (1 + 0.1)⁵
```

You can practice creating the timeline for Project C. Here are the numbers to
check: –35,000 + 16,363 + 8,264 + 9,015 + 5,464 + 2,483. Adding the numbers for
the NPV, the total is $6,589.

Internal rate of return

The *internal rate of return* (IRR) is the interest rate that makes the PV of costs
equal to the PV of benefits. It's the discount rate that makes the net present
value of those cash flows equal to zero. This is a lot like NPV. But, in this
case, you solve for r — the discount rate. There are noted problems with
using IRR, mainly because of the possibility for defining more than one
interest rate. IRR is generally used as a complement to NPV.

```
Initial investment = CF₁ ÷ (1 + r)¹ + CF₂ ÷(1 + r)² + CF₃ ÷ (1 +
                     r)³ + CFₙ ÷ (1 + r)ⁿ
```

where

```
CF_x = cash flow in period x
n = the number of periods
r = the internal rate of return or discount rate
```

On the exam, you may have to plug in some of the answers and work backwards. In the case of Project A in Table 8-1, you know the NPV at 10 percent is roughly $10,000. Because you want to determine at what rate this would be zero, you have to increase the interest rate.

```
Project A = -27,500 + 10,000 ÷ (1 + r)¹ + 10,000 ÷ (1 + r)² +
            10,000 ÷ (1 + r)³ + 10,000 ÷ (1 + r)⁴ + 10,000 ÷ (1
            + r)⁵
```

If you plug in a rate of 20 percent for r, you get 2,406 for Project A. If you plug in a rate of 30%, you get –3,144. Therefore, the rate is in the middle.

Follow these steps to solve discounted cash flow and time value of money problems on the exam:

1. Read the problem thoroughly.

2. Determine if it is a PV, FV, or NPV problem. The exam may try to confuse you with the right answer to the wrong formula. You might get the answer to one of the responses when you solve for FV, but the question may be asking for PV.

3. Create a timeline. This can help determine the type of problem and the formula you need to use.

4. Put cash flows and arrows on the timeline. The sequence of inflows and outflows is significant.

5. Determine if the solution involves a single cash flow or a mixed flow.

6. Plug in the formula. Make sure it's the right formula.

7. Do the math.

8. Check your math with a (financial) calculator.

   Some answers may vary slightly due to rounding. If you don't get the exact amount, pick the closest. (For exam responses, the closest number is the best answer, even if the exact figure isn't one of your options.)

Prep Test

1 Systems engineering, value engineering, value analysis, function analysis, and quality function deployment are examples of:

   A Expert judgment methods

   B Product analysis

   C Alternatives identification

   D Scope planning methods

2 _____ includes the systems, activities, and data that permit information to flow in a project.

   A The project management information system

   B Project status reports

   C Information distribution

   D Documentation control

3 Project justification, major deliverables, and project objectives are part of the:

   A Scope statement

   B Project strategy

   C Product strategy

   D Business strategy

4 Growing your knowledge about the project is called _____:

   A Rolling wave planning

   B Rolling thunder planning

   C Progressive iteration

   D Iterative planning

5 The future value of $2,000 invested for two years at 8.5% will be?

   A $2,170

   B $2,355

   C $2,555

   D $2,772

6 What would a single payment of $35,000 two years from now be worth today with a 10% interest rate?

   A $42,350

   B $28,926

   C $31,818

   D $26,296

7 What is the IRR of Project B in Table 8-1?

    A 12.5%

    B 15.5%

    C 29.8%

    D 35%

8 The sponsor of the project wants you to forget about developing a formal project plan. He wants you to dive into the work right away. What do you do?

    A Do as instructed. Start the team working on the project immediately.

    B Refuse to comply. Start working on developing the initial project plan, drafting a scope statement (with major deliverables quantified), and developing a WBS. When these activities are completed, ask the sponsor and client representative to sign off on those documents. Then start the team working.

    C Discuss the reasons why projects fail with the sponsor. Persuade the sponsor that the key reasons why projects fail include a lack of agreed upon scope and a lack of planning. Then document that discussion as part of the project records. Begin the planning process and share the resulting documents with the sponsor.

    D Explain to the sponsor that the project depends on beginning with an adequate planning foundation. Planning is necessary to execute and control the project. Begin the planning process and share the resulting documents with the sponsor.

Answers

1 **B.** This pattern gives examples and asks for the definition. It tests your ability to demonstrate your understanding of the relationship among facts, principles, and methods. The *-ing* gives you a clue that it's a tool and technique. *See "Planning the scope."*

2 **A.** This pattern requires you to know the definition. It's the simplest type of question. *See "Establishing a PMIS."*

3 **A.** This pattern asks for the definition. It tests your ability to demonstrate your understanding of the relationship among facts, principles, and methods. *See "Planning and Defining Scope".*

4 **A.** This pattern asks for the definition. It tests your ability to demonstrate your understanding of the relationship among facts, principles, and methods. *See "Using rolling wave planning."*

5 **B.** $FV = 2,000 (1.085)^2 = 2,000 \times 1.177 = 2,355$. *See "Understanding Formulas for the Time Value of Money."*

6 **B.** $PV = 35,000 \div (1 + .10)^2 = 35,000 \div (1.21) = 28,926$. *See "Understanding Formulas for the Time Value of Money."*

7 **C.** Initial investment $= CF_1 \div (1+r)^1 + CF_2 \div (1 + r)^2 + CF_3 \div (1 + r)^3 + CF_n \div (1 + r)^n$. Initial investment is noted as −27,500 to indicate this is subtracted. Let's guess the r is 20%. Plug in the numbers: $14,000 \div (1 + 0.2)^1 + 12,000 \div (1 + 0.2)^2 + 13,000 \div (1 + .2)^3 + 8,000 \div (1 + 0.2)^4 + 3,000 \div (1 + 0.2)^5$. This translates to −27,500 $= 14,000 \div (1.1) + 12,000 \div (1.21) + 13,000 \div (1.33) + 8,000 \div (1.46) + 3,000 \div (1.6)$ = 11,212. So 20% is too low. By solving for r, we're trying to get the amount close to 0. Try plugging in 30%. $14,000 \div (1.3) + 12,000 \div (1.69) + 13,000 \div (2.19) + 8,000 \div (2.85) + 3,000 \div (3.7)$ = −104. That means r is below 30%. *See "Internal rate of return."*

8 **C.** Discussing the reasons why projects fail with the sponsor is the best answer. A and B are train wrecks waiting to happen; with A, you won't deliver the project, and B will get you fired. D is a good answer but incomplete.

Chapter 9

Creating the Work Breakdown Structure

. . . .

Exam Objectives

▶ Using a work breakdown structure (WBS) and decomposing the work

▶ Relating the WBS to the activity list

▶ Creating a resource matrix

▶ Creating a staff management plan

▶ Using the WBS for staffing

▶ Planning for procurement and solicitation

▶ Contracting for services and supplies

▶ Developing the schedule

▶ Harnessing earned value management

. . . .

*T*his chapter presents the planning tools and concepts that the exam measures. The range of material is broad. Entire books have been written on each of these major topics. We condense the material to what you need for the exam.

Pay special attention to the definitions and examples for the work breakdown structure (WBS), network diagrams, and CPM (critical path method). Project managers love the WBS, so make sure that you're familiar with it.

This chapter covers how to use a WBS for staffing and how to create a responsibility assignment matrix (RAM). You can develop a sample RAM for your project on the CD. This chapter gives you the lowdown on Procurement Planning and Solicitation Planning, developing a schedule, and applying earned value.

Quick Assessment

WBS

1 A work breakdown structure is a _____ grouping of project elements that organizes and defines the total scope of the project.

2 The _____ links the scope to the schedule.

3 The WBS links scope to _____ and to _____.

4 The staffing management plan is first developed in the _____ process of Project Human Resource Management.

Procurement
Contracts5

5 If you want to limit your risk in purchasing services from a subcontractor, select a _____ contract type.

6 You're on a three-year project with a long development cycle and have significant test requirements. You determine that the performing organization can't make several subcomponents, so you'll have to procure them. In order to control the seller and share some savings, you would select a _____ contract.

Developing
the
Schedule7

7 You're the project manager on a research and development project with lots of uncertainty. After decomposing the work and developing your WBS, the engineers have found that you are missing some deliverables and that you need to add some corrections to the project's scope. The document you'll update is called a _____, and the process of updating is called a _____.

8 In a detailed planning meeting, a programmer tells you that developing a new reporting module will take four weeks. You ask for a best-case scenario, and the programmer estimates it could take as long as ten weeks to complete. Next, you ask how long it would take if everything went perfectly, and the programmer replies that he might be able to complete the reports and reuse another reporting module. Under those conditions, he estimates that it could take one week. The estimated task duration using PERT would be _____.

Answers

1   Deliverable-oriented. The concept is deliverable-orientation rather than task-orientation. This pattern asks for you to know the definition. It's the simplest type of question. See "Using a Work Breakdown Structure."

2   WBS. This pattern asks for the process interactions. See "Using a Work Breakdown Structure."

3   Time and cost. WBS links Scope to Time through the activity list, Scope to Cost in Resource Planning and HR Organizational Planning. This pattern asks for the process interactions. It tests your understanding of the relationship among facts, principles, and methods. See "Using a Work Breakdown Structure," "Relating the WBS to the activity list," and "Creating a responsibility assignment matrix."

4   Organizational Planning. This pattern is the order of events. This question tests your understanding of the relationship among facts, component processes, and methods. See "Organizational Planning."

5   Firm fixed price. This pattern asks for the definition of the process. It tests your understanding of the relationship among facts, principles, and methods. See "Contracting for services and supplies."

6   Cost plus incentive fee. This pattern asks for the definition of the process. It tests your understanding of the relationship among facts, principles, and methods. See "Contracting for services and supplies."

7   WBS and refinement. This pattern asks for the definition of the process. It tests your understanding of the relationship among facts, principles, and methods. See "Developing the Schedule."

8   The mean is 4.5 weeks with a standard deviation of 1.5 weeks and a variance of 1.2 weeks. See "Estimating techniques and formulas."

Using a Work Breakdown Structure

Work breakdown structure (WBS) is a scope definition tool that organizes the work and provides a basis for project estimates. It looks similar to an org chart, but it diagrams the categories of a project rather than shows who's who in an organization. Its purpose is to include all the work required to complete the project. If you start entering tasks into a scheduling tool, you'll find out somewhere in the middle or end of the project that you left out important activities. By dividing the objectives into smaller, more manageable chunks, the WBS identifies responsibilities to the level of either departments or individuals and identifies the work at the task level.

Figure 9-1 shows a WBS for your PMP Exam Prep Project. This breakdown has three levels: Level 1 shows study materials and exam administration. Level 2 identifies resources. Level 3 lists steps for studying the materials.

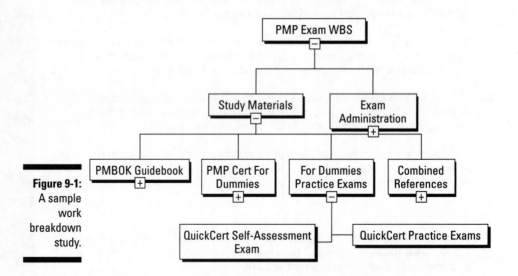

Figure 9-1:
A sample
work
breakdown
study.

Figure 9-2 shows another view of the WBS. This view breaks down the study plan by the parts of this book, following the project life cycle.

In Figure 9-1, the WBS starts by identifying the highest levels of work in the project. Each lower level breaks the groupings into smaller chunks. The breakdown continues to as many levels of detail as you need. There is no fixed number of levels for a proper decomposition. In general, you want to continue breaking down tasks until they are small enough for one person or one team to control and manage effectively. By looking at different views of the project, you'll determine if you've adequately covered the scope.

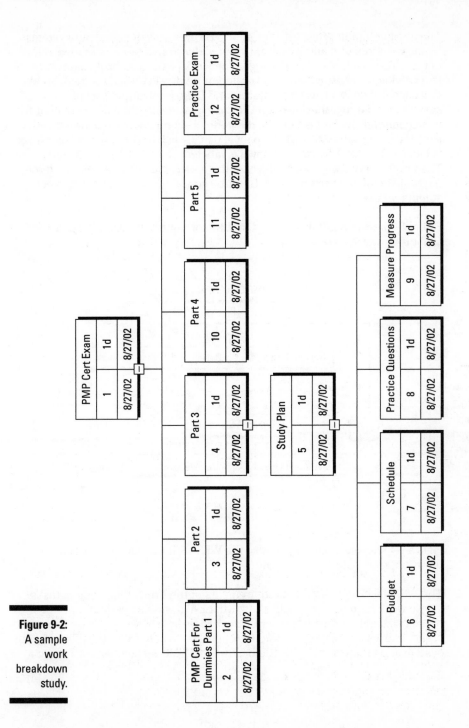

Figure 9-2:
A sample
work
breakdown
study.

The most common types (or views) of WBS are by system and subsystems, by life-cycle phases, and by organizational division of labor. The lowest level of the WBS is called a *work package*. The work package is broken down to the level of deliverables, which is lower and more detailed than the task break-down level. The WBS, work packages, and the organization's accounting system are tied together through the *code of accounts*. Similar in concept to an accounting chart of accounts, the code of accounts uniquely identifies each element in the WBS. The top level usually is labeled 1; the second level is labeled 1.1, 1.2, 1.3; the third level is labeled as 1.1.1, 1.1.2, 1.1.3; and so on. The first level is always at the level of the *project* life cycle (as opposed to anything involving the product). Don't be confused if you see the project summary labeled as Level 0.

Figure 9-3 shows another view of the WBS for your PMP Exam Prep Project by skill or knowledge area.

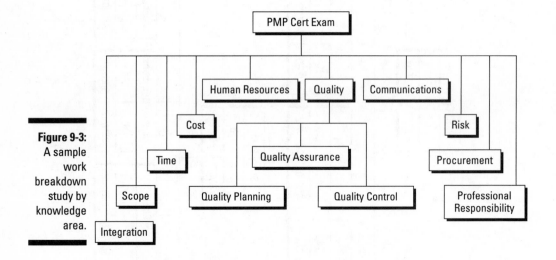

Figure 9-3: A sample work breakdown study by knowledge area.

Figure 9-4 shows a planning view of the WBS with the code of accounts, duration, start date, and end date.

The WBS describes the work requirements of the project in terms of tasks. These work requirements help show what skills will be needed to perform those tasks. WBS Chart Pro from Critical Tools links with Microsoft Project to create impressive planning and control charts. Install WBS Chart Pro on your system and create a WBS. It's the best way to become familiar with using a WBS.

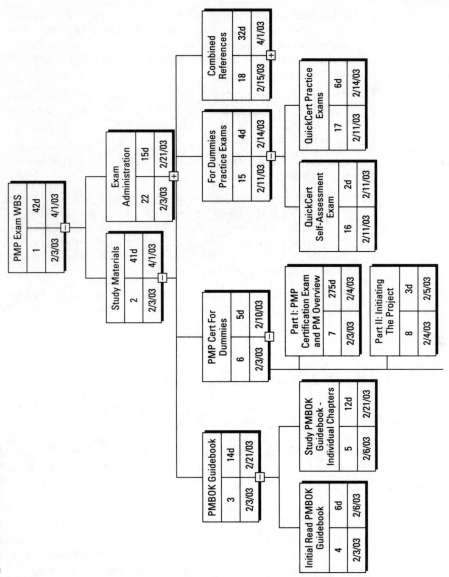

Figure 9-4:
A sample work breakdown study by knowledge area.

Here are some WBS definitions you need to know for the exam:

✔ **WBS:** A deliverable-oriented grouping of project elements that organizes and defines the total scope of the project. Remember that WBS is *deliverable-oriented* rather than *task-oriented*. Each element should be defined not as a task but as a tangible result of the work. Work not shown in the WBS is outside the scope of the project. Any in-scope work obviously missing from the WBS must be added to its structure. It defines the project's scope baseline.

- **WBS dictionary:** Defines each element in the WBS. It includes a description of work packages (in case you forget what the abbreviations mean) and other planning information such as schedule dates, costs, and staff assignments. The WBS dictionary is part of the supporting detail documentation.

- **Cost control system:** Any system of keeping costs within the bounds of budgets. It's established by matching business needs to the work package. The work package is mapped to the organization's chart of accounts via the WBS code of accounts.

- **Code of accounts:** Any unique numbering system that identifies each WBS element.

- **Cost account:** A level in the budget element breakdown structure. It defines what work will be performed and who will perform it. As an accounting systems identifier, the cost account provides a crucial integration point for scope, cost, and schedule. It's also called a control account. It's generally either one level above the work package or at the lowest summation level in the WBS.

- **Work package:** A deliverable at the lowest level of the WBS. A work package may be divided into activities. These activities are rolled into cost accounts.

Decomposing the work

Decomposition involves identifying the major project deliverables so that they can be controlled in later phases. Using a hierarchical tree-structure approach, you break down the deliverables into smaller, more manageable components. The process of decomposition is complete when all deliverables are defined in sufficient detail to support future project activities (planning, executing, and controlling). Make sure that there are no gaps or overlaps.

You must decompose each deliverable into its elements. Make sure that the elements don't have gaps or overlaps. Use tangible, verifiable results to describe elements so that they're measurable. This process enables you to develop cost and duration estimates, as well as identify specific results for each level of the WBS. The last decomposition step is to verify that you have correctly detailed the elements of all deliverables. You'll use these outputs in other processes for scheduling, budgeting, and assigning to a responsibility party (department, team, or person).

Updating the scope statement from WBS

The two-way link between the WBS and Scope Planning and Definition is one of the important updates to the 2000 *PMBOK Guide*. If you or any team member finds a change in scope from your preliminary planning work, now is your chance to correct it. When your decomposition work is done, update or modify the scope statement as needed. Then communicate the changes to the stakeholders as defined in your communications plan.

PMI methodology specifies how the processes feed back into each other as control points, how everything must be documented, and the need for communicating with appropriate stakeholders.

Relating the WBS to the activity list

Throughout the book, we describe how an output of one PM process becomes the input to other PM processes. In the case of the WBS, it links Scope to Time through the activity list. (We explain how the WBS interacts and integrates with Cost and HR later in the chapter.)

All activities that must be performed to produce the deliverables identified in the WBS need to be identified, placed in sequential order, and their durations estimated. The first Time Management process is to define the activities. Activity Definition involves identifying and documenting the work that the team must perform to produce all product deliverables. The resulting output is an *activity list,* which will be used in subsequent Time Management processes to create a schedule. (For more information on process interactions, see "Developing the schedule," later in this chapter.)

Creating a responsibility assignment matrix

The responsibility assignment matrix (RAM) is the integrating link from the WBS to HR. The WBS links to Cost (Resource Planning) and then interacts with HR (Organization Planning). The staffing requirements are a subset of all resource requirements (which are contained in the Cost process). This book's CD includes a sample RAM. The PMI methodology gives this area scant coverage. Here are a few terms that you need to know for the exam:

- **Resource:** Anything that's assigned to an activity or needed to complete an activity. This includes services, equipment, people, materials, and so on.

- **Resource availability:** The extent to which a needed resource can work on your project. For example, a person's availability may vary over time. People are assigned to other duties, or they might be on vacation when you need them for your project. The skill that you desire for completing the assignment doesn't necessarily belong to a specific individual. It could be a generic skill available from a resource pool.

✔ **Responsibility assignment matrix (RAM):** Shows who does what and when that person will do it (for specific work packages or project phases). The RAM attributes responsibilities and accountabilities (for example, who creates, inspects, and signs off on the deliverables?). It's also called a linear responsibility chart (LRC).

✔ **Organizational breakdown structure (OBS):** A hierarchical structure that depicts how the project organization relates work packages to various organizational units. It establishes organizational responsibility and accountability for performing the work.

✔ **Resources histogram:** Shows resource requirements, usage, and availability along a timeline. Resource usage is shown in staff hours. Time periods are shown as days, weeks, or months. Usage always relates to a specific task or job function. It's often incorporated into the staffing management plan.

Planning for needed resources

Resource Planning is the process of determining how to staff your project. You can find more on other cost processes later in this chapter.

Resource requirements define what physical resources (people, equipment, and materials) and what quantities of each are needed to perform project activities. The final step in Resource Planning is determining the time phase when you'll need the resources. At this planning stage, you're concerned primarily with staff resources, not with consultants or vendors. Staffing is the output of the Resource Planning process in Cost Management — determining resources and quantities needed for material, equipment, and people.

The six inputs to Resource Planning are as follows:

✔ **WBS:** Identifies the project elements that require resources.

✔ **Historical information:** Identifies required resources used in similar work on previous projects.

✔ **Scope statement:** Contains the project justification and the project objectives.

✔ **Resource pool description:** Identifies available project resources.

✔ **Organizational policies:** The performing organization may impact some of your decisions — they'll be a constraint. These are policies regarding staffing, rentals, and purchasing supplies and equipment.

✔ **Activity duration estimates:** The best estimates of the time that it will take to perform the work. The estimates become an output from a Time Management process called Activity Duration Estimating.

These are the two tools and techniques to Resource Planning:

✔ **Expert judgment:** Used to assess the inputs to this process. It's provided by any subject-matter expert, group, or individual, including:

- Other units within your organization
- Consultants
- Professional or technical associations
- Industry advisory groups
- Alternatives identification

✔ **PM software:** Helps you organize resource pools, define resource availabilities and their rates, and define resource calendars.

Here is the one output to Resource Planning:

✔ **Resource requirements:** Describe the types (for example, skill levels) and numbers of resources required by each element of the WBS.

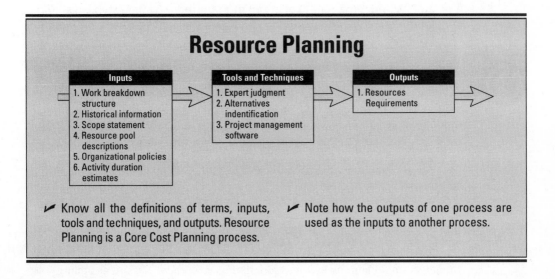

Resource Planning

Inputs	Tools and Techniques	Outputs
1. Work breakdown structure 2. Historical information 3. Scope statement 4. Resource pool descriptions 5. Organizational policies 6. Activity duration estimates	1. Expert judgment 2. Alternatives indentification 3. Project management software	1. Resources Requirements

✔ Know all the definitions of terms, inputs, tools and techniques, and outputs. Resource Planning is a Core Cost Planning process.

✔ Note how the outputs of one process are used as the inputs to another process.

Creating a Staff Management Plan

At the project discovery or conception phase, the project manager must consider how to staff the project. During this project phase, staffing estimates are at a high level — ballpark guesses. As you progress, staffing estimates become more detailed. Staffing is a good example of how processes integrate, interact, and overlap and feed back to refine requirements more precisely. Here's the timeline for the staffing phase: Define resource requirements, define actual staffing requirements, create a staffing management plan, and select and acquire the team. That's a lot of planning. It encompasses many knowledge areas: Cost, HR, and Procurement.

- ✔ **Staffing requirements:** Define the kinds of competencies from individuals and groups within a specific timeframe during the project. Staffing requirements are an input to the Organizational Planning process in Project HR Management.

- ✔ **Staffing management plan:** Defines how and when people will be added to and removed from the project. During the conception phase, the plan can be informal and broadly based. During later planning stages, it will become more formal and detailed. It's an *output* of the Organizational Planning process in Project HR Management. The staffing management plan is a subsidiary element of the project plan.

- ✔ **Staff Acquisition and Procurement Planning:** The final steps in staffing your team. Staff Acquisition is an HR process, and Procurement Planning is a Procurement process.

Select appropriate techniques for team relationships, which will likely be both new and temporary.

Your approach to staffing can change over time. As the project advances to the next phase, team composition and size may need to change. Choose the staffing techniques that are appropriate to your current needs.

As a project manager, you must comply with the organization's HR administrative requirements.

Organizational Planning

Organizational Planning involves identifying, documenting, and assigning project roles, responsibilities, and reporting relationships. Individuals and groups assigned to the project may be internal to the performing organization, or they may come from outside. Internal groups are usually composed of specific functional departments, such as IT, engineering, marketing, or accounting. HR is an important area because people are your project's most valuable resources.

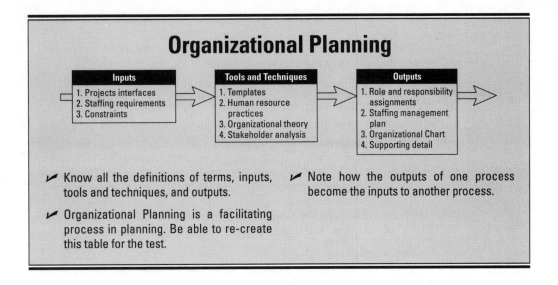

Organizational Planning

Inputs	Tools and Techniques	Outputs
1. Projects interfaces 2. Staffing requirements 3. Constraints	1. Templates 2. Human resource practices 3. Organizational theory 4. Stakeholder analysis	1. Role and responsibility assignments 2. Staffing management plan 3. Organizational Chart 4. Supporting detail

✔ Know all the definitions of terms, inputs, tools and techniques, and outputs.

✔ Organizational Planning is a facilitating process in planning. Be able to re-create this table for the test.

✔ Note how the outputs of one process become the inputs to another process.

These are the three inputs to Organizational Planning:

✔ **Project interfaces:** Fall into the following categories:

- **Organizational interfaces:** Formal and informal reporting relationships among different organizational units.

- **Technical interfaces:** Formal and informal reporting relationships among technical disciplines. (Recall that the Mars Lander crashed after one team calibrated its instruments in feet, the other in meters.)

- **Interpersonal interfaces:** Formal and informal reporting relationships among different individuals working on the project.

✔ **Staffing requirements:** Define the skills required of individuals or groups and the desired time frame within which they'll be needed.

✔ **Constraints:** Factors that limit the project team's options. They entail the following:

- Organizational structure of the performing organization — for example, strong matrix, weak matrix, or functional.

- Collective bargaining agreements with unions or other employee groups. These may impose certain roles and reporting relationships.

- Preferences of the project management team.

- Expected staff assignments. They often depend on the skills and capabilities of the staff, and how the project is organized may depend on their skills.

The four tools and techniques to Organizational Planning are as follows:

- ✔ **Templates:** A template from a similar project can help define roles and responsibilities or reporting relationships.

- ✔ **HR practices:** Can help you plan the structure of your project team.

- ✔ **Organizational theory:** Describes how an organization should be structured.

- ✔ **Stakeholder analysis:** Ensures stakeholders' needs and expectations are met. The *PMBOK Guide* gives this area scant attention.

Here are the four outputs to Organizational Planning:

- ✔ **Roles and responsibility assignments:** The appropriate stakeholders — who does what and when they will do it.

- ✔ **Staffing management plan:** Describes when and how human resources will join and leave the project team. Resources histograms that show resource requirements, their usage, and availability along a timeline are often incorporated into the staffing management plan. The staffing management plan is a subsidiary element of the project plan.

- ✔ **Organization chart:** Displays the reporting relationships in a graphic format. The OBS is a specific org chart that indicates which organizational unit is responsible for particular work items.

- ✔ **Supporting detail:** Generally includes the following:

  - • **Organizational impact:** Describes the alternatives that are precluded by organizing your project in a particular way.

  - • **Job descriptions:** Outlines the skills and characteristics involved in performing a given job.

  - • **Training needs:** Outlines how to develop skills needed to perform a job. If the assigned resources need to acquire new skills, identify what they will need and how they will receive it.

Staff Acquisition

Staff Acquisition involves getting the people resources needed (individuals or groups) assigned to and working on the project. The project manager doesn't always have direct control over these resources because many of them will be assigned to the team by other managers. The person you most desire to have on your team may be busy on another project or report to a functional manager who has other priorities. Because you're not likely to always get the best resources for your team, you must ensure that the people who are available meet project requirements.

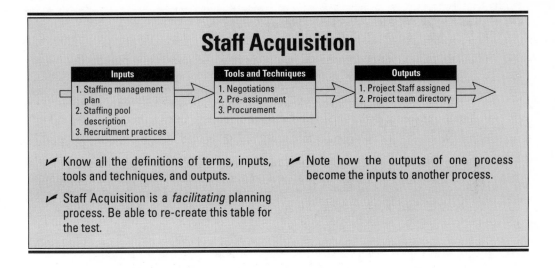

Staff Acquisition

Inputs	Tools and Techniques	Outputs
1. Staffing management plan 2. Staffing pool description 3. Recruitment practices	1. Negotiations 2. Pre-assignment 3. Procurement	1. Project Staff assigned 2. Project team directory

✔ Know all the definitions of terms, inputs, tools and techniques, and outputs.

✔ Staff Acquisition is a *facilitating* planning process. Be able to re-create this table for the test.

✔ Note how the outputs of one process become the inputs to another process.

These are the three inputs to Staff Acquisition:

✔ **Staffing management plan:** The main Organizational Planning output.

✔ **Staffing-pool description:** Includes the characteristics of potential staff, their experience, interests, characteristics, and availability.

✔ **Recruitment practices:** Include various organizational policies, guidelines, and procedures governing staff assignments. These are a constraint on staffing your project.

The three tools and techniques to Staff Acquisition are as follows:

✔ **Negotiations:** Ensure that you'll have appropriate resources at the required time. You typically negotiate with functional managers or other project managers.

✔ **Preassignment:** Usually occurs if staff must be assigned because they were promised in a competitive proposal, contract, or SOW (statement of work). It also happens internally if staff is preassigned in the project charter.

✔ **Procurement:** Recruiting people outside the organization. This technique entails hiring consultants and contractors.

Here are the two outputs to Staff Acquisition:

✔ **Project staff assignments:** Indicate who will work on the project full time, part time, or variably.

✔ **Project team directory:** Lists all project team members and key stakeholders. It can be a simple, informal list or very detailed. Make sure it suits the needs of the project.

Planning for Procurement

Two important processes take place during planning in the purchasing arena: Procurement Planning and Solicitation Planning. Both are facilitating processes. How they interact with other planning processes depends on the nature of the project. Procurement and Solicitation Planning are performed intermittently and as needed during project planning. Although they don't have to take place in any particular order, they are not optional.

For the exam, you need to know how Procurement Planning and Solicitation Planning interact and integrate with other processes, especially the schedule processes. You are likely to see exam questions asking you to select the best type of contract and what the financial benefits or costs will be of using a particular contract type.

Procurement Planning

The *Procurement Planning* process determines how project needs can best be met by sourcing products or services outside the organization. This includes consideration of potential subcontracts, different contract types, what to procure, and when to procure it. Most of this planning happens at the same time as the scope development process. When buying something, keep in mind that you'll want to influence or control the seller to perform.

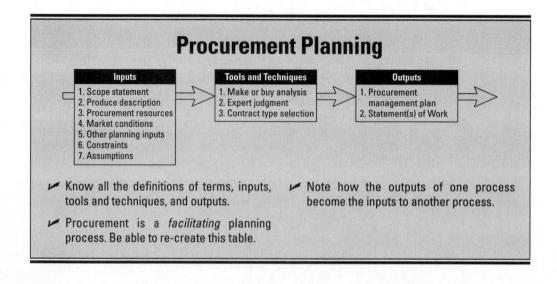

Procurement Planning

Inputs	Tools and Techniques	Outputs
1. Scope statement	1. Make or buy analysis	1. Procurement management plan
2. Produce description	2. Expert judgment	2. Statement(s) of Work
3. Procurement resources	3. Contract type selection	
4. Market conditions		
5. Other planning inputs		
6. Constraints		
7. Assumptions		

✔ Know all the definitions of terms, inputs, tools and techniques, and outputs.

✔ Procurement is a *facilitating* planning process. Be able to re-create this table.

✔ Note how the outputs of one process become the inputs to another process.

The seven inputs to Procurement Planning are as follows:

✔ **Scope statement:** Describes current project needs and strategies.

✔ **Product description:** Defines the end product of the project and provides important information about any technical issues or concerns.

✔ **Procurement resources:** The resources and expertise needed to support project procurement activities.

✔ **Market conditions:** Affect available products and services that have an impact on your decision-making.

✔ **Other planning outputs:** A catch-all phrase that includes such items as:

- Cost and schedule estimates

- Quality management plans

- Cash-flow projections

- WBS

- Identified risks

- Planned staffing needs

✔ **Constraints:** Factors that limit the buyer's options, such as availability of funds.

✔ **Assumptions:** Factors that, for planning purposes, will be considered to be true, real, or certain.

These are the three tools and techniques to Procurement Planning:

✔ **Make-or-buy analysis:** Determines whether it's more cost effective for the performing organization to produce the product or purchase it from an outside vendor.

✔ **Expert judgment:** Can be sought from groups or individuals with specialized knowledge or training.

✔ **Contract-type selection:** An important factor in your efforts to influence and control the seller's performance. Different contracts are appropriate for different kinds of work. (For more information on contract types, see "Contracting for services and supplies," later in this chapter, and Appendix A.)

The two outputs to Procurement Planning are as follows:

✔ **Procurement management plan:** A subsidiary of the project plan. It describes how the remaining procurement processes (from Solicitation Planning through Contract Closeout) will be managed.

✔ **Statement of work (SOW):** Describes the procurement items in sufficient detail for prospective sellers to determine if they are capable of providing the items. It should include a description of any collateral services required for the procured item, such as equipment purchase, installation, and initial training.

Solicitation Planning

Solicitation Planning involves documenting the product requirements and identifying potential sources in preparation to support solicitation.

Here are the three inputs to Solicitation Planning:

✔ **Procurement management plan:** Describes how to manage the procurement processes (Solicitation Planning through Contract Closeout).

✔ **SOW (statement of work):** Describes the procurement items in sufficient detail for prospective sellers to determine if they can provide the items.

✔ **Other planning outputs:** Includes preliminary cost and schedule estimates, quality management plans, cash-flow projections, the WBS, identified risks, and planned staffing and involves any modifications to other planning processes as a result of Procurement Planning. For the exam, remember that if you don't coordinate solicitation documents to the schedule, you risk not having the materials, equipment, or people you need at specific times.

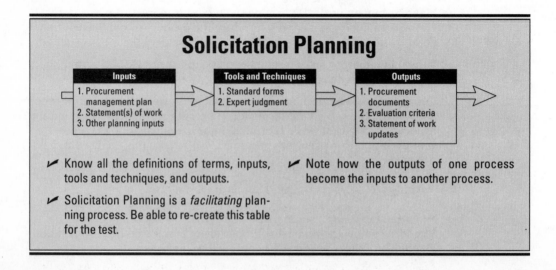

Here are the two tools and techniques to Solicitation Planning:

- ✔ **Standard forms:** Include standardized contracts, descriptions of procurement items, and bid documents.
- ✔ **Expert judgment:** Can be sought from groups or individuals with specialized knowledge or training.

Outputs to Solicitation Planning are as follows:

- ✔ **Procurement documents:** These solicit proposals from potential buyers:
  - Request for proposal (RFP)
  - Request for quotation (RFQ)
  - Invitation to bid
  - Invitation for negotiation
  - Contractor initial response

  Procurement documents should include the following:
  - The project's SOW
  - Description of the desired format of the response
  - Required contractual provisions
  - Evaluation criteria to rate or score proposals (objective or subjective)
  - Overall or life-cycle cost
  - Technical capabilities
  - Management approach
  - Financial capacity
- ✔ **SOW updates:** Modifications to existing SOWs. They're usually identified during Solicitation Planning.

Contracting for services and supplies

All contracts share certain fundamentals:

- ✔ **Offer:** The consent to specific terms by both parties. An offer must be made. Acceptance of the agreement can be written or spoken.
- ✔ **Consideration:** Something of value given in exchange for the product or service rendered.
- ✔ **Legal capacity:** The ability to contract, or enter into, a valid agreement. All contracts must have legal purposes, which cannot violate any public policy or laws.

Trade-offs of different contract types allocate and balance cost, schedule, and technical risks between the buyer and seller. The project manager must select the contract type that places the appropriate degree of risk, responsibility, and incentives on the seller for performance. The following list explores some of the contract types with their associated risks; this is a subject area ripe for test questions:

✔ **Fixed price** contracts lock in a total price. They're generally used for well-defined products. Variations include

- **Fixed price plus incentive fee (FPIF):** Provides bonuses for delivering projects under budget and imposes penalties for exceeding the budget.

- **Firm fixed price (FFP):** Used on projects with solid specifications, when the project's deliverables aren't a core competency of the performing organization. FFPs shift risks to the seller, who is responsible for performance, costs, and resulting profits (or losses).

- **Fixed price award fee:** Provides a bonus to the seller based on performance. Bonuses are often calculated based on a sliding scale of quality or cost targets, particularly if the seller's performance can't be measured objectively until delivery.

✔ **Cost reimbursable contact:** Covers actual costs expended by the seller. In a cost-plus contract, a fee in excess of cost is the only firm number, which may be a dollar amount or a percentage of overall expenditures.

- **Cost plus percentage of cost (CPPC):** Provides for all direct costs plus a percentage for the seller's profit. CPPCs are prohibited in federal contracts.

- **Cost plus fixed fee (CPFF):** Generally used for R&D contracts. Allowable costs are reimbursed, but the negotiated fee or profit is fixed. CPFF generally has higher uncertainty, higher risk, and less defined scope than other types. If there is a change order or contract change, the fixed fee changes. Risks rest with the buyer; the seller has little incentive to control costs.

- **Cost plus incentive fee (CPIF):** Permits the buyer and seller to share savings, which are based on predetermined percentages. These contacts have performance incentives for the vendor. They're generally used on longer projects with development and test requirements. See Appendix B for the formula.

✔ **Direct costs:** Cover only those costs incurred for work on the project. Time & material (T&M) is a contract type often used when the buyer wants full control, the scope is unclear, and work must start immediately. Profits are factored into the seller's hourly rates.

✔ **Indirect costs:** Overhead allocated to the project by the performing organization — the cost of doing business.

✔ **Unit price contracts:** Provide for a set dollar amount per unit of service rendered. The contract's total value depends on the quantity of units required to complete the work.

✔ **Purchase order (PO):** Used for simple commodity purchases. It's normally unilateral, issued by the buyer as a promise to pay for the contracted item when standard-cost goods or services are required.

✔ **Letter contract:** A written, preliminary contractual instrument authorizing the seller to begin performing services or delivering goods.

Developing the Schedule

Developing the schedule involves several activities. You must define the scope of the work, define the activities, estimate how long the activities will take to accomplish, sequence the activities, and associate costs with the activities. Somewhere along the way, things suddenly get complicated. That's where the discipline of the WBS comes in. The next few sections break down this material into smaller components — the three Time processes that you need to know for planning.

Defining activities

Activity Definition involves identifying and documenting the specific activities that must be performed in order to produce the deliverables and subdeliverables identified in the WBS.

Activity Definition has six inputs:

✔ **WBS:** The primary input to Activity Definition.

✔ **Scope statement:** Must be considered explicitly during Activity Definition. Project justification and objectives are especially important.

✔ **Historical information:** Activities required on similar projects should be considered in defining project activities.

✔ **Constraints:** Factors that limit the team's options.

✔ **Assumptions:** Factors that, for planning purposes, will be considered to be true, real, or certain.

✔ **Expert judgment:** Expert judgment guided by historical information should be used whenever possible. Subject-matter experts can help. (Remember the concept of lessons learned, an organizational output of previous project efforts.)

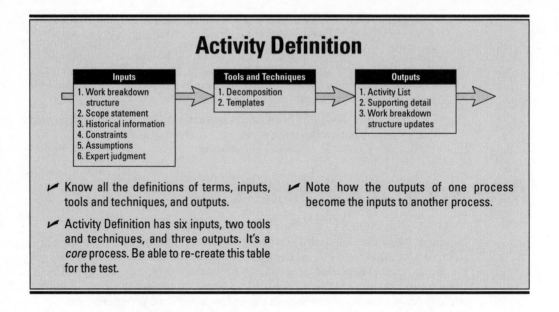

Activity Definition

Inputs	Tools and Techniques	Outputs
1. Work breakdown structure 2. Scope statement 3. Historical information 4. Constraints 5. Assumptions 6. Expert judgment	1. Decomposition 2. Templates	1. Activity List 2. Supporting detail 3. Work breakdown structure updates

✔ Know all the definitions of terms, inputs, tools and techniques, and outputs.

✔ Activity Definition has six inputs, two tools and techniques, and three outputs. It's a *core* process. Be able to re-create this table for the test.

✔ Note how the outputs of one process become the inputs to another process.

The two tools and techniques for Activity Definition are as follows:

✔ **Decomposition:** Dividing project elements into smaller, more manageable components. Decomposition in Activity Definition and in Scope Definition differ; the final outputs in Activity Definition are activities (action steps), and the final outputs in Scope Definition are deliverables (tangible items).

✔ **Templates:** Previous project templates help you jump-start the process. Use a completed activity list from another project as a guide.

There are three outputs for Activity Definition:

✔ **Activity list:** Includes all activities that will be performed on the project. This is an extension of the WBS that ensures completeness and excludes activities not required. Descriptions of each activity should ensure that stakeholders understand how the work will be done.

✔ **Supporting detail:** Includes assumptions, constraints, and anything else that's relevant. Document and organize this detail for use in subsequent PM processes.

✔ **WBS updates:** Missing deliverables, clarifications, or corrections. This output creates a feedback loop by which you get to tie up loose ends. Update the WBS and related documents, such as cost estimates. These updates are often called *refinements*. Refinements are typical of R&D projects.

Sequencing activities

Activity Sequencing involves identifying and documenting interactivity dependencies, which must be sequenced accurately to support later development of a realistic and achievable schedule.

The second Time Management process is to sequence the activities.

These are the six inputs to Activity Sequencing:

- ✔ **Activity list:** Includes all activities performed on the project.

- ✔ **Product description:** Product characteristics. These often affect Activity Sequencing.

- ✔ **Mandatory dependencies:** Inherent in the nature of the work being done. They often involve physical limitations. Constraints caused by mandatory dependencies are called *hard logic*.

- ✔ **Discretionary dependencies:** Defined by the project management team. Constraints caused by discretionary dependencies are called *soft logic*.

- ✔ **External dependencies:** Involve a relationship between project and nonproject activities.

- ✔ **Milestones:** Need to be a part of Activity Sequencing to ensure the requirements for the milestone events are being met.

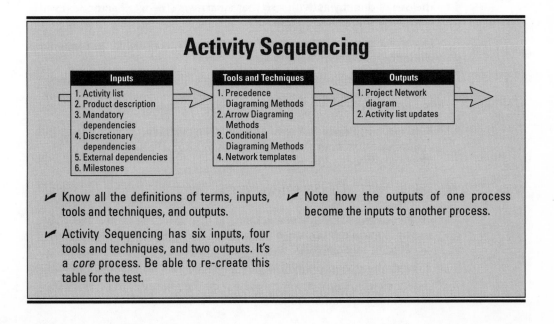

Activity Sequencing

Inputs	Tools and Techniques	Outputs
1. Activity list	1. Precedence Diagraming Methods	1. Project Network diagram
2. Product description	2. Arrow Diagraming Methods	2. Activity list updates
3. Mandatory dependencies	3. Conditional Diagraming Methods	
4. Discretionary dependencies	4. Network templates	
5. External dependencies		
6. Milestones		

✔ Know all the definitions of terms, inputs, tools and techniques, and outputs.

✔ Activity Sequencing has six inputs, four tools and techniques, and two outputs. It's a *core* process. Be able to re-create this table for the test.

✔ Note how the outputs of one process become the inputs to another process.

The four tools and techniques to Activity Sequencing are as follows:

✔ **Precedence Diagramming Method (PDM):** Constructing a project network diagram by using nodes to represent the activities and connecting them with arrows to show the dependencies between tasks. This charting method is also called *activity-on-node (AON)*. Four types of dependencies are

- **Finish-to-start:** The *from,* or predecessor, activity must finish before the *to,* or successor, activity can start. This is the most commonly used dependency.

- **Finish-to-finish:** Activities must finish in a specific sequence; the *from,* or predecessor, activity must finish before the *to,* or successor, activity can finish.

- **Start-to-start:** The *from,* or predecessor, activity must start before the *to,* or successor, activity can start.

- **Start-to-finish:** The *from,* or predecessor, activity must start before the *to,* or successor, activity can finish. Only professional scheduling engineers use this dependency.

Figure 9-5 shows the different PDM dependencies.

✔ **Arrow diagramming method (ADM):** Constructing a project network diagram by using arrows to represent the activities and connecting them at nodes to show the dependencies. It's also called *activity-on-arrow (AOA)*. This method uses only finish-to-start activities and may require the use of dummy activities so that all arrows (the work activities) will have nodes at which to terminate.

Figure 9-6 shows ADM using the AOA method. The dashed lines represent a dummy, or placeholder, activity.

✔ **Conditional diagramming methods:** Allow for non-sequential activities such as loops or conditional branches, neither of which is possible in the PDM or ADM.

✔ **Network templates:** Can expedite the preparation of project network diagrams. Subnets are especially useful in projects that have several identical or nearly identical features.

Here are the two outputs to Activity Sequencing:

✔ **Project network diagram:** A schematic display of the project's activities and the logical relationships (dependencies) among them. Often it's incorrectly called a PERT chart.

✔ **Activity list updates:** Allow a feedback loop if a network diagram reveals instances where an activity must be redefined in order to diagram the correct logical relationships.

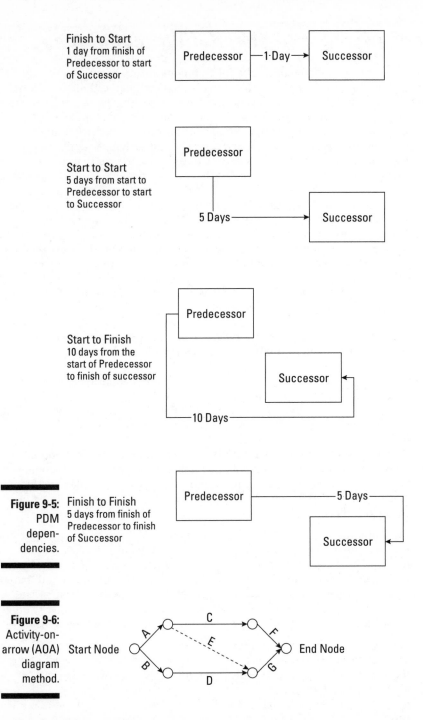

Finish to Start
1 day from finish of
Predecessor to start
of Successor

Start to Start
5 days from start to
Predecessor to start
to Successor

Start to Finish
10 days from the
start of Predecessor
to finish of successor

Figure 9-5:
PDM
depen-
dencies.

Finish to Finish
5 days from finish of
Predecessor to finish
of Successor

Figure 9-6:
Activity-on-
arrow (AOA)
diagram
method.

Sequencing and scheduling techniques

If you're using sequencing and scheduling techniques to detail your study plan, you've already sequenced the activities and estimated their durations. Next, you'll want to graph them according to your project logic. This *network diagram* charts a view of the activity sequence and relationships of your project data. It's linked together in chains or paths, from the beginning to the completion of your project. Boxes representing activities (aptly called activity boxes) are connected in a path with one-way arrows to indicate precedence.

The first activity is placed at a start node on the left side of the diagram, and the links continue for each activity until reaching the end node on the right side. The diagram gets complicated if several activities can be performed simultaneously: Parallel activities allow work to be completed faster than if the activities were arranged serially in a straight line. This arrangement increases the coordination of handoffs and management of resources for parallel activities. This network diagram is also called a flowchart, PERT chart, logic drawing, or logic diagram.

Figure 9-7 shows a typical network diagram. In this view, tasks are sequenced, and durations are noted in the top row as the middle number.

Almost all exams have some questions about networks, identifying the critical path and determining float or slack on an activity. To answer these questions, you have to calculate a forward and backward path through the network. The following list discusses forward and backward paths:

- **Activity:** Has an expected duration, an expected cost, and expected resource requirements. Diagramming helps you identify and document the activities that must be performed to produce deliverables. At this stage of the process, activities almost always have no *float* (defined in the next bullet).

- **Critical path method (CPM):** Works by making two separate paths through the network. A *forward pass* through the entire network determines the early start and early finish dates. The earliest finish date for the last task in the network establishes the earliest project end date. Next, CPM uses a second, *backward pass* to calculate the late start and late finish dates. The difference between the late date and the early date of a task is the amount of *total slack* (also called *total float*) on a task. Critical tasks have zero slack.

- **Critical path:** Charts the tasks in a network that drive the project end date. The critical path of a project network diagram shows a series of activities that determines the earliest completion of the project. Contrary to what you might expect, it's the *longest* duration path through the chain. And the longest path is the *minimum* project completion time because it constrains all the other paths.

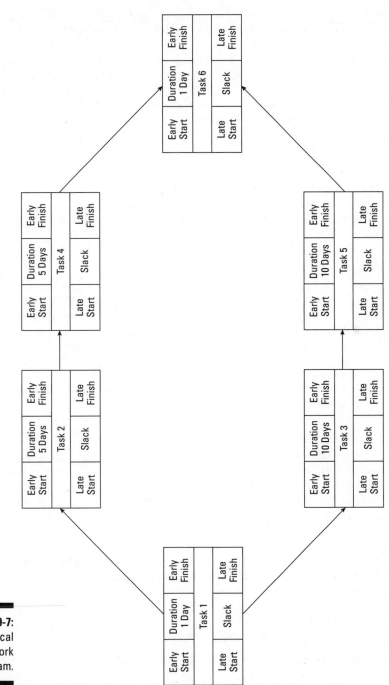

Figure 9-7:
Typical
network
diagram.

> When you delay an activity on the critical path, the entire project will be delayed by that same duration (unless you can speed up another activity that's also on the critical path by the same amount so the net result is zero). The critical path occasionally changes as activities are completed ahead or behind schedule. Although normally calculated for the entire project, the critical path can also be determined for a shorter period such as a milestone or subproject. The critical path is usually defined as those activities with float less than or equal to a specified value, often zero.

Diagramming networks

The next two sections detail the steps you must take to calculate the critical path within a network diagram.

Calculating the forward pass

The start node begins with zero as the early start (ES) date for the first task. Add the duration of the task to calculate the early finish (EF). Add any *lags,* the wait time between two tasks. This yields the ES of the next or successor task. If there are two or multiple predecessor tasks, take the latest (which has a higher number) of the EFs of the predecessors to identify the ES of the successor. Continue through each path until you reach the end/finish node. If there are multiple activities at the end, the latest EF becomes the project duration, and the LF (late finish) is the conclusion of all the activities coming off the finish node.

Calculating the backward pass

Start calculating the backward pass from the end/finish node and work backward toward the start node. Subtract the duration from the LF. This number is the late start (LS). Subtract any lags (from the LS), and the result becomes the LF of the predecessor task. If there are two or multiple successor tasks, take the earliest LS (which has the lowest number) as the LF of the predecessor. Continue calculating to the start node.

Check for float, the difference between the ES and LS. Note that one of the paths (invariably, the longest one) will not have any float — its float will be zero. This is the critical path.

```
Float or Slack = Late Start - Early Start or Late Finish -
                 Early Finish
```

```
Early Finish = Early Start + Duration
```

```
Late Start = Late Finish - Duration
```

Defining leads, lags, and float

Figure 9-8 shows leads and lags in a network diagram. The following list defines leads, lags, and float:

- ✔ **Lead:** The minimum necessary lapse of time between the start of one activity and the start of an overlapping activity.

- ✔ **Lag:** The waiting time between two tasks (also called *negative lead*). Waiting for concrete to harden, plaster to set before painting, paint to dry before applying a second coat, or an equipment order to arrive before installation are all examples of lags.

- ✔ **Float or slack:** The amount of time an activity may be delayed from its early start without delaying the project finish date. It's calculated as the difference between the required end date and expected project completion date. Negative slack on the critical path indicates the project is behind schedule. If the slack is greater than 0, you have some leeway time available. If the slack equals 0, the early and late dates are the same; therefore, this is a critical task because no slippage is possible. If the slack is less than 0, the schedule can't hit the completion date.

- ✔ **Free float:** The amount of time an activity or task can be delayed without delaying the early start of its successor.

- ✔ **Float or total float:** The amount of time an activity may be delayed from early start without delaying the project finish date.

Simple activity duration estimates are risky for several reasons. For one thing, you might not meet the dates. The estimates might be understated or overstated. *Path risk* is the sum of all individual risks.

Lead Time

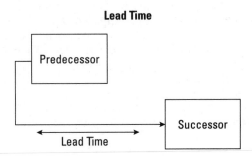

Figure 9-8:
Network
diagram
leads and
lags.

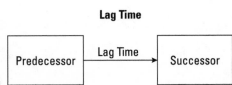

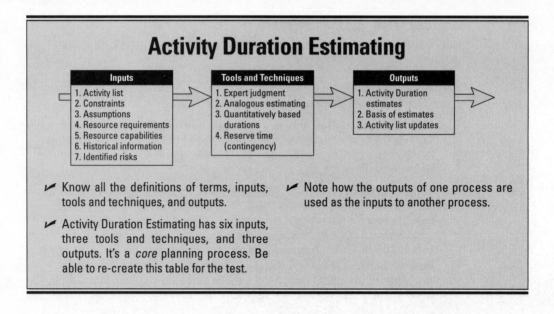

Activity Duration Estimating

Inputs	Tools and Techniques	Outputs

1. Activity list
2. Constraints
3. Assumptions
4. Resource requirements
5. Resource capabilities
6. Historical information
7. Identified risks
	1. Expert judgment
	2. Analogous estimating
	3. Quantitatively based
	   durations
	4. Reserve time
	   (contingency)
		1. Activity Duration
		   estimates
		2. Basis of estimates
		3. Activity list updates

✔ Know all the definitions of terms, inputs, tools and techniques, and outputs.

✔ Activity Duration Estimating has six inputs, three tools and techniques, and three outputs. It's a *core* planning process. Be able to re-create this table for the test.

✔ Note how the outputs of one process are used as the inputs to another process.

Figure 9-9 shows a convergence of three paths toward the finish date. The figure shows a well-known risk of *convergence,* or *merge bias.* This bias is introduced because of the following statistical probabilities. The probability of Activity A finishing at the same time as the other activities is 50 percent. Because each of the three activities has the same probability rate, you'd write the equation as

```
0.5 × 0.5 × 0.5 = 0.125
```

That's a 12.5 percent probability that all the activities will finish on time. The finish date is driven by the latest of the converging paths. A delay on any of the paths might affect the finish date. Unless resources are added, some activities must be delayed or stretched out. For example, CPM scheduling allows *resource leveling,* a reallocation of resources, which usually stretches out the timeline and delays the project. For the exam, you should know the following components of schedule risk:

✔ Risk of the activity duration

✔ Risk of duration along a path

✔ Risk at a point where parallel paths merge

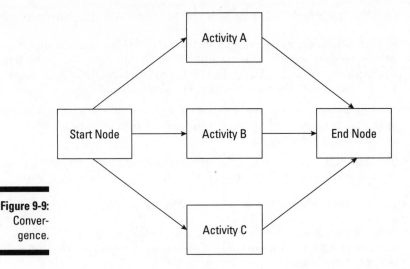

Figure 9-9: Conver-gence.

Estimating effort — Activity Durations

The third Time process is Activity Duration Estimating. This process involves assessing the number of work periods likely to be needed to complete each identified activity. Figure 3-4 (in Chapter 3) shows that Activity Duration Estimating and Activity Sequencing occur at the same time.

Here are the six inputs for Activity Duration Estimating:

✔ **Activity list:** Includes all activities that will be performed on the project. This is an extension of the WBS that ensures completeness and excludes activities not required.

✔ **Constraints:** Restrictions that will affect the performance of the project. When contracts are involved, special considerations are often required for communications.

✔ **Assumptions:** Factors that for planning purposes are considered to be true, real, or certain. They imply a certain degree of risk.

✔ **Resource requirements:** Controlling factors on activity duration. The duration of most activities will be significantly influenced by the resources assigned to them.

✔ **Resource capabilities:** Staff and material resources assigned to them will affect the duration of most activities.

✔ **Historical information:** May be available for review from project records, commercial duration-estimating databases, and team knowledge.

The three tools and techniques for Activity Duration Estimating are as follows:

- ✔ **Expert judgment:** Judgment guided by historical information should be used whenever possible. An example is the Delphi Technique, which is a forecasting technique that relies on gathering expert opinions. After several iterations, the experts reach consensus of opinions.

- ✔ **Analogous estimating:** Uses the duration of a previous, similar activity as the basis for estimating the duration of a future activity. It's also called *top-down estimating.*

- ✔ **Simulation:** Calculates multiple durations with different sets of assumptions. The most common is the Monte Carlo analysis.

Here are the three outputs for Activity Duration Estimating:

- ✔ **Activity duration estimates:** Quantitative assessments of the likely number of work periods — such as hours, days, weeks, or months — that will be required to complete an activity.

- ✔ **Basis of estimates:** Includes the assumptions made in developing your estimates, which must be documented.

- ✔ **Activity list updates:** This feedback loop ensures completeness.

Estimating techniques and formulas

Estimates of effort can be classified according to level of detail, accuracy, and their intended use. For example, *order of magnitude* estimates are used in the planning and initial evaluation stage of a project. *Semi-detailed estimates* are used in the preliminary or conceptual design stage of a project. *Definitive* (or detailed) *estimates* are used in the detailed design, engineering, and construction stages of a project. The work effort and duration of each individual task needs to be estimated. Such task-based estimating is the most accurate, but it's also the hardest because of the high level of detail involved.

PERT (program evaluation and review technique) is a technique that emphasizes meeting schedules with flexibility on cost. Adhering to schedule is assumed to be more important than adhering to budget. This technique is seldom used anymore, but PERT-like techniques are used in CPM calculations. Therefore, you only need to consider this later PERT-like technique for the exam. It's referred to as having a *PERT distribution* rather than a normal distribution. In the normal distribution, you'd simply select the most likely estimate. The most likely estimate will be either a mean value or weighted average. With PERT distribution, you'll use three time estimates per single activity: Optimistic, Most Likely, and Pessimistic.

The formulas for estimating activities are as follows:

- **Beta distribution using PERT-weighted average approximations:**

  ```
  Mean μ = (O + 4M + P) ÷ 6
  Standard Deviation σ = (P - O) ÷ 6 or √ Variance
  Variance = Standard Deviation raised to a power of 2
  ```

  or

  ```
  σ² = (P - O) ÷ 6²
  ```

- **CPM:**

  ```
  CPM = Most likely estimate only
  ```

- **Triangular distribution:**

  ```
  Mean μ = (O + M + P) ÷ 3
  Standard Deviation = √ Variance
  Variance = (P - O)² + (M - P) (M - O) ÷ 18
  σ² = (P - O) ÷ 3²
  O = Optimistic, M = Most Likely, and P = Pessimistic
  ```

It's generally better to use a triangular distribution because it produces more conservative results than the beta distribution does. Adding individual triangular duration estimates creates a bell-shaped path duration — a curve described by the Central Limit Theorem. However, you'll get the best estimates using Monte Carlo simulations. Monte Carlo techniques collect a series of the three time estimates (Optimistic, Most Likely, and Pessimistic), apply all three estimates for every task, and then run all combinations of the variables to estimate the schedule's distribution.

The questions that follow are sample word problems that you're likely to see on the exam. Assume the optimistic commuting time is 15 minutes, the most likely time is 30 minutes, and the pessimistic time is 60 minutes.

Using the PERT weighted average, what's the expected time that Gerald can make it to his office in Los Angeles?

It's [15 + 4 (30) + 60] ÷ 6 = 32.5 minutes.

Using the CPM average, what's the expected time for Pete to travel to his office in Atlanta?

It's 30 minutes, the figure you were given in the assumptions. This is a trick question because CPM uses only one number.

Using the triangular weighted average, what's the expected time that Pete used to get to his office in Atlanta?

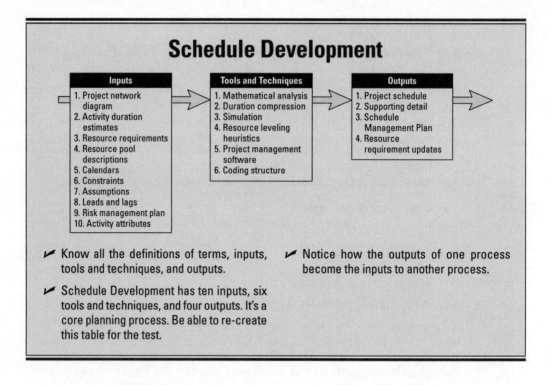

Schedule Development

Inputs	Tools and Techniques	Outputs
1. Project network diagram 2. Activity duration estimates 3. Resource requirements 4. Resource pool descriptions 5. Calendars 6. Constraints 7. Assumptions 8. Leads and lags 9. Risk management plan 10. Activity attributes	1. Mathematical analysis 2. Duration compression 3. Simulation 4. Resource leveling heuristics 5. Project management software 6. Coding structure	1. Project schedule 2. Supporting detail 3. Schedule Management Plan 4. Resource requirement updates

✔ Know all the definitions of terms, inputs, tools and techniques, and outputs.

✔ Schedule Development has ten inputs, six tools and techniques, and four outputs. It's a core planning process. Be able to re-create this table for the test.

✔ Notice how the outputs of one process become the inputs to another process.

It's 15 + 30 + 60 ÷ 3 = 35 minutes. When Pete lived in Southern California and commuted from Los Angeles to Irvine, the estimates showed more dramatic variations. The Optimistic time was 50 minutes (at 4 a.m., no traffic, and a radar detector), the Most Likely time was 75 minutes (before rush hour at 7 a.m.), and the Pessimistic time was 180 minutes (during peak rush hour in bumper-to-bumper traffic).

What would have been the expected times for Pete's old route using PERT, CPM, and Triangular distributions?

The answers are 88, 75, and 176 minutes respectively. If you had to estimate this activity, which estimate would you select? If you selected the Most Likely estimate, your task will probably run over the allotted schedule. Imagine the consequences if all tasks in your network slipped by 117 or even 235 percent (those are the differences between your estimate of 75 and the other two values — 88 and 176).

A relative newcomer in operations research techniques is *critical chain method (CCM),* which is based on the Theory of Constraints (TOC). Critical Chain Method modifies the schedule to allow for constraints such as resource limitations, organizational rules, training, or other measures that act as policy restraints. You can find some additional information on TOC and CCM on the Web site for this book.

Developing the schedule

Schedule Development is the process of determining the start and finish dates for all project activities. You analyze activity sequences, activity durations, and resource requirements to create the project schedule.

Schedule Development has ten inputs; that's more inputs than you'll see on any other process on the test:

- **Project network diagram:** A schematic display of the project's activities and the logical relationships (dependencies) among them. Don't make the common mistake of calling this a PERT chart.

- **Activity duration estimates:** The best estimates of the time it will take to perform the work.

- **Resource requirements:** Define what physical resources (people, equipment, and materials) and what quantities of each are needed to perform project activities.

- **Resource pool descriptions:** Identify the required resources, listing who will be available, when, and in what patterns, as necessary for schedule development.

- **Calendars:** Identify the time when work is allowed. *Project calendars* affect all resources. *Resource calendars* affect a specific resource or category of resource.

- **Constraints:** Constraints to consider during schedule development include

    - **Imposed dates:** These can be stipulated by a project sponsor, customers, or external factors such as a trade show from which the marketing department wants to get publicity for the product. Having to complete your deliverables by a specified date is always a major constraint.

    - **Key events or major milestones:** These may impose constraints for completing deliverables. Handoffs of deliverables between groups may impose constraints — for example, a requirement for just-in-time delivery. Such constraints may be requested by the project sponsor, customers, or other stakeholders. Once scheduled, these dates become expected, and moving them can be difficult.

- **Assumptions:** Factors that, for planning purposes, are considered to be true, real, or certain.

- **Leads and lags:** The *lead* is the minimum necessary lapse of time between the start of one activity and the start of an overlapping activity. The *lag* is the waiting time between two tasks (negative lead) such as waiting for concrete to harden or paint to dry. These are similar concepts and easily confused, so be sure you know the distinction.

✔ **Risk management plan:** A subsidiary part of the project plan. It documents the procedures to manage risk throughout the project. (This input is new to the 2000 *PMBOK Guide.*)

✔ **Activity attributes:** Describe various characteristics of the activities you're scheduling — who's responsible, the WBS order, the location where the work will be performed, and the level (detail or summary). These characteristics are important for selection and sorting of activities. (This input is new to the 2000 *PMBOK Guide.*)

The six tools and techniques for Schedule Development are as follows:

✔ **Mathematical analysis:** Calculating theoretical early and late start and finish dates for all project activities without any resource pool limitations. Your goal is to show dependencies on predecessor and successor tasks. The most common analysis techniques are as follows:

- **Critical path method (CPM):** Calculates a single, *deterministic* early and late start and finish date for each activity based on specified, sequential network logic and a single duration estimate. Deterministic distinguishes traditional networks from probabilistic networks. (Deterministic means the duration can be predicted exactly rather than as a range of probabilities.) CPM uses the most likely estimate for activity duration. CPM's goal is identifying activities with the least scheduling flexibility by calculating float.

- **Graphical evaluation and review technique (GERT):** Allows for probabilistic treatment of both network logic and activity duration estimates. Some activities may not be performed at all. GERT allows for loops or conditional branches; none of the other methods permit loops. Loops might include testing, rework, and retesting.

- **PERT:** Uses sequential network logic and weighted-average duration estimates to calculate project duration. Although PERT is an older technique that is seldom used anymore, PERT-like estimates are often used in CPM calculations. Today's PERT-like estimates use a weighted average (mean) to estimate durations.

✔ **Duration compression methods:** Ways to shorten the project schedule without changing the project scope. You apply them after you've completed activity duration estimating and before finalizing the schedule. Two techniques for doing so are detailed in the following list:

- **Crashing:** Used when you are worried about time and cost considerations are secondary. You analyze the trade-offs between cost and schedule to obtain the greatest compression for the least incremental costs. It's typically achieved by adding resources.

- **Fast-tracking:** Provides compression by working resources in parallel or overlapping activities that would normally be sequential. This involves replacing sequential relationships (finish-to-start) with parallel relationships (start-to-start). This strategy may increase rework and risk, however. Start by fast-tracking the tasks on the critical path, remembering that critical tasks have zero float.

✔ **Simulation:** Calculates multiple durations with different sets of assumptions. The most common is Monte Carlo analysis, discussed earlier in this chapter, in which a distribution of probable results is defined for each activity and used to calculate a distribution of probable results for the total project.

✔ **Resource leveling heuristics:** Use mathematical analysis to produce a preliminary schedule. Resource leveling heuristics are used when the schedule requires more resources during certain time periods than are available, or requires changes in resource levels that are not manageable. Then applying resource leveling can result in a project duration that is longer than the preliminary schedule.

Resource constrained scheduling is a special case of resource leveling in which the *heuristic* (rule of thumb) involved is a limitation on the quantity of resources available. Resource reallocation from noncritical to critical path activities can be an effective way to bring the schedule back, or as close as possible, to the originally intended overall duration. By using positive float available on noncritical paths, develop a revised schedule by smoothing or leveling the peaks and valleys of resource utilization. Fast-tracking can further reduce overall project durations, and critical chain techniques can help you modify the schedule to account for using limited resources.

✔ **Project management software:** Widely used to assist with schedule development.

✔ **Coding structure:** All activities should be defined for easy retrieval, sorting, and extracting of data. Categories within the coding structure can be defined by the activities' attributes: responsibilities, geographic location, project phase, schedule level, WBS classification, or activity type. (This input is new to the 2000 *PMBOK Guide.*)

Here are the four outputs for Schedule Development:

✔ **Project schedule:** Includes at a minimum the planned start and expected finish dates for each detailed activity. (Your schedule is preliminary until resource assignments have been confirmed in Project Plan Development.) You can present the schedule graphically in one of the following formats:

- **Project network diagrams:** Show sequenced tasks with dates added.

- **Bar charts:** Show start dates, end dates, and expected durations for activities as horizontal bars on a timescale. Sometimes, bar charts will also show dependencies. Usually, they're called *Gantt charts* and are used in almost all PM presentations because they're intuitive and easy to read. An example of a bar chart is shown in Figure 9-10.

• **Milestone charts:** Similar to bar charts. They identify the scheduled start or completion of major deliverables and key external interfaces. We've included a trial version of Kidasa's Milestones Professional 2002 on this book's CD. You need to be familiar with creating and using milestone charts for the exam. An example of a milestone chart is shown in Figure 9-11.

✔ **Supporting details:** Include at least documentation of all identified assumptions and constraints. Some examples are resource histograms, alternative schedules, and cash-flow schedules.

✔ **Schedule management plan:** Defines how changes to the schedule will be managed.

✔ **Resource requirement updates:** A result of resource leveling and activity list updates. Both may have a significant effect on preliminary estimates of resource requirements, which need to be documented.

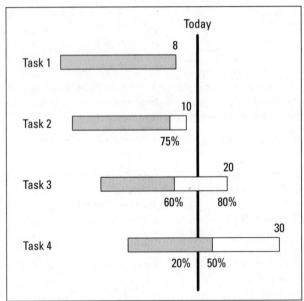

Figure 9-10:
A bar chart.

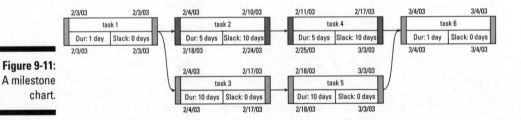

Figure 9-11:
A milestone
chart.

Building the Budget and Spending Plan

During planning, you need to consider three Project Cost Management areas. We cover Resource Planning earlier in the chapter. In the next few sections, we cover Cost Estimating and Cost Budgeting. Both are core processes in planning. Remember that they must happen in essentially the same order on every project.

Estimating costs

Cost Estimating is the process of collecting and predicting the costs over the life cycle of a project or phase of a project, developing cost estimates for all the resources needed to complete project activities. Professional cost engineers and accountants can help.

The eight inputs to Cost Estimating are as follows:

- ✔ **WBS:** A deliverable-oriented grouping of project elements that organizes and defines the total scope of the project. Work that's not in the WBS is outside the scope of the project.

- ✔ **Resource requirements:** Describe the types (for example, skill levels) and numbers of resources required by each element of the WBS.

- ✔ **Resource rates:** The unit rates for each resource that are used to calculate project costs.

- ✔ **Activity duration estimates:** The best estimates of the time that it will take to perform the work. This is an output from a Time Management process, Activity Duration Estimating, which affects cost estimates where the project budget allows for the cost of financing.

- ✔ **Estimating publications:** Provide commercial cost data.

- ✔ **Historical information:** The cost of many categories of resources is available from the following sources:

    - **Project files:** Previous project records may provide sufficient detail to assist in developing your new estimates.

    - **Commercial cost-estimating databases:** These contain actual costs and cost estimates for you to use.

    - **Project team knowledge:** Individual team members may remember previous actuals or estimates.

- ✔ **Chart of accounts (COA):** Describes the coding structure or the budget categories that the performing organization uses to report financial information in its general ledger. The account categories define where you'll allocate project costs.

> ✔ **Risks:** These have been added to the new *PMBOK Guide* to show the importance of considering the impacts of both opportunities and threats for costs estimates for each activity.

These are the five tools and techniques to Cost Estimating:

> ✔ **Analogous estimating, or top-down estimating:** A form of expert judgment because it uses actual costs from previous, similar projects to estimate current costs. Although it's less costly than other estimates, it's the least accurate. It's frequently used to estimate total project costs when a limited amount of detailed information is available.

> ✔ **Parametric modeling:** Uses project characteristics as the parameters in a mathematical model to predict project costs. Models may be simple (typical construction cost per square foot) or complex (simulations using statistics or function point analysis to estimate software development durations). The costs and accuracy of parametric models vary.

> ✔ **Bottom-up estimating:** Estimating the cost of individual activities or work packages and then adding the individual estimates to arrive at a project total. Defining smaller activities or work packages increases both the cost and accuracy of the estimate.

> ✔ **Computerized tools:** PM software, spreadsheets, simulation tools, and statistical packages can help estimate costs.

> ✔ **Other cost-estimating tools:** Includes vendor bid analyses.

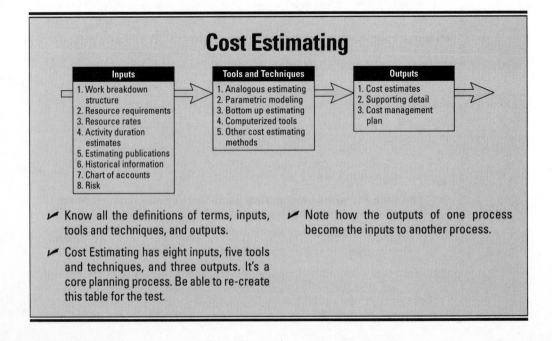

Cost Estimating

Inputs	Tools and Techniques	Outputs
1. Work breakdown structure 2. Resource requirements 3. Resource rates 4. Activity duration estimates 5. Estimating publications 6. Historical information 7. Chart of accounts 8. Risk	1. Analogous estimating 2. Parametric modeling 3. Bottom up estimating 4. Computerized tools 5. Other cost estimating methods	1. Cost estimates 2. Supporting detail 3. Cost management plan

✔ Know all the definitions of terms, inputs, tools and techniques, and outputs.

✔ Cost Estimating has eight inputs, five tools and techniques, and three outputs. It's a core planning process. Be able to re-create this table for the test.

✔ Note how the outputs of one process become the inputs to another process.

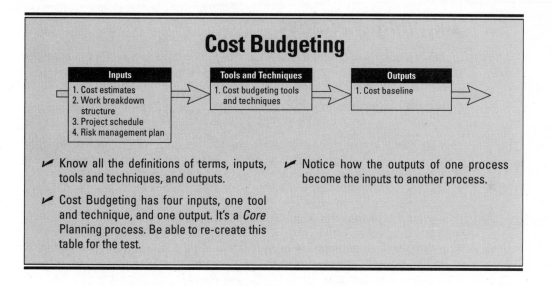

Cost Budgeting

Inputs	Tools and Techniques	Outputs
1. Cost estimates 2. Work breakdown structure 3. Project schedule 4. Risk management plan	1. Cost budgeting tools and techniques	1. Cost baseline

✔ Know all the definitions of terms, inputs, tools and techniques, and outputs.

✔ Cost Budgeting has four inputs, one tool and technique, and one output. It's a *Core* Planning process. Be able to re-create this table for the test.

✔ Notice how the outputs of one process become the inputs to another process.

The three outputs to Cost Estimating are as follows:

✔ **Cost estimates:** Quantitative assessments of the likely costs of the resources required to complete project activities. Make sure that you do risk and cost contingency planning. Cost estimates types include

- **Order of magnitude, conceptual, and preliminary estimates:** These are –25 to +75 percent accurate. They're the least accurate. They're used in the planning and initial evaluation stage of a project.

- **Budget estimates:** These are –10 to +25 percent accurate. They provide the middle level of accuracy. They're used in the preliminary or conceptual design stage. They're also called *semi-detailed.*

- **Analogy estimates:** These are –10 to +25 percent accurate. They're actual costs from previous, similar projects used to estimate current costs.

- **Definitive and control estimates:** These are –5 to +10 percent accurate. They are the most accurate. They're used in the detailed design, engineering, and construction stages.

✔ **Supporting details:** Should include the description of the scope of work estimated, references to WBS, the basis of the estimate, assumptions, and the range of possible results (for example: $10,000 (10%).

✔ **Cost management plan:** Describes how cost variances will be managed. It's a subsidiary part of the project plan.

Defining a budget

Defining a budget is one of the hardest things you'll do as a project manager. It's a critical activity because the sponsor and customer will always want to know the all-important answer to the question: How much will this project cost? In the Cost Budgeting process, you'll discover that the Resource Planning and Cost Estimating processes are tightly linked.

Cost Budgeting is the process of allocating cost estimates to individual work activities. You must also consolidate these costs into a budget, standards, and baselines so the project can be measured and controlled over the life cycle.

The project budget is the planned cost of each activity at the lowest level, which is then rolled into a project total. The budget shows the *time-phased* financial requirements for the project. Time-phased means that your budget is broken down by time — for example, $100 for Period 1, $120 for Period 2, and so on. Baselines provide the initial reference levels against which the project is monitored and controlled.

- **Baseline cost** is the intended dollar cost of an activity when the schedule was baselined.

- **Cost baseline** is the cost anticipated at the start of a project, or initial project budget. The cost baseline is the standard by which project performance is measured.

The baseline budget remains frozen until it is reset. Resetting the baseline is done when the scope of the project has been changed significantly, for example after a negotiated change. At that point, the original or current baseline becomes invalid and should not be compared with the current budget.

- **Budget estimates:** Approximations prepared early in a project to prove the business case or secure resources. Estimates can be made by order of magnitude, heuristics, or parametric models. Again, heuristics are rules of thumb, simplifications, or educated guesses that reduce or limit the search for solutions in an area that is difficult or poorly understood. Some examples are costs per square foot (construction), pages per day (film and TV production), or lines of code per day (IT). Parametric estimates use statistical models to predict costs. They are more accurate than the other two estimating methods.

- **Contingency reserves:** Materials, resources, market conditions, technology changes, and risk situations that are in scope as defined by the project charter, but aren't covered in the budget. This is a separate quantity of time and money set aside to cover *known unknowns*. These reserves are intended to cover specific risks identified in the Risk Management process.

✔ **Management reserves:** Cover unforeseen activities and become a budget account for management purposes; these funds are never assigned to execute a particular project task. If you're ever forced to spend these funds, your project is in serious trouble, and you're likely to be thrown to some hungry alligators as a snack. This is a separate budget account set aside to cover *unknown unknowns*.

The four inputs to Cost Budgeting are as follows:

✔ **Cost estimates:** Quantitative assessments of the likely costs of the resources required to complete project activities. Make sure that you do risk planning and have a cost contingency plan.

✔ **WBS:** A deliverable-oriented grouping of project elements that organizes and defines the total scope of the project. Work not in the WBS is outside the scope of the project.

✔ **Project schedule:** Includes planned start and expected finish dates for the activities or work packages in order to allocate costs. This information is needed to allocate costs to appropriate time periods.

✔ **Risk management plan:** A subsidiary part of the project plan that contains procedures to manage risk throughout the project. It was added to the new *PMBOK Guide* to reflect the importance of cost contingency, which can be estimated from the accuracy of estimates.

This is the one set of tools and techniques to Cost Budgeting:

✔ **Cost estimating tools and techniques:** A catch-all category to describe any and all tools that can be applied to estimate costs.

This is the one output to Cost Budgeting:

✔ **Cost baseline:** A *time-phased* budget that will be used to measure and monitor cost performance on the project. It's developed by summing estimated costs by period and is usually displayed in the form of an S-curve. Larger projects may have multiple cost baselines to measure different aspects of cost performance. For example, a spending plan or cash flow forecast is a cost baseline for measuring disbursements.

Figure 9-12 shows the S-curve of a time-phased budget, meaning that it is plotted against time. The cumulative budget has a curve that's flat at the beginning and ends, and has a sharp rise in the middle.

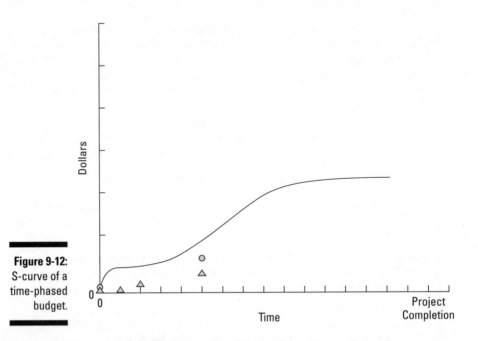

Figure 9-12:
S-curve of a
time-phased
budget.

Harnessing Earned Value Management

One of the benefits of joining the PMI and attending local chapter meetings is that you get to hear PM experts like Quentin Fleming. His book on *earned value management (EVM)* is suggested reading for the exam.

Earned value analysis (EVA) can help project managers predict final costs and schedules. The most persuasive reason why any project should employ EVM is for this early warning signal. Identifying problems early will enable you to react before the situation becomes uncontrollable.

EVM measures actual costs against budgeted costs for a measurable amount of work scheduled to be performed at a specific time. This corresponds to a completed deliverable or milestone. EVM represents much more than an accounting system; it covers cost, schedule, and technical health of the project. It shows real variances of your project so you can fix them.

Planning for earned value analysis

By knowing just three values, EVA makes it possible for you to determine the health of the project. It makes possible procedures and systems for capturing actual resource utilization, labor hours, and costs. This type of analysis has become necessary because many organizations' accounting systems don't handle project work well. Historically, the terms were usurped by the U.S. Department of Defense, which used some confusing acronyms. The *PMBOK Guide* is transitioning to the newer terms. Most of the software tools and references continue to use the old terms and formulas. You must be able to translate the old notation into the newer terms.

Here are the current definitions of three terms you must know for the exam:

- **Planned value (PV):** Formerly *budgeted cost of work scheduled* (BCWS). PV shows the work scheduled to be performed, as well as the authorized budget to accomplish the scheduled work. As the performance measurement baseline, PV indicates how much work should be done.

- **Earned value (EV):** Formerly *budgeted cost of work performed* (BCWP). EV shows the physical work actually accomplished as well as the authorized budget for this work. It shows the progress the project makes. It's expressed in terms of the value of work completed as compared to your baseline budget. When the project is completed, EV equals PV (BCWP = BCWS).

- **Actual cost (AC):** Formerly *actual cost of work performed (ACWP).* AC shows the real cost of the work that the team has completed. This number comes from the organization's accounting system.

EV analysis can be performed on either dollar costs or hourly rates. These are readily translatable from one to the other. Expect exam questions with a mixture of costs and hourly rates (such as a labor rate) with time durations. You'll have to take hourly rates × duration to derive the costs. Or you might be given a percentage — for example, the labor rate is $10 per hour, the task takes 10 days (80 hours) to complete, and the task is 50 percent complete.

Analyzing formulas for earned value

The formulas in this section use the three earned values that you need to know for the exam. Expect EV questions on the exam. The math on these questions is simple. Memorize these formulas and plug in the numbers. The formulas are used in executing and controlling the project, so we also cover them in Appendix A.

Memorize the following formulas by using naturally occurring groups. CV and CPI use the same values; CV uses subtraction, CPI uses division, and CV% repeats the CV formula, as do SV and SPI.

- **Cost variance:**

```
Cost Variance = EV - AC or BCWP - ACWP
Variance = Planned - Actual
```

- **Schedule variance:**

  ```
  Schedule Variance = EV - PV or BCWP - BCWS
  ```

  If the variance is less than 0, the work completed is less than what was planned.

- **Cost performance index:**

  ```
  Cost Performance Index = EV ÷ AC or BCWP ÷ ACWP
  ```

  CPI tells how what percentage return you're getting out of each dollar spent on the project. For every dollar spent, you're getting $1.15 in return. If the result is greater than 1, the CPI is good. If it's less than 1, the CPI is bad. Cumulative CPI rarely varies by 10 percent once a project is 20 percent complete. Many project managers use TCPI to forecast final costs.

  ```
  TCPI = (BAC - EV) ÷ (BAC - AC)
  ```

- **Schedule performance index:**

  ```
  Schedule Performance Index = EV ÷ PV or BCWP ÷ BCWS
  ```

  SPI tells how much (what percentage) you're getting out of each dollar spent on the schedule.

- **Cost variance in %:** `Cost Variance in % = CV ÷ EV`

- **Schedule variance in %:** `Schedule Variance in % = SV ÷ PV`

- **Estimate at completion (EAC):** This is an educated guess. Several formulas have been proposed to derive EAC. EAC tells what the final cost will be based on project performance and risk quantification.

- **Estimate to completion (ETC):** This tells you how much more it's going to cost.

  `AC + ETC` is used when you believe the original estimates are flawed.

  `AC + BAC - EV` is used when you don't expect future variances in the rate of work being performed.

  `AC + (BAC - EV) ÷ TCPI` is used when you expect future variances.

  BAC is the budget at completion, the total budgeted cost.

  ```
  EAC = BAC ÷ CPI
  Estimate to Completion (ETC) = EAC - AC or (BAC - EV) ÷ CPI
  ```

- **Variance at completion (VAR):** `Variance at Completion (VAR) = BAC - EAC`

- **Percent spent:** `Percent Spent = AC ÷ BAC`

- **Budget at completion (BAC):** Tells how much is budgeted for the total project.

Prep Test

1 Using Figure 9-7, what techniques do you perform to determine the critical path?

- **A** ○ Perform a forward pass.
- **B** ○ Perform a backward pass.
- **C** ○ Perform a forward pass and backward pass and calculate the slack for all activities and paths.
- **D** ○ Calculate the early start, early finish, late start, and late finish for all activities and paths.

2 Using Figure 9-7, the early start date for Task 2 is:

- **A** ○ 1
- **B** ○ 2
- **C** ○ 3
- **D** ○ 4

3 Using Figure 9-7, the late start date for Task 2 is:

- **A** ○ 2
- **B** ○ 4
- **C** ○ 6
- **D** ○ 12

4 Using Figure 9-7, the early finish date for Task 4 is:

- **A** ○ 10
- **B** ○ 13
- **C** ○ 12
- **D** ○ 17

5 Using Figure 9-7, the early start date for Task 4 is:

- **A** ○ 6
- **B** ○ 7
- **C** ○ 8
- **D** ○ 17

6 Using Figure 9-7, the slack for Task 4 is:

- **A** ○ 0
- **B** ○ 4
- **C** ○ 5
- **D** ○ 10

7 The project in Figure 9-7 will take _____ days to complete.

A ○ 12
B ○ 21
C ○ 25
D ○ 32

8 The same programmer is working on Task 2 and Task 4. He indicates on his status report that he has completed Task 2 and has some extra time because he isn't scheduled to start on Task 4 for a few days. You look at the resource usage, and he isn't scheduled for another task. What should you tell him to do?

A ○ Ask the functional manager whether she needs the programmer for ten days.
B ○ Spend the extra ten days polishing the code to ensure quality.
C ○ Ask the programmer to start Task 5 as early as possible.
D ○ Inspect the work to verify that it is complete.

9 In Figure 9-7, you find that the same resource must be used on all tasks. You determine that his time is over allocated, so you level the resources. Specifically, what is most likely to happen?

A ○ The project end date will lengthen.
B ○ The critical path will change.
C ○ The slack on noncritical paths will change.
D ○ The project will run 14 days over the planned schedule.

10 The hourly cost for a grip, a semi-skilled laborer, on a movie production crew is $28 per hour. The subcontracting project manager from Ask Pete Productions knows that the labor union's fringe benefits costs are 30 percent of hourly wages. Stupendous Pictures, the movie studio that is the performing organization, has overhead costs of 50 percent of wages plus the fringes. What are the fringe costs?

A ○ $36.40
B ○ $50.40
C ○ $54.60
D ○ Unable to calculate from information given

Answers

1 **C.** You can determine the critical path by determining which path has zero slack. This is a tough question because several answers could be correct, but all the other choices are incomplete in some way. The critical path is the longest path in the network; the forward pass tells the early start and finish, but gives you the early completion date. The backward path tells the late finish and late start, but if you only work backwards, you'd still not know the exact end date. Answer D is a poor choice; although you need to calculate all of these items, the answer omits calculating the slack. *See "Developing the Schedule."*

2 **B.** *See "Developing the Schedule."*

3 **D.** *See "Developing the Schedule."*

4 **B.** *See "Developing the Schedule."*

5 **C.** *See "Developing the Schedule."*

6 **D.** *See "Developing the Schedule."*

7 **C.** *See "Developing the Schedule."*

8 **B.** The best answer is to use this extra time for the programmer to add quality to the code. The question asks what to do with the extra time using an available resource. Optimization of code performance and ensuring code stability are often overlooked in IT projects. This is a tough situational question because several of the answers look right. Because the question doesn't mention whether the organizational structure is functional or fully projectized, you can eliminate answer A. You can eliminate C because adding another programmer to a task can often add a delay instead of shortening the task. For example, the programmer might not be familiar with the task and would need additional ramp-up time. D is a correct statement, just not the best answer; you or the appropriate team member should inspect all work regardless of schedule considerations. The pattern is the single most important thing a project manager should do is.

9 **D.** This is the most specific answer. The question asks you to specify what is the Most Likely duration. You should give a specific number of days. It is true that the project end date will lengthen, but this statement is not specific enough. The critical path isn't changed in this example, although it might under certain conditions. The slack on noncritical paths will certainly change, but again this is too general an answer. The slack on Tasks 2 and 4 is reduced to five days. This question tests your ability to demonstrate your understanding of the relationship among facts, principles, and methods.

10 **C.** If the hourly rate is $28, the fringes cost $8.40. The basis of the overhead calculation calls for you to subtotal wages plus fringes for $36.40. Then calculate $36.40 \times 1.5 = $54.60. Practice calculating the fully burdened rate cost estimates.

Chapter 10

Establishing Project Controls

● ●

Exam Objectives

▶ Developing the project plan

▶ Authorizing work

▶ Planning stakeholder communications

▶ Improving processes by ensuring quality

▶ Identifying and planning for risk

● ●

*T*his chapter concludes the all-important planning processes. The planning category accounts for the highest number of exam questions of any of the process groups. To complete your understanding of planning, you need to master the main facilitating planning processes of quality, risk, and communications. (If you've skipped the last two chapters, read them and master the core planning processes because those definitely appear on the exam.) We also cover several areas on the exam that address planning but aren't specifically mentioned in the *PMBOK Guide*.

In this chapter, we summarize the major points of the gurus of modern Quality Theory. Their leading-edge thinking composes much of what professional project managers know about quality today.

Then, because risk planning processes are relatively less important for the exam based on sheer number of questions, we speed past several of them. We explain five out of the six risk processes — the ones you need to study in relation to planning (the sixth is a controlling process). To prepare adequately for the exam, understand the principles and the process flow involved in managing risk. We cover the risk formulas in Appendix A. Then, know the definitions, and finally memorize all the inputs, tools and techniques, and outputs.

Quick Assessment

Communi-
cations

1 The communications management plan is an output of the _____ process.

2 Variance analysis, trend analysis, and earned value analysis are tools and techniques of the _____ process.

3 The main output of the Information Distribution process is _____.

4 Gathering, generating, and disseminating information in order to formalize the acceptance of the product by the sponsor, client, or customer is called _____.

5 Performance-measurement documentation is created during the _____ process.

6 Requests for changes to some aspect of the project are called _____.

7 A method for developing a systematic and logical view of the information needs of the stakeholders and of the sources for meeting those needs is called _____.

8 As you move into another project phase, your five-member team adds five more people. The number of communication channels you now have is _____.

9 Of the areas quality, schedule, and cost, _____ is/are more important than the others.

10 The risk management plan is developed during _____.

Answers

1 Information Distribution. This pattern is the order of events. This question tests your understanding of the relationships among facts, component processes, and methods. Know when the various plans are created. See "Maintaining the plan as a living document."

2 Performance Reporting. This is the tool and technique pattern for a specific process. See "Sharing findings with stakeholders."

3 Project records. This is the output pattern for a specific process. See "Maintaining the plan as a living document."

4 Administrative Closure. This pattern asks you to complete the definition. See "Sharing findings with stakeholders."

5 Administrative Closure. This is the input pattern. This question tests your understanding of the relationships among facts, component processes, and methods. See "Sharing findings with stakeholders."

6 Change requests. This pattern asks you to complete the definition. See "Maintaining the plan as a living document."

7 Stakeholder analysis. This is the tool and technique pattern. See "Planning Stakeholder Communications."

8 45. Using the formula, $n(n-1) \div 2$ where n represents the number of people on the team, calculate $10(10-1) = 90$; $90 \div 2 = 45$. If the question asked how many *more* channels, you solve two separate channel equations and then subtract to find the difference. The five-person team starts with $5(5-1) = 20$; $20 \div 2 = 10$ channels. Then you find the difference: $45 - 10 = 35$. That is, you'd be adding 35 more channels by adding five additional people to the team. See "Applying the formula for communications channels."

9 All of them. They are all equally important! This pattern asks you to distinguish between terms that are closely related. This question tests your understanding of the relationships among facts, component processes, and methods. Know when the various plans are created.

10 Risk Management Planning. This pattern is the order of events. This question tests your understanding of the relationship among facts, component processes, and methods. Know when the various plans are created. See "Identifying and Planning for Risk."

Creating the Project Plan

By this point, you already know that the project plan is a combination document composed of several subsidiary plans from each of the knowledge areas. To round out the plan, you collect lots of supplemental material as supporting detail. You also include other technical documents, or, if the work is complex, you might even add an entire technical subsidiary plan.

Maintaining the plan as a living document

Remember that the project plan is an integrated document that must be updated continually throughout the project. Formal project management methodology actually prevents you from ignoring the integrated plan because its process feedback loops generate updates to the plan. The project plan document is a tool that serves you and the team. Furthermore, updating the subsidiary plans is important as well — hence the emphasis on an *integrated* plan. And, after you've updated the project plan, you must follow the guidelines in the communications plan for distributing the revisions to stakeholders.

A mantra for the exam is this: Project requirements evolve over time. As the work progresses, you chart new territory, update your planning documents, and sometimes revise or correct them. In Chapter 9, you ended the core planning processes by establishing several baselines: scope, cost, and schedule. During other project planning processes, you determine how to manage such changes, how to measure them against the baseline, and how to integrate them into the project. This integrated plan — incorporating the WBS, performance reports, and change requests — helps you manage the project.

Creating subsidiary plans

Your planning efforts should result in the creation of subsidiary plans from each knowledge area. Subsidiary management plans include

- Scope management plan
- Time schedule management plan
- Cost management plan
- Quality management plan
- Human resource management plan

✔ Communications management plan

✔ Risk management plan

✔ Procurement management plan

Project integration management is omitted from the subsidiary plans. Integration is an overall process that combines all these subsidiary plans into the project plan.

Planning for future changes

As you create the project plan, keep in mind that facts and circumstances change. As you progress into other phases or stages, you may need to alter the plan to reflect these changes. Know how the methodology requires you to handle these updates. Remember also that change control has a dual nature: it's both *proactive* and *reactive*. In the proactive sense, your ability to manage changes as they occur is a Planning process — steps you took in advance to identify risks and determine how you would deal with them should they occur. In a reactive sense, change control is a continual controlling process, something the project manager is supposed to be doing all the time. To manage any change, you need a *change control system*. The *PMBOK Guide* defines a change control system as "a collection of formal, documented procedures that defines the steps by which official project documents may be changed. It includes the paperwork, tracking systems, and approval levels necessary for authorizing changes." Memorize this definition!

Some organizations already have change control procedures in place. You can and should use them. Otherwise the PM team must devise a change control system for the project. Early in the project, form agreements on how to handle your change control. Decide on what

✔ Reviews will be made of proposed changes

✔ Approval levels to require

✔ Action to take in simple cases when a formal review isn't necessary

✔ Action to take in emergencies

You also need to agree on a document *versioning* procedure and a configuration management procedure so all stakeholders know which set of revisions is current.

Obtaining written approvals for buy-in

A prudent business practice is to obtain written approvals before you begin the work. When disagreements occur later, having a document with the customers' signatures on it is helpful. Having all the scope documents approved is also helpful. These approvals establish a baseline for managing the ongoing project over its life cycle, so maintain orderly records of these authorizations, expenditures, and accomplishments.

Authorizing Work to Be Performed

Especially on larger projects, document all work authorized or de-authorized in a work authorization system (WAS). The WAS can be formal or informal, and it can be manual (pencil and paper) or automated (program-generated). *System* in this sense doesn't mean computerized. Make the WAS easy for people to use, because during the control portions of the project, it provides checklists to ensure all work has been performed. A WAS also provides a useful check and balance for changes. For example, the WAS should require approval of change requests, and the translation of associated activities into specific work authorizations. This process assures work won't go forward without the necessary approvals. If the activity isn't authorized, don't let the staff work on it. The process of documenting of changes and how they're converted into work authorizations can provide an audit trail, which can improve project control. Issue change requests whenever problems that require attention arise on the project. During the review of the *Challenger* accident, for example, the investigating commissions found that 96 percent of the work authorizations had errors. A reliable WAS could have at least prevented the errors and possibly the accident.

Planning Stakeholder Communications

The PM process of Communications Management incorporates all the processes required to ensure timely and appropriate development, collection, dissemination, storage, and disposition of project information. The detailed project plan — the entire plan that includes all subsidiary plans of the different knowledge areas — must be documented formally and elaborated upon as part of your discovery process. (Recall that requirements ultimately flow from the process of discovering what stakeholders really want and need.) Document the deliverables of the project as well as the project processes.

The formal document that serves as a guide for solving the information and communications requirements of the stakeholders is the *communications management plan.*

On a small or short-duration project, the effort in producing records doesn't need to be as great as it is on a larger project. Also, records don't need to be as detailed on small project as on larger ones. The effort and detailing are the responsibility of the PM team, according to the standards of the performing organization.

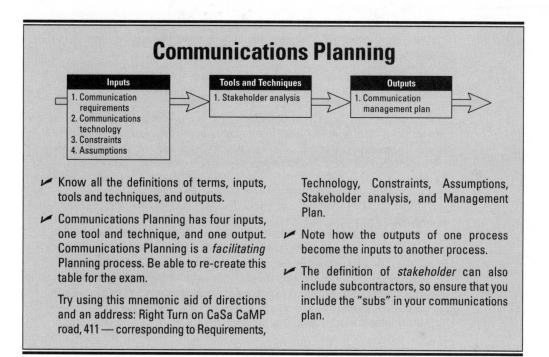

Communications Planning

Inputs	Tools and Techniques	Outputs
1. Communication requirements 2. Communications technology 3. Constraints 4. Assumptions	1. Stakeholder analysis	1. Communication management plan

✔ Know all the definitions of terms, inputs, tools and techniques, and outputs.

✔ Communications Planning has four inputs, one tool and technique, and one output. Communications Planning is a *facilitating* Planning process. Be able to re-create this table for the exam.

Try using this mnemonic aid of directions and an address: Right Turn on CaSa CaMP road, 411 — corresponding to Requirements, Technology, Constraints, Assumptions, Stakeholder analysis, and Management Plan.

✔ Note how the outputs of one process become the inputs to another process.

✔ The definition of *stakeholder* can also include subcontractors, so ensure that you include the "subs" in your communications plan.

Communications Planning has four inputs:

✔ **Communication requirements:** Include

- Who needs what type of information

- When they need the information

- How to distribute the information to them

Define the requirements by balancing the information needed (including its format and type) with an analysis of the value of that information. Your project will probably include multiple functional departments and some technical departments. Each department will have a different set of information requirements. Apply the formula for determining the number of communication channels to ensure that you include all stakeholders in your Communications Planning. (See "Applying the formula for communications channels," later in this chapter.)

✔ **Communications technology:** The methods and tools used to transfer information among stakeholders. This area includes brief face-to-face conversations to elaborate knowledge repository databases and online schedules. New technologies give us more communication options: e-mail, videoconferences, voice mail, streaming video, newsletters, and Web sites. As project teams spread out over increasingly larger geographic areas, these technologies can keep everyone informed.

 ✔ **Constraints:** Restrictions that affect the performance of the project. When contracts are involved, special considerations are often required for communications.

 ✔ **Assumptions:** Factors that for planning purposes, are considered to be true, real, or certain. They imply a certain degree of risk.

Memorize the preceding definitions for constraints and assumptions. Both are repeated many times in various processes — sometimes as process inputs, other times as process outputs. When you know these two definitions, you have a shortcut wherever they're repeated in the process descriptions.

Communication Planning has only one tool and technique.

 ✔ **Stakeholder analysis:** Provides the methods and techniques to determine a systematic and logical view of the information requirements of stakeholders, and how to meet those needs. The PM team is responsible for determining the stakeholders' requirements, as well as managing and influencing those requirements in order to produce a successful project. Notice how stakeholder analysis uses all four of the inputs to Communication Planning to create the output, the communications management plan, which follows.

Communications Planning has only one output:

 ✔ **Communications management plan (CMP):** An evolving document and a subsidiary component of the project plan, the CMP describes how to handle all communication on the project. The CMP can be formal or informal, detailed or high-level, depending on the needs of the project. The plan contains the methods and procedures used to collect, update, and store information. Often, it specifies a distribution list of stakeholders and the methods used to distribute various types of information. This plan describes what materials are distributed — including details on content, formats, levels of detail, and definitions. The plan contains a distribution schedule for each important communication, especially recurring events and documents for key milestones. You also need to plan how to handle updates to the CMP throughout the project.

Sharing findings with stakeholders

Each project stakeholder has a different need for information. Here's how to create, execute, and control an organized communications management plan to satisfy the most finicky stakeholder.

Know all the PMI definitions of terms, inputs, tools and techniques, and outputs of all four processes for Communications Planning, Information Distribution, Performance Reporting, and Administrative Closure. Exam questions we've seen include topics like:

✔ The formula for communications channels

✔ Hair-splitting definitions of terms

✔ Which processes are defined as core and facilitating processes

✔ When the communications management plan first appears (for the record, it's first in Communications Planning)

Applying the formula for communications channels

As team size increases, the number of communication paths increases geometrically (see Figure 10-1). With smaller teams, you can have more face-to-face time to communicate. With increasing team sizes, you must develop alternatives to having every team member talk to every other member.

The formula for the number of people with whom you must share information is

```
n(n - 1) ÷ 2
n = the number of people
```

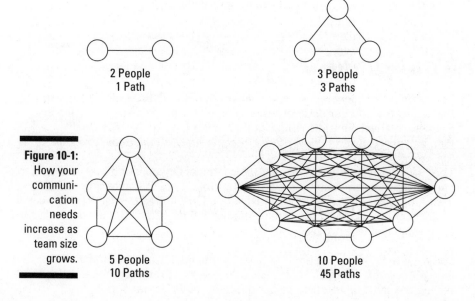

Figure 10-1: How your communication needs increase as team size grows.

Assume that everyone talks to everyone else on the team. When two people are on the team, it has only one communication channel. When the team has three people, it has two channels; four people, six channels; five people, ten channels; ten people, 45 channels. On a project with 50 people, the team is communicating along 1,225 channels. The greater the number of channels, or communication paths, the more time the team spends just communicating!

From a risk management perspective, more communication pathways mean more opportunities for miscommunication. Larger projects require tools and techniques for streamlining communications:

✔ Newsletters

✔ E-mail

✔ Project Web sites

✔ Progress report distribution lists

✔ Videoconferences

These types of formal documentation are among the best ways to ensure proper communication. Communicating forces people to make agreements. Having a consensus of opinions can prevent future problems.

You can apply this formula in developing the communications management plan. The plan answers the question of how to ensure that all stakeholders have the information they need when they need it.

Improving Quality

The exam covers several areas in quality not in the *PMBOK Guide*. Perhaps that's because a larger body of research and literature exists on quality as a general management discipline. In this section, we review the Quality Planning process and review other concepts that you need for the exam.

The *PMBOK Guide* follows the ISO (International Organization for Standardization) in defining *quality* as the "totality of characteristics of an entity that bear on its ability to satisfy stated or implied needs." The critical project context is that transforming implied needs into stated needs is a Scope Management process.

You need to know the distinction between the *quality* and the *grade* of an entity. According to the ISO, *grade* is a "category or rank given to entities having the same functional use but different requirements for quality." Although low quality is a problem, low grade may not be. A burger at McDonald's may be a lower-grade meal than a Porterhouse steak, but the burger is made according to a high-quality standard set by the fast-food vendor. As another example, many *lite* software versions have limited features (are low grade), but the program still works to a high level of quality (no bugs or crashes, comes with a good manual, has high usability). Because of its full feature set, the complete version of the software has a higher grade. You and the PM team determine, and later deliver on, quality and grade requirements.

The *PMBOK Guide* has two other mantras for quality. The first cautions against the concept of *gold plating,* which is simply loading additional features and functions that are not necessary for the scope of the project or for the specifications of the product. Gold plating doesn't add value; you'll burn through your schedule and budget to deliver the extra features. The second mantra states that the performing organization must cover the cost of quality improvements. Projects are temporary and may not last long enough to reap any rewards in quality improvements.

Project quality management includes those processes required to ensure that the project satisfies the needs for which it was undertaken. The concept of quality management follows the ISO definition (which is like quality guru Crosby's): "All activities of the overall management function that determine the quality policy, objectives, and responsibilities and implements them by means such as Quality Planning, Quality Control, Quality Assurance, and Quality Improvement, within the quality system."

Quality Planning

The PM process of *Quality Planning* involves identifying the quality standards that are relevant to the project and determining how to meet them. Quality Planning is a facilitating process in planning.

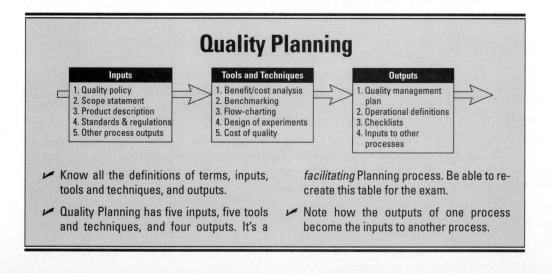

Quality Planning

Inputs	Tools and Techniques	Outputs
1. Quality policy	1. Benefit/cost analysis	1. Quality management plan
2. Scope statement	2. Benchmarking	2. Operational definitions
3. Product description	3. Flow-charting	3. Checklists
4. Standards & regulations	4. Design of experiments	4. Inputs to other processes
5. Other process outputs	5. Cost of quality	

✔ Know all the definitions of terms, inputs, tools and techniques, and outputs.

✔ Quality Planning has five inputs, five tools and techniques, and four outputs. It's a

facilitating Planning process. Be able to re-create this table for the exam.

✔ Note how the outputs of one process become the inputs to another process.

Quality Planning has five inputs:

- ✔ **Quality policy:** Defined by the ISO as the "overall intentions and direction of an organization with regard to quality as formally expressed by top management." The performing organization's quality policy can serve as the policy for the project. When such a policy doesn't exist, make one. The PM team's responsibility is to ensure that all stakeholders are fully aware of quality policy.

- ✔ **Scope statement:** Provides a documented basis for making future project decisions and for confirming or developing common understanding of project scope among stakeholders. The scope statement describes major product deliverables and objectives that define the project.

- ✔ **Product description:** Documents the characteristics of the product or service that the project was undertaken to create. The product description details various technical issues or concerns that may impact Quality Planning.

- ✔ **Standards and regulations:** Inputs from authorities outside the performing organization may impact Quality Planning.

- ✔ **Other process outputs:** Outputs from the other PM knowledge areas may impact Quality Planning.

Quality Planning has five tools and techniques:

- ✔ **Benefit/cost analysis:** Involves estimating tangible and intangible benefits (returns) and costs (outlays) of meeting quality requirements and then using financial measures to assess the relative desirability of the identified alternatives.

- ✔ **Benchmarking:** Compares actual or planned project practices to other projects to generate ideas for improvement and to provide a standard against which to measure performance.

- ✔ **Flow-charting:** Involves creating any diagram detailing how elements of a system relate to one another. Flow-charting techniques commonly used in quality management include:

  - **Cause-and-effect diagrams:** Show how causes and sub-causes relate and create potential problems or effects. The diagrams pinpoint root problems from the bottom up. They're also called *Fishbone* diagrams or *Ishikawa* diagrams. (See Figure 10-2.)

  - **Process flow charts:** These show how various elements interrelate. Flow charts help identify types of quality problems and where they might occur. They can help in developing approaches to dealing with the quality problems.

✔ **Design of Experiments:** An analytical technique that helps identify which variables have the most influence on the overall outcome and helps determine an optimal solution from a relatively limited number of cases. Design of Experiments helps you determine where to put most of your effort.

✔ **Cost of quality:** The financial cost incurred to ensure quality. These costs are associated with preventing, finding, and correcting defects, including costs of all quality processes: Planning, Assurance, and Control.

- **Prevention costs:** The cost of conformance. Prevention costs arise from activities designed to prevent inferior quality. Commonly encountered examples of inferior quality in IT include: coding errors, application design omissions or design errors, poor documentation, and un-maintainable code. Prevention costs can also include training, surveys, and implementation of the quality system itself.

- **Appraisal costs:** Arise from activities such as inspection and testing designed to find problems.

- **Failure costs:** Result from nonconformance. Failure costs can be internal or external to the performing organization.

- **Internal failure costs:** Rework, fixing software bugs, rejects, downtime, dealing with customer complaints, and scrap.

- **External failure costs:** Warranties, recalls, and handling customer complaints.

Quality Planning has four outputs:

✔ **Quality management plan:** A subsidiary component of the project plan. QMP describes how the PM team implements the quality policy. For the project, it covers

- Quality Control

- Quality Assurance

- Quality Improvement

✔ **Operational definitions:** Also called *metrics*. They describe the specifics of *what something is* (such as a work procedure or operation) and *how the Quality Control process measures it.* For example, convert a general objective of "increase success rate" to "increase success rate by 15 percent in two months" to make it specific.

✔ **Checklists:** Verify required steps have been performed or followed.

✔ **Inputs to other processes:** Provides the feedback loops to other processes to determine if Quality Planning can identify a need for further activity in another knowledge area.

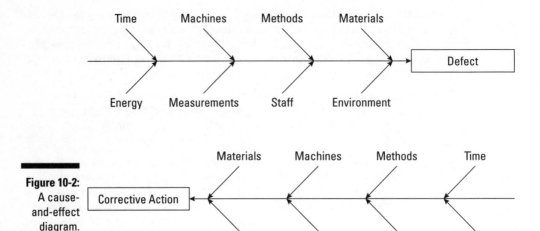

Figure 10-2:
A cause-
and-effect
diagram.

Approaching quality

This section introduces some other concepts, characteristics, attributes, and definitions of terms that reflect on quality. They're likely to be in the exam questions.

A mantra of the *PMBOK Guide* methodology is that quality addresses both the management of the project as well as the product of the project. Focusing your attention on quality issues improves your PM skills and the product. Quality isn't an assignable task to some distant QC manager or department. Quality must be designed into and monitored in every process of the project. Another mantra is that the performing organization must underwrite improvements in product quality — because the major causes of quality problems are systems, which are management's responsibility. Management also has the responsibility of providing needed resources, so management has *overall* responsibility for quality. Because the project team performs the actual work, it is *ultimately* responsible for quality, but the project manager is *primarily* responsible for the project's quality. Any way you figure it, you're on the hook! If you get this "Who is responsible?" exam question, check the qualifier words.

Traditional thinking was that management defined quality — as when Henry Ford said that customers can have any color auto they want as long as it's black. Modern thinking is that the customer defines quality. Because we know that customers vote on quality with their purchasing habits, customer satisfaction is paramount. Customer satisfaction involves understanding, managing, and influencing various needs and expectations, and then ensuring those needs and expectations are met or exceeded. Deming expanded this concept to "delighting," rather than merely satisfying, customers. (See "Philosophies of the QC gurus" in this chapter.)

Two other key tenets of modern quality management are: "Quality is planned in; it can't be inspected in." In this context, the term *planning* includes the all-important design phase. The concept of having limited tolerance for errors implies a goal of having as few defects as possible. The ultimate goal of all processes is to avoid any defects as in zero defects.

A zero-defect philosophy is similar to the six-sigma approach. Six Sigma methodology, a relative newcomer, is based on the notion that tighter control limits provide better products. Until Six Sigma was proposed, the traditional approach used three sigma, or three standard deviations from the mean. We explain just what those statistics mean in Appendix A. Because these categories described 99 percent of all possible outcomes, that three-sigma level was defined as quality. But was the three-sigma level good enough? Would you accept a 1 percent error rate? That means we'd have a water shortage, electricity blackout, gas turn-off, telephone and Internet disconnects for 15 minutes every day. We couldn't drink the water, surf the Web, or watch TV for four days of the year. We'd get food poisoning once a year. We've changed our views of acceptable quality; where we once accepted thousand rejects, we now accept fewer than one hundred per million products.

These key principles of general Quality Theory, not covered in the *PMBOK Guide,* may be on the exam:

- ✔ **The customer is the next person in the process:** Recognizes how tasks and products are transferred downstream in internal systems. Only after the product meets all the specifications and requirements is it transferred downstream to next person in the process. This way of thinking about quality eliminates poor workmanship and incorrectly assembled components.

- ✔ **Do the right thing right the first time:** Engenders the concept that doing the job right the first time is easier and cheaper than repeating the work if a defect is found. This approach requires a trained staff that has all the required skills and tools.

- ✔ **Kaizen or continuous improvement process:** Having a continual stream of tiny, incremental improvements is better than having occasional big ones. Deming said he'd rather have 1,000 improvements of 1 percent than one improvement of 1,000 percent. Kaizen focuses on 11 principles:

  - Constancy of purpose

  - Commitment to quality

  - Customer focus and involvement

  - Process orientation

  - Continuous improvement

  - System-centered management

  - Investment in knowledge

- Teamwork

- Conserving human resources

- Total involvement

- Perpetual commitment.

✔ **Producibility:** Assesses whether you can make a new product with existing technology, human resources, skills, knowledge, and materials at a cost compatible with market expectations. Producibility is a critical assessment in developing new products.

✔ **Usability:** Examines the performance, function, and condition of a product to see if it performs its intended function under the prescribed conditions.

✔ **Availability:** Measures the probability of performance to perform a required function under normal conditions. The key parts of availability are

- **Reliability:** How equipment performs under specified conditions over time. Reliability is computed by two *mean time between failure* (MTBF) methods: *Predicted MTBF* uses a probabilistic tree diagram to determine sequential failures among components over time. Predicted MTBF is the least desirable method—it doesn't account for environmental variations that can degrade components. *Actual MTBF* uses historical data to compute the average time between failures.

- **Maintainability, or mean time to repair (MTTR):** The capability of a product to be fixed within a specified, average period of time.

✔ **Operability:** Measures a product's expected conditional use. Operability is the capability of a product when people operate it over time and under normal conditions without significant degradation of the output.

Cost of quality

Until the 1940s, defects and other errors were accepted as a cost of doing business. Management viewed ensuring quality as an unnecessary, extra cost. Senior execs and quality managers had a serious communications gap. Since then, the emerging philosophies of the leading quality managers changed that view forever. They discovered the notion of the cost of not achieving quality. Cost became the common language communicating the need for quality to senior executives.

Cost of quality is the total price of all quality efforts. It's a Quality Planning tool and technique. These costs can run from 20 to 40 percent of sales. Cost of Quality has been a key principle of quality for 50 years and is cornerstone of Total Quality Management (TQM). Generally used statistics (which may appear on the exam) are that 85 percent of costs are the responsibility of management; only 15 percent are due to workers. The typical project should have a goal of 3 to 5 percent of the total value as the cost of a quality program, depending on the type of project and its total dollar value.

Let's explore two specific aspects of the cost of quality. The first cost includes all work to build a product or service to conform to requirements. The second cost includes the cost of all work resulting from nonconformance:

- ✔ **Cost of conformance:** This includes

  - Costs for planning

  - A policy of building right the first time

  - Training

  - Process control

  - Field-testing

  - Product design validation

  - Process validation

  - Testing and evaluation

  - Statistical process control (SPC)

  - Quality audits

  - Maintenance

  - Calibration

- ✔ **Cost of nonconformance:** This includes

  - Rework

  - Scrap

  - Expediting

  - Additional material and inventory

  - Warranty repairs or service

  - Complaint handling

  - Liability judgments

  - Product recalls

Philosophies of the QC gurus

The leading business thinkers in quality in the later part of the last century have all been referred to as *gurus.* They were generally highly trained in statistics, engineering, or operations research. While they could back up their ideas with statistics, most of their innovative techniques were rooted in pragmatism. All of them downplayed mathematical theory in favor of clarity and practicality. The math is at a fairly simple level so everyone can understand it, so don't let it intimidate you. The calculations that we help you master in Appendix A are fairly simple. You may see a few math and statistical questions on the exam. As well, you may see some questions on quality definitions and the philosophies of these gurus. In particular, understand where these members of the quality club agree and disagree. Know their main points and their various definitions of quality. Sorting out their unique points of view can be particularly challenging because they often modified or expanded upon each other's work.

W. Edwards Deming

Deming was the father figure of the modern quality revolution, which he led for almost 70 years. He's the dean of quality gurus, and most project managers have heard of him. His statistical sampling and process control techniques applied to manufacturing processes improved the quality of Japanese manufacturing so much that he's largely regarded as starting Japan's leadership role in international business.

A statistician by training, Deming's approach used statistical methods and compliance from the QC viewpoint. As a management visionary for most of his 90 years, he stressed management leadership, taking long-term positions, continuous improvement, improved efficiency, participation by everyone in quality, and doing it right the first time. In sharp contrast to the theories of some of his colleagues, he felt zero defects were unattainable. His 14 Points are still considered leading management theory.

Deming expanded on Shewhart's concept of common and special causes of variation (which we explain shortly). Deming used Shewhart's cycle of improvement: Plan, Do, Check, Act (PDCA). After Deming took this technique to Japan, PDCA became known as Deming's cycle. As the results from his teachings paid off in Japan, his reputation grew to legendary proportions. Deming taught that *special causes* of variation in a product (or process) prevented it from remaining in equilibrium — in a statistical sense — and he distinguished these special causes from *common causes*:

Special and common process variation causes are different.

 ✔ **Special causes:** Easily identified changes from fleeting events like changes of operator, machine, shift, or procedure.

 ✔ **Common causes:** All other causes of defects after special causes have been identified. Common causes include variation due to design, process, operation, or system. While operators can identify these causes of variations, it takes management authority to eliminate them. Deming believed that managers who didn't understand the distinction between variations could make matters worse.

Deming's 14 Points from his book *Out of the Crisis* have one aim — "to make it possible for people to work with joy." Here they are:

- ✔ Create constancy of purpose toward improvement of product and service, with the aim to become competitive, stay in business, and provide jobs.

- ✔ Adopt the new philosophy (of quality). Management takes on leadership for change.

- ✔ Cease dependence on inspection to achieve quality.

- ✔ End the practice of awarding business on the basis of price tag. Instead, minimize total cost. Move toward a single supplier for any one item, on a long-term relationship of loyalty and trust.

- ✔ Improve constantly and forever the system of production and service, to improve quality and productivity, and thus constantly decrease costs.

- ✔ Institute training on the job.

- ✔ Institute leadership. The aim of supervision should be to help people and machines to do a better job. Supervision of management is in need of overhaul as well as supervision of production workers.

- ✔ Drive out fear, so that everyone may work effectively for the company.

- ✔ Break down barriers between departments. People must work as a team.

- ✔ Eliminate slogans, exhortations, and targets for the work force asking for zero defects and new levels of productivity.

- ✔ Eliminate work standards (quotas) on the factory floor. Eliminate management by objective, by numbers, and by numerical goals.

- ✔ Remove barriers that rob the hourly worker, management, and engineering of his right to joy of workmanship. The responsibility of supervisors must be changed from sheer numbers to quality. This means abolishment of the annual merit rating and of management by objective.

- ✔ Institute a vigorous program of education and self-improvement.

- ✔ Put everybody in the company to work to accomplish the transformation.

These are Deming's Seven Deadly Diseases:

- ✔ Lack of constancy of purpose (of the company for the long term to stay in business). He's referring to products and services that will have a market, keep the company in business, and provide jobs. Consistency of purpose includes:

  - • Research.

  - • Learning from experiences.

  - • Applying them to create innovative products.

- ✔ Emphasis on short-term profits. Short-term thinking is the opposite of constancy of purpose. It's fed by fear of unfriendly takeovers and by demands from bankers and owners for short-term increases.

- ✔ The devastating effects of personnel review systems, evaluation of performance, merit rating, annual review, or annual appraisals. He referred to the traditional practice of management by objectives as "Management by Fear."

- ✔ Mobility of management due to job-hopping and layoffs.

- ✔ Use of visible figures only for management, with little or no consideration of figures that are unknown or unknowable.

- ✔ Excessive medical costs.

- ✔ Excessive warranty costs, fueled by speculative lawyers working for contingency fees.

In the views he formed late in his career, Deming increased management accountability of the costs of potential improvement from the generally used level of 85 percent to 94 percent. Deming summarized his experience in his *System of Profound Knowledge.* It describes four interrelated parts:

- ✔ **Appreciation for a system:** Emphasizes the need for managers to understand the relationships between functions and activities. Everyone should understand that the long-term aim is for everybody to gain — employees, shareholders, customers, suppliers, and the environment. Failure to accomplish the aim causes loss to everybody in the system.

- ✔ **Knowledge of statistical theory:** Includes knowledge about variation, process capability, control charts, interactions, and loss function. (For more on control charts, see Appendix A.) All these need to be understood to accomplish effective leadership and teamwork.

- ✔ **Theory of knowledge:** States that all plans require prediction based on past experience. Success cannot be copied unless the theory is understood.

- ✔ **Knowledge of psychology:** Necessary to understand human interactions. Leaders must understand the differences between people and optimize them. People have intrinsic motivation to succeed in many areas. Extrinsic motivators in employment may smother intrinsic motivation. These include pay rises and performance grading.

Joseph M. Juran

Dr. Juran broadened the statistical origins of quality. Juran added a human dimension and emphasized continuous awareness of the customer in all processes. Like Deming, he emphasized total involvement of everyone. Then Juran added that Quality Control should be an integral part of Management Control. This breakthrough idea has now evolved into Total Quality Management. In fact, many concepts on the exam belong to Juran. For example, Juran's pioneering work requires that you know Pareto diagrams on the exam.

In the late 1930s, Juran applied Pareto's 80 ÷ 20 principle to quality. This separates the "vital few" causes of quality problems from the "useful many" in their activities.

Juran thought higher quality encompassed two aspects:

- ✔ More features that meet customers' needs
- ✔ Fewer defects

His Quality Planning Road Map consists of the following concepts. Quality does not happen by accident; it must be planned. The key to implementing company-wide quality planning rests on identifying customers and their needs; establishing optimal quality goals; creating measurements of quality; planning processes capable of meeting quality goals under various operating conditions; and producing results in improved market share, premium prices, and error reduction. His formula for results is

- ✔ Establish specific goals
- ✔ Establish plans for reaching the goals
- ✔ Assign clear responsibility
- ✔ Base the rewards on results achieved

Emphasizing special knowledge and tools for managing quality, Juran thought mastering the Quality Planning process prevents new chronic problems. He believed management-controllable defects account for over 80 percent of quality problems. He disagreed with two quality ideas from his colleagues: Crosby's zero defects (ZD) and quality circles. Juran thought ZD was based on the mistaken idea that the majority of quality problems are caused by careless workers. Although Quality Circles had enjoyed some success in Japan, Juran was unconvinced that they would work in Western countries.

Philip Crosby

Crosby considers traditional Quality Control, the definition of what quality tolerances are acceptable, and release of substandard products as management failures. His definition of quality is conformance to requirements.

Although Crosby emphasizes a top-down approach from specialists spreading the quality improvement message throughout the organization, not everyone agrees with his philosophy on how to achieve quality. With his negative views on traditional Quality Controls, he's pretty controversial. In fact, he's so controversial that he's never received any encouragement from the quality establishment, especially with the concept of ZD. To Crosby, ZD begins with management not planning for workers to make mistakes. The three-sigma tolerances aren't close enough, and in this respect, his approach is closer to Six Sigma. He believes senior management is entirely responsible for reaching this level of quality. Management sets the tone on quality; and workers follow their example. To stretch the point further, Crosby's message is that most companies' organizations and systems allow or even encourage deviation from what's required to achieve quality improvements. His measurements indicate that manufacturing companies in particular spend 20 percent of revenues doing things wrong and reworking products. For service companies, waste must be expressed not as a percentage of revenue but of operating expenses — amounting to as much as 35 percent.

Crosby's theme of "Quality is Free" is that every dollar not spent fixing mistakes and reworking tasks translates directly into profits. He believes in giving all workers whatever training and tools they need to improve quality so that they can apply prevention. For this, he uses a process model, in which work is a series of actions to produce a desired result. This process model ensures a clear definition and understanding of requirements for every member of the organization — including suppliers and customers.

Crosby's four absolutes of Quality Management:

✔ Quality is conformance to requirements, not as goodness nor 'elegance. It's always cheaper to "do it right the first time."

✔ The system of quality is prevention, not appraisal.

✔ The performance standard is zero defects, not "that's close enough."

✔ The measurement of quality is the price of nonconformance, not indexes. Nonconformance is the cost of doing things wrong.

Crosby's 14 steps to improving quality:

✔ Management commitment

✔ Quality improvement team

✔ Measurement

✔ Cost of quality

✔ Quality awareness

✔ Corrective action

✔ Zero defects planning

✔ Employee education

✔ Zero defects day

✔ Goal setting

✔ Error cause removal

✔ Recognition

✔ Quality councils

✔ Do it over again

Genichi Taguchi

Taguchi was an engineer, and his methodology is geared to engineering. In contrast to Western definitions on the attributes of quality, Taguchi was the first person to equate quality with cost. By quantifying the losses due to lack of quality over the life span of a product, he wanted to be able to show management the total monetary impact on the company of failing to produce quality. He helped revolutionize the post-WWII Japanese manufacturing process through cost savings. His main work is on how product and process designs impact on both life cycle costs and on quality.

Under the Taguchi method, the Quality Loss Function focuses on quantifying losses associated with controlling, or failing to control, process variability. The goal is to minimize the factors that cause variation. He emphasized quality cannot be ensured through inspection, statistical Quality Control, or rework. Quality must be designed in a product or service through the appropriate design of both the processes and the product. The concept of *prevention over inspection* is the cost of avoiding mistakes. Intuitively, prevention is less expensive than the cost of correcting mistakes.

Taguchi created a three-step approach called quality by design, which includes: *system design*, *parameter design*, and *tolerance design*. By selecting robust design parameters, products are more flexible and tolerant. It's a prototyping method that identifies the optimal settings for a robust product that can survive manufacturing. *System design* essentially creates a prototype. *Parameter design* minimizes features or processes that are least sensitive to changing environmental conditions and other uncontrollable (noise) factors. *Tolerance design* minimizes the impact of factors with the largest impact on variation. This three-step design technique helps determine the value (break-even point) of improving a process to reduce variability, which he called "noise." He estimated that 85 percent of failures occur in the process, not with the worker. Taguchi's methodology for implementing robust design in the preceding three areas takes a four-step procedure:

- Formulate the problem
- Plan the experiment
- Analyze the results
- Confirm the experiment

One of Taguchi's major contributions is his use of Design of Experiments, explained previously in this chapter. He changed the long-held belief that the only proper way to conduct an experiment was to vary only one factor at a time while locking all other variables as a fixed constant. The typical analysis currently used was Monte Carlo technique. Monte Carlo analysis requires hundreds or even thousands of iterative tests to estimate the mean and variance. In the days before inexpensive desktop computers, this testing was very time-consuming and costly. The time lag for determining a solution kept the process out of control even longer, so Taguchi designed experiments in which he varied several factors at once in preset patterns. Basically, he used matrix algebra in the analysis of variance, taking orthogonal arrays to isolate the effects of three independent factors (such as time, temperature, and concentration) using as few as eight experiments. From this type of experimental design, you determine detailed information on how each factor affects quality and how much the factors interact in a cost-effective manner.

Kaoru Ishikawa

Ishikawa is best known for starting the Quality Circle movement in Japan in the early 1960s, a movement characterized by participation from top management all the way to the lowest-ranking workers in the organization. He knew the importance of tools: control charts, run charts, histograms, scatter diagrams, Pareto diagrams, Binomial probability, sampling inspections, and flow charts. He educated factory foremen (called "on-the-spot leaders" in Japan) about quality by making statistical techniques accessible to all levels. He emphasized good data collection and presentation, like Pareto diagrams to prioritize quality improvements, and his Cause-and-Effect diagrams (discussed previously in this chapter) that look like a fishbone. He thought the diagrams were simple group tools for brainstorming. For analyzing causes of variation, he stressed the importance of systematic tools, such as control charts and scatter diagrams.

A Quality Circle is a small, voluntary group of five to ten workers. A foreman, assistant foreman, work leader, or even a worker leads the group in regularly scheduled meetings. They use statistical Quality Control to achieve significant results in quality improvement, cost reduction, productivity, and safety. They teach seven tools to all employees: Pareto diagrams, Cause-and-Effect diagrams, stratification, check sheets, histograms, scatter diagrams, and Shewhart's control charts and graphs. The circles implement solutions themselves. While Japan has over 10 million Quality Circle members, the practice is falling into disuse because of management's lack of interest or excessive intervention. The philosophy is that even a minor enhancement from the Quality Circle adds up to a much larger progress for the entire company.

Crosby and Juran warned against Quality Circles. Crosby didn't think the approach solved poor employee motivation, quality, or productivity. And, as we've said, Juran doubted their effectiveness in the West.

Shigeo Shingo and Zero Defects

In Japan, Shingo developed the concept of Poka-Yoke, which is translated to "Defects = 0"or mistake-proofing. This concept has become known in the west as ZD or zero defects. A common belief today is that statistical QC methods like inspection can't reduce defects to zero. ZD works by having source inspection systems halt processes upon spotting a defect. Machines designed around this concept give immediate feedback and help define the cause, and then the staff can prevent the defect's source from recurring. This procedure of detecting and correcting defects at the source of the problem eliminates the need for statistical sampling.

Quality definitions from each guru

The *PMBOK Guide's* definition of *quality* is: "totality of characteristics of an entity that bear on its ability to satisfy stated or implied needs." Other theorists approach quality definitions from a different perspective: quality is the conformance to requirements or specifications, fitness of use, satisfying stated or implied needs. For the exam, know the distinctions between the PMI definition and those of these theorists. The themes of the major theorists are

- ✔ Deming's is "reduction of variance."

- ✔ Juran's is "fitness for use." Higher quality covered two aspects — a greater number of features that meet customers' needs and fewer defects.

- ✔ Taguchi's is "The quality of a product is the (minimum) loss imparted by the product to the society from the time product is shipped."

- ✔ Crosby advocated "conformance to requirements."

Identifying and Planning for Risk

Risk is the possibility of suffering harm or loss — anything that prevents you from achieving the project's goals and objectives. Risk has two sides: *Opportunities* are the positive outcomes as a result of risk, and *threats* are the negative outcomes as a result of potential risk. PM methodology focuses on risk definition, management risk planning, risk identification, quantification, risk response development, and risk control.

Project risk management involves the processes concerned with identifying, analyzing, and responding to uncertainty. The most likely cause of poor risk management is lack of a prioritized list of risks.

The *2000 PMBOK Guide's* chapter on the Risk Management process has been completely rewritten. It has expanded the entire risk section into several new processes, indicating the importance of managing risks on projects. In this view, PM is a management tool to reduce project risk.

The theme in the risk processes is to get all stakeholders to help identify risks, determine their impacts, and develop responses. Then publish the project risks and monitor them throughout the project.

Risk Management Planning (RMP) is how to approach and plan risk management activities. RMP is essentially a scope process for risk, and this process is a new addition to PM methodology. Risk is among the last steps in the core planning processes before developing the project plan.

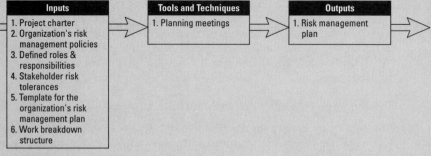

Risk Management Planning

Inputs	Tools and Techniques	Outputs
1. Project charter 2. Organization's risk management policies 3. Defined roles & responsibilities 4. Stakeholder risk tolerances 5. Template for the organization's risk management plan 6. Work breakdown structure	1. Planning meetings	1. Risk management plan

✔ Know all the definitions of terms, inputs, tools and techniques, and outputs.

✔ Risk is composed of six processes; five are planning processes and one is a controlling process. Risk Management Planning is the only core process of Planning and one of the last in the planning group. The other risk processes are all facilitating processes.

✔ Risk Management Planning has six inputs, one tool and technique, and one output. Be able to re-create this table for the exam.

✔ Connect the outputs of Risk Management Planning process and the inputs of the next process, Risk Identification. Linking these interactions can help you remember both processes. Continue these links with the rest of the risk processes.

Risk Planning concerns the approach for planning risk management activities. Risk Identification determines which risk events require your attention. Qualitative Risk Analysis helps you prioritize the effects of risk on the objectives of your project. Quantitative Risk Analysis estimates probabilities and impacts of each risk occurring, and then prioritizes the risks. Risk Response Planning enables the team to response to risk events.

Risk Management Planning has six inputs:

✔ **Project charter:** Formally recognizes the existence of a project.

✔ **Organization's risk management policies:** Provide a predefined approach to risk analysis and response for your project.

✔ **Defined roles and responsibilities:** Provide authority levels for decision-making. They also affect risk planning.

✔ **Stakeholder risk tolerances:** Indicators of how stakeholders might react in different situations and risk events. These are different for all organizations and people. You'll notice them in policy statements or in actions. They include the different profiles:

- Risk Taker

- Risk Averse

- Risk Neutral

✔ **Template for the organization's risk management plan:** A pro forma standard for use by the project.

✔ **WBS:** A deliverable-oriented grouping of project elements that organizes and defines the total scope of the project.

Risk Management Planning has one tool and technique:

✔ **Planning Meetings:** Develop the RMP. Everyone responsible for planning and executing activities should help create the RMP.

Risk Management Planning has one output:

✔ **Risk management plan (RMP):** Documents the procedures used to manage how risk is handled throughout the project. RMP doesn't address any responses or solve any individual risks. That's the role of Risk Response Plan. In addition to documenting the results of the Risk Identification and Risk Quantification processes, the RMP addresses who is responsible for managing various areas of risk. In a roles and responsibilities section, the RMP sets forth the reporting formats of how the initial identification and quantification outputs are maintained, how contingency plans are implemented, and how reserves are allocated. An RMP may be formal or informal, highly detailed or broadly framed, based on the needs of the project. It is a subsidiary element of the overall project plan.

  • **Methodology:** Defines approaches, tools, and data sources used to perform risk management on the project.

  • **Roles and responsibilities:** Define lead, support, and risk management team membership for each type of action in the plan.

  • **Budget:** The anticipated cost of performing project risk management activities.

  • **Timing:** Describes how often the risk management process is performed throughout the project life cycle.

  • **Scoring and interpretation:** Methods for performing Qualitative and Quantitative Risk Analysis to ensure consistency.

  • **Thresholds:** The targets against which the project team measures the effectiveness of the risk response plan execution.

  • **Reporting formats:** Define how the results of the risk management processes is documented, analyzed, and communicated to the project team and stakeholders.

  • **Tracking:** Documents all facets of risk activities for the benefit of current project, future needs, and lessons learned. Tracking also documents if and how the risk process is audited.

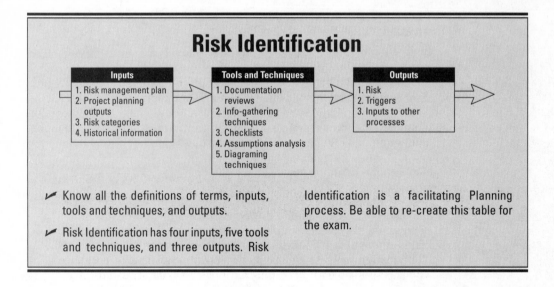

Risk Identification

Inputs	Tools and Techniques	Outputs
1. Risk management plan	1. Documentation reviews	1. Risk
2. Project planning outputs	2. Info-gathering techniques	2. Triggers
3. Risk categories	3. Checklists	3. Inputs to other processes
4. Historical information	4. Assumptions analysis	
	5. Diagraming techniques	

✔ Know all the definitions of terms, inputs, tools and techniques, and outputs.

✔ Risk Identification has four inputs, five tools and techniques, and three outputs. Risk

Identification is a facilitating Planning process. Be able to re-create this table for the exam.

Identifying risk

The PM process of *Risk Identification* involves

✔ Determining which risks are most likely to influence the project

✔ Documenting their specific characteristics and symptoms

✔ Categorizing the types of risk that you'll face

The RMP is an input to this process. Two types of risks generally faced are

✔ **Business risks** (opportunity for gain or loss)

✔ **Pure risks** (only loss)

Pure risks are *insurable*.

Risk Identification has four inputs:

✔ **Risk management plan (RMP):** Contains the procedures used to manage risk throughout the project.

✔ **Project planning outputs:** Reviews other process outputs to identify the risks across the entire project. Looks at product description (unproven technologies, innovations, or inventions involve greater risk), project charter, WBS, cost and duration estimates (for aggressive schedules and limited amount of information in making the estimates), staffing plan (for skills that are hard to replace or acquire), procurement management plan (for timing of market conditions).

✔ **Risk categories:** Organize and identify risks. Risks are generally categorized in terms of *technical, quality, PM, organizational, scope, schedule, cost,* and *external.*

- **Technical, quality, or performance risks** include unproven technology, unrealistic performance goals, and changes to technology or to industry standards. Technical risks involve identifying errors or defects. They're normally addressed first because they impact on costs and schedules. Quality risks involve failure to complete tasks to the required level of technical or quality performance.

- **PM risks** include poor allocation of time and resources, inadequate project plan, and poor use of PM methodologies.

- **Organizational risks** include inconsistent project objectives, lack of prioritization of projects, insufficient or lack of funding, and resource conflicts with other projects. Scope risk involves how scope changes and resulting corrective actions to reach your required deliverables. Schedule risks involve how to complete tasks within estimated time limits, or risks associated with dependency network logic. Cost risks involve completing tasks within the estimated budget.

- **External risks** include shifting legal or regulatory environment, labor issues, changing owner priorities, country risk, and Force Majeure risks.

✔ **Historical information:** Drawn from project records or archives, commercial databases, team member experiences and knowledge.

Risk Identification has five tools and techniques:

✔ **Documentation reviews:** Provide a structure review of project plans and assumptions, at different level of detail for the total project and detailed scope level.

✔ **Information-gathering techniques:** Include the following:

- **Brainstorming:** Developed in the 1950s by a psychologist as a simple way to help people think creatively in a group situation without feeling inhibited or being criticized. Brainstorming is used extensively in initial planning and in creating risk scenarios.

- **Delphi method:** Derives a consensus solution to a specific problem among panel of experts in an iterative fashion. In the next iteration, each expert refines his own estimate as well as the others'. The process continues until group responses converge to a consensus. The Delphi method is used for large and critical risk impacts.

- **Interviewing:** Explores issues with various stakeholders, or project managers. Subject-matter experts might also be called in to identify potential risks.

- **Strengths, Weaknesses, Opportunities and Threat (SWOT) Analysis:** Provides a framework for identifying critical issues. When dealing with complex situations with limited time, addressing all the issues involved often doesn't pay. Strengths and weaknesses are internal factors; opportunities and threats are external factors. Caution: SWOT Analysis can be very subjective.

✔ **Checklists:** Provided by previous projects. Checklists are organized by source of risk, including project context, process outputs, product and technology issues, and internal sources.

✔ **Assumptions analysis:** Explores the assumptions and identifies potential risks.

✔ **Diagramming techniques:** Help you understand various cause-and-effect relationships. Examples are Cause-and-Effect (Fishbone or Ishikawa) diagrams, System or Process flow charts, and Influence diagrams.

Risk Identification has three outputs:

✔ **Risks:** Uncertain events or conditions that have a positive or negative effect on the project when they occur.

✔ **Triggers:** Symptoms of risk; indirect manifestation of actual risk events like poor morale.

✔ **Inputs to other processes:** Usually constraints or assumptions.

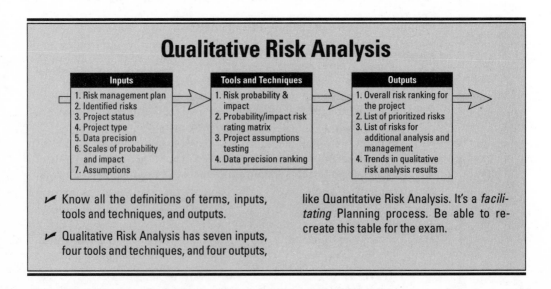

Qualitative Risk Analysis

Inputs	Tools and Techniques	Outputs
1. Risk management plan	1. Risk probability & impact	1. Overall risk ranking for the project
2. Identified risks	2. Probability/impact risk rating matrix	2. List of prioritized risks
3. Project status	3. Project assumptions testing	3. List of risks for additional analysis and management
4. Project type	4. Data precision ranking	4. Trends in qualitative risk analysis results
5. Data precision		
6. Scales of probability and impact		
7. Assumptions		

✔ Know all the definitions of terms, inputs, tools and techniques, and outputs.

✔ Qualitative Risk Analysis has seven inputs, four tools and techniques, and four outputs, like Quantitative Risk Analysis. It's a *facilitating* Planning process. Be able to re-create this table for the exam.

Qualifying risks

Qualitative Risk Analysis is assessing the impact and likelihood of identified risks.

Qualitative Risk Analysis has seven inputs:

- ✔ **Risk management plan:** Documents the procedures used to manage risk throughout the project.

- ✔ **Identified risks:** Taken from previous Risk Identification process. Evaluate these risks for their potential impacts on the project.

- ✔ **Project status:** Identifies risks through the project life cycle.

- ✔ **Project type:** Determines the amount of risk you can expect. Common or recurrent type projects have less risk, while state-of-the-art, first-time technology, or highly complex projects have more uncertainty.

- ✔ **Data precision:** Tests the value of data. Data precision measures the extent of data available, reliability of the data, and source of the data.

- ✔ **Scales of probability and impact:** Assesses the two key dimensions of risk (*probability of occurring* and *impact on project*).

- ✔ **Assumptions:** Identified during Risk Identification need evaluation.

Qualitative Risk Analysis has four tools and techniques:

- ✔ **Risk probability and impact:** The two dimensions of specific risks. *Risk probability* is the likelihood that a risk will occur. *Risk consequences,* or impact, are the effects on project objectives if the risk event occurs.

- ✔ **Probability/impact risk rating matrix:** A matrix constructed for assigning ratings to risks or conditions on combining probability and impact scales. The Risk Probability scale falls between 0.0 (no probability) and 1.0 (certainty). Ordinal scales are ranked-order values, such as *very low, low, moderate, high,* and *very high.* Cardinal scales assign values to these impacts. These values are usually linear (0.1, 0.3, 0.5, 0.7, 0.9) or nonlinear (.05, 0.1, 0.2, 0.4, 0.8).

- ✔ **Project assumptions testing:** Performed against two criteria: *assumption stability* and the *consequences on the project* if the assumption is false.

- ✔ **Data precision ranking:** A technique to evaluate the degree to which the data is useful for risk management. Data should be unbiased and accurate. The process involves examining:

  - Extent of understanding of the risk
  - Data available about the risk
  - Quality of the data
  - Reliability and integrity of the data

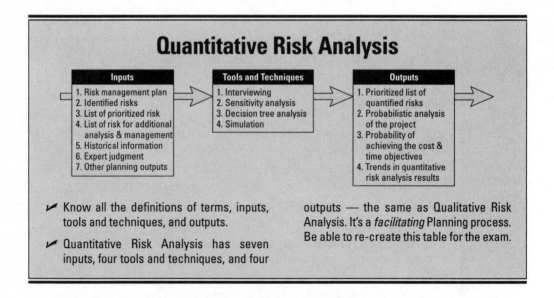

Quantitative Risk Analysis

Inputs	Tools and Techniques	Outputs
1. Risk management plan	1. Interviewing	1. Prioritized list of quantified risks
2. Identified risks	2. Sensitivity analysis	2. Probabilistic analysis of the project
3. List of prioritized risk	3. Decision tree analysis	3. Probability of achieving the cost & time objectives
4. List of risk for additional analysis & management	4. Simulation	4. Trends in quantitative risk analysis results
5. Historical information		
6. Expert judgment		
7. Other planning outputs		

✔ Know all the definitions of terms, inputs, tools and techniques, and outputs.

✔ Quantitative Risk Analysis has seven inputs, four tools and techniques, and four outputs — the same as Qualitative Risk Analysis. It's a *facilitating* Planning process. Be able to re-create this table for the exam.

Qualitative Risk Analysis has four outputs:

✔ **Overall risk ranking for the project:** Indicates the overall risk position of a project relative to other projects by comparing risk scores.

✔ **List of prioritized risks:** Include those grouped by: rank (high, moderate, low); WBS level; risks requiring immediate response; risks that can be handled later, as well as risks that affect cost, schedule, functionality, and quality. Significant risks should have a description of the basis for the assessed probability and impact.

✔ **List of risks for additional analysis and management:** Itemizes moderate and high risks that are candidates for further analysis, including Qualitative and Quantitative Risk Analysis, as well as risk management action.

✔ **Trends in Qualitative Risk Analysis results:** Become apparent as the analysis is repeated and can make risk response more or less urgent and important.

Quantifying risks

Quantitative Risk Analysis is a process that numerically analyzes the probability of each risk and its consequence on objectives. This process uses techniques such as Monte Carlo simulations and decision analysis to:

✔ Determine probability of achieving a specific project objective.

✔ Quantify the risk exposure for the project, as well as determine the size of cost and schedule contingency reserves that may be needed.

✔ Identify risks requiring the most attention by quantifying their relative contribution to project risk.

✔ Identify achievable and realistic cost, schedule, or scope targets.

Quantitative Risk Analysis has seven inputs:

✔ **Risk management plan:** Documents the procedures used to manage risk throughout the project.

✔ **Identified risks:** Evaluates risks in the previous Risk Identification process for their potential impacts on the project.

✔ **List of prioritized risks:** Includes those grouped by: rank (high, moderate, low); WBS level; risks requiring immediate response; risks that can be handled later, and risk that affect cost, schedule, functionality, and quality.

✔ **List of risks for additional analysis and management:** Indicates that moderate and high risks are candidates for further analysis, including quantitative and risk analysis, and risk management action.

✔ **Historical information:** Drawn from previous projects concerning how they handled risks, studies of similar projects by risk specialists, and risk databases available.

✔ **Expert judgment:** Determines whether risks have a probability of occurrence (ranked high, medium, or low) and the level of impact (ranked severe, moderate, or limited).

✔ **Other planning outputs:** Includes schedule logic and duration estimates, WBS list of all cost elements, and models of project technical objectives.

Quantitative Risk Analysis has four tools and techniques:

✔ **Interviewing:** Using project stakeholders and subject-matter experts to quantify the probability and consequences of risks on project objectives. The information needed depends upon the type of probability distributions that will be used.

✔ **Sensitivity analysis:** Helps determine which risks have the greatest impact on the project. It's the simplest form of risk analysis. Sensitivity analysis examines the change of a single project variable to analyze its effect on the project plan. By defining the variation for each component, you obtain probabilities of risk estimates, but only for variables highly impacting cost, time, or economic return. Advantages include identifying a range of possible outcomes and making decisions that are more realistic. Weaknesses are: treating variables individually, limiting the combinations of variables studied, and the fact that a sensitivity diagram doesn't indicate probability of occurrence.

✔ **Decision tree analysis:** Identifies possible options or outcomes (see Figure 10-3). It forces consideration of the probability of each outcome — usually a success or failure option — but it can also include other choices. You quantify each likelihood and place a value on each outcome. You generally apply decision-tree analysis to uncertainties issues having to do with cost or time. Solving the decision tree indicates which decision yields the greatest expected value when all the uncertain implications, costs, rewards, and subsequent decisions are quantified.

✔ **Simulation:** Uses a model of a system to analyze the behavior or performance of the system. Examples are

- Monte Carlo

- Critical Path

- PERT

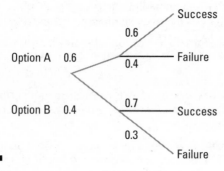

Figure 10-3:
A decision
tree.

What is the probability that Option B will be selected and will be successful?

Answer: 28%

Quantitative Risk Analysis has four outputs:

✔ **Prioritized list of quantified risks:** Shows which pose the greatest threat or opportunity to the project and a measure of their impact.

✔ **Probabilistic analysis of the project:** Forecasts potential project schedule and cost results, listing the possible completion dates, or project duration, and costs with their associated confidence levels.

✔ **Probability of achieving the cost and time objectives:** Assessed under the current project plan and with the current knowledge of the project risks.

✔ **Trends in Quantitative Risk Analysis results:** Become apparent as the analysis is repeated.

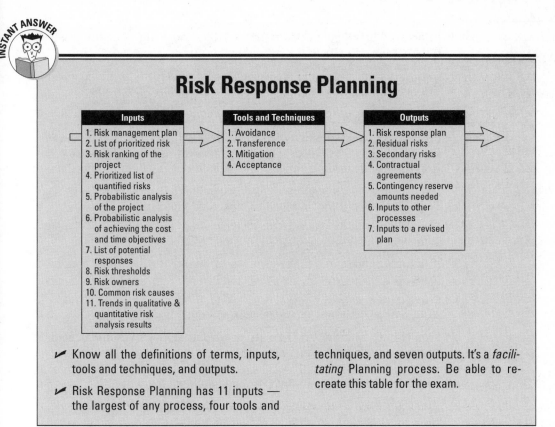

Risk Response Planning

Inputs	Tools and Techniques	Outputs
1. Risk management plan 2. List of prioritized risk 3. Risk ranking of the project 4. Prioritized list of quantified risks 5. Probabilistic analysis of the project 6. Probabilistic analysis of achieving the cost and time objectives 7. List of potential responses 8. Risk thresholds 9. Risk owners 10. Common risk causes 11. Trends in qualitative & quantitative risk analysis results	1. Avoidance 2. Transference 3. Mitigation 4. Acceptance	1. Risk response plan 2. Residual risks 3. Secondary risks 4. Contractual agreements 5. Contingency reserve amounts needed 6. Inputs to other processes 7. Inputs to a revised plan

✔ Know all the definitions of terms, inputs, tools and techniques, and outputs.

✔ Risk Response Planning has 11 inputs — the largest of any process, four tools and

techniques, and seven outputs. It's a *facilitating* Planning process. Be able to re-create this table for the exam.

Developing responses for risks

Risk Response Planning involves developing options and determining actions to enhance opportunities to reduce threats to project objectives.

Risk Response Planning has 11 inputs:

> ✔ **Risk management plan:** Documents the procedures to manage risk throughout the project.

> ✔ **List of prioritized risks:** Itemizes those grouped by: rank (high, moderate, low); WBS level; risks requiring immediate response; risks that can be handled later, and risk that affect cost, schedule, functionality, and quality. Significant risks should have a description of the basis for the assessed probability and impact.

> ✔ **Risk ranking of the project:** Indicates the overall risk position of a project relative to other projects by comparing risk scores.

✔ **Prioritized list of quantified risks:** Identifies those that pose the greatest threat or opportunity to the project and proposes some means of measuring their impact.

✔ **Probabilistic analysis of the project:** Forecasts potential project schedule and cost results, listing the possible completion dates, or project duration, and costs with their associated confidence levels.

✔ **Probability of achieving the cost and time objectives:** Assessed under the current project plan and with the current knowledge of the project risks.

✔ **List of potential responses:** Identifies specific risks or categories of risk. These lists specify the actions the team will take.

✔ **Risk thresholds:** The acceptable level of risk to the organization, which influences risk response planning.

✔ **Risk owners:** Identifies staff to provide accountability for managing responses.

✔ **Common risk causes:** Several risks driven by a common cause. This reveals opportunities to mitigate many risks with one response.

✔ **Trends in Qualitative and Quantitative Risk Analysis results:** Become apparent as the analysis is repeated.

Risk Response Planning has four tools and techniques:

✔ **Avoidance:** The elimination or reduction of risks. Eliminating the cause eliminates the risk. While you can never eliminate all risks, certain specific risk events can be eliminated.

✔ **Transference:** Includes insurance or warranties, both of which are means of deflecting or sharing risks.

✔ **Mitigation:** A reduction of risk. Reduce the expected monetary value by reducing the probability of occurrence. For example, float can mitigate potential schedule risks.

✔ **Acceptance:** Accepts or retains consequences. In *active acceptance,* you develop a contingency plan. In *passive acceptance,* you don't act and accept lower profits — if activities run over schedule.

Risk Response Planning has seven outputs:

✔ **Risk response plan:** Documents the procedures to manage risk events. Addresses Risk Identification, owners and responsibilities, results from qualification and quantification processes, agreed responses for each risk, the level of residual risk to remain after the strategy is implemented, budget and times for responses, and contingency plans.

✔ **Residual risks:** Remain after avoidance, transfer, or mitigation responses have been taken.

✔ **Secondary risks:** Arise in direct result of implementing a risk response.

✔ **Contractual agreements:** Specify each party's responsibility for specific risks, for insurance, services, and other items to avoid or mitigate threats. Types of coverage include

  • Direct property damage insures principal assets: equipment, materials, property, auto, or servers.

  • Indirect consequential loss is an indirect loss suffered by third party due to the contractor.

  • Legal liability includes design errors, public bodily injury, and project-performance failures.

  • Personnel refers to bodily injury.

  • Wrap-up insurance can be provided in a single integrated package.

✔ **Contingency reserve amounts needed:** Probabilistic analysis of the project and the risk thresholds to help the project manager determine the amount of buffer or contingency reserve needed to reduce the risk of overruns of project objectives to a level acceptable in the organization.

✔ **Inputs to other processes:** Responses to risk may require expenditures of additional time, cost, or resources that become changes to the plan.

✔ **Inputs to a revised plan:** Feedback mechanisms that integrate the risk response plan with the project plan to ensure that agreed upon actions are implemented and monitored.

Prep Test

1 The communications management plan first appears as an output of the _____ process.

A ○ Communications Initiation

B ○ Communications Planning

C ○ Communications Execution

D ○ Communications Control

2 _____ generates, gathers, and disseminates information to formalize phase or project completion.

A ○ Scope Verification

B ○ Performance Reporting

C ○ Administrative Closure

D ○ Project Communications Management

3 According to Crosby, quality is defined as _____.

A ○ Reduction of variance

B ○ Fitness for use

C ○ Conformance to requirements

D ○ Minimum loss imparted by the product to the society from the time product is shipped

4 Quality is _____.

A ○ The minimum loss imparted by the product to the society from the time product is shipped

B ○ Totality of characteristics of an entity that bear on its ability to satisfy stated or implied needs

C ○ More features that meet customers' needs and fewer defects

D ○ The conformance to requirements or specifications, fitness of use, satisfy stated or implied needs

5 _____ defines the actions or steps that the risk owners will take if a risk event suddenly occurs.

A ○ Risk management plan

B ○ Risk response plan

C ○ Contingency plan

D ○ Risk control plan

6 You have a risk of shooting a movie sequence that involves blowing up a building. You don't want the crew to accept the risk of injury, even though the studio's production executive tells you there are ample safeguards, and the production is insured. You especially don't want the star to be involved because any injuries could delay the remainder of your shooting schedule. What is the best way to handle the situation?

A ○ Shoot the stars on a sound stage and use computer graphics to insert the stars in the explosion sequence.

B ○ Insure the crew for additional amount found by the 50 percent probability of the explosion causing damage by the number of people on the crew and the personnel insurance rate to cover bodily harm.

C ○ Transfer the risk to a second camera unit and make them obtain their own insurance.

D ○ Accept the exec's appraisal of the situation and shoot the explosion in the building with the star. Get the studio exec's written authorization to shoot in the dangerous location. If anything goes wrong, cite the written authorization.

7 You are trying to determine the extent of the risk in the preceding explosion scenario. What methods would help you quantify the risks?

A ○ Decision trees

B ○ Simulation

C ○ Pareto diagram

D ○ Monte Carlo analysis

8 Contingency reserves in the project budget are used for _____.

A ○ Covering specific cost account overruns

B ○ Covering missed cost and schedule and scope objectives

C ○ Covering unknown unknowns

D ○ Covering items that management reserves don't cover

9 The risk response plan is the output of _____.

A ○ Risk Planning

B ○ Risk Identification

C ○ Risk Response Planning

D ○ Risk Management Planning

10 _____ quantify(ies) the risk of various schedule alternatives, different project strategies, different quality variables, different paths through the network, and individual activities.

A ○ Decision trees

B ○ Simulation

C ○ Monte Carlo analysis

D ○ Critical Path analysis

Answers

1 **B.** This pattern is the order of events. This question tests your understanding of the relationships among facts, component processes, and methods. *See "Sharing findings with stakeholders."*

2 **D.** This pattern asks for the definition of the process. *See the* PMBOK Guide, *p. 117.*

3 **C.** This pattern asks for the definition of the process. *See "Quality definitions from each guru."*

4 **B.** This is the *PMBOK Guide* and ISO definition. The others are the definitions of other quality theorists. This pattern asks for the definition. *See "Quality definitions from each guru."*

5 **B.** Risk response plan covers reactions to specific risks as well as identifying the risk owners' roles and responsibilities. Risk management plan covers how the risk area will be managed. Although contingency plan is a good answer, it is a subset of risk response plan and may not assign responsibilities. This pattern asks you to distinguish between terms that are closely related. *See "Identifying and Planning for Risk" and the* PMBOK Guide, *p. 144.*

6 **A.** Avoidance of the risk by using new technology is the best answer. B and C provide for transference; and D, acceptance of the consequences. Each still has some major residual risks for the project. D might save your job by placing the burden of the decision on the studio exec, but if you're responsible for the project, don't let a dysfunctional exec reduce the project's chances of success. The pattern is the best way to handle the situation.

7 **A.** Decision trees help establish probabilities by forcing choices. This is the tool and technique pattern. *See "Identifying and Planning for Risk."*

8 **B.** This is a definition pattern. *See "Developing responses for risks" and the* PMBOK Guide, *pp. 144, 199.*

9 **C.** Risk Response Planning. This is the output pattern. *See "Developing responses for risks" and* PMBOK Guide, *p. 143.*

10 **C.** Monte Carlo analysis is a generic approach to solving probability problems. Simulation is a good answer, but it's too general. Decision trees aren't used to quantify different paths through a network. Critical path analysis isn't used in quality processes, only time processes. This pattern asks for examples of the tools and techniques.

Part IV
Executing the Project

The 5th Wave   By Rich Tennant

"Why, of course. I'd be very interested in seeing this new milestone in the project."

In this part...

Execution of *PMP, The Movie* begins with the "first day of principal photography." It's an exciting time. You resisted the temptation to dive into production right away and have spent lots of time planning. You've polished the various subsidiary plans. Now, everyone knows his role and responsibilities. The actors know their lines. The crew knows what sets to build, what equipment is required, and each day's shooting location. Production is where the action is, where creative dreams must become realities, and where you'll spend most of your budget.

The project management team is ready. The First Assistant Director (AD) initially scheduled for the crew to shoot a page and a half of the script per day and subsequently refined that estimate for individual activities. He's locked a schedule down and even has some pre-planned contingency "cover sets" in case of rain while shooting outside. The shooting pace closely matches the director's needs. The Unit Production Manager (UPM) has completed a budget and spending plan. During the formative phases of the project, the studio's senior managers who authorized the movie had some WAG ("wild-ass guess") estimates stuck in their minds. Those serious schedule and budget constraints became hotly contested areas for negotiation during the detailed planning phase of the project. Now the UPM has some "wiggle room" covering his contingencies.

As filming begins, we find the director rehearsing the actors. The producer, UPM, and AD confer as they "work the plan." Early on, the AD will execute the communication plan, which calls for daily meetings with the Director, Designer, Director of Photography, Wardrobe, Property Master, and a dozen more managers. The UPM will be responsible for the spending plan. He knows this is where the bulk of the budget will be spent and must account for every last paperclip. He'll check his detailed budget against it, providing information to the studio execs on variances and estimates to complete the movie.

Here's where we make the product, a few cans of film.

Chapter 11

Procuring Resources, Managing, and Reporting Progress

● ●

Exam Objectives

▶ Executing the plan

▶ Soliciting and sourcing materials, equipment, and supplies

▶ Administrating contracts

▶ Implementing resources

▶ Communicating with stakeholders

▶ Assuring quality

▶ Measuring progress with metrics

*E*xecuting the project plan, managing the project's myriad of details, and reporting on results are the exciting parts of the project manager's job. Being in the middle of the action is fun and is probably why you became a project manager in the first place. You feel the rush of adrenaline and can't wait to get to the office in the morning. Naturally, you hope everyone else on the project feels the same excitement you do.

In this chapter, we reveal why Project Plan Execution is the core to the executing processes. As an overall Integration process, we show you the importance of process flows — pointing out where Project Plan Execution interacts and overlaps with all the other executing processes. This executing section has only seven processes to remember. We show you how to master the techniques of purchasing items and handling contracts. We also cover how to develop, motivate, and influence the project team so you can make them feel as excited about the project as you do. And we reveal how to report back to the stakeholders on the project's performance. Finally, you'll ace the exam questions on providing confidence that the project will satisfy the relevant quality standards and selecting which metrics to measure your progress.

Quick Assessment

Executing the Plan

1 During the middle of the project, a customer comes to you with a new wish list of items to add to the project. The wish list is called _____.

2 Product skills and knowledge, work authorization system, status review meetings, project management information systems, organizational procedures, and organizational policies are all tools and techniques of the executing process except for _____.

3 The main output of the Information Distribution process is _____.

Administrative Closure

4 Gathering, generating, and disseminating information in order to formalize the acceptance of the product by the sponsor, client, or customer is called _____.

5 Performance-measurement documentation is created during the _____ process.

6 Requests for changes to some aspect of the project are outputs of _____.

7 The interpersonal communications within the team or organization structure are _____.

8 QC audits, continuous-improvement targets, and personnel guidelines are examples of _____.

Developing the Schedule7

9 A certain project manager who doesn't believe his team is working hard enough on the project uses threats, coercion, and a kick in the seat of the pants. This project manager is using _____.

10 For the birthday of one of the key team members who has worked very hard on the project, you have the rest of the team surprise him with a cake. This is an example of _____.

Answers

1   Change request. This pattern is the order of events. Know when the various plans are created. See "Executing the Project Plan."

2   Performance Reporting. All the other processes are integrative in Project Plan Execution. See "Executing the Project Plan" and "Administrating contracts."

3   Project records. See "Distributing Information."

4   Administrative Closure. See "Distributing Information."

5   Input to Administrative Closure. See "Distributing Information."

6   Project Execution. Work results and change requests are the outputs of Project Execution.

7   Unofficial. See "Distributing Information."

8   Organizational policies. See "Executing the Project Plan."

9   Theory X management style. See "Motivating the team."

10   Team-building activities. See "Developing the team."

Executing the Project Plan

The Executing processes include seven process interactions.

- ✔ Project Plan Execution entails performing the activities and tasks to produce the final objectives of the project — carrying out the project plan.

- ✔ Quality Assurance evaluates project performance on a regular basis to ensure you meet standards.

- ✔ Team Development includes developing the team and individual skills.

- ✔ Information Distribution of project information ensures stakeholders have it in a timely manner. You hold progress meetings to keep stakeholders informed.

- ✔ During Solicitation, you obtain quotations, bids, and proposals in order to make purchases.

- ✔ Source Selection is the key step in deciding which suppliers are most appropriate for your purchases.

- ✔ Contract Administration entails managing relationships with suppliers.

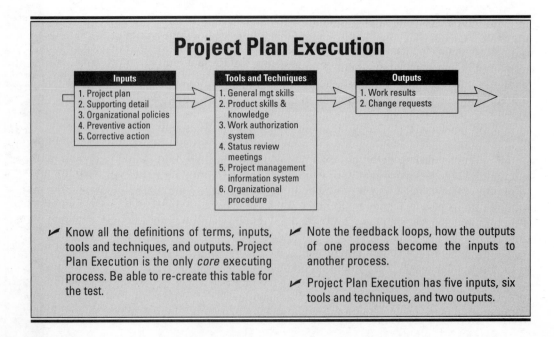

Project Plan Execution

Inputs	Tools and Techniques	Outputs
1. Project plan 2. Supporting detail 3. Organizational policies 4. Preventive action 5. Corrective action	1. General mgt skills 2. Product skills & knowledge 3. Work authorization system 4. Status review meetings 5. Project management information system 6. Organizational procedure	1. Work results 2. Change requests

✔ Know all the definitions of terms, inputs, tools and techniques, and outputs. Project Plan Execution is the only *core* executing process. Be able to re-create this table for the test.

✔ Note the feedback loops, how the outputs of one process become the inputs to another process.

✔ Project Plan Execution has five inputs, six tools and techniques, and two outputs.

A mantra of the methodology is that the project manager must manage the expectations of superiors, sponsors, and customers by proactively defining and solving issues or problems. It's not good PM practice to go to any of these stakeholders as soon as you notice a problem. You must make sure that you have some options for them to discuss and evaluate, especially, if you want them to make a decision.

Project Plan Execution is a core process in execution. It is the main process for carrying out the project plan and is the most costly aspect of project management. During this core Integration process, you manage organizational resources and the interfaces to the rest of the performing organization.

Project Plan Execution has five inputs:

✔ **Project plan:** The formal, approved document used to guide project execution and control.

✔ **Supporting detail:** Additional information or documentation generated during development of the project plan. These details are outputs from other planning processes like technical documentation and documentation of relevant standards.

✔ **Organizational policies:** Provide constraints to your project. They include formal and informal policies, such as QC audits, continuous-improvement targets, and personnel guidelines.

✔ **Preventative action:** Anything that reduces the probability of potential consequences of project risk events. This input is a new addition to this version of the *PMBOK Guide*.

✔ **Corrective action:** Anything that brings your expected performance back in line with the project plan. They're outputs from the other knowledge areas.

Project Plan Execution has six tools and techniques:

✔ **General management skills:** Include leadership, communication, negotiation skills, problem solving, and influencing the organization.

✔ **Product skills and knowledge:** Defined as part of resource planning and provided by the people you select for your team.

✔ **Work authorization system:** Any formal procedure for sanctioning project work to ensure completion. It can involve written or verbal authorizations to begin work.

✔ **Status review meetings:** Provide a regular exchange of information about the project with stakeholders.

✔ **Project management information system (PMIS):** Tools and techniques (either automated or manual) to provide for the collection, dissemination, and storage of information from other PM processes.

✔ **Organizational procedures:** Formal and informal procedures often useful during project execution. Some policies are

- QC audits

- Continuous-improvement targets

- Personnel guidelines

Project Plan Execution has two outputs:

✔ **Work results:** The outcome of activities performed. Work results are fed into the performance reporting process and are what you monitor throughout all aspects of the project.

✔ **Change requests:** Formal requests, usually by the customer but possibly also from other team members, that expand or shrink project scope, modify costs and schedule estimates, as well as impact resources. These requests can be oral or written, direct or indirect, externally or internally initiated, and legally mandated or optional.

Know the pattern of the relationship between corrective action and change requests. In Integration during Project Plan Execution, corrective action is an input, and change requests are outputs. In Overall Change Control, those inputs and outputs switch so that corrective action is the output while change requests are the inputs. This feedback loop is also the pattern for the other change control processes where corrective action is always an output, and change requests are always inputs. The other change requests exception is in Communications — Performance Reporting.

Procuring Resources

The approach in all procurement processes is always from the *buyer's* side for the exam. In this context, you are the buyer. If you are performing PM services along with other deliverables under a contract, then sometimes you have to reconsider the processes from the seller's side in the real world.

Soliciting

Solicitation involves obtaining information in the form of bids and proposals from prospective sellers. The sellers trying to win your business bear most of the effort of gathering the information.

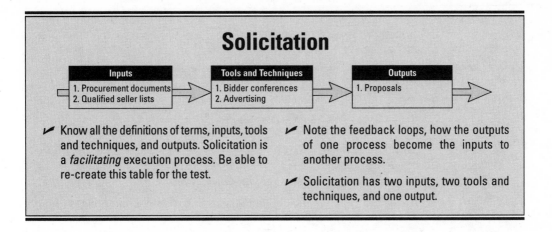

Solicitation has two inputs:

☛ **Procurement documents:** Solicit proposals from potential buyers. They include:

  • Request for proposal (RFP)

  • Request for quotation (RFQ)

  • Invitation to bid

  • Invitation for negotiation

  • Contractor initial response

☛ **Qualified seller lists:** The preferred vendors for a product or service. The performing organization usually has a list of preferred suppliers.

Solicitation has two tools and techniques:

☛ **Bidder conferences:** Provide mutual understandings in meetings. Bidder conferences give you a chance to exchange key information.

☛ **Advertising:** Request for services, supplies, materials, and equipments completed primarily on government projects to ensure equal access to bidding opportunities.

Solicitation has one output:

☛ **Proposals:** Entail the seller preparing documents that describe its willingness and ability to provide the service or product. Proposals become an important part of the project records. In some cases, they become the statement of work (SOW). In any event, the proposals are used to develop formal contracts. In many cases, the contract has the winning proposal attached as one of the supporting detail sections.

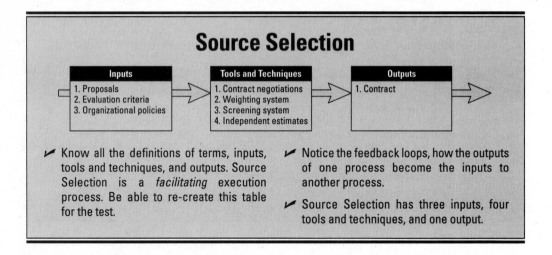

Source Selection

Inputs	Tools and Techniques	Outputs
1. Proposals	1. Contract negotiations	1. Contract
2. Evaluation criteria	2. Weighting system	
3. Organizational policies	3. Screening system	
	4. Independent estimates	

✔ Know all the definitions of terms, inputs, tools and techniques, and outputs. Source Selection is a *facilitating* execution process. Be able to re-create this table for the test.

✔ Notice the feedback loops, how the outputs of one process become the inputs to another process.

✔ Source Selection has three inputs, four tools and techniques, and one output.

Selecting sources of materials

During Source Selection, you use the proposals and evaluation criteria that you developed in Solicitation Planning. Source Selection is seldom a straightforward process, and you must exercise judgment as you analyze the answers from the sellers to determine the best bid. The lowest price may not always be the best for the project or result in lowest total project cost. If the low-price bidder omits something in the contract or delivery dates don't fit your needs, you might have to cancel the contract and pay more for rush delivery. You must look at the seller's approach and price.

> ✔ *Approach* involves the technical aspects of the seller's proposal.
>
> ✔ *Price* involves the commerce side.

In many cases, a single vendor can't supply all your needs. You might need multiple sources for the same item or service. When you've selected the winning bids, you enter into negotiations and develop final contracts.

Source Selection has three inputs:

> ✔ **Proposals:** Seller-prepared documents that describe the seller's ability and willingness to provide the requested product. They're an output of Solicitation Planning.
>
> ✔ **Evaluation criteria:** Establish ratings or scores for proposals. The criteria can be objective or subjective. They can be limited to price considerations, especially if the item is a readily available commodity.

The sellers' documents should show an understanding of your project needs, the overall or life-cycle cost, their technical capabilities, their management approach, and their financial capacity.

✔ **Organizational policies:** May impact your decision. They can come from any of the organizations involved in the project.

Source Selection has four tools and techniques:

✔ **Contract negotiation:** The clarification and mutual agreement on structure and requirements of a contract prior to signing. The subjects covered usually include: responsibilities and authorities, applicable terms and law, financing and price, and technical and business management. During this process, be sure you understand the risks associated with the different type of contracts. (See Chapter 9 for a list of different contract types and their risks.)

✔ **Weighting system:** Used to quantify data in three steps to minimize personal prejudices of source selection: First, they assign numerical weight to evaluation criteria. Second, they rate the sellers. Finally, they multiply weights by rating and totaling overall score.

✔ **Screening system:** Establish minimum performance criteria.

✔ **Independent estimates (or should cost estimates):** Prepared by the project procuring organization to determine any significant differences. These differences could mean the seller didn't understand the SOW or omitted something in the SOW.

Source Selection has just one output:

✔ **Contract:** A mutually binding agreement that obligates a seller to provide goods or services and the buyer to make payment. It establishes a legal relationship that is subject to remedy in court. Most organizations have policies and procedures concerning who can sign a contract, referred to as a *delegation of procurement authority.* The winning proposal is part of the supporting detail to the contract. Most organizations also require legal review and approval of contracts.

Administrating contracts

Contract Administration ensures that the seller's performance meets your contractual requirements. It also involves managing vendor relationships, especially important with change requests. Contract Administration entails maintaining formal correspondence with the seller and expediting requests for payment with the performing organization. Nothing is more frustrating to a project manager than a vendor holding up shipments because he hasn't gotten paid. The project team must consider legal ramifications of all actions taken when administering the contract. Contract Administration interacts with several processes:

✔ Project Plan Execution to authorize and perform the work

✔ Performance Reporting to monitor costs and the schedule

✔ Quality Control to verify that the seller's output meets the teams' quality requirements

✔ Integrated Change Control to handle contract changes

Contract Administration has four inputs:

✔ **Contract:** A mutually binding, legal agreement that obligates a seller to provide goods or services and the buyer to make payment.

✔ **Work results:** The seller's deliverables, quality standards, and actual costs.

✔ **Change requests:** Modifications to the contract or its description of the product or service. If the seller's work is unsatisfactory, the project manager can terminate the contract. The state of the project manager and seller disagreeing on compensation for contested changes is called a *claim, dispute,* or *appeal.*

✔ **Seller invoices:** Submitted periodically and requesting payment for work performed. The contract defines invoice requirements and supporting documentation.

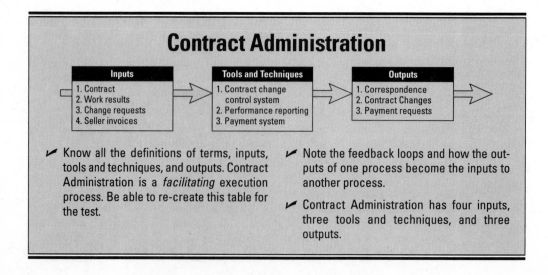

Contract Administration

Inputs	Tools and Techniques	Outputs
1. Contract	1. Contract change	1. Correspondence
2. Work results	control system	2. Contract Changes
3. Change requests	2. Performance reporting	3. Payment requests
4. Seller invoices	3. Payment system	

✔ Know all the definitions of terms, inputs, tools and techniques, and outputs. Contract Administration is a *facilitating* execution process. Be able to re-create this table for the test.

✔ Note the feedback loops and how the outputs of one process become the inputs to another process.

✔ Contract Administration has four inputs, three tools and techniques, and three outputs.

Contract Administration has three tools and techniques:

- **Contract change control system:** Defines how a contract may be modified. It includes paperwork, tracking system, dispute resolution procedures, and the hierarchy of approval levels.

- **Performance reporting:** Tells the PM team how effectively the seller is achieving the contractual objectives. Performance Reporting is generated by the communications process as part of the overall process of controlling the project.

- **Payment system:** Usually an organization's accounts payable (AP) process.

Contract Administration has three outputs:

- **Correspondence:** Retained as a way of documenting and clarifying the contract's terms and conditions. Contracts usually require written documentation such as warnings of unsatisfactory performance and contract changes or clarifications. The project manager is responsible for giving the seller formal notice of the contract's completion.

- **Contract changes:** Both approved and unapproved changes. Changes are fed back through the planning and procurement processes. The project plan or other relevant documentation is updated when necessary.

- **Payment requests:** (Or *payments* if the project has its own internal system.) Issued when you are using an external payment system. Sellers are demotivated if payment requests stall in the payment system. In many organizations, you must manage the interface to AP for timely payment to sellers. Otherwise, sellers delay your shipments or charge extra.

Implementing Resources

Projects involve people as resources. No matter how well you plan and control the project, people still must perform the work. Naturally, you might wonder, how does a project manager find the people, and how does a project manager motivate them to do the work? The exam covers these needs:

- Organizing the team

- Developing team skills

- Motivating the team

- Removing conflict causes

- Exercising your power as a project manager

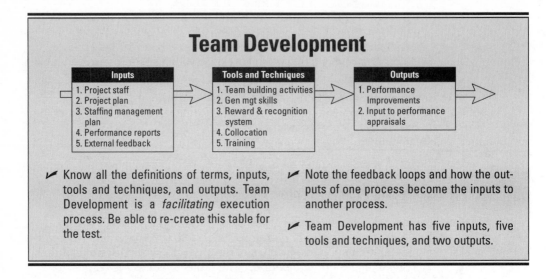

Team Development

Inputs	Tools and Techniques	Outputs
1. Project staff	1. Team building activities	1. Performance
2. Project plan	2. Gen mgt skills	Improvements
3. Staffing management	3. Reward & recognition	2. Input to performance
plan	system	appraisals
4. Performance reports	4. Collocation	
5. External feedback	5. Training	

✔ Know all the definitions of terms, inputs, tools and techniques, and outputs. Team Development is a *facilitating* execution process. Be able to re-create this table for the test.

✔ Note the feedback loops and how the outputs of one process become the inputs to another process.

✔ Team Development has five inputs, five tools and techniques, and two outputs.

Developing the team

To develop the team, the project manager must enhance team members' abilities. The project manager also must enhance the team to function as a coordinated unit. This is critical on uncertain projects, such as risky research and development projects. The *PMBOK Guide* indicates the groundwork necessary to developing a team requires developing each person in both managerial and technical areas. This can be complicated if you're working in a matrix organization; team members report to both a functional manager and a project manager. But the *PMBOK Guide* clearly indicates, "The effective management of this dual reporting relationship is often a critical success factor for the project and is generally the responsibility of the project manager." Although team development is categorized as an executing process, it occurs throughout the project. Having a dysfunctional team with otherwise good performers is a symptom of an impending risk.

Team Development has five inputs:

✔ **Project staff:** An output of Staff Acquisition, where it's *project staff assigned.* The key is that particular skill sets for individuals and the team are available to support the project. Staff may be assigned full time, part time, or variably, based on project needs.

✔ **Project plan:** Incorporates the integrated documents that provide the baseline for controlling changes.

✔ **Staffing management plan:** Documents the timings and methods by which people will join and leave the project team. As the main output of Organizational Planning, it lists all the required skills you'll need on the project. The gap between the plan's skill requirements and the actual project staff's skills indicate the team's training needs.

✔ **Performance reports:** Alert the project team to issues that can cause problems in the future. Know the distinction between status and progress reports. *Status* reports describe the project's current standings. *Progress* reports describe the team's accomplishments.

✔ **External feedback:** Criticism from outside the project helps the project team make periodic measurements of performance.

Team Development has five tools and techniques:

✔ **Team-building activities:** Any actions that improve team performance.

✔ **General management skills:** Include leadership, communication, negotiation skills, problem solving, and influencing the organization.

✔ **Reward and recognition system:** Motivates people through intrinsic factors like responsibility, promotions, and achievement, as well as extrinsic factors like pay raises, status, and working conditions. If rewards are given in a timely and public manner, they promote desired behavior.

✔ **Collocation:** Places team members in the same physical location.

✔ **Training:** Enhances your team's skills, knowledge, and capabilities. Training costs need to be considered in developing the project.

Team Development has two outputs:

✔ **Performance improvements:** Includes anything that improves individual skills, enhances the ability of the team to function as a team, or identifies more efficient methods of working.

✔ **Input for performance appraisals:** Comprises evaluations of each staff member's contribution to the project. You use the evaluations for periodic or annual performance reviews according to the organization's HR policy.

Motivating the team

You need to know three motivational theories for the exam. The *PMBOK Guide* doesn't cover these personnel management approaches. They relate to work motivation.

Maslow's hierarchy of needs

Abraham Maslow's *hierarchy of needs* was a radical departure from the current standard psychological approaches of Sigmund Freud (Determinism) and B. F. Skinner (Behaviorism). Maslow's theory states that people are motivated by unsatisfied needs. Lower-level needs, such as eating or sleeping, must be satisfied before higher-level needs, such as intellectual curiosity, can be satisfied. Maslow ranked human needs in the following order, from lowest to highest:

✔ **Physiological** needs are requirements of hunger, thirst, bodily comforts, medical care, emergency attention, rescue, and coping.

✔ **Security** needs are about safety and security, keeping out of danger, safety planning, food supplies, and shelter requirements.

✔ **Social** needs relate to belonging, affiliating with others, social acceptance, social self-help, finding love, escaping bad feelings and alienation, and gaining a sense of belonging.

✔ **Esteem** includes needs of ego self-help, finding healthy pride, finding direction, being empowered in business to achieve, being competent, and gaining approval and recognition.

✔ **Self actualization** needs involve finding self-fulfillment and realizing one's potential. These needs are cognitive — to know, to understand, and to explore things that give life direction and meaning.

McGregor's theories of X and Y

Doug McGregor's *Theories of X and Y* describes how managers can motivate different types of people. Since 1960, McGregor's notions have profoundly affected management philosophy. He described the norms, values, and opinions that managers have about the staff. His focus is from a management perspective. He influenced personnel policies, Total Quality Management (TQM), and the continued practice of staff appraisal (which Deming fought against). Unfortunately, studies to quantify or provide support for these theories don't exist, but McGregor has held a place in the management mindset for so long that his two theories have become established dogma.

✔ **Theory X** (the authoritarian management style) states that people prefer to be directed and controlled. Workers are lazy, selfish, and hate work. Money is their only motivation. In response, management must structure work, inspections, instructions, and punishments. Tasks must be well defined and specific. Management controls workers through the use of rewards, promises, incentives, close supervision, rules and regulations, threats, or even sanctions.

✔ **Theory Y** (the participative management style) states that people prefer to work without supervision. A humanistic or self-actualization approach to managing workers, Theory Y is sometimes called the *Human Resource model*. When workers feel committed to their jobs, they exercise responsibility, self-direction, and self-control. They're motivated by factors other than money. They enjoy work, exercise imagination, ingenuity, and find creative solutions. Management can utilize the worker's unused intellectual potential. A Theory Y manager takes the time to explain things, understands the needs of the individual, and engages in joint-problem solving with all staff.

Ouchi's Theory Z management

In the 1980s, William Ouchi at UCLA described how Japanese companies produce high employee commitment, motivation, and productivity. Because Ouchi calls his theory of motivation *Theory Z*, it naturally invites comparisons to McGregor's theories. (For the exam, you should consider the three theories as a continuum.) However, the focus on Theory Z is from the employee's perspective rather than McGregor's management perspective.

Theory Z (the Japanese management style) places freedom to act and trust with workers, who have strong loyalties to the organization. Japanese employees are guaranteed a position for life and are extremely loyal to their companies. They're responsible and use teamwork to solve problems. Theory Z emphasizes more secure employment, increased career prospects, and increased worker participation in making decisions. This approach develops respect between managers and workers.

Herzenberg's theory

Frederick Herzenberg believed past job attitude theories made no sense. Herzenberg's core insight was that job satisfaction and job dissatisfaction aren't opposites, but completely separate scales or modalities. He coined the motivational term *KITA,* for *kick in the ass,* which has both a negative and a positive side — the stick or the carrot. We have Herzenberg to thank for *management by motivation* and all the *job enrichment* programs.

In the late 1950s, Herzenberg described job performance by his *Two Factor Theory* (or *Motivation-Hygiene Theory*):

- **Hygiene factors** (dissatisfiers) make people unhappy. They can't motivate workers, but if you get them wrong, motivation declines. If they're absent or mishandled, workers are unhappy. Satisfaction from hygiene factors is only temporary. Hygiene factors include:

  - Company policy (if unclear or unfair)

  - Relationship with supervisor

  - Work conditions

  - Salary

  - Status

  - Job security

  - Relationship with subordinates

- **Motivating factors** (satisfiers) come from job content. The most important factors for lasting attitude changes are

  - Self-actualization

  - Professional growth

  - Recognition (for achievement)

Other motivating factors are

- A sense of achievement
- Recognition
- Responsibility

When the hygiene factors are addressed, motivator factors increase job satisfaction and performance.

Assuring your authority

Some questions on the exam might ask you to distinguish which sources or types of authority or power some hypothetical PM uses in a particular situation. Become familiar with the following terms. As a project manager you can exercise five types of power (see Chapter 7):

- ✔ Formal (legitimate)
- ✔ Reward
- ✔ Penalty (punishments are coercive)
- ✔ Expert (the source of your power is earned by your skills and knowledge)
- ✔ Referent (your authority comes from a higher level position, or influence, charisma, or personality)

The best types of power to use are *expert* (because it shows leadership by example) and *reward* (the best motivator). The worst type of power to use is *penalty*.

Just by virtue of the project manager's position in the organization, you have *formal, reward,* and *penalty* power. You may also have *expert* power by virtue of your background, education, or experience. And you will have *referent* authority if management gives you their support.

Tolerating conflicts

Sources of conflict include

- **The inevitable consequence of organizational interactions:** Can be beneficial to the project. For example, two team members champion different approaches to solving a problem or recommend different designs. Often, such conflicts can be resolved by the involved people directly identifying the root causes with the assistance of their immediate supervisor. Just make sure that these conflicts don't become personal.

✔ **The nature of the project:** Can cause conflict within the organization if the existence of your team threatens to make other departmental functions or workers obsolete. Frequently, IT projects automate clerical tasks and eliminate many jobs in the process. For example, PCs on almost everyone's desktop eliminated the typing pool, creating conflicts among senior managers and with the eliminated typing pool.

A project manager's power is limited when obtaining resources from functional managers.

Ranked by frequency, the sources of conflicts include

✔ Schedules

✔ Project priorities

✔ Resources

✔ Technical opinions

✔ Administrative procedures

✔ Cost

Some typical ways to avoid the most common conflicts include

✔ Informing the team about issues

✔ Clearly assigning tasks and obtaining feedback about your shared understanding

✔ Providing challenging and interesting work assignments

Communicating

Exam questions may apply these key ideas:

✔ **The sender-receiver model:** The sender makes the information concise and complete. The receiver ensures that the information is received, is complete, and is understood correctly.

✔ **The feedback loop:** The loop ensures that the receiver understood what the sender intended. For example, don't assume that the receiver understands the information; make sure by having the receiver restate the message in his own words and ask any questions he might have about what it means.

Channel movement can be associated with *directions:*

✔ *Vertical communication* is up and down the management hierarchy.

✔ *Horizontal communication* is between peers.

The sender encodes messages and the receiver decodes based on the receiver's education, experience, language, and culture. Senders should encode messages carefully. Be sure you know about nonverbal communication. For example, Pete has managed plenty of programmers from India, a culture where they respond nonverbally by nodding in disagreement to indicate "No," shaking their heads in agreement and meaning "Yes." It's just the opposite nonverbal cue of what he expected.

✔ *Paralingual* refers to pitch and tone.

✔ *Active listening* is when the receiver

- Confirms he's listening

- Confirms agreement

- Asks for clarification

✔ *Effective listening* is

- Watching the speaker

- Thinking before speaking

- Asking questions

- Repeating what the speaker says

- Providing feedback

Information Distribution

Inputs	Tools and Techniques	Outputs
1. Work results 2. Communication management plan 3. Project plan	1. Communication skills 2. Info retrieval systems 3. Info distribution methods	1. Project records 2. Project reports 3. Project presentations

✔ Know all the definitions of terms, inputs, tools and techniques, and outputs. Project Communications Management is a *facilitating* execution process. Be able to re-create this table for the test.

✔ Information Distribution has three inputs, three tools and techniques, and three outputs. Try using the mnemonic aid of *Information Distribution has three eyes* or *Distribution 333*. We're fond of the *three eyes* because the word *distribution* has three i's. It also completes the three processes in the Project Communications Management mnemonic: Our courier, Cyclopes, Distributes Info to Puerto Rico and closes in Atlantic City. It helps you remember: Information Distribution, Performance Reporting and Administrative Closure.

✔ Note how the outputs of one process become the inputs to another process.

Distributing Information

Information Distribution involves making information that stakeholders need on a timely basis. By properly executing the communications management plan, using the information retrieval and distribution tools you have available, and responding to unexpected requests for information, you can ensure all stakeholders have the information they need.

Information Distribution has three inputs.

- ✔ **Work results:** The results of activities performed to accomplish the project. Information on work results — completed and incomplete scheduled assignments and deliverables, actual and committed budget costs, how quality assurance standards map to the results, and so on — is collected as the team executes the project. The work results are gathered and analyzed during information distribution as an Executing process. Work results become an input to Performance Reporting as part of a controlling process.

- ✔ **Communications management plan:** Describes how all communication on the project is handled. It contains the methods and procedures used to collect, update, and store information. This plan describes what materials are distributed — including details on content, formats, levels of detail, and definitions. The plan contains a distribution schedule for each important communication, especially recurring events and documents for key milestones.

- ✔ **Project plan:** The formal, approved document used to guide project execution and control. Keep in mind that the plan is more than just a schedule. It contains all the subsidiary plans of all knowledge areas — like the communications management plan.

Information Distribution has three tools and techniques. (We are combining Information Retrieval and Information Distribution Systems into a single explanation because they are so closely related, but be sure you understand they are two separate tools for the exam.)

- ✔ **Communications skills:** Those skills involving information exchanges. They overlap general management skills.

- ✔ **Information retrieval and information distribution systems:** These are tools in the Information Distribution process. They can be simple paper files, bound notebooks (sometimes referred to as *credenza-ware*), or they can be stored electronically as files or in a database. Retrieval systems (tools) are either filing systems or software. Microsoft SharePoint and Lotus Notes are two examples of application software. Distribution systems (tools) include project meetings, correspondence, databases stored in a data warehouse, and video or audio conferences.

Information Distribution has three outputs.

- ✔ **Project records:** Organized for easy accessibility. Team members will keep their own personal records for their assigned areas. Their personal records are often more detailed than the official project records. Project records include *correspondence, documents, and memos*

- ✔ **Project reports:** Formal reports on status and issues. Many organizations have set standard formats for their appearance. On this, refer to the standard that the organization has set.

- ✔ **Project presentations:** Describe how the reports and records are presented to stakeholders. Presentation can be formal or informal. A great deal of a project manager's job involves doing these stakeholder presentations. That's why some estimates indicate that up to 90 percent of a project manager's role is in communicating.

Three categories of communications channels are in the project environment. Choose the appropriate one for your message. *Formal* communications fall inside the organization's formal guidelines dealing with policies, goals, priorities, and management directives. *Informal* communications fall outside the organization's formal guidelines. *Unofficial* interpersonal communications are within the team or organization structure.

Whenever you publish a document, a plan, a task, or review an instruction, get feedback to ensure the rest of the stakeholders share your understanding.

Assuring Quality

Quality Assurance is planned and systematic activities implemented within the quality system to provide confidence that the project will satisfy the relevant quality standards. The key in measuring quality is that the project and product delivers on what it promised. That's the concept of *conformance to requirements.* The product must satisfy real needs is the concept of *fitness of use.* Quality Assurance includes both prevention costs and appraisal costs. *Prevention costs* are associated with the design and planning of a QM program. *Appraisal costs* cover direct inspection and appraisal of the product quality either in the plant or out in the field. Failures or defects inside the plant are *internal failures.* Failures in the field are *external failures.*

Quality Assurance has three inputs:

- ✔ **Quality management plan:** A subsidiary component of the project plan. It describes how the PM team implements the quality policy. It should cover quality control, quality assurance, and quality improvement.

✔ **Results of quality control measurements:** Records of quality testing and measurements, presented in a format useful for comparison and analysis.

✔ **Operational definitions (also called metrics):** Describe an element and how the element is measured by the Quality Control process. An element can relate to either the project or product.

Quality Assurance has two tools and techniques:

✔ **Quality planning tools and techniques:** Include benefit/cost analysis, benchmarking, flow-charting, and Design of Experiments. (Chapter 10 has detailed descriptions.)

✔ **Quality audits:** A structured review of other QM activities to identify the lessons learned that can improve the performance of this project and other projects in the organization. Such audits are an independent review of quality management activities to a performance standard.

Quality Assurance has one output:

✔ **Quality improvements:** Actions that increase the effectiveness and efficiency of the project and provide added benefits to stakeholders. Implementing them usually involves preparing change requests or taking corrective action in accord with procedures for overall change control.

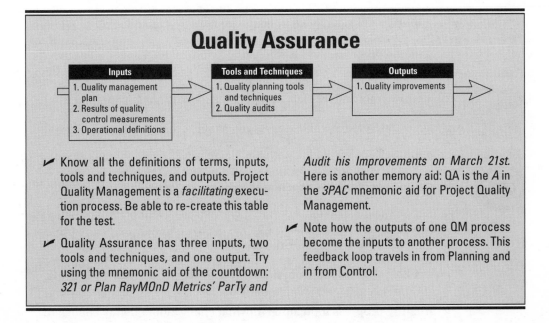

Quality Assurance

Inputs	Tools and Techniques	Outputs
1. Quality management plan	1. Quality planning tools and techniques	1. Quality improvements
2. Results of quality control measurements	2. Quality audits	
3. Operational definitions		

✔ Know all the definitions of terms, inputs, tools and techniques, and outputs. Project Quality Management is a *facilitating* execution process. Be able to re-create this table for the test.

✔ Quality Assurance has three inputs, two tools and techniques, and one output. Try using the mnemonic aid of the countdown: *321* or *Plan RayMOnD Metrics' ParTy and*

Audit his Improvements on March 21st. Here is another memory aid: QA is the *A* in the *3PAC* mnemonic aid for Project Quality Management.

✔ Note how the outputs of one QM process become the inputs to another process. This feedback loop travels in from Planning and in from Control.

Watch for trick questions like this: Among the challenges in reviewing the material from the perspective of a project life cycle is that the process interactions between Quality Planning, Assurance, and Control begin to interact and overlap so much, they become inseparable. In fact, in the initial versions of the methodology, prior to the PMI's standardizing on the ISO 9000 series, Planning and Assurance were one combined process. If you look at QA carefully, you can easily get confused about the logical order of when certain processes happen. For example, *Results of QC Measurements* is an input to QA. Where do these measurements come from? Because the results form an input to QA, you'd think you haven't yet collected the data or performed the analysis. What is this inconsistency? Maybe you're thinking it's an error, that the Results of QC Measurements shouldn't be an input. Because the QA tools and techniques section repeats all the same ones from Quality Planning, you might be tempted to think that Results of QC Measurements should be a QA output. Nope! The measurements come from the tools and techniques from the Quality *Control* processes. The answer may be obvious because the question has QC as the defining part of the term. These results will also come from the outputs of specific *product* processes.

The QM key is that *the processes interact and integrate.* Don't be fooled by hairsplitting distinctions; know the flow of all processes for the exam.

Measuring Progress with Metrics

Time spent during the planning phase to describe characteristics you'd like to measure now begins to pay off. Only the things you measure actually get done. In PMI methodology, you collect these measurements and sample data during the execution processes; when you're using control processes, you analyze and interpret the data. You may send some feedback to the execution of the process. This is another example of why the methodology stresses how processes interact and overlap. Always measure *cost, time, scope,* and *risk.*

When you anticipate a problem area, you should cover these secondary metrics: *Integration, Quality, HR, Communications, and Procurement.*

Metrics for product processes aren't well covered on the exam because they're usually specific to a particular industry or technology.

The timing intervals for these metrics are also considerations. If you schedule them too closely or can't collect enough data, the numbers may be worthless. These metrics help you analyze the project so you can correct in time:

- **Weekly progress indicators:** Include *spending rates (burn rate), actual labor hours,* and *completed milestones.*

- **Monthly progress indicators:** Any that change infrequently enough to be measured weekly.

✔ **Phase gate indicators:** Include summations of *Milestones, Weekly progress indicators and reports,* and *Monthly metrics.*

✔ **Project completion indicators:** Measure whether you've fulfilled the strategic goals the project set out to solve.

✔ **Cost metrics:** Evaluate project performance against the budget. The beginning cost metrics are divided into two areas:

　• **Selection metrics:** Involve benefit/cost, return on investment (ROI), net present value (NPV), and internal rate of return (IRR).

　• **Monitoring metrics:** Generally involve accounting functions like variances of the actual costs against the planned budget. Cost monitoring metrics increasingly involve earned value analysis.

✔ **Time metrics (TM, or scheduling):** Concern performance measured against the schedule. Some metrics likely to use for this purpose include *earned value (EV) analysis, milestones (*whether ahead of schedule or indicating slippage), and *critical path.*

✔ **Scope metrics (SM):** Generally refer to product scope as opposed to project scope. Product scope metrics include *customer expectations, objectives, and requirements, quality measurements,* and *requirements changes.*

✔ **Risk metrics (RM):** Generally characterize risk by the consequences and probability. The formula expected monetary value (EMV) is an example. (See Appendix A.) Risk metrics consider which risks no longer affect the project. At a minimum, the RM process should examine these risk areas: *Cost, Performance,* and *Schedule.*

You should also include risk considerations in contracts — product liabilities, for example. If your metrics can help you avoid one risk on your project, the savings can pay for all the project's risk management activities.

Prep Test

1 All the following are tools and techniques of Project Plan Execution except _____.

A ○ Product skills and knowledge

B ○ Work authorization system

C ○ Status review meetings

D ○ Organizational policies

2 During a weekly status meeting, you discover that a programming lead is taking the team in a direction that conflicts with the customer's needs. Because you know about the reporting needs of the customer, you decide to alter the designs. What kind of authority are you exercising?

A ○ Formal

B ○ Expert

C ○ Referent

D ○ Legitimate

3 Which of the following is not a procurement document?

A ○ Request for proposal (RFP)

B ○ Request for quotation (RFQ)

C ○ Invitation to bid

D ○ Invitation for proposal

4 In a functional matrix organization, the staff members work on your project about 40 percent of the time, and the other 60 percent return to performing their regular duties. As part of the project, you need to have some of the staff trained on a new software application. Who is responsible for the training?

A ○ The project manager

B ○ The functional manager

C ○ The staff members

D ○ The sponsor

5 The team began on a shaky basis. One of the key customers doesn't like its initial work and has confided to you that several team members should be fired. To your delight, they turn the situation around and devise a new way of doing things that the functional managers want to make an organizational standard. The sponsor asks key team members to make a presentation to senior management. They are exercising their _____ needs.

A ○ Social

B ○ Esteem

C ○ Ego

D ○ Self-actualization

6 Messages are _____ by sender and _____ by receiver based on receiver's education, experience, language, and culture.

A ○ Decoded, encoded

B ○ Decoded, understood

C ○ Encoded, decoded

D ○ Encoded, understood

7 The following statement reflects which theory of motivation? Workers need a sense of achievement, recognition, responsibility, self-actualization, professional growth, and recognition for achievement.

A ○ Theory X

B ○ Theory Y

C ○ Theory Z

D ○ Motivation-Hygiene Theory

8 Something that reduces the probability of potential consequences of a risk occurring on your project is called _____.

A ○ Corrective action

B ○ Preventative action

C ○ Contingency action

D ○ Workaround

9 In response to your request for a proposal, a seller replies with a bid much lower than the others. What should you do?

A ○ Ensure that the seller understands the SOW, and then accept the low bid.

B ○ Ensure that the seller understands the SOW, the bid doesn't leave anything out, and then accept the low bid along with a higher bid from another seller that that you're sure can deliver.

C ○ Ensure that the seller understands the SOW, hasn't omitted anything, has the technology, and can meet your delivery dates.

D ○ Toss out the low bid and pick a vendor that you're sure can deliver.

10 Which is an output of Project Plan Execution?

A ○ Preventative action

B ○ Progress reports

C ○ Change requests

D ○ Corrective action

Answers

1 **D.** This question is tricky, trying to confuse you with organizational procedures, which is a tool or technique. This is an exception pattern. *See "Executing the Project Plan."*

2 **B.** *See "Assuring your authority."*

3 **D.** This is an exception pattern. *See "Soliciting."*

4 **A.** Team development is complicated when team members are accountable to both a functional manager and project manager. "The effective management of this dual reporting relationship is often a critical success factor for the project and is generally the responsibility of the project manager." This pattern asks for you to include your knowledge of a process. It tests your understanding of the relationships among facts, principles, and methods. *See "Developing the team" and the* PMBOK Guide, *p. 114.*

5 **B.** Esteem includes needs of ego self-help, finding healthy pride, direction, empowerment in business to achieve, be competent, and gain approval and recognition. This pattern asks you to distinguish between terms that are closely related. *See "Motivating the team."*

6 **C.** This pattern asks you to distinguish between terms that are closely related. *See "Distributing Information."*

7 **D.** This pattern asks you to distinguish between terms that are closely related. *See "Motivating the team."*

8 **B.** Corrective action includes anything that brings your expected performance back in line with the project plan. This pattern asks you to distinguish between terms that are closely related. *See "Executing the Project Plan."*

9 **C.** A is incomplete. B is a good answer that covers most contingencies, averages out costs, and reduces risk from single source suppliers. However, B omits schedule considerations. D is the best choice only if you are risk adverse and the cost of the item is not the most important factor. This is a thought-provoking question with lots of possible permutations. This is the pattern what should the project manager do. *See "Selecting sources of materials."*

10 **C.** Preventative and corrective action are inputs. This is an output pattern. *See "Executing the Project Plan."*

Part V
Controlling and Closing the Project

The 5th Wave   By Rich Tennant

"The funny thing is he's spent 9 hours organizing his computer desktop."

In this part...

Controlling and closing a project is like flying and landing an airplane. This part of *PMP, The Movie* shouldn't turn into a disaster movie. Instead, it should be a light comedy that the whole family can enjoy.

Pilots say that a good landing is one you can walk away from. After a *great* landing, you can reuse the plane. With the help of this part, you'll show that you deserve your wings. These are steps you follow for a smooth and steady flight, a gentle landing, and a simple roll to the hangar.

Contact! And your scarf blows in the wind as the cameras roll.

Chapter 12

Ensuring Plan Compliance

. . . .

Exam Objectives

▶ Integrating overall change control

▶ Measuring compliance

▶ Improving quality

▶ Inspecting work

. . . .

*N*o matter how well you plan, nothing ever goes entirely as you anticipated. In fact, chaos theory predicts that an event as small as a butter-
fly flapping its wings in China could create thunderstorms in North America.
Unexpected changes happen, and you're responsible for managing them.

In this chapter, you discover the important aspects of controlling the
inevitable changes to your project. There are two sides to monitoring
progress and controlling changes — the risk side and the opportunity side.
Understanding the methodology requires knowing how to manage both risk
and opportunity. No matter how events unfold, you're responsible for ensuring that changes are beneficial to your project. You find out about the overall
process of monitoring project activities and controlling changes. You also discover the Integrated Change Control process, and then the change control
processes of seven other skills sets. We help you master the aspects of taking
corrective actions to get your project back on track — or even make it better.

Quick Assessment

Overall Change Control

1   The Inputs to Overall Change Control include _____.

2   Successful completion of project scope is measured against the _____.

3   The formal change control processes omit only one of the skill sets as defined by the knowledge areas. Which knowledge area does not have a change control process?

4   The outputs to Overall Change Control are _____.

Updating Subsidiary Plans

5   Why should you bother to update the subsidiary management plans?

6   A scope change has occurred and requires additional planning. What documents do you update?

Project Metrics

7   Some of the metrics that you might track include _____.

Measuring Compliance 9

8   What is the distinction between Scope Verification and Quality Control?

Answers

1   The project plan, change requests, and performance reports. See the *PMBOK Guide* p. 42 and "Integrating Overall Change Control." This pattern asks for you to include all inputs.

2   Project plan. This question tests your ability to demonstrate your understanding of the relationship among facts, principles, and methods. See Chapter 6.

3   Human Resources. This question asks for the exclusion pattern. It tests your ability to demonstrate your understanding of the relationship among facts, principles, and methods. See the *PMBOK Guide* p. 108 and "Integrating Overall Change Control."

4   Project plan updates, corrective action, lessons learned. This question asks for the output. See the *PMBOK Guide* p. 108 and "Integrating Overall Change Control."

5   Plan updates and subsidiary plans might require modifications or outright revisions as a result of change requests or corrective actions. Failure to update the plans entails adding risks to the project. You might omit a desired feature and not communicate it to the appropriate stakeholders. This question tests your ability to demonstrate your understanding of the relationship among principles and methods. See "Updating Subsidiary Plans."

6   Any of the subsidiary management plans and the project plan. Don't forget to communicate the changes. This pattern asks for process steps. It tests your ability to demonstrate your understanding of the relationship among facts, principles, and methods. See "Updating Subsidiary Plans."

7   Cost performance, schedule performance, technical performance. This pattern asks for examples. It tests your ability to demonstrate your understanding of the relationship among facts, principles, and methods. See "Verifying Scope and Work Results."

8   Scope Verification is primarily concerned with the acceptance of the work results. Quality Control's main concern is determining the correctness of the work results. This pattern asks you to distinguish between terms that are closely related to determining process characteristics. You have to know the purpose of the 39 process interactions. See "Verifying Scope and Work Results."

Integrating Overall Change Control

Integrated Change Control covers those factors that ensure changes made to the project are beneficial. You must first identify that a change has actually occurred and has been requested, and then manage the resulting changes. In the last *PMBOK Guide* update, this process was renamed from *overall* to *integrated* to better show the interdependencies between processes.

You can think of this project-wide process of change control in the same way as the other knowledge areas; they also contain subsidiary plans that roll up into the single, integrated project plan. This project-wide change control process impacts other knowledge areas and provides a feedback loop to coordinate changes across all of them. The methodology stresses the importance of documenting approved changes in the project plan, the reasons why these changes are beneficial, and any alternatives. Update changes in the project scope definition because they affect cost, risk, quality, and staffing — the performance measurement baseline. Changes to the product scope must also be documented. Expect exam questions in these areas.

When do you use monitoring and controlling processes? The process of controlling isn't time dependent. It starts after initial planning, and it overlaps execution. It continues throughout the project until you reach project closure. They are processes that occur in every phase. They can overlap phases or subprojects.

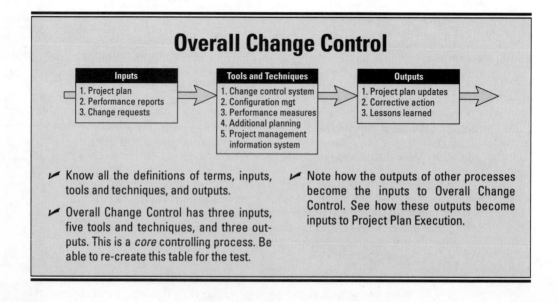

Overall Change Control

Inputs	Tools and Techniques	Outputs
1. Project plan 2. Performance reports 3. Change requests	1. Change control system 2. Configuration mgt 3. Performance measures 4. Additional planning 5. Project management information system	1. Project plan updates 2. Corrective action 3. Lessons learned

✔ Know all the definitions of terms, inputs, tools and techniques, and outputs.

✔ Overall Change Control has three inputs, five tools and techniques, and three outputs. This is a *core* controlling process. Be able to re-create this table for the test.

✔ Note how the outputs of other processes become the inputs to Overall Change Control. See how these outputs become inputs to Project Plan Execution.

The formal change control processes omit only one of the skill sets as defined by the knowledge areas. Human Resources is the only process that's missing a separate subsidiary change control process. First, staff assignments and staff changes overlap general management functions and are usually covered under the organization's HR policies and procedures. Second, there are two main eventualities — bringing additional people onto the project or terminating them from the project. These should have been covered in the staffing management plan during Organizational Planning. If the scope changes so drastically that you need additional resources, use the same Staff Acquisition process that you set up initially.

The three inputs to Overall Change Control are as follows:

✔ **Project plan:** The formal, approved document used to guide project execution and control. It provides the baseline for measuring and controlling. It includes the schedule and budget, as well as the knowledge area subsidiary plans such as the communications plan, risk management plan, and quality plan. Most importantly, the project plan sets a baseline by which you can measure progress and control changes.

✔ **Performance reports:** Can alert the project team to issues that could cause problems in the future. Know the distinction between *status* and *progress* reports. Status reports describe the project's current standings. Progress reports describe the team's accomplishments. For some examples of difference types of reports, see Chapter 13.

✔ **Change requests:** Take many forms: oral or written, direct or indirect, externally or internally initiated, legally mandated or optional. Changes may expand or shrink the scope of the product or project. Change requests are generally the result of:

   • External events (such as new governmental regulations)

   • Errors or omissions in defining the product scope (which is a key reason why many software development projects get in trouble)

   • Errors or omissions in defining the project scope

   • A value-added change (such as taking advantage of new technology)

The tools and techniques to Overall Change Control are as follows:

✔ **Change control system:** A collection of formal, documented procedures that define how project performance will be monitored and evaluated. It also includes the steps for changing official project documents. It includes paperwork, tracking systems, processes, and the level of approvals necessary to authorize the changes.

✔ **Configuration management:** A subset of the change control system that ensures the product is correct and complete. Documents the procedures used to apply technical and administrative direction and surveillance for the following:

- Identifying and documenting the functional and physical characteristics of an item or a system

- Controlling any changes to identified characteristics

- Recording and reporting both the change and its status

- Auditing items and systems to verify conformance to requirements

✔ **Performance measurements:** Help you determine if variances from the plan require corrective action.

✔ **Additional planning:** May be required to generate new or revised plans in the other knowledge areas.

✔ **Project management information system (PMIS):** A collection of tools and techniques (which can be either automated or manual) used to store and disseminate information from the other PM processes. These are tools that project management offices provide.

These are the three outputs to Overall Change Control:

✔ **Project plan updates:** Any modifications to the project plan or to supporting detail.

✔ **Corrective action:** Any action that brings your expected performance back in line with the project plan. Corrective actions are outputs from the other knowledge areas and various control processes. Taking action implies identifying the sources of problems, developing a plan to correct them, and implementing a plan. Don't forget to communicate what corrective actions you're taking to everyone involved.

✔ **Lesson learned:** Information to be documented and carried forward to other phases and projects. This includes the causes of variances, the reasoning behind the corrective action chosen, and other types of lessons learned.

Improving Quality

Quality Control (QC) involves monitoring specific project results to determine if they comply with relevant quality standards and identifying ways to eliminate causes of unsatisfactory performance. QC's main concern is determining the correctness of the work results.

The four inputs to Quality Control are as follows:

✔ **Work results:** Results of activities performed to accomplish the project become inputs to its control processes. You can measure the results by using metrics you defined during planning. Examples of metrics include the percent of deliverables completed, costs incurred, and schedule ahead or slippage. (See Chapter 11.)

✔ **Quality management plan:** Describes how the team will implement its quality policy.

✔ **Operational definitions:** Also called metrics. These distinctions describe in detail the specifics of what something is and how it'll be measured in the QC process.

✔ **Checklists:** Structured tools, usually industry- or activity-specific, used to verify that a set of required steps has been performed. Many organizations have standardized checklists available to ensure consistency in frequently performed activities. They're generally available from professional associations or commercial providers.

Here are the six tools and techniques to Quality Control:

✔ **Inspection:** Activities such as measuring, examining, and testing undertaken to determine if results conform to requirements. It's also referred to by specific industry terms such as reviews (multiple types), product reviews, audits, and walk-throughs.

✔ **Control charts:** Graphically display the results of a process. They help you determine if the process is statistically in control.

✔ **Pareto diagrams:** Histograms, ordered by frequency of occurrence, that show how many results were generated by type or category of identified cause. The ranking of categories can be used to guide your corrective action. That is, you fix the problems that are causing the most defects. Juran based this charting method on Pareto's 80/20 rule — 80 percent of the problems are caused by 20 percent of the problems or defects.

✔ **Statistical sampling:** Choosing part of a population of interest for inspection. Appropriate sampling can often reduce the cost of quality control. A good grasp on statistical sampling techniques may be required for your project.

✔ **Flow-charting:** A graphical method of analysis that helps determine how and where quality problems occur. It can help you develop approaches to resolving the problems. Such diagrams can show how various elements of a system interrelate. Flow charts commonly used in Quality Management (QM) include cause-and-effect diagrams and system or process flow charts.

✔ **Trend analysis:** Using mathematical techniques to forecast future outcomes based on historical results. You monitor technical performance to determine how many defects or errors have been identified and corrected, as well as any remaining uncorrected. You also monitor cost and schedule performance.

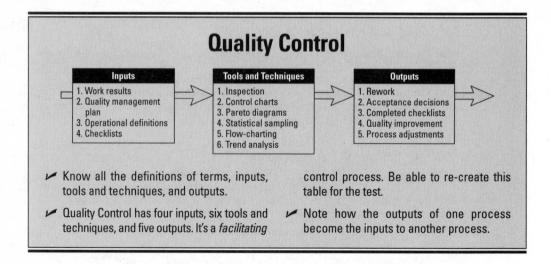

Quality Control

Inputs	Tools and Techniques	Outputs
1. Work results 2. Quality management plan 3. Operational definitions 4. Checklists	1. Inspection 2. Control charts 3. Pareto diagrams 4. Statistical sampling 5. Flow-charting 6. Trend analysis	1. Rework 2. Acceptance decisions 3. Completed checklists 4. Quality improvement 5. Process adjustments

✔ Know all the definitions of terms, inputs, tools and techniques, and outputs.

✔ Quality Control has four inputs, six tools and techniques, and five outputs. It's a *facilitating*

control process. Be able to re-create this table for the test.

✔ Note how the outputs of one process become the inputs to another process.

The five outputs to Quality Control are as follows:

✔ **Rework:** Any action taken to bring a defective or nonconforming item into compliance with requirements or specifications. Rework, especially unanticipated rework, is a frequent cause of project overruns in most application areas.

✔ **Acceptance decisions:** The results of inspecting items delivered to you. You either accept or reject them. Rejected items may require rework.

✔ **Completed checklists:** Whenever this type of control is used, these documents should become part of the project records.

✔ **Quality improvements:** Outputs from the related process of Quality Assurance (QA). They represent actions intended to increase the effectiveness and efficiency of the project. They provide added benefits to stakeholders. In most cases, implementing quality improvements requires preparation of change requests or taking corrective action. Any improvements are managed according to procedures for Overall Change Control.

✔ **Process adjustments:** Immediate corrective or preventive action as a result of Quality Control measurements.

As project manager, you're responsible for preparing and maintaining the quality management plan (QMP), ensuring that Quality Assurance (QA) and Quality Control (QC) are conducted according to the approved plan. The QMP contains the overall scope and the detailed objectives of the quality aspects for the project, specific deliverables that can be measured, and the responsible organization and staff who'll perform the quality functions.

Measuring Compliance

We want to jump backwards for a brief refresher so you'll remember the flow of process interactions. During the initiation and planning processes, the team creates and refines the scope statement. The scope statement could be created at a very high level during Initiation, but it is formally created as an output of Scope Planning. During Scope Definition, the scope statement is updated as a result of creating the work breakdown structure (WBS). The scope statement describes both the product deliverables and the project objectives. During the planning portion of the project (Scope Planning and Scope Definition), these objectives and deliverables are defined clearly and provide your starting baseline. *Product deliverables* are a list of features that the product or service will have. Delivering these features makes the project successful. *Project objectives* are the quantifiable criteria that should be met for the project to be considered successful. These criteria should include performance metrics by which you'll judge the success of the project, such as cost, schedule, and quality.

Your team members should know the precise metrics they'll use to monitor completion and evaluate progress. Both the product deliverables and the project objectives (as contained in the scope statement) are inputs to Scope Verification. They're part of the feedback loop of the process interactions as you find out in "Verifying Scope and Work Results," later in this chapter.

Inspecting tasks

The metrics you use will vary by industry, product definition, and project needs. The exam doesn't get into specific metrics that vary by industry, but it does cover project metrics of cost and schedule, as well as general metrics in quality. Metrics you might consider tracking include measuring *features* (characteristics and functions), *performance* (operating characteristics), reliability (how the system operates over time), conformance (compliance with established requirements), durability (useful product life span), serviceability (ease of repairs, upgrades, and maintenance), and aesthetics (visual, tactile, and auditory product qualities).

Control charts

Control charts track a process by making periodic measurements. The control chart has an upper control limit (UCL) and a lower control limit (LCL) for sampling successive measurements taken over a period of time. The series of measurements is a *run*. The control limits have been traditionally defined as three sigma (standard deviations) from the mean; recently some organizations that are more concerned with accuracy and precision use six sigma for tighter controls. The charts signal if the process is *in control* or *out of control*. If the process centers near the mean, it's in control. When the process crosses the UCL or the LCL, it's at the extremes and becomes out of control. That signals you to investigate the process and check if anything is wrong.

Variations in quality may be introduced into the process by assignable causes. Some examples of assignable causes include differences among machines, workers, and materials. The distance between the UCL and LCL is called the *range*. Anything inside the range is in control. A series of exceptions rules help you detect out of control or abnormal conditions. One exception is called the *rule of 7s:* A run of seven consecutive data points on one side of the mean (either plus or minus) has a tiny probability that it's due to random variation. It's a general rule indicating that the process is drifting out of control. Be careful here. The seven consecutive points must be on the same side of the mean and cannot cross the mean, as shown in Figure 12-1. As we discuss in Appendix A, the probability that this trend is due to an assignable cause or a special variation is extremely low — 0.0156 (that's 1.56 percent).

When a process is in control, it shouldn't be adjusted. The only reason to change the process is to provide improvements.

Pareto diagrams

Figure 12-2 shows a Pareto diagram. This type of chart helps you focus your efforts by selecting the vital few causes from many other potentially distracting factors.

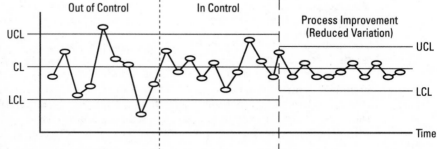

Figure 12-1: This control chart shows three types of control variants.

Project Metrics

Controlling the project means paying relentless attention to a variety of details. When getting results is crucial, exercising control over the situation requires you to collect metrics. These metrics give you detailed information on your current status and progress to date. Applying metrics tells you the *who, what, when,* and *where* of taking corrective action. These are similar to the criteria journalists apply to determine whether they have all the essential facts for a story. The only item left out is the *how,* and that's something you determine through planning.

Pareto Diagram

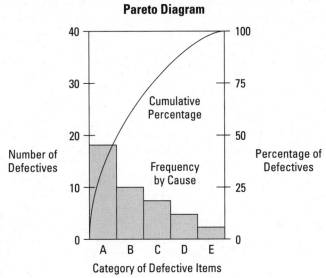

Figure 12-2:
Pareto
diagram.

Performance measurements (defined during planning) help you objectively determine if variances from the plan on each activity or work package require any corrective action. This control process entails scrutinizing the pertinent details of all deliverables, slipping tasks, and variances in schedule or cost. You want to focus on higher-value and higher-risk work packages that have the potential to set the project back. For example, one measurement might be the percent of major milestones that the team achieved versus its planned targets. If these controls indicate rework or other corrective actions are needed to bring the process back into compliance, these items will have to measured or inspected again.

One type of measurement process that's popular with quality circles follows the Plan-Do-Study-Act (PDSA) approach, developed by Walter A. Shewhart in the 1930s. It breaks the measurement process into four separate activities: plan, do, study, and act. The PDSA approach corresponds to these measurement activities:

✔ Plan — define measurement goals

✔ Do — perform the measurement process

✔ Study — collect and analyze the measurements

✔ Act — correct and improve the process

These measurements help you identify problems when they are small. The key is to identify issues and solve problems early in the project when there is still time to take corrective action. You don't want to let them escalate into bigger problems. When you get close to the end of the project, you have little ability to influence cost, schedule, and quality performance.

Progress measurements generally relate to the schedule. Each progress measurement is made at the work package level. Each work package has a start date and finish date as the measurement criteria. Work packages also have to satisfy specific completion criteria, not just the effort that has gone into creating them. Remember, you're measuring for results, too.

Cost performance measurements relate to the budget. Cost is still considered the best measurement of productivity. These measurements are also at the work package level. During the planning portion of the project, you estimate costs for labor, equipment, and material for each activity or task. Each work package has its own miniature baseline. Comparing actual costs to estimated costs enables you to know how well your project is progressing. Cost performance measurements can tell you about variances between planned expenditures (cash outflows) and actual figures, but they can't predict whether the project is on budget or what the completed cost will be. Because of the nine combinations between schedules and budgets in Table 12-1, you generally use earned value measurements to track cost performance and schedule performance. Earned value (EV) provides the missing link between cost accounting and scheduling. We cover the EV formulas in Appendix A.

Table 12-1 shows various schedule and budget performance combinations focusing on schedule performance. Values are measured in dollars. (See Appendix A, Figures A-16 and A-17.)

Table 12-1	Schedule and Budget Performance Using Earned Value Metrics			
PV (BCWS)	**EV (BCWP)**	**AC (ACWP)**	**Schedule Performance**	**Budget Performance**
On Schedule Where PV = EV				
100	100	100	On schedule	On budget
100	100	75	On schedule	Under budget
100	100	150	On schedule	Over budget
Ahead of Schedule Where PV < EV				
75	100	100	Ahead of schedule	On budget
75	100	150	Ahead of schedule	Over budget
100	150	100	Ahead of schedule	Under budget

PV (BCWS)	EV (BCWP)	AC (ACWP)	Schedule Performance	Budget Performance
Behind Schedule Where PV > EV				
150	100	75	Behind schedule	Under budget
100	75	150	Behind schedule	Over budget
150	100	100	Behind schedule	On budget

Table 12-2 shows various schedule and budget performance combinations focusing on budget performance. The values are the same as in Table 12-1, but they're sorted by budget. Values are measured in dollars.

Table 12-2	Budget and Schedule Performance Using Earned Value Metrics			
PV (BCWS)	EV (BCWP)	AC (ACWP)	Schedule Performance	Budget Performance
On Budget Where AC = EV				
100	100	100	On schedule	On budget
75	100	100	Ahead of schedule	On budget
150	100	100	Behind schedule	On budget
Over Budget Where AC > EV				
100	75	150	Behind schedule	Over budget
75	100	150	Ahead of schedule	Over budget
100	100	150	On schedule	Over budget

(continued)

Table 12-2 *(continued)*

PV (BCWS)	EV (BCWP)	AC (ACWP)	Schedule Performance	Budget Performance
Under Budget Where AC < EV				
150	100	75	Behind schedule	Under budget
100	150	100	Ahead of schedule	Under budget
100	100	75	On schedule	Under budget

Measurement goals differ depending on the management level within the project. At the overall project or project manager level, goals include measuring schedule compliance, resource availability and usage, and changeability of requirements. At the team leader level, measurement goals include detailed technical performance and progress measures, such as software size and requirements growth. This measurement process provides an objective method for quantifying all the activities performed on your project. For each work package, measurements should give a complete picture of your real progress. In a software application development example, a measurement process may collect earned value data from the cost accounting system, development metrics from the programmers, and technical performance metrics from software engineers and quality control testers. The measurement process provides data to the project manager from important activities, allowing a feedback loop for immediate corrective action.

Verifying Scope and Work Results

Scope Verification is the process of formalizing acceptance of the project scope by key stakeholders, especially the customer and sponsor. It requires reviewing work products and results to ensure that all product or service features and functions are complete, correct, and satisfactory.

The *PMBOK Guide* makes a big distinction between Scope Verification and Quality Control. Scope Verification is primarily concerned with *acceptance* of the work results. QC's main concern is in determining the *correctness* of the work results.

How do you inspect the deliverables? WBS provides a detailed graphic view of project scope. The low-level tasks on the WBS become the basis for monitoring progress because each is a measurable unit of work, an individual work package with an expected deliverable. The summary tasks represent higher levels in the WBS. They're not executed but represent combinations of multiple work packages.

Controlling work packages usually involves scheduling for durations no longer than one status reporting period. If your status reporting period is two weeks, the longest work package you'd want to schedule is 80 hours. If your status reporting period is one week, the longest work package you'd want to schedule is 40 hours.

In special circumstances, it's necessary to control work packages in smaller increments, sometimes even an hour in duration. Coordinating "inch stones" or "inch pebbles" (the diminutive form of milestones) can be necessary when the project is under extreme time pressure. Here are some examples:

- The repair of crucial equipment that must be taken offline

- An overnight office move

- A new computer system conversion (overnight or weekend)

- Shooting our movie production (which proceeds by capturing as little as eight minutes of usable film at a time)

To help you visualize the process for the exam, here's an example of how we would control the film schedule for a sequence that involves a major stunt. This stunt occurs near a building that's being demolished by a crew of pyrotechnic experts. They will implode the building, and the movie crew will film the collapse as part of the action sequence. The film production crew must coordinate with the demolition crew. Assuming you're managing the film production crew, the demolition crew is not under your control because they are outside of your project. But you must work within the demolition crew's scheduled time frame and coordinate with them to get your action sequence.

The schedule for filming the explosion must be planned in seconds and minutes. The coordination with the detonation crew must be controlled in real time, as the implosion is happening. Because you have only one chance to get it right, you must coordinate with multiple teams. Coordinating includes various functional managers and their staffs. You have multiple camera crews to get the shot from multiple angles and for redundancy. One camera crew shoots a wide shot of the building's collapse, a second shoots a close-up of the actors driving up in their jeep, a third crew shoots a tracking shot on guide rails moving in concert with the jeep, a fourth crew shoots some close-ups of the building as it falls, a crew on a high crane shoots from a high perspective, and the final crew in a helicopter captures it all from above.

Your special-effects pyrotechnic crew sets up the day before, rigging gas pipes with holes to simulate fires in the scene's foreground as a jeep drives up. A team composed of technicians called grips and gaffers takes care of rigging the lights on the set. You also have crews for property, an ambulance with paramedics, safety consultants from your insurance bonding company, studio executives, television news crews and newspaper reporters with their photographers, crowd control officers, union officials (their business representatives), security guards, police (who check various permits and enforce parking restrictions), writers for the TV pilot, photographers, publicists, and even Web camera and computer techs who will be covering the text chat over a promotional Web site with the actors after the stunt.

You assign an assistant director with the detonation crew as a coordinator. Immediately before the detonation crew is ready to implode the building, have your staff in place and ready to act. When the director says "action," the entire film crew jumps into motion. Seconds later, the building is detonated with the camera crew filming the implosion in real time. Hundreds of people work together to complete this exciting action sequence in the movie.

The two inputs to Scope Verification are as follows:

✔ **Work results:** Describe which deliverables have been fully or partially completed, as well as what costs have been incurred or committed. They're the outcome of activities performed and are fed into the performance reporting process.

✔ **Product documentation:** Any paperwork describing the project's products must be available for review.

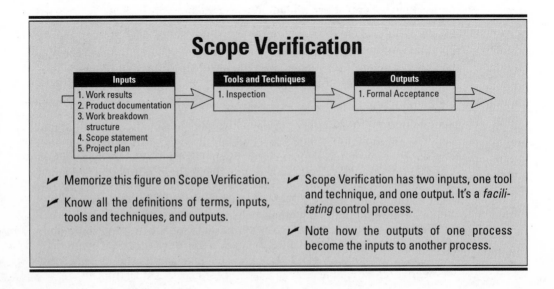

Scope Verification

Inputs	Tools and Techniques	Outputs
1. Work results 2. Product documentation 3. Work breakdown structure 4. Scope statement 5. Project plan	1. Inspection	1. Formal Acceptance

✔ Memorize this figure on Scope Verification.

✔ Know all the definitions of terms, inputs, tools and techniques, and outputs.

✔ Scope Verification has two inputs, one tool and technique, and one output. It's a *facilitating* control process.

✔ Note how the outputs of one process become the inputs to another process.

This is the one group of tools and techniques to Scope Verification:

> ✔ **Inspection:** Activities such as measuring, examining, and testing undertaken to determine if results conform to requirements. The purpose is to identify any particulars on variances, omissions, deficiencies, gaps, and errors. Be sure to compare any exceptions against the project documentation, which serves as the baseline.

This is the one output to Scope Verification:

> ✔ **Formal acceptance:** Documentation of approving the product of the project, or phase, needs to be prepared. Often the client or sponsor needs to sign off on formal documents as a part of wrapping up the project. However, this signed acceptance document must be distributed to others.

Controlling Scope Changes

Spotting *scope creep* can be a difficult chore, because its development can be imperceptible. The big change requests are easy to spot because they happen all at once. If you have multiple change requests that are all rather small, they can add up to a much larger change. Without warning, you can break out with scope creep.

For example, managing change requests is the single most demanding challenge for software teams. These change requests come from incomplete requirements, stiff competition, tough customers, and changing business needs. All that little stuff builds up. Scope creep can result from the unplanned changes, additions of minor features, or reworking of a few screens and reports as a favor for marketing or accounting. Some of these changes may benefit the project and can be introduced easily, but they may prolong the schedule, push costs over budget, or reduce other features or objectives to met imposed deadlines.

Change control procedures enable you to understand and manage change requests. You need to control the scope of both the product and the project. You coordinate with key stakeholders, including managers and possibly even a change control board according to your scope management plan. As a group, you evaluate each request and determine the impact of changes. For example, you have to figure out if you have enough time, money, and resources to handle the requested change.

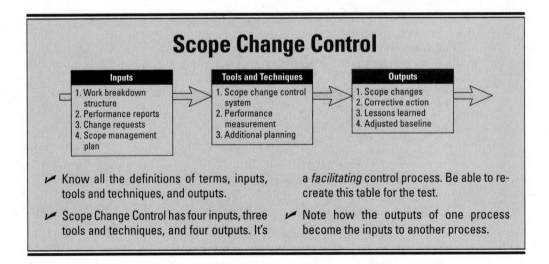

Scope Change Control

Inputs	Tools and Techniques	Outputs
1. Work breakdown structure	1. Scope change control system	1. Scope changes
2. Performance reports	2. Performance measurement	2. Corrective action
3. Change requests	3. Additional planning	3. Lessons learned
4. Scope management plan		4. Adjusted baseline

✔ Know all the definitions of terms, inputs, tools and techniques, and outputs.

✔ Scope Change Control has four inputs, three tools and techniques, and four outputs. It's a *facilitating* control process. Be able to recreate this table for the test.

✔ Note how the outputs of one process become the inputs to another process.

The four inputs to Scope Change Control are as follows:

✔ **Work breakdown structure (WBS):** A scope definition tool that organizes the work and provides a basis for project estimates. It defines the project's scope baseline; along with the Resource Assignment Matrix RAM), assigns responsibilities for performing the work; and provides the basis for measuring and reporting about scope performance. (See Chapter 9.)

✔ **Performance reports:** Can alert the project team to issues that could cause problems. Status reports describe the project's current standings. Progress reports describe the team's accomplishments. They provide background information on scope performance such as which interim products have been completed and which have not.

✔ **Change requests:** May require expanding the scope or may actually permit it to shrink. Change requests are generally the result of external events such as governmental regulations, errors or omissions in scope definition of the product or project, and value-added changes.

✔ **Scope management plan:** The subsidiary portion of the project plan. It describes how the project scope will be managed, how changes will be identified and classified, how changes will be integrated into the project, and what the required procedures are for making changes.

These are the three tools and techniques to Scope Change Control:

✔ **Scope change control system:** Defines the procedures by which the scope of the project may be changed. It includes the paperwork, tracking systems, and approval levels necessary for authorizing changes.

✔ **Performance measurement:** Techniques to assess the magnitude of any variations that occur in the performance of the project.

✔ **Additional planning:** Activities that may be necessary to the project plan or subsidiary plans in order to adjust to changes.

Here are the three outputs of Scope Change Control:

✔ **Scope changes:** Any modifications to the authorized project scope as defined by the approved WBS. Scope changes often require adjustments to cost, time, quality, or other project objectives.

✔ **Corrective action:** Anything that brings your expected performance back in line with the project plan. These actions are outputs from the other knowledge areas.

✔ **Lessons learned:** Assessments that include the causes of variances, reasoning behind corrective actions, and other types of lessons learned as a result of scope change.

Updating Subsidiary Plans

The process of controlling changes provides an important feedback mechanism. The impact of change requests can ripple through your project — including the subsidiary plans for all knowledge areas. This feedback loop travels in both directions — from Integration, at the overall top level, to specific knowledge areas. For example, quality improvement changes need to be reflected in the integrated project plan. Extra planning to accommodate these quality changes may be required for new or revised plans, which in turn can impact the other knowledge areas. The change request for a quality improvement might require schedule or budget changes, which must be included in the integrated project plan. So update all subsidiary elements of the project plan. Remember that the plan updates (an output of Integrated Change Control) include any modifications to the project plan or to the supporting detail. You need to document alternatives, your decisions, and the impacts on the project and product. You also need to communicate the changes as indicated in the communications management plan.

For example, managing change requests is the most demanding challenge for software teams. These change requests come from incomplete requirements, competition, tough customers, and changing business needs.

Prep Test

1 The inputs to Overall Change Control include all of the following except:

A ○ Project plan

B ○ Performance measurement

C ○ Performance reports

D ○ Change requests

2 The tools and techniques to Overall Change Control include:

A ○ Performance reports

B ○ Performance reporting

C ○ Performance measurement

D ○ Project reporting tools and techniques

3 Scope changes include all of the following examples except:

A ○ A variation in government-mandated regulations and standards.

B ○ Failure to include a required product design feature in a Web-based customer order tracking system.

C ○ Introducing emerging technology not available when the scope was originally defined in order to reduce costs and provide value-added changes.

D ○ The project is behind schedule. To meet the customer's deadlines, you reduce the features in the customer relationship management system.

4 Configuration management is a technique used in the _____ process.

A ○ Integrated Change Control

B ○ Quality Change Control

C ○ Scope Change Control

D ○ Risk Change Control

5 During a design review meeting, the chief architect discovers an incompatibility with existing systems. This design error prevents the new application from meeting all the technical performance objectives the customers require. If left unattended, you're sure your project will be canceled. What do you do as project manager?

A ○ Notify the stakeholders of the error and request they terminate the project.

B ○ Call a meeting of the change control board and put in a change order.

C ○ Develop alternative solutions to this design problem or develop a new design.

D ○ Determine the impact of the scope change and then request a meeting with your sponsor to update him on the issues and let him decide if the project should be terminated.

6 Work results are accepted as completed in the _____ process and approved for correctness in the _____ process.

A ○ Scope Verification, Integrated Change Control

B ○ Scope Verification, Quality Control

C ○ Scope Change Control, Quality Control

D ○ Quality Control, Scope Verification

7 At the photo lab, you analyze sensitometric and chemical control charts on a photographic chemical processing to monitor gamma index, minimum and maximum density, average density, gross fog, temperature, pH, and specific gravity. You find a single point outside the lower control limit. This indicates that _____.

A ○ A source of common cause variation is present.

B ○ A source of special cause variation is present.

C ○ The process is still in control.

D ○ A source of system variation is present.

8 You have just started on a turn-around software development project that is six months behind schedule. You determine the software specifications are a mess, but your sponsor expects you to write quality test case documents and complete the testing in a shorter timeframe than originally scheduled. When is development and testing completed?

A ○ After you've inspected every line of code and tested every feature and function

B ○ When you've checked the software against the quantifiable acceptance criteria defined in the operational definitions

C ○ When you've checked the software against the quality management plan

D ○ When you've checked the software against the product description

9 In Statistical Process Control using control charts, among the series of rules that can detect out-of-control conditions is _____.

A ○ The Rule of 6s, six runs on one side of the center line (mean)

B ○ The Rule of 7s, seven consecutive points within the normal range

C ○ The Rule of 8s, eight consecutive points oscillating back and forth

D ○ The Rule of 5s, five consecutive points occurring near the control limit

Answers

1 **B.** Performance measurement is a tool and technique and not an input to Overall Change Control. This is the exception pattern. *See the* PMBOK Guide *p. 48 and "Integrating Overall Change Control."*

2 **C.** Performance measurement is a tool and technique of Overall Change Control. This is the pattern match. *See the* PMBOK Guide *p. 48 and "Integrating Overall Change Control."*

3 **D.** This is a hair-splitting question because scope changes can involve either increasing or reducing scope. In A and C, you won't be held responsible for the changes. In B, you might be responsible for failing to identify all the requirements; if the customer was highly involved in defining the requirements and signed off on them, the omission is a scope change that the customer will request as an additional feature. The other options are standard types of scope changes. In D, you're on the hook for a lack of performance. This requires you to show your understanding of the relationship among facts and principles. *See the* PMBOK Guide *p. 63 and "Integrating Overall Change Control."*

4 **A.** Configuration management is a technique in Integrated Change Control. This pattern applies the tools and techniques of the different process areas. *See the* PMBOK Guide *p. 49 and "Integrating Overall Change Control."*

5 **C.** Maybe an alternative will prevent you from requesting that the project be terminated in choices A and D. Eliminate B because you might not know what the change entails. Because this requires some action, the pattern asks for a tool or technique. This is additional planning in Scope Change Control. *See the* PMBOK Guide *p. 63 and "Integrating Overall Change Control."*

6 **B.** Work results are accepted for *completeness* in the Scope Verification process and approved for *correctness* in the Quality Control process. This tests your understanding of the purpose of each process. Scope Control looks for the satisfactory completion of all deliverables; Quality Control checks quality (conforming to requirements) and performance of each objective. *See the* PMBOK Guide *p. 61 and "Verifying Scope and Work Results."*

7 **B.** You can eliminate the answer C, the mismatched *in control* choice. Common cause variation and system variation refer to same thing: the naturally occurring fluctuation or variation inherent in all processes. Special cause variation is typically present when caused by some problem or extraordinary occurrence in the system.

8 **B.** Check the software against the quantifiable acceptance criteria defined in the operational definitions, also called metrics.

9 **B.** The other options are also measures of out of control, but PMI specifically references the Rule of 7s.

Chapter 13

Taking Corrective Action

• •

Exam Objectives

▶ Implementing your risk response plan

▶ Taking corrective action

▶ Controlling schedule changes

▶ Controlling cost changes

▶ Communicating performance to stakeholders

• •

*T*his is the second chapter in the controlling process group. Remember that almost all of the nine knowledge areas contain a controlling process; the exceptions are Procurement and HR. In Chapter 12, we cover the controlling processes of Overall Change Control, Quality Change Control, and Scope Change Control. In this chapter, you'll master what's important for the exam in risk control (Risk Response Control and Risk Monitoring and Control), as well as Schedule Control, Budget Control, and Performance Reporting.

We alert you to the need for taking decisive action in responding to risks and risk changes as your project moves along. Risk Monitoring and Control is the process of keeping track of the identified risks, monitoring residual risks and identifying new risks, ensuring the execution of risk plans, and evaluating their effectiveness in reducing risk. You'll master controlling changes to the different project baselines for controlling the schedule and budget. We familiarize you with the concepts involved in reporting project performance to your stakeholders.

Controlling processes account for approximately 45 exam questions, 23 percent of the total questions. Concentrate a good deal of your study efforts here. While the controlling area officially ranks third in importance based on the number of questions, the difference between this area and the number of questions in planning and execution is less than 1 percent. For all practical purposes, planning, execution, and controlling are all tied for first place in your study emphasis.

Quick Assessment

Controlling Risk

1 You're halfway through a major software implementation project when you get word that your chief software architect has stormed off the project. This is an example of _____.

2 You're halfway through a major software implementation project when you get word that your chief software architect has stormed off the project. What do you do?

3 You're halfway through a major software implementation project when you get word that your current design can't meet your operating requirements. What do you do?

4 The new design is an example of a(n) _____.

Schedule Control

5 The sponsor of the software project asks, "What's the first schedule implication?"

6 Now that you have the schedule change request, what do you do next?

Cost Control

7 You promise to give the sponsor complete details on the updated costs. What are you promising to deliver?

8 How will you estimate the final project cost?

Answers

1   Additional risk identification and analysis, a previously unidentified risk. This is an input of Risk Monitoring and Control. Although this is a situational question, it asks you to identify the input pattern. See "Controlling Risks."

2   Implement your workaround plans and take corrective action. You use the risk response plan output to implement the workarounds and corrective actions you chose during planning. The question asks you to identify the output pattern. See "Controlling Risks."

3   Submit a change request, implement workaround plans, and take corrective action. The output pattern question asks you to identify additional outputs. See "Controlling Risks."

4   Scope change. The question asks you to identify the input pattern and tests your knowledge of processes and methods. See "Controlling Risks."

5   Although the exact details are still unknown at this point, the start and finish dates of your already-approved schedule will change. Revisions are a special type of schedule update used as a response to scope changes. Making revisions usually involves resetting the project baseline. The question asks you to identify the output pattern (schedule updates are outputs) and tests your knowledge of processes and methods. See "Controlling Schedule Changes."

6   Use the change request as an input and use the Schedule Control change system, additional planning, and project management software to develop the revised schedule. The pattern of this question asks you to identify tools and techniques. See "Controlling Schedule Changes."

7   Revised cost estimates, budget updates, corrective actions, estimate at completion, and lessons learned. The question asks you to identify the outputs and tests your knowledge of processes and methods. See "Controlling Cost Changes."

8   Actual costs to date plus a new estimate for all remaining work. You use this method when past performance shows that the original estimating assumptions were fundamentally flawed or are no longer relevant due to a scope change. The question asks you to identify a formula pattern and tests your knowledge of processes and methods. See "Controlling Risks."

Controlling Risks

After you've formalized the risk management plan (RMP), Risk Monitoring and Control is the subsequent process of keeping track of the identified risks, monitoring residual risks and identifying new risks, ensuring the execution of risk plans, and evaluating the plans' effectiveness in reducing risk.

The inputs to Risk Monitoring and Control are as follows:

- **Risk management plan (RMP):** The RMP is the subsidiary part of the integrated project plan. It documents procedures for managing risk throughout the project. It details identification and quantification of risk, responsibilities for managing risks, how contingency plans will be implemented, and how reserves will be allocated.

- **Risk response plan:** This plan documents the procedures for managing risk events. It addresses risk identification, owners and responsibilities, results from qualification and quantification processes, agreed responses for each risk, the level of residual risk to remain after the strategy is implemented, budgets and times for responses, and contingency plans.

- **Project communication:** Work results and other project records provide information about project performance and risks. Reports to monitor and control risks commonly include issues logs, action item lists, and jeopardy warnings (also called escalation notices).

- **Additional risk identification and analysis:** As project performance is measured and reported, unidentified potential risks may surface.

- **Scope changes:** They require new risk analysis and response plans.

These are the five tools and techniques to Risk Monitoring and Control:

- **Project risk response audits:** Throughout the life cycle of the project, risk auditors examine and document the effectiveness of your risk response in avoiding, transferring, or mitigating risk occurrence, as well as the effectiveness of the risk owner.

- **Periodic project risk reviews:** Such reviews should be regularly scheduled to monitor the progress and any changes to the project.

- **Earned value analysis:** EVA is used for monitoring overall project performance against a baseline plan. If a project deviates significantly from the baseline, update your risk identification and analysis. See Appendix A for EVA formulas, charts, and examples.

- **Technical performance measurement:** This compares technical accomplishments during execution to the plan's schedule of technical achievement. For example, omitting a milestone introduces scope risks.

✓ **Additional risk response planning:** If an unanticipated risk emerges, or if its impact on objectives is greater than expected, the planned response may not be adequate. You might require additional response planning to control risk. This provides a feedback loop.

These are the six outputs to Risk Monitoring and Control:

✓ **Corrective action:** This encompasses anything that brings your expected performance back in line with the project plan. At this stage, it involves carrying out either your contingency plan or workaround.

✓ **Workaround plans:** These are unplanned responses to emerging risks that were not previously identified or accepted.

✓ **Project change requests:** Implementing a contingency plan or workaround frequently requires changing the risk responses described in the project plan. Know the process flow and feedback loop.

✓ **Updates to risk response plan:** Document the risks that occur. Risks that don't occur should also be noted and closed out in the risk response plan. It's important to keep this up-to-date, and it becomes a permanent addition to project records, eventually feeding into lessons learned.

✓ **Risk database:** This is a repository for collection, maintenance, and analysis of data. It's used in risk management processes. Maintaining this database is very important for your project records.

✓ **Updates to risk identification checklists:** Because these updates help in the risk management of future projects, the checklists are vital tools.

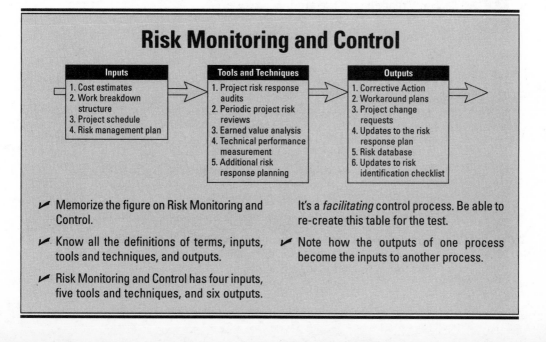

Risk Monitoring and Control

Inputs	Tools and Techniques	Outputs
1. Cost estimates 2. Work breakdown structure 3. Project schedule 4. Risk management plan	1. Project risk response audits 2. Periodic project risk reviews 3. Earned value analysis 4. Technical performance measurement 5. Additional risk response planning	1. Corrective Action 2. Workaround plans 3. Project change requests 4. Updates to the risk response plan 5. Risk database 6. Updates to risk identification checklist

✓ Memorize the figure on Risk Monitoring and Control.

✓ Know all the definitions of terms, inputs, tools and techniques, and outputs.

✓ Risk Monitoring and Control has four inputs, five tools and techniques, and six outputs.

It's a *facilitating* control process. Be able to re-create this table for the test.

✓ Note how the outputs of one process become the inputs to another process.

Mastering risk controls

The key to understanding risks is to identify what constitutes the *triggering event.* You analyze, qualify, and quantify risks to minimize threats and maximize opportunities. Closely monitor risks throughout the project. Revisit your risk list periodically. Are the risks still valid? Perhaps a particular risk is no longer important. Or you might uncover additional risks from new events or change requests. You must update the risk plans as you proceed. If you document your actions, stating why you made certain choices, and describe the results, you'll provide a good record for understanding upcoming risks, risks in future phases, and any risks that might affect the next project.

Handling change requests

Almost all controlling processes have change requests, so memorize the definition of this term and know the patterns. In exam questions, change requests may be described by using slight variations in terms. A change request fits a general pattern — as an *input* of control processes. The two exceptions where it's an output are Performance Reporting and Project Plan Execution. These are feedback loops in the process flow. The Quality process omits this feedback pattern; improvements are implemented immediately.

Anyone on the team can make a change request: a customer, a sponsor, or any stakeholder. You'll get change requests because a new technology has become available, government regulation forces it, or customers want new features that change the product's scope.

All proposed modifications are handled via change requests, which must be tracked. You manage them according to your change control system and configuration management procedures. These are both tools and techniques in Integrated Change Control, the global-level process that governs changes to both your project and the product.

You'll often have the authority to approve the decision yourself. If you do, it's important to document the change. Those requests increase scope or alter schedule, costs, or quality baselines. In these cases, you have to invoke your change control system. If your organization has a formal change control board (CCB) procedure for this process, call a meeting of the CCB, get its formal approval, document the results, and communicate the results to the team.

Change requests are the most important factor in controlling *scope creep,* the way most projects get out of hand and exceed their available resources. As a rule, the larger the number of change requests, the less planning that went into the initial project planning stages.

Triple constraint

On pressure-cooker projects, change requests often require that you consider the alternatives among the triple-constraint variables. The triple constraint is the competitive trade-off among cost/budget, time/schedule, and scope/quality. You may choose any two variables (from time, cost, or quality), but the third variable must be flexible for reasonable results. You can have it better, cheaper, or faster, but not all at the same time. Some PM practitioners consider this to be outdated, recognizing *scope* as a necessary fourth variable of project management.

Taking corrective action

Corrective action is anything that changes the expected future performance of the project. You want to bring your actual results back into line with your desired results, and you don't want variances to reoccur. For the exam, remember these two key corrective action process flows, or feedback loops:

- ✔ Changes you make to adjust deviations from the project plan must be updated in subsidiary plans. You must communicate those changes to the rest of the team according to the communications plan.

  Corrective action fits a general pattern — it's an output of *all* control processes. It's a response to inputs of change requests, work results, or performance reports. Corrective action creates a feedback loop in Integration as an input to Project Plan Execution.

- ✔ Implementing contingency plans is a risk management process.

During the risk planning process, you identify key assumptions that are beyond your control, and you quantify their probability of occurrence. You should identify alternative plans for successfully achieving your goals and objectives. You prepare workarounds for such things as alternative schedules or reordering key activity sequences in response to types of disasters. These workarounds should reduce the impacts of particular risk events. Evaluate your liabilities in a worst-case scenario that anticipates early termination of the project. Always plan for project closeout. As an intermediate work product, develop a subsidiary management plan to be invoked if specific risks occurred. Provide for a contingency allowance in the budget.

If your expected results have failed to appear, implement your contingency plan or your mitigation plan. The contingency plan provides an alternative course of action to cope with this risk. You should've planned well enough so you understand its budget, schedule, quality, and implications. Be aware of the controversy that is sure to arise when you dip into contingency reserves. Be able to explain the unexpected results, why they happened, and how your plan provides a workaround. When you need additional funds, management, accountants, and customers wonder how your mandate has changed.

Controlling Schedule Changes

Schedule Control involves managing changes to the schedule (or baseline). You determine factors affecting the schedule, how they can be influenced (how to reduce delays, for example), whether these changes benefit the product or project, if the variances are so great you must revise the schedule baseline, and how to manage schedule changes. The major activities include monitoring the schedule performance of project activities to detect variances from the original schedule baseline, updating authorized changes in the schedule baseline documentation, and informing stakeholders of authorized changes. Earned value analysis shows schedule performance. You need to determine why you have positive and negative variances. For example, if you have a positive schedule variance, is someone cutting corners to look good?

Here are the four inputs to Schedule Control:

✔ **Project schedule:** As a subsidiary part of the integrated project plan, the approved schedule is called the *schedule baseline.* You *re-baseline* when the schedule becomes unrealistic. Re-baselining occurs when you do any major update so you can better control the schedule.

✔ **Performance reports:** These reports provide information on schedule execution — showing if planned dates have been met. Performance reports also alert you to issues that may cause problems in the future.

✔ **Change requests:** Requests take many forms — oral or written, direct or indirect, externally or internally initiated, and legally mandated or optional. Changes may require extending or accelerating the schedule.

✔ **Scope management plan:** This plan describes how changes will be integrated into the project. It's a subsidiary part of the project plan.

The four tools and techniques to Schedule Control are as follows:

✔ **Schedule change control system:** This defines the procedures for changing the project schedule. It includes the paperwork, tracking systems, and approval levels necessary for authorizing changes.

✔ **Performance measurement techniques:** These techniques help you assess the magnitude of any variations that occur in project performance. An important part of Schedule Control is to decide if the schedule variation requires corrective action.

✔ **Additional planning:** Prospective changes may require new or revised activity duration estimates, modified activity sequences, or analysis of alternative schedules.

✔ **Project management software:** This is software a project manager or team uses. In the context of Controlling on the exam, it is schedule development, tracking, and reporting software. It helps level resources, automates mathematical network analysis, and presents what-if scenarios for schedule alternatives. Examples include scheduling software, such as Microsoft Project and Project Server, Milestones, and PERT Chart EXPERT, and such Monte Carlo simulation software as @RISK.

These are the three outputs to Schedule Control:

✔ **Schedule updates:** Include any modification to the schedule used to manage the project. It's used to measure performance. A special category of schedule updates, *revisions,* describes changes to start and finish dates in the approved project schedule. Revisions usually require resetting the project baseline.

✔ **Corrective action:** Encompasses anything that brings your expected future schedule back in line with the project plan. These actions are outputs from the other knowledge areas.

✔ **Lessons learned:** Document causes of variances, the reasoning behind corrective actions, and other of lessons learned from schedule change.

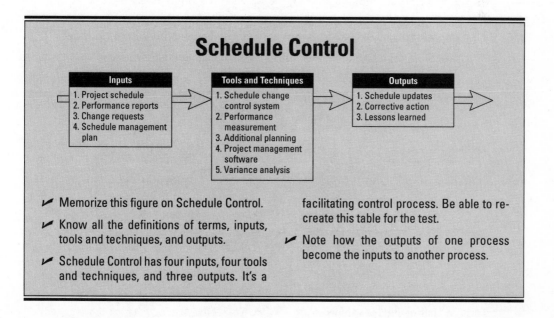

Schedule Control

Inputs	Tools and Techniques	Outputs

1. Project schedule
2. Performance reports
3. Change requests
4. Schedule management
   plan
	1. Schedule change
	   control system
	2. Performance
	   measurement
	3. Additional planning
	4. Project management
	   software
	5. Variance analysis
		1. Schedule updates
		2. Corrective action
		3. Lessons learned

✔ Memorize this figure on Schedule Control.

✔ Know all the definitions of terms, inputs, tools and techniques, and outputs.

✔ Schedule Control has four inputs, four tools and techniques, and three outputs. It's a facilitating control process. Be able to re-create this table for the test.

✔ Note how the outputs of one process become the inputs to another process.

Controlling Cost Changes

Cost Control involves controlling changes to the project budget (or baseline). During this process, you try to determine what factors impact costs, how these factors can be influenced (how to reduce overages, for example), whether these changes are beneficial to the product or project, whether the variances are so great that you need to revise the cost baseline, and how to manage the cost changes. The major activities you'll perform include monitoring the cost performance of the project activities to detect variances from the original cost baseline, updating authorized changes in the cost baseline documentation, and informing appropriate stakeholders of authorized changes. You'll have positive and negative variances; you'll have to determine why they occurred. For example, is someone cutting corners to make a positive cost variance?

Here are the four inputs to Cost Control:

- ✔ **Cost baseline:** Includes a time-phased budget used to measure and monitor cost performance on the project. You add up estimated costs by period to develop your original budget. The cost baseline is usually shown as cost-by-period and can be charted in the form of an S-curve.

- ✔ **Performance reports:** Provide information on cost performance, such as which budgets have been met and which have not.

- ✔ **Change requests:** Take many forms: oral or written, direct or indirect, externally or internally initiated, and legally mandated or optional.

- ✔ **Cost management plan:** Describes managing cost variances.

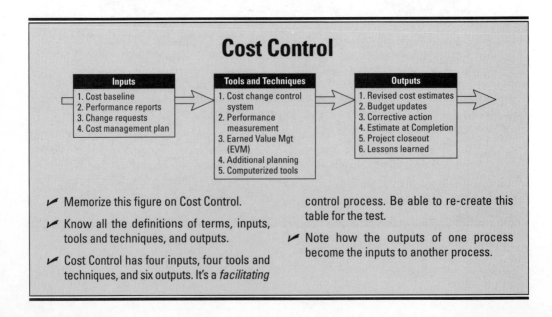

Cost Control

Inputs	Tools and Techniques	Outputs
1. Cost baseline	1. Cost change control system	1. Revised cost estimates
2. Performance reports	2. Performance measurement	2. Budget updates
3. Change requests	3. Earned Value Mgt (EVM)	3. Corrective action
4. Cost management plan	4. Additional planning	4. Estimate at Completion
	5. Computerized tools	5. Project closeout
		6. Lessons learned

- ✔ Memorize this figure on Cost Control.

- ✔ Know all the definitions of terms, inputs, tools and techniques, and outputs.

- ✔ Cost Control has four inputs, four tools and techniques, and six outputs. It's a *facilitating*

control process. Be able to re-create this table for the test.

- ✔ Note how the outputs of one process become the inputs to another process.

The four tools and techniques to Cost Control are as follows:

✔ **Cost change control system:** Defines the procedure by which the cost baseline may be changed. It includes the paperwork, tracking systems, and approval levels necessary for authorizing changes.

✔ **Performance measurement techniques:** Help you assess the magnitude of any variations that do occur. Earned value analysis is especially useful for cost control. An important part of cost control is determining variance causes and deciding if the variance requires corrective action.

✔ **Additional planning:** Prospective changes may require new or revised cost estimates or analysis of alternative approaches.

✔ **Computerized tools:** PM software or spreadsheets that track planned versus actual costs or that forecast the effects of cost changes.

These are the six outputs to Cost Control:

✔ **Revised cost estimates:** Help you manage the project.

✔ **Budget updates:** Require changes to an approved cost baseline. The numbers are generally revised only in response to scope changes. Cost variance may be so severe that re-baselining is needed in order to provide a realistic measure of performance.

✔ **Corrective action:** Anything done to bring expected future project performance into line with the project plan.

✔ **Estimate at completion (EAC):** A forecast of total project costs based on project performance. The most common variations are

- **Actual costs to date plus the remaining project budget modified by a performance factor.** This approach is most often used when current variances are typical of future variances.

- **Actual costs to date plus a new estimate for all remaining work.** This is most often used when past performance shows that the original estimating assumptions were fundamentally flawed or are no longer relevant due to a change in conditions.

- **Actual costs to date plus the remaining budget.** This approach is used when current variances are atypical and you do not expect a similar variance to occur in the future.

✔ **Project closeout:** Processes and procedures for closing or canceling the project.

✔ **Lessons learned:** You must document the causes of variances, reasons behind the corrective action chosen, and other lessons learned.

Communicating Performance

Performance Reporting is collecting and distributing information to stakeholders on how the project is performing — how the team is achieving project objectives. This process involves progress reports, status reports, and forecasts. Stakeholders watch trade-offs among schedule, quality, and cost. The triple constraint, risk, procurement, and staff topics are included in reports. (See the "Triple constraint" sidebar, elsewhere in this chapter.)

Here are the three inputs to Performance Reporting:

- ✓ **Project plan:** The formal, approved document to guide project execution and control. It includes the schedule, budget, and the knowledge area subsidiary plans such as the communications plan, risk management plan, and quality plan. The plan sets a baseline to measure progress.

- ✓ **Work results:** The results of activities performed to accomplish the project. Work results are analyzed with the tools and techniques to be described shortly and are used to control the project. You can measure them by using such metrics as percent of deliverables completed, costs incurred, and schedule ahead or slippage. (See Chapter 11.)

- ✓ **Other project records:** A catchall phrase for other documents. These could be blueprints, technical documents, or specifications documents. Use whatever you can get that will help control the project.

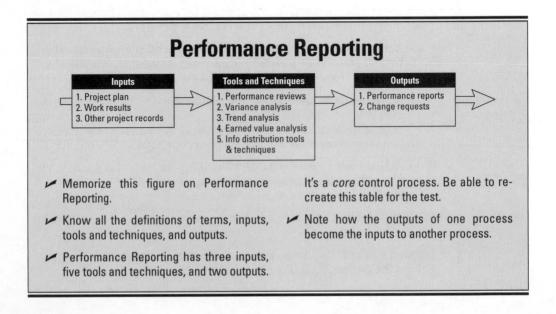

Performance Reporting

Inputs	Tools and Techniques	Outputs
1. Project plan	1. Performance reviews	1. Performance reports
2. Work results	2. Variance analysis	2. Change requests
3. Other project records	3. Trend analysis	
	4. Earned value analysis	
	5. Info distribution tools & techniques	

- ✓ Memorize this figure on Performance Reporting.

- ✓ Know all the definitions of terms, inputs, tools and techniques, and outputs.

- ✓ Performance Reporting has three inputs, five tools and techniques, and two outputs.

- ✓ It's a *core* control process. Be able to re-create this table for the test.

- ✓ Note how the outputs of one process become the inputs to another process.

The five tools and techniques to Performance Reporting are as follows:

- ✔ **Performance reviews:** Project meetings are held to evaluate status and progress. Don't hold a review meeting with an unprepared team. Make sure that team members use some of the relevant tools and techniques to get you the information you need to control the project.

- ✔ **Variance analysis:** Compares results to planned results. Generally, the analysis is cost- and schedule-related. That's why the project plan is an input. The project plan provides the baseline for the planned results.

- ✔ **Trend analysis:** Examines project results over the dimension of time to see if patterns show performance improvements or deterioration. Chapter 11 has details on trend analysis, especially as it relates to quality control.

- ✔ **Earned value analysis:** Integrates scope, cost, and schedule measures. It's the most common method of measuring a project's progress. It compares actual results to planned results. See Appendix A for the EV formulas. All calculations are based on three key measures:

    - **Planned value (PV):** The portion of the approved cost estimate planned to be spent on activity during a given period. (The old term is budgeted cost of work — BCWS.)

    - **Actual cost (AC):** The total of direct and indirect costs incurred in accomplishing work on activity in a given period. (The old term is actual cost of work performed — ACWP.)

    - **Earned value (EV):** The value of work actually completed. (The old term is budgeted cost of work performed — BCWP.)

    Know both sets of terms and be able to translate them. PMI says the EV format on the exam uses a new term followed by an old term in parentheses. For example, it may appear as earned value (budgeted cost of work performed). But not all questions follow this format.

- ✔ **Information distribution tools and techniques:** This includes all the tools and techniques mentioned in Information Distribution. The *PMBOK Guide* covers this topic. (See Chapter 11 for details.)

These are the two outputs from Performance Reporting:

- ✔ **Performance reports:** Contain organized and summarized results of project reports, correspondence, documents, and memos. They should also present the results of any analysis performed by the team. Charts and graphs neatly summarize information for busy executives. This alerts the team to issues that could cause future problems.

    - **Status reports** describe the project's current standing.

    - **Progress reports** describe the team's accomplishments.

- **Trend reports** describe the project results over time, usually for the duration of your status reporting period.

- **Forecast reports** predict future project status. They include indicators of scope, schedule, cost, quality, risk, and procurement.

- **Variance reports** compare actual results against the baseline.

✔ **Change requests:** Ask for modifications to some deliverable or objective. These formal documents can also involve changes to a contract, even including contract termination.

Prep Test

1 Taking over a troubled project as project manager, you want to find out the team's accomplishments. Where do you look?

- **A** ○ Status reports
- **B** ○ Progress reports
- **C** ○ Trend reports
- **D** ○ Variance reports

2 To get up to speed on the new project, the best technique is to _____.

- **A** ○ Hold a performance review.
- **B** ○ Obtain performance reports.
- **C** ○ Obtain status reports.
- **D** ○ Check the work results.

3 To get up to speed on the new project, the best technique to use is _____.

- **A** ○ Performance measurement techniques
- **B** ○ Earned value analysis
- **C** ○ Technical performance measurements
- **D** ○ Variance analysis

4 To get up to speed on the project, which document should you read first?

- **A** ○ Product description
- **B** ○ Schedule
- **C** ○ Technology management plan
- **D** ○ Project plan

5 After implementing your workaround plans, what do you do next?

- **A** ○ Hold a performance review.
- **B** ○ Measure technical performance.
- **C** ○ Update the risk response plan.
- **D** ○ Check the work results.

6 An unanticipated risk comes out of left field, which process will be affected the most?

- **A** ○ Risk Monitoring and Control
- **B** ○ Risk Response Planning
- **C** ○ Risk Identification
- **D** ○ Risk Quantification

7 After you make a revision to the schedule baseline, what do you do next?

A ○ Check the work results.

B ○ Measure performance.

C ○ Update the project plan.

D ○ Notify stakeholders according to the communications plan.

8 All of the following are outputs of Risk Monitoring and Control except:

A ○ Workaround plans

B ○ Corrective action

C ○ Change requests

D ○ Lessons learned

9 After introducing a new technology, the project sponsor requests a revised estimate to complete. You determine that the original cost estimates no longer hold. The best formula to use is _____.

A ○ Actual costs to date plus the remaining project budget modified by a performance factor

B ○ Actual costs to date plus a new estimate for all remaining work

C ○ Actual costs to date plus the remaining budget

D ○ Actual costs to date plus the remaining budget

10 The summation of all direct and indirect costs incurred in accomplishing work on an activity in a given period is called _____.

A ○ Planned value

B ○ Earned value

C ○ Actual cost

D ○ Budgeted cost of work

Answers

1 **B.** Progress reports describe accomplishments. This pattern requires you to distinguish between terms that are closely related. It tests your knowledge of the detailed processes in performance reports. *See "Communicating Performance."*

2 **A.** It's the only technique listed; the others are inputs and outputs. This is the tool and technique pattern. *See "Communicating Performance."*

3 **B.** The others are good answers, but they're not the best answers. This pattern asks you to distinguish between terms that are closely related. *See "Communicating Performance."*

4 **D.** The key word is *first*. The pattern is the project manager should do the single most important thing first. It asks for project, not product, which eliminates A.

5 **C.** The key word is *next*. A, B, and D would happen later in time. This pattern is the order of events. *See "Controlling Risks."*

6 **B.** If an unanticipated risk emerges, the planned response may not be adequate. You might require additional response planning to control risk. The key word is *most*. This question tests your ability to demonstrate your understanding of the differences among processes. *See "Controlling Risks."*

7 **D.** You could take all of these actions. The key word is *next*. It's most important to communicate these changes to stakeholders who might be responsible for the new delivery date. This pattern is the order of events. *See "Communicating Performance."*

8 **D.** Almost all the knowledge areas contain a lessons-learned process. In Risk, lessons learned are derived from the risk database. The key word is *except*. This is an exception pattern. Did the pair *corrective action and change requests* fool you? They normally don't appear together as outputs; they're usually an input and output. *See "Controlling Risks."*

9 **B.** This is most often used when past performance shows that the original estimating assumptions are no longer relevant due to a change in conditions. It tests your ability to demonstrate your understanding of the relationship among facts, principles, and methods. *See "Communicating Performance."*

10 **C.** Actual cost (AC) is the total of direct and indirect costs incurred in accomplishing work on activity in a given period. This pattern asks for the definition. *See "Communicating Performance."*

Chapter 14

Closing the Project

· ·

Exam Objectives

▶ Repeating closeout at each phase

▶ Evaluating work packages

▶ Handling administrative closeout

▶ Examining contract closeout

· ·

*P*roject closing accounts for approximately 16 exam questions. That represents only 8 percent of the total questions on the exam. Because closing represents a minority of questions, concentrate your study efforts on higher payback areas first. Don't skip this area, but give it appropriate attention.

Quick Assessment

Repeating
Closeout at
Each Phase

1   You are assigned to a new project with an existing customer. This customer has balked at signing off on previous projects. What steps can you take as a project manager to ensure the customer will sign off on your new project?

2   What is the distinction between Administrative Closure and Contract Closeout?

3   Who is involved in Administrative Closure?

4   Who is involved in Contract Closeout?

Retaining
the know-
ledgebase

5   Successful completion of the project requires finalizing the _____ document.

Releasing
Resources

6   What document helps you decide when to release a team member?

Contract
Closeout

7   What are the outputs of Contract Closeout?

8   Final payment requests are handled in which process?

Answers

1 Negotiate the project scope with the customer, manage the customer's expectations, involve the customer in all phases, and have the customer sign off on all important documents that include requirements and deliverables. This pattern asks for you to include your knowledge of steps before the Administrative Closure process. To identify those steps, you have to work through the methodology backwards. See the *PMBOK Guide* p. 42 and "Repeating Closeout at Each Phase."

2 Administrative Closure relates to documenting your project results, acceptance of the product and of the project by the customer according to the given specifications, customer feedback, lessons learned, and archiving the information for future projects. Contract Closeout relates to the procurements during the project. It involves product verification, contract conditions, and terms. This question tests your understanding of the differences among processes. See "Contract Closeout."

3 Administrative Closure processes involve the project team, sponsor, and customer. This question asks for the inclusion pattern. This question tests your understanding of the relationship among facts, principles, and processes. See "Repeating Closeout at Each Phase."

4 Contract Closeout processes involve your contract administrator and, indirectly, your suppliers and subcontractors. This asks for the inclusion pattern. This tests your understanding of the relationship among facts, principles, and processes. See "Repeating Closeout at Each Phase."

5 Project closure. An example of the inclusion pattern, this question asks for an output. See "Closing Down Administrative Functions."

6 The staffing management plan should cover the releasing of resources. This question asks for the inclusion pattern. This question tests your ability to demonstrate your understanding of the relationship among processes. See "Handling Staff During Closing."

7 The two outputs are contract file and formal acceptance and closure. See the *PMBOK Guide* p. 159 and "Contract Closeout." This question asks for process outputs.

8 Payment requests are a feedback loop to the executing process of Contract Administration — another Procurement process. This question tests your understanding of the relationship among facts, principles, and processes. See "Contract Closeout" and the *PMBOK Guide* p. 158.

Repeating Closeout at Each Phase

Although it's not as exciting as developing the product or delivering the final version of the product, closeout involves important accounting and communicating activities.

Closeout doesn't happen just at the end of your project; you need to perform the same closeout steps at the end of each project phase.

During Administrative Closure, the closeout processes involve the project team, the sponsor, and the customer. During this time, you confirm with the project team and sponsor that all phase deliverables and requirements have been fulfilled and that the requirements of the performing organization have been completed. The phase deliverables include documenting project and product performance reviews, budget and cost reports, and lessons learned.

You also confirm that the customer formally accepts the product of the project and your teams' progress as being complete. As the project manager, you plan (at the project's start) how to obtain the customer's acceptance. (Recall the acceptance criteria that you defined during the initial scope process, as described in Chapter 6. Each work package has an acceptance criterion. Each phase has its deliverables and acceptance criteria.) The complexity of acceptance depends on many factors such as the size of the project, whether it's an internal or an external project, the nature of the product, industry standards, and the organizations and people involved. It might be a short approval (on smaller projects, perhaps just one signature), or on a large project, it could be an intricate process involving a committee from many departments.

We've seen lots of projects that require testing and evaluation steps before customers or sponsors are willing to sign off on their acceptance. By involving customers throughout the project, you ensure that they're satisfied at the end of each phase. Of course, satisfying customers is the main goal of any project. It's up to you as the project manager to balance the stakeholders' various interests and convey to them what's possible and what's not. If customers are involved in the project details and know why the team makes certain decisions, they will more readily accept some compromises on the final product. But if you don't keep customers informed, they might have different expectations and balk at approval. In some cases, payments are made based on the customer's approval. Anything that might delay payments is a red flag. Another reason to manage customer expectations carefully is that phase ends, or toll gates, are kill points where a sponsor or customer can terminate a project early. An unhappy customer might terminate the project in the middle.

As an output of this step, formal acceptance documentation should be prepared and distributed. This documentation shows that the clients or sponsors have accepted the product of the project, or phase. Having thus documented their approval helps during the next phase. For example, you ensure that the team is on track with the project, and you limit scope creep.

During Contract Closeout, closeout processes involve your contract administrator and, indirectly, your suppliers and subcontractors. This step provides a feedback loop to ensure that all contract terms have been met. Closeout might be hampered if there are outstanding items or work remaining. In most organizations, your formal acceptance of procurement contracts enables the suppliers and subcontractors to get paid. This step keeps valuable procurement knowledge inside the organization and contributes to improvements in the next phase or in the next project.

Exam questions on project closure include definitions as well as situational questions.

Evaluating Work Packages

When you set up the work breakdown structure (WBS), you ensure that each work package has a criterion for completion. Don't allow tasks to be considered complete until all those completion criteria are met. Otherwise, your official status will indicate you're further along than you actually are, which can cause problems. Unrealistic schedules don't benefit anyone. If you make the work packages easy to understand and track, and if the people performing the work understand their responsibilities, it will be easier for you to approve the work. You might have to negotiate with functional managers to ensure that the work gets completed because you often won't have authority over the people performing the work. In evaluating work packages, the project manager is generally more concerned with inspecting the quality and scope of the deliverables for completeness. Like quality guru Crosby says (see Chapter 10), it's faster and cheaper to do it right the first time.

Retaining the Knowledgebase

To retain the knowledgebase for future projects and future phases of your project, complete these three processes:

✔ **Conduct a phase review, or project post mortem.** This consists of two formal processes:

- Administrative Closure (a Communications process)
- Contract Closeout (a Procurement process)

You conduct both processes before the team disperses at the end of a project or before key staff leave at the end of a phase. Include the perspective of all stakeholders, including customers, sponsors, team members, subcontractors, and functional managers. You want to capture details on successful and unsuccessful activities — noting what worked, what didn't work, and why. Include general activities, milestone- or phase-specific activities, and PM process controls.

✔ **Document lessons learned.** If you've examined the historical records of other projects, that will give you some insight into what you need to capture for your own historical records. You may have looked at plan versus actual performances to see how accurate cost-schedule estimates were. You may have examined various logs (such as the issues log and the risk log) to see how the team responded to challenges and how those challenges were met.

If you're working on a phase-end closeout, you might have to handle some transition tasks such as creating turnover memos and wish lists of features and handling open tasks and unresolved issues.

✔ **Archive project records.** Often during the review, you'll find that key members have more detailed records on matters than were generally available to the entire team. You might want to incorporate these records into the formal project archives.

Closing Down Administrative Functions

Closing the administrative functions takes place at the end of every phase as well as at the end of the project. Because projects are temporary, project closeout briefings and lessons-learned documents provide important feedback. They keep valuable knowledge inside the organization and contribute to improvements in the next cycle of projects. Talk openly about failures as well successes. As far as the methodology is concerned, if you haven't completed this step, the project isn't completed.

Administrative Closure has three inputs, three tools and techniques, and three outputs. Try using the mnemonic aid of *Administrative Closure 333.* Or remember that there are three *i*'s in Administrative.

Here are the three inputs:

✔ **Performance measurement documentation:** This type of input includes all the performance-related documents used to guide, record, and analyze project planning, execution, and control. They include status, progress, and forecast reports, in addition to the original project plan.

Mainly, project managers are concerned with documents that provide information on cost, schedule, and quality. But the documents can also deal with risk and procurement.

✔ **Product documentation:** These documents show the results of activities performed to create the product or service that the project was chartered to achieve. These include plans, technical documents, design documents, specifications, blueprints, drawings, and electronic files. The names vary depending on the application area. The original documents in the charter provide a baseline to measure results and changes. You'll factor in the product change requests and then compare this result to the final product to see if the product met its target.

✔ **Other project records:** This is catchall category for other documents that might be relevant. See Chapter 13 for details.

These are the three tools and techniques to Administrative Closure:

✔ **Performance Reporting tools and techniques:** This provides a feedback loop, solving the information needs of the various stakeholders and showing the interaction of all the tools used during the Performance Reporting phase just described. These tools and techniques include performance reviews, variance analysis, trend analysis, and earned value analysis. See Chapter 13 for the definitions of the tools and techniques for Performance Reporting.

✔ **Project reports:** These are formal reports on status and issues. See Chapter 10 for details.

✔ **Project presentations:** These are how the reports and records are presented to stakeholders. Check out Chapter 10.

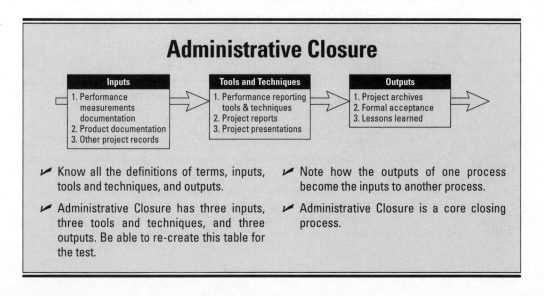

Administrative Closure

Inputs	Tools and Techniques	Outputs
1. Performance measurements documentation 2. Product documentation 3. Other project records	1. Performance reporting tools & techniques 2. Project reports 3. Project presentations	1. Project archives 2. Formal acceptance 3. Lessons learned

✔ Know all the definitions of terms, inputs, tools and techniques, and outputs.

✔ Administrative Closure has three inputs, three tools and techniques, and three outputs. Be able to re-create this table for the test.

✔ Note how the outputs of one process become the inputs to another process.

✔ Administrative Closure is a core closing process.

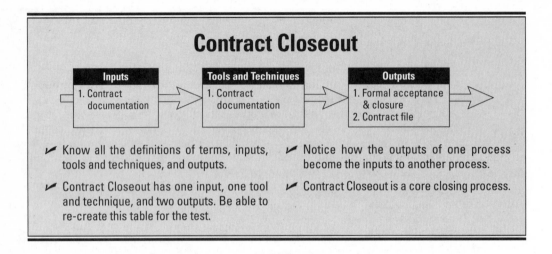

Contract Closeout

Inputs		Tools and Techniques		Outputs
1. Contract documentation		1. Contract documentation		1. Formal acceptance & closure 2. Contract file

✔ Know all the definitions of terms, inputs, tools and techniques, and outputs.

✔ Contract Closeout has one input, one tool and technique, and two outputs. Be able to re-create this table for the test.

✔ Notice how the outputs of one process become the inputs to another process.

✔ Contract Closeout is a core closing process.

Here are the three outputs to Administrative Closure:

✔ **Project archives:** This is the long-term storage of all project activity records. The information should be complete and indexed for easy retrieval. All databases should be updated with the appropriate information. Pay special attention to financial records, especially if the project was completed under contract or if large procurements have been made.

✔ **Project closure:** This documentation confirms that the customer formally accepts the product of the project, that all requirements have been fulfilled, and that the requirements of the delivering organization have also been met. These requirements may include staff performance reviews, budget/cost reports, and lessons-learned documents. Exam questions on project closure include definitions as well as situational questions.

✔ **Lessons learned:** This documentation includes detailed information on how common and unusual project events were resolved. These documents shed light on the causes of variances on the project, how the team resolved the variances, and the reasoning behind the team's actions. This document becomes part of the organization's knowledgebase so the information can be applied to future projects.

Lessons learned reappear as an output in all controlling processes.

Project closeout briefings and lessons-learned meetings need to take place before the project ends and the project team disperses. Otherwise, you'll miss a great opportunity to gather information that could benefit future projects. You might even have an end-of-phase, lessons-learned review meeting.

Good formal documentation is important, especially if you loose a key team member, inherit a project from someone else, or become involved in a dispute with a client or subcontractor.

If you are working for a large organization or are working under a contract, you're likely to face a post-project audit. This project review could happen at a phase end to determine if the project should continue, right after the project is completed, or even a year later while you're busy managing another project. Be aware that the year's time is the fiscal year for the performing organization or the client's fiscal year, not the calendar year.

Sometimes a project management office will do this audit. Even if the audit is delayed, consider this as part of the closing process; use the same steps in handling lessons learned and project closure in the Administrative Closure process. One of our colleagues, a consulting project manager, went through this audit process twice: once for his client's auditors as part of the official project closure and again for his consulting company's internal auditors — almost six months after he closed down the project. Dealing with internal auditors or an independent, outside consulting firm usually strikes fear in the hearts of most managers, project managers, and functional managers alike. The potential for being audited is increasingly important to remember in the post-Enron climate of corporate accountability. But if you've directed the team to keep updating the project documentation, you should be in good shape.

The purpose of such an audit isn't to pass or fail. It's to explain what you did, the reasons you made certain choices, and the processes you used. The auditors essentially perform Quality Assurance (QA) on your project for the performing company. As with any audit, they examine the processes you used and determine if those processes were sound and verifiable. Because you're using the generally accepted PM practices, you should have nothing to fear. Be sure that you can provide your documentation from the following areas: planning stages, requirements gathering, scope definition (the product and project), testing, and the entire QA plan, as well as customer involvement and approval.

Contract Closeout

Here is the one input to Contract Closeout:

- ✔ **Contract documentation:** This includes, but is not limited to, the contract along with all supporting schedules, requested and approved contract changes, any seller-developed technical documentation, seller performance reports, financial documents, and the results of any contract-related inspections.

Here is the one group of tools and techniques to Contract Closeout:

> ✔ **Procurement audits:** These are structured reviews of the Procurement process, from Procurement Planning through Contract Administration. The objective of a procurement audit is to identify successes and failures that warrant transfer to other procurement items on this project or to other projects.

Here are the two outputs to Contract Closeout:

> ✔ **Formal acceptance and closure:** The person responsible for Contract Administration provides the seller with formal written notice that the contract has been completed.
>
> ✔ **Contract file:** This is a complete set of indexed records. Compile them for inclusion with the final project records.

Be sure that you know the major differences between Administrative Closure and Contract Closeout. It's a favorite exam topic.

What is the main difference between Contract Closeout and Administrative Closure? Is it a product verification step? Or, is it a project verification step?

Contract Closeout relates to the procurements you make during the course of the project. It involves product verification. The contract conditions and terms are verified at the time of Contract Closeout. The contract document is verified with the audited results, the contract is closed out officially, and the supplier receives final payment. The feedback loop for payment requests goes back to the executing process of Contract Administration — another Procurement process.

Administrative Closure relates to documenting your project results, final acceptance of the product and of the project by the customer according to the given specifications, customer feedback, lessons learned, and archiving the information for use in future projects. You must apply Administrative Closure to each phase of the project.

In Contract Closeout and Administrative Closure, product verification is similar in terms of lessons learned. During Contract Closeout, you develop lessons learned along with your suppliers and subcontractors. During Administrative Closure, the lessons learned involve the project team and the customer.

Handling Staff During Closing

Expect to see a few closing questions related to releasing resources, rewarding performance, and contract profits. We offer a few sample questions so you get used to the format, and we cover the contract profit formulas in Appendix A.

Releasing resources

One of the difficult things a project manager faces during closing activities is trying to determine when to release or redeploy staff. This responsibility varies by organization and by industry. The biggest risks are that you might release staff members too soon, and they might not be available to return to the project if the need arises. Or you release them too late, which is a waste of resources that could be applied elsewhere. In both cases, poor timing is costly to the project. Your decision will vary depending on the policies of the performing organization and the organizational structure.

The staffing management plan should include a section that describes when and how resources should be removed from the project. In almost every case, the staff knows that the project is coming to an end. If they don't have another project to go to, they may make up work to fill the time. If you find team members doing this, you should release them. This is one of those tricky areas where experience helps. Also, morale can suffer from uncertainty about the next assignment, and this can affect performance. If staffers are actively looking for their next assignments, they might not pay as much attention to completing their current assignments. Generally speaking, when staffers have completed all the work packages to which they are assigned, they should be released.

Rewarding performance

You create a reward and recognition system during the Team Development process, as described in Chapter 11. Now it's time to promote and reinforce the performance behavior you wanted. Some organizations have formal reward and recognition systems. On many projects, you have to develop your own. There are unwritten rules about rewarding performance on projects that depend on your organization; some relate to rewarding voluntary overtime to meet an aggressive schedule, some to rewarding top performers, and some to rewarding the entire team.

The types of questions we've seen on the rewards-related exam questions have involved types of motivation a project manager can use, as well as the ethics of rewards. A project manager who gives a bonus to a staffer for outstanding work is using reward motivation. But if a project manager carpools with the team member, does the bonus create the appearance of impropriety? The PMI answer is that the team should decide on how to allocate the bonus for all team members. If you're doing an intensive 360-degree review on a smaller project, this is a good idea. And if you're on a large project, it might be the fairest way to handle the situation. However, if you're developing a merit-based system, it might be difficult for the team to know everyone's individual contributions.

Prep Test

1 Conducting a phase review or project post mortem consists of formal processes including _____, which is a _____ process.

- **A** ○ Administrative Closure, Procurement
- **B** ○ Administrative Closure, Communications
- **C** ○ Contract Closeout, Communications
- **D** ○ Contract Closeout, Integration

2 Conducting a phase review or project post mortem consists of formal processes including _____, which is a _____ process.

- **A** ○ Administrative Closure, Integration
- **B** ○ Administrative Closure, Procurement
- **C** ○ Contract Closeout, Communications
- **D** ○ Contract Closeout, Procurement

3 Conducting the Administrative Closure process begins with _____, _____, and _____.

- **A** ○ Performance measurement documentation, product documentation, other project records
- **B** ○ Contract documentation, procurement audits, performance measurement documentation
- **C** ○ Project reports, product documentation, and performance metrics
- **D** ○ Product documentation, performance reports, change requests

4 Which of the following is a tool and technique of Contract Closeout?

- **A** ○ Performance Reporting tools and techniques
- **B** ○ Payment system
- **C** ○ Contract change control system
- **D** ○ Procurement audits

5 Reviewing project performance and key deliverables at the end of a phase is called a _____.

- **A** ○ Stage gate
- **B** ○ Kill point
- **C** ○ Hammock
- **D** ○ Milestone

6 During the _____ process, the client and sponsor should formally accept the project as completed.

A ○ Overall Acceptance

B ○ Administrative Closure

C ○ Contract Administration

D ○ Contract Closeout

7 Your project is ahead of schedule during final customer acceptance. The product meets all the specifications and came in under budget. Your customer refuses to accept the product unless you make several changes. What do you do?

A ○ Obtain all the changes and estimate their cost. If the total costs of the changes are within the budget, just do the extra work and bill for the original budget.

B ○ Send your estimated cost changes to your customer as a part of a contract revision.

C ○ Tell the customer to file a formal change request. Then pass this through your change control procedures.

D ○ Insist that you've completed the project and have delivered the product specs.

8 The purpose of a phase end review of deliverables and project performance is to _____.

A ○ Adjust schedule and cost baselines based on performance to date.

B ○ Manage customer expectations about project deliverables.

C ○ Decide if the project should continue to the next phase.

D ○ Confirm that all deliverables and requirements have been fulfilled.

9 An unwritten rule of thumb on software projects in your organization is to reward the top 10 percent of performers on your project team. You feel everyone has contributed above and beyond the norm. What do you do?

A ○ Reward just the top 10 percent.

B ○ Split the bonus among the entire team.

C ○ Ask the sponsor for additional bonuses for the team.

D ○ Ask the team how they want to split the bonus pool.

10 When do you release the team?

A ○ After Administrative Closure

B ○ After Contract Closeout

C ○ According to the staffing management plan

D ○ As soon as their work packages are completed

Answers

1 **B.** This pattern variant asks you to demonstrate your knowledge of the 39 process interactions and to determine in which of the 39 knowledge areas the process belongs. *See "Closing Down Administrative Functions."*

2 **D.** This is a variant of question 1. This pattern variant asks you to demonstrate your knowledge of the 39 process interactions and to determine in which of the nine knowledge areas the process belongs. *See "Contract Closeout."*

3 **A.** You should eliminate B with contract documentation, which is an input to Contract Closeout, and procurement audits is a tool and technique of Contract Closeout. C can be eliminated because project reports belong to tools and techniques. D can be eliminated because performance reports and change requests are outputs of Performance Reporting. *See "Closing Down Administrative Functions."*

4 **D.** Procurement audits is the only tool and technique in Contract Closeout. It can be eliminated because Performance Reporting tools and techniques belong to Administrative Closure. B can be eliminated because payment systems belong in Contract Administration. C can be eliminated because contract change control system belongs in Contract Administration. *See "Contract Closeout."*

5 **B.** B is the best answer. Kill points are also commonly called phase ends or toll gates. *See "Repeating Closeout at Each Phase."*

6 **B.** There is no A choice; C and D deal with the closing of Procurement processes — your organization's obligations to your suppliers. *See "Closing Down Administrative Functions."*

7 **C.** Although A looks like a good answer, it misses the mark in following procedures. If you complete the extra work, your status reports will give false impression of productivity (or lack of it) to your performing organization. If the contract terms reward you for coming in under budget, you lose out if you add the requested changes without any additional increase in costs. B is incomplete because even if the customer agrees to the increased costs as part of the revised contract, you still have to go through the change control process — possibly a change control board — and distribute the changes to the rest of the team. D is not the best choice because it's rare that a conversation goes well when you just say to a customer, "We're done. Pay us. Goodbye." *See "Repeating Closeout at Each Phase."*

8 **C.** C is the best answer. B is also a good answer, but it includes only the product deliverables and doesn't include anything about the project performance. D is out of sequence — if you confirmed that all requirements were completed, you'd be at the project closeout instead of the phase closeout. *See "Repeating Closeout at Each Phase."*

9 **D.** The purpose of rewarding the team is to motivate them to increase their performance for the next phase or project. Sometimes, the team will know more about the real contributions of individuals and can make a better decision than you can. This is the kind of situational question the exam asks. We'd go out on a limb and ask the sponsor to award extra bonuses if the team deserved it. But the sponsor might not have those extra funds, so the gesture might be futile. If you selected A, then you'd be de-motivating the other 90 percent. In effect, you'd be sending them the message that their effort wasn't as appreciated as the others. If you selected B, then you'd be fair but not giving the team their chance to recognize extra efforts. It's not uncommon for a team to split the award with double shares going to top performers. *See "Rewarding performance."*

10 **C.** The staffing management plan should include a section that describes when and how resources should be removed from the project. The biggest risks are that you might release staff members too soon, and they might not be available to return to the project, or you release them too late. *See "Releasing resources."*

Part VI
The Part of Tens

The 5th Wave   By Rich Tennant

Oh come on—how fatal can it be?

FATAL ERROR

In this part...

The Part of Tens is a tradition of ...*For Dummies* books. This part features a pair of quick chapters that summarize tips you can use to maximize your exam performance.

Chapter 15

Ten Test Preparation Tips

In This Chapter

▶ Take care of administrative stuff

▶ Define your study plan

▶ Stay motivated

▶ Do your homework

▶ Understand question patterns

▶ Memorize terms

▶ Get a handle on process flow

▶ Strategies for question types

Take Care of Admin Stuff

Here are a few administrative things you need to do prior to taking the exam:

✔ **Download the Certification Handbook.** It's a PDF file you'll use as a reference for the application process. You can also download the Certification Handbook at:

```
www.pmi.org/certification/ExamAdmin/CertificationHandbook
    03-2002.pdf
```

✔ **Apply online for the exam.** Go to certificationapp.pmi.org/. You may want to join PMI now (www.pmi.org) to take advantage of the PMI member discount. The member discount plus the exam fee equals the non-member exam fee. It's a great deal! You'll have to join PMI after you get your PMP certification anyway in order to keep up your continuing education requirements. For details, see Chapter 1.

✔ **Schedule the exam.** After you get your eligibility letter, contact a Prometric Test Center (the exam contractor) to schedule an exam appointment. You can schedule your exam for any day or time that the Prometric Test Center has available.

To verify your identity, the testing center requires your PMI ID#, so have it handy. Because you've already paid PMI for taking the exam, you don't have to pay any fees to Prometric. When dealing with Prometric, you have the option of using its Web site (www.prometric.com) or automated telephone response system.

After you've scheduled your exam, write down Prometric's exam confirmation number or print out the page.

Here are the documents you'll need to take with you to the exam center:

✔ Your application letter from PMI, which contains the PMI Registration Code. Not having this number could actually prevent you from sitting for the exam.

✔ Prometric's exam confirmation number.

✔ Two forms of identification. One must have your picture. Most people use a driver's license and a credit card. Make sure that both forms of ID match; the proctors won't accept a credit card with *Pete* and a driver's license with *Peter.*

Take a trip to the exam site before your appointment to get familiar with the route.

Define Your Study Plan

Do an initial feasibility assessment of your level of knowledge in relation to the *PMBOK Guide*. Determine the areas where you'll need to study and concentrate your efforts.

On the CD, we offer a simplified study plan that allows you to practice the same methodology used on the exam. Customize your PEPP study plan with some of the tools we've included on the CD and on the Web site.

✔ Review the study plan templates.

✔ Create your study plan's scope statement as a word processing document.

✔ Develop your WBS by decomposing all of your exam deliverables with WBS Chart Pro.

✔ Sequence your activities and work through the network by using PERT Chart EXPERT.

✔ Use Milestones to plan and track your milestones, and use Microsoft Project to create the schedule baseline and track your progress.

✔ Use Excel to plot out your budget baseline to see if it's an S-curve.

✔ At the end of each chapter, monitor and control your study plan by using earned value measurements. Post your EV metrics — such as SV, CV, SPI, and CPI — near your study materials, perhaps next to your computer monitor.

Following this study method will help you familiarize yourself with the methodology you need to know to ace the exam.

Define a study plan and stick to it. It's better to study for an hour a day than to cram all weekend. It's also better to make studying a regular daily practice than to cram the week before the exam.

Stay Motivated

Studying for the PMP exam is time consuming and demanding. Here are some suggestions on how to make the process easier and more enjoyable:

✔ Keep your study materials handy wherever you go. Any time you're waiting or have a few minutes to kill, read the definitions and skim the chapters of this book.

✔ Take practice exams and look at what you got right, what you got wrong, and what you've learned since your previous attempt.

✔ Use the simulation exam from the Computer Based Training (CBT) course on the accompanying CD. Because the exam format is also computer-based, the simulation exam will help prepare you for the real exam.

Keep the scores as a motivator to do better. We know the material isn't fun; in fact, we know firsthand just how dry it is. Try making your study session a quiz to challenge yourself.

Do Your Homework

Because you need to know many ordered lists and definitions for the exam, concentrate your efforts at the highest levels. The high-level ordered lists are

✔ The five process groups

✔ The nine knowledge areas

✔ The 39 component processes

When you start memorizing the ordered lists for the nine knowledge areas and the 39 component processes, the first step is to become familiar with the definitions. Don't focus your energy on memorizing the definitions just yet. Focus your effort on memorizing the lists, in order. Later, you can dive into the definitions.

Here are some key terms you need to know:

- Constraints
- Assumptions
- Every management (subsidiary project) plan and its supporting detail
- The feedback loop for (subsidiary or knowledge area) project plan updates. (They may be called something else depending on their knowledge areas — for example, *schedule updates* rather than *time updates*.)
- Historical information (always an input)
- Organizational policies (always an input)
- Organizational procedures (almost always a technique)
- Corrective actions
- Change requests
- Lessons learned (always an output)
- Work results (output of execution, an input to control)
- The work breakdown structure
- Decomposition
- Expert judgment
- Project charter
- Scope statement
- Statement of work

It's easier to learn these ordered lists as pairs or groupings of terms. For example, it's easy to see the logical grouping among corrective action, change requests, and lessons learned. An example of pairing is with any subsidiary management plan in any knowledge area; it's paired with some type of supporting detail. Other pairs include assumptions and constraints, work results (exact definitions change in different knowledge areas), and change requests.

Be on the lookout for how the processes for each of the following terms flow, how the output of one process becomes the input of another:

- ✔ Assumptions and constraints
- ✔ Change requests and corrective action
- ✔ The management plans (as an output of planning and an input to both execution and control)

Make note of their exceptions — for example, where change requests are an input or where they are an output.

Execution outputs include the paired items' work results (the exact definition may be different in different knowledge areas) and change requests. Know in which process the subsidiary project plan for that process starts or first appears. It will generally start in a planning process. Be careful because some planning processes don't necessarily include *planning* in the term. For example, the schedule management plan is an output to Schedule Development.

In the controlling processes, the only two processes that don't include the word *control* are Scope Verification (Scope) and Performance Reporting (in Communications). Both are overall processes.

Make sure that you know the differences between the core and facilitating processes in each knowledge area. Know the tools and techniques, especially where they involve further analysis. Know the tools and techniques of the risk area especially, including Performance Reporting in Communications, Time, Quality, and Cost.

Look for Question Patterns

Being able to detect patterns in the questions helps you eliminate bad choices and select the correct answer. Here are our guidelines for deciphering repeated patterns:

- ✔ Is the question looking for a match to the pattern or the exception to the pattern?
- ✔ Is the question looking for an input, tool and technique, or an output?
- ✔ What process group does the question cover?
- ✔ What are the process results? These objectives are *outputs*.
- ✔ What knowledge area does the question cover?

Two basic types of patterns are *matching* and *exception:*

✔ **Matching:** A question that calls for a matching pattern names a series of items and asks you to pick the item in the responses that's most nearly like the others. For example, *banana* is a match for apple, orange, and grapefruit.

Possible exam question: Which of the following processes *belongs* to Risk?

✔ **Exception:** The exception pattern presents you with a list of items and asks you to identify the one that doesn't belong: Among apple, brick, orange, and grapefruit, *brick* is the exception. Another term for an exception pattern is a *mismatch.*

Possible exam question: Which of the following processes *does not belong* to Risk?

Look for key words and phrases in the question such as:

✔ Best or worst

✔ First or last

✔ Belongs to or does not belong

✔ Must or except for

✔ Most effective or least effective

✔ First or last

✔ Greatest or least

✔ Most helpful or least helpful

✔ Not including

✔ Key activity

✔ Preferred response

Remember the Process Interactions

Here are some tips to help you figure out whether something is an input, a tool or technique, or an output:

✔ **Inputs** are documents, or documentable items, that will be acted upon.

✔ **Tools and techniques** are mechanisms applied to inputs to create outputs.

✔ **Outputs** are documents, or documentable items, that result from a process.

Beware of study materials that use old terms from the 1996 *PMBOK Guide*. The entire risk section has been rewritten, and the old terms are no longer valid. For example, insurance used to be considered a type of mitigation. As of the 2000 edition, insurance is now considered a type of transference.

Know the Component Process Interactions

On our Web site, you'll find a downloadable, wall-sized chart that will help you memorize the 436 component process interactions. It shows the 186 inputs, 137 tools and techniques, and 113 outputs to each of the 39 component processes. It's already grouped by knowledge area. We recommend that you print several copies of this chart so you can make notes on them. With these copies in hand, you'll be able to study the material in different ways:

✔ Try color-coding each of the 39 component processes and grouping them by their five process groups. This should yield you a 6- to 8-point return on your exam score.

✔ After your first reading of this book and the *PMBOK Guide*, try indicating whether the 39 component processes are core or facilitating processes. This short exercise yields about a 3- to 5-point return.

✔ Link the outputs of one process to the inputs of another process. Knowing how the process flows can yield an 8- to 10-point return.

Recognize Question Types

You'll see several common question formats on the exam. Here are a few formats and insights for analyzing them. For example, a question will be set up with a scenario that contains the problem you have to solve. Long, involved setups generally ask the question in the last few sentences. Having set up a situation, variations of question types include

✔ **What did the project manager forget to do?**

For this type of question, determine which process group is involved, what knowledge area is important, which component process is relevant, and whether the question is looking for an input, a tool and technique, or an output. Then select what's missing.

✔ **What could the project manager do to avoid the problem?**

The right answer solves the problem rather than covering it up or mitigating it.

✔ **What's the worst thing to do?**

✔ **What's the most important thing to do?**

   The correct answer always has the biggest impact or payback on the project.

✔ **What's the least preferred method?**

✔ **What should the project manager do first?**

   The correct answer always has the biggest impact or payback on the project.

✔ **What must the project manager avoid?**

However accurate any answer might appear, pick the choice that answers the question from the PMI point of view. Testing for the project manager mindset is PMI's major objective in designing the questions.

Do the Math

The math you need to know for the exam isn't difficult. The statistics are actually entry-level. The math will probably involve less than 10–15 percent of the questions. Several math questions ask you to determine the best choice. Some questions refer to a graph and ask you to determine project performance.

Appendix A covers the formulas. Mastering math problems is a three-step process:

1. Memorize the formulas.

2. Select the right formula for the job.

3. Plug in the numbers and calculate.

You not only must memorize the formulas, but also understand the type of analysis each formula is intended to support. Practice plugging the numbers into the formulas and solving the equations. If you're familiar with the formulas and solving problems, you'll save valuable time during the exam.

Chapter 16

Ten Tips for Exam Day

In This Chapter

▶ Preparing the day before the exam

▶ Arriving at the test center

▶ Starting the exam

▶ Analyzing question patterns

▶ Making mental notes

Before You Get to the Test Center

Make the most of your final few days of studying. Don't be surprised if you have butterflies dancing in your stomach. Any exam is a major stress trigger.

Day before

The day before the exam, all that you should need to do is to make sure you have the necessary materials for the exam.

✔ Get the folder with your application letter from PMI. It contains your PMI Registration Code.

✔ Check your calculator. If you're the cautious type, replace the batteries and make sure the calculator's turned off.

✔ Look over your map to the exam site.

✔ Have a healthy dinner. We recommend brain food — fish for dinner the night before and eggs for breakfast on exam day (or other high-protein foods if you're a vegetarian) — supplemented with lecithin and choline as memory enhancers.

✔ Get a good night's rest.

✔ Check your wallet for two forms of identification. One needs a photo.

Both names on your identification must match. The testing center won't accept a credit card with *Pete* on it and a driver's license with *Peter*.

Exam day

On exam day, grab your test kit and some snacks, such as a candy bar, energy bar, or banana, and a few bottles of water. Dress comfortably for the test. Exam rooms can be cool because of air conditioning, so you may want to bring a sweater.

Kick-start your brain by repeating the 39 process interactions, and review each of the core and facilitating processes according to the five process groups.

At the Test Center

You can anticipate these steps at the test center.

Registration

Get to the test center in plenty of time. Prometric (formerly Sylvan) suggests arriving 30 minutes before the exam. This gives the test center time to process your paperwork and download your exam to a PC workstation. If you're early, you might be able to start a few minutes early.

Get the lay of the test site before beginning the test and then sign in. The sign-in process will be easier on the proctors because you'll have your test kit with all the documentation they need to verify who you are. While they're processing your paperwork and downloading your exam to your PC, find the restroom and use it; four hours is a long time between restroom breaks.

If you leave the exam for a restroom break, the clock continues to count down. Minimize your breaks!

Because of the ticking clock, don't plan on eating, drinking, or going to the restroom for the next few hours. Although you are permitted to leave the exam room, you don't get those minutes back.

Exam tools

The exam is computer-based. The desktop will be familiar — a PC running Windows. As with most online tests, you don't need the keyboard. You only need the mouse. The test is all multiple choice.

Prometric provides a locker where you can store your wallet or purse, break snacks, and water. The only things you're permitted to take into the exam room are a calculator and a locker key. You can ask the Prometric proctor for these exam tools:

✔ A calculator, if you forget yours or your battery dies during the exam.

✔ Pencils and scratch paper. You get about five sheets of paper to start the exam. If you want more paper, just ask for it.

✔ Earplugs.

You must return exam tools to the proctor when you finish.

Settling in

After you're assigned to a testing cubicle, make yourself comfortable. You will be sitting in front of a computer monitor at a small desk in a small cubicle. Before the exam starts, adjust the chair and height of the monitor. If you want, kick off your shoes.

If you used the Computer Based Training (CBT) exam simulator on the CD, you've seen the computer-based exam format and the types of questions.

Taking the tutorial

You can take a 15-minute tutorial on how all the commands work for the computer-based test. Review the tutorial on marking questions for review. It really helps to mark questions if you are unsure of the answer or if you want to skip ahead because they'd take longer to answer. Don't use up all 15 minutes of the tutorial. You should only need about two to three minutes for this. At the end of the timed tutorial, the exam starts. Welcome to the show!

Use most of the 15-minute tutorial time to do a "brain dump" on the scratch paper. (That's why you asked for more paper.) Write these out:

✔ All the formulas in the Cheat Sheet located in the front of this book

✔ Earned value formulas

✔ Time estimating formulas for CPM, beta distributions, and triangular distributions

✔ Charts showing the knowledge areas and the 39 component processes — you can put these charts on another page for easier reference

Get familiar with the screen.

  ✔ Find buttons and controls.
  ✔ Be able to move forward and backwards through the questions.

Two important controls for you to scan visually and note for the next four hours are the *question number* and the *time clock*. These reference points help you keep track of your pace. You have four hours to answer 200 questions; that's 72 seconds per question. If you pace yourself and answer the easier questions first, time for completing all 200 questions shouldn't be a problem.

You need 137 correct answers out of 200. Anything over 137 passes. You get the same grade if you score a 137 or a perfect 200, so don't sweat the number.

Beginning the Exam

The question format is simple. For each question, you click one of the radio buttons marked A, B, C, or D for the best choice. You can use either the keyboard or the mouse to make the selection. After answering, you can move forward to the next question or move back to the previous question.

The exam consists of 200 questions in random order. Prepare yourself mentally to jump around. Candidates tell us the first ten questions scare them because they're so tough. If you think the introductory questions are harder than you expected, it's okay to skip ahead. Just mark the challenging questions. The obvious questions are few and far apart, but you will get some. By the time you reach question 20, you'll have hit your stride.

If you've done your homework, the single most common reason you'll give the wrong answer is because you misread the question! This is a pitfall for people who are well prepared. They've seen so many practice questions, they assume they've seen the question before, or they miss a key word.

Analyze the Question Patterns

In reading questions, determine the pattern, the formula, or some aspect of the pattern. Do this step *as you read the question*. Don't let any of the suggested answers influence the pattern that you select. (That's one way trick questions can trick you. They have trick answers that seem correct if you don't fully understand the pattern!) Determining the pattern for the question will make it easier for you to find the right answer and eliminate the wrong ones. As you read each question, make sure that you understand what is actually being asked. Don't answer with an input if the question asks for an output. Don't use the PERT formulas if the question asks for a triangular distribution. Avoid this trap by first eliminating wrong answers.

You can deduce many correct answers by a process of elimination. Out of 200 questions, 125–150 of the questions are straightforward. They require you to know the *PMBOK Guide* standards, but there is little ambiguity in the answer choices. In the remaining 5–10 questions, you won't know how to answer. Don't waste your time trying to solve them; mark them and return later. Expect the remaining questions to be tough, with ambiguous choices. You can usually eliminate two responses and have two likely answers.

Think carefully about your answers, especially in Professional Responsibility, where most questions are situational. Use your knowledge of the standard PM concepts as expressed in the *PMBOK Guide* and use your PM experience. Remember the principles we highlight in the chapters as PMI mantras. Review the discussion in Chapter 2 on analyzing the patterns in questions. You'll find some answers that are very close calls, and you must use your knowledge and experience to choose between them. When in doubt, answer questions from the PMI point of view. We believe the priority order for answer selection is *PMBOK Guide* (sometimes both answers can be correct; it depends upon the question), training, education, and real-world experience.

Make Notes

Watch for extraneous details in questions. Extra details are there to throw you off the track. Part of being test-wise is to be able to determine what information is relevant. Often in scenarios, the real question is contained in the last two sentences. Don't worry if you reread the question several times.

Although the order of exam questions is random, watch for questions that use the same scenarios. For example, a set of questions may relate to a diagram. Within a set, you'll likely find details that are irrelevant *only to that question.* Another question in the exam may use the extra data. To complicate matters, the random questions disperse the scenario throughout the test. Two questions in the same scenario might be separated by 50 questions. Unless you're looking for a pattern, you won't notice. A *later* question in the set might give you exactly the information you need to solve a previous question. So don't be afraid to mark questions for review later and to review your answers.

Watch for questions using a *network diagram* or *earned value table.* Mark them on the screen for later review. If you see a network diagram or earned value table on the test, expect that more than one question will refer to it.

Use your scratch paper to save your calculations. If you must redo a forward/backward pass for a Late Start/Late Finish or Early Start/Early Finish, the calculations can waste time.

For questions that belong to the same set, check your scratch paper notes as a timesaver. Your answer to the first problem can help you answer the next questions in the set without redoing your math. Or it can provide additional information that helps you answer the question. (Just make sure that both questions are indeed related, use the same table, or use the identical scenario.)

Create a simple information retrieval system: Use a different sheet of paper for each type of formula. Use one sheet for earned value, another page for network diagrams, and so on. On each sheet, mark the question number with your solution. By using the Go to Question Number command on the PC, you can check whether the previous question relates to your current one. If you think a second EV question is unrelated to the first EV question, just use another piece of paper for the second one. If you organize your scratch paper in this simple way, you'll find those related questions. Write legibly on your scratch paper! Don't worry about writing so small you must cram the other formulas all on one page. With organization, you can make things easier.

During the exam, take the time to stand up and stretch. Every 50 questions is a good target for a stretch and pace check.

Some prep course experts tell you to track your progress in three categories: questions that you're sure you've answered correctly, those you narrow down to two choices, and those that are a guess. This type of tracking can't help you answer questions, and it can't help you increase your score. You're better off not keeping a running total. Instead, concentrate on getting right answers.

Review your work. Check calculations. Review questions you've marked or skipped.

After you click the End Exam button, it's *over*. You can't get back into the exam. Your result appears instantly.

Part VII

Appendixes

Well heck, Justin - that's darn impressive! What else can that little programmable robot of yours do? How about sewing up and dressing that incision?

In this part...

These are Appendixes (or appendices, depending on the dictionary), but not Afterthoughts. We've included three key resources here that you can use any time. There's an appendix with the crucial formulas you need to know for the exam. A practice test that will gauge your readiness when you think you're ready for your closeup. And a guide for integrating the CD into your study plan.

Appendix A

Important Formulas

• •

▶ PM statistics
▶ Estimating time formulas
▶ Risk formulas
▶ Earned value analysis
▶ Cost accounting formulas

• •

The Quantitative View of Project Management

One of the complaints we hear from candidates is that the math on the exam is hard. That point of view is simply wrong. The actual math and the formulas that contain it are easy. It's just that the people who write the various training materials take a perverse pleasure in making math harder than it has to be.

The math is not especially difficult. Mastering the math is a three-step process:

1. Memorize the formulas.

2. Decide which formula applies to a given word problem on the exam.

3. Plug in the numbers and calculate.

The challenging part is Step 2, which requires you to understand the usage and application of each formula. But we help you make quick work of that in this appendix.

You will encounter questions that are poorly written, not necessary because they split hairs on definitions (although many of them do), but because they didn't explain the problem well enough or lack English grammar skills! Many questions simply need rephrasing or rewording. The formulas that you see in this appendix are easy to solve. If you just remember the formulas, *pick the right one for the problem,* plug in the numbers, and do the math, you'll master the quantitative portion of the exam.

A century ago, British Prime Minister Benjamin Disraeli categorized misleading information in three groups: "lies, damned lies, and statistics." This section is a quick overview of some of the terms used on the exam relating to formulas. In this appendix, we start with some basic statistics.

Expect to spend some time studying each formula before it makes sense. Many people expect to read mathematical formulas at the same speed as normal text. They get scared when they can't follow along at the same pace. Studying formulas doesn't work that simply; you may spend several hours studying before you understand and master just one formula. So allow yourself the luxury of reading this section at a pace comfortable enough for you to master the material. It contains important information that you'll certainly see on the exam. We recommend using Excel to work through the formulas one step at a time. We also have a few spreadsheets with the formulas up on the Web site as a shortcut for you.

PM Statistics for Dummies

Here's a recap of statistical terms you need to know for the exam. Be careful: we've worded the definitions in the technical jargon of the profession. Even if you think you know the common-sense or everyday definitions, study the meanings given here — it's another requirement for adopting the PM mindset.

Experiment: A systematic evaluation of the occurrence of a phenomenon (represented by one or more dependent variables), or of changes in a phenomenon, under well-specified, controlled conditions (represented by one or more independent variables). Examples of experiments include counting people who watch a movie at a theater and sampling a crayon manufacturing process.

Descriptive statistics: Summary numbers that describe the characteristics of a sample of items or events. The exam covers measures of central tendency like the *mean, median,* and *mode,* as well as measures of variation like *range* and *standard deviation.* Meaningful summaries of the characteristics of a sample can also be displayed graphically using charts such as histograms or bar charts.

Statistics: The method of collecting, organizing, analyzing, and reporting on numerical data derived from a sample. Know the distinction between a *statistic* and a *parameter.* A *statistic* is a number that summarizes some quality of a sample taken from a larger population (a part of the entire population — you might think of it as "something's missing from my enchilada"). However, a *parameter* characterizes a population (the "whole enchilada"). On the exam, the wording is like this: The sample's mean is a statistic; the population's mean is a parameter.

Central Limit Theorem: States that the sampling distribution of the mean approaches a *normal distribution* (with its familiar bell-shaped curve) as the sample size increases. It really doesn't matter what the real population distribution looks like.

Sampling distribution: The hypothetical distribution of a statistic, such as a mean or a variance, derived from a sample. In theory, you can obtain this type of distribution by drawing many independent samples of the same size from one overall population — calculating, say, the mean for each sample and then compiling a sampling distribution of the means themselves. The same could be done, in theory, for the variance and the other *moments* (principle characteristics) of a distribution. If the data are reasonably well behaved, the mean of the sampling distribution is the same value as the mean of the population.

Sample: A (hopefully) representative subset of the elements of a population. By measuring elements in a representative sample, you can make inferences about the population.

Normal distribution: A collection of many sample points (called a *probability density*) that forms a specific type of bell-shaped, symmetrical curve. A single peak at its center is where the mean, median, and mode of the distribution all coincide (see Figure A-1). The two tails of this type of distribution extend indefinitely out to either side, never quite touching the x-axis. That's termed being *asymptotic* to the x-axis. A normal distribution can be meaningfully described by its *moments,* or principal statistics. The moments of such a distribution are its *(arithmetic) mean, variance, standard deviation, skewness,* and *kurtosis.* (This appendix defines all these terms.)

Figure A-1 shows the bell-curved, normal distribution.

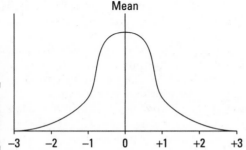

Figure A-1:
Normal
distribution.

Standard normal distribution: A normal distribution in which the mean is zero and the standard deviation is one.

(Arithmetic) mean: The sum of the values of all events in a sample or population divided by the number of events. The mean is a measure of central tendency or location. The mean, or average, of the five values — 1, 8, 3, 6, and 2 is $1 + 8 + 3 + 6 + 2 = 20$; $20 \div 5 = 4$. The symbol **μ (MU)** denotes the arithmetic mean ; it's the parameter for a population, while $\bar{x}$ **(Xbar)** is the statistic for a sample. Remember, a *statistic* is a number that summarizes some quality of a sample taken from a larger population (a part of the entire population). However, a *parameter* characterizes a population (the "whole enchilada"). On the exam, the wording is like this: Xbar, the sample's mean is a statistic; Mu, the population's mean is a parameter.

Median: The value in the middle of the range of ordered values. Within the set of ordered values, the media has just as many values above it as below it. The median is easiest to find when you have an odd number of values. When you have an even number of values, the median is the average of the two middle values. Another term for the median is the *50th percentile.* For symmetrical distributions (like the bell-shaped normal distribution), the median corresponds with the mean and is the center of the distribution. You can estimate the center of a distribution by the value of the median in a sample. If the distribution has "heavier tails" (see the definition of *kurtosis* later in this appendix) than the normal distribution, then the sample median is usually a more precise estimator of the distribution center than the sample mean. Consider the set of values: 350, 190, 174, 298, and 388. Sorting these into order, and taking the middle value gives the answer for the median value: 174, 190, **298**, 350, 388. The median is 298. If you get an even number of values in the exam question, average the middle two. The median value is some-times more representative of the center of a skewed sample than is the mean.

Mode: Within a set of values, the value that occurs with the greatest frequency (most often). Mode is the single value most typical of all the values in the distribution. Multiple modes in a sample (for example, a sample with two or more "humps") can sometimes indicate you're looking at items or events that should be sorted into two or more different distributions rather than into just one.

Variance: A measure of dispersion. Variance is the average of the squared deviations from the mean — where a "deviation" is the distance between the mean and each item in the population or sample. (In the case of a normal or near-normal distribution, if the deviations weren't squared before they are added together and averaged, the positive deviations from the mean would cancel out the negative deviations from the mean. The variance would be essentially zero!) For a sample variance, use the divisor $(n - 1)$; for the population variance, use the divisor (n).

Standard deviation (SD): A measure of dispersion. Standard deviation is the positive square root of the variance. Standard deviation is represented in the notation by σ, the Greek letter sigma. The historical norm in measuring quality has been three sigma (3σ), and some new emphasis on QM has reduced this tolerance level to six sigma. The Six Sigma quality methodology improves process capabilities by 20,000 times when compared to three sigma. In the QA process control context, six sigma is defined as 3.4 defects per million opportunities — that's only on one side of the mean. An advantage of the standard deviation (as compared to the variance) is that it expresses dispersion in the same units as the original values in the sample. For example, the standard deviation of a distance measurement is measured in feet; the variance is measured in "feet squared." When using the sample to estimate the sample SD, the divisor (n − 1) is typically used instead of (n) to calculate an estimate of the population average. The (n − 1) reduces a bias in the estimate that can creep into the calculations due to the relatively small size of the sample in comparison to the size of the whole population. The important thing to remember for the exam is that the standard deviation is just a form of average. It measures the average deviation from the mean, and is therefore the "yardstick" for measuring the deviance of a sample value from the "run of the mill," or the typical values of the sample. (The meaning of the expression "run of the mill" should be clear in the context of the quality of manufactured goods.)

Confidence interval: Assume that mu and sigma are, respectively, the mean and the standard deviation of a sampling distribution of a statistic Q. Assume further that the sampling distribution of Q is so large that you are reasonable in assuming that it is normally distributed (via the Central Limit Theorem). Given these assumptions, you can expect to find an actual, obtained, sample value of Q within the range of mu − 2 sigma to m + 2 sigma about 95.45 percent of the time. This range within the sampling distribution of Q is called the *95 percent confidence interval* for Q The limits of a confidence interval for the sampling distribution of a statistic such as Q are usually expressed in terms of some multiple of its respective sigma. The interval can be set up at any level of confidence, right up to m" plus or minus 6 sigma, or more. If the actual value of Q were found to be outside the predetermined bounds for whatever you are studying, you may suspect that such an unusual value of Q indicates a significant nonrandom difference between the obtained sample and the total population, at least in terms of Q Confidence intervals are routinely applied to a variety of descriptive statistics and to "test" statistics.

Variation: Indicates inefficiency and waste in a process. You're likely to see this term in reference to quality concerns. Management has the responsibility to reduce process variation to a minimum. Reduced variation makes the process more predictable, with process outputs closer to the desired value. To deal with variation, you must be able to quantify it. If you can't quantify it, you can't tell whether your process improvements were successful. First, make sure the process is stable. Next, use the appropriate distribution — usually, a normal distribution — to set reference points as your baseline. This should contain the everyday, random chance, or common-cause variations. *Common-cause variation* refers to normal fluctuations or variations inherent in all processes. Outside the process limits of the normal distribution are the special-cause variations. *Special-cause variation* is due to a problem or extraordinary occurrence. Finally, you need to monitor the process using control charts, and then identify and correct any special causes that upset the normal processes. Special causes indicate specific factors affecting the distribution's shape. After troubleshooting special causes, you can work on systemic changes to reduce the common-cause variation.

Control charts: Track a process by making periodic measurements. The Control chart has an upper control limit (UCL) and a lower control limit (LCL) for sampling successive measurements taken over a period of time. The series of measurements is termed a *run*. The control limits have been traditionally defined as three sigma (standard deviations) from the mean. Recently, some organizations more concerned with accuracy and precision use six sigma for tighter controls. The control charts signal whether the process is in or out of control. If the process centers near the mean, it's in control. When the process crosses the UCL or the LCL, it's at the extremes and becomes out of control. That signals you to investigate the process, find out what's wrong, and correct it. Assignable causes can introduce variations in quality into the process. Some examples of *assignable causes* include differences among machines, workers, and materials. The *range* represents those values between the UCL and LCL. Anything inside the range is in control. Outside of the UCL and LCL are the specification limits, which represent the customer's quality requirements. A process is out of control when a data point falls *outside* of the UCL or LCL, or when non-random samples are *within* the UCL and LCL.

A series of exceptions, or rules, for these non-random samples help you detect out of control, or abnormal, conditions. One of these exception rules is called the *Rule of 7s:* A run of seven consecutive data points (samples) on one side of the mean (either plus or minus) has a tiny probability that it's due to random variation. As a rule of thumb, a run of seven consecutive points indicates that the process is drifting out of control. Be careful here. The seven consecutive points must be on the *same side* of the mean and cannot cross it. An extremely low probability exists that this process shift is due to an assignable cause or to a random variation — 0.0156 (that's 1.56 percent). The Rule of 7 formula is $(.5)^{n-1}$, which is 0.5 (an equally likely chance of hitting or missing) to the n–1 Power. Therefore, the probability that a run of seven data points on either side of the mean is due to random variation is $(.5)^{7-1} = (.5)^6 = .0156 = 1.56$ percent.

Some other variations include:

- 1σ violations occur where 4 of 5 points on the same side of the center-line (mean) exceed 1σ from the centerline (mean).

- 2σ violations occur where two or more points on the same side of the centerline (mean) are greater than 2σ from the centerline.

- 3σ violations occur where a single point is greater than 3σ from the centerline (mean).

✔ Six successive points that increase or decrease form a *trend*.

✔ Eight successive points on the same side of the centerline (mean).

✔ 10 of 14 successive points on the same side of the centerline (mean).

The concept for control charts is pretty simple. If you can see a pattern that is not random (due to common-cause variation), then some other extraordinary occurrence is happening that needs to be analyzed and corrected. Those types of problems are termed *special-cause variations*.

See Figure A-2 to see a control chart in control and Figure A-3 to see one out of control.

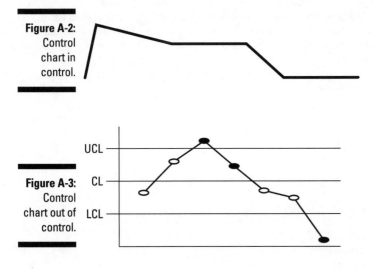

Figure A-2: Control chart in control.

Figure A-3: Control chart out of control.

Figure A-4 illustrates the Rule of 7s.

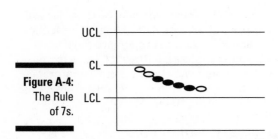

Figure A-4: The Rule of 7s.

Figure A-5 shows control charts with Zones C, B, A (which correspond to 3σ on each side of mean) and specification limits that are outside of the control limits.

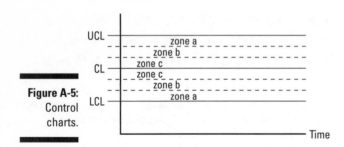

Figure A-5:
Control
charts.

Expected value: The expected value of a truly random variable is simply the arithmetic mean. For a discrete random variable, the expected value is the weighted average of the possible values of the random variable, the weights being the probabilities that those values will occur. For a continuous random variable, use the values of the probability density instead of probabilities, and the integral replaces the summation operator.

Histogram: A histogram is a graph of a set of data (see Figure A-6). A histogram appears as a bar chart.

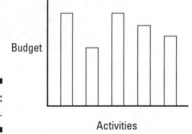

Figure A-6:
A histogram.

Figure A-7 shows a *Pareto* diagram.

Six-Sigma: The six standard deviation limits drawn on some process control charts rather than the traditional three standard deviation limits. Production processes are in control when the sample is within six standard deviations of the overall process mean (rather than the traditional three). The narrow bands of these limits when charted represent very tight controls. Motorola popularized the use of Six Sigma methodology. It forces manufacturing process to limit output variability to very strict limits.

Skewness: Measures the lack of symmetry of a distribution. Skewness is *positively skewed* if its charted curve leans to the right or if the curve tails off toward the high end of the scale. Simply, if positively skewed, the right tail is longer than the left tail. Skewness is *negatively skewed* if the curve leans to the left; it tails off toward the low end of the scale.

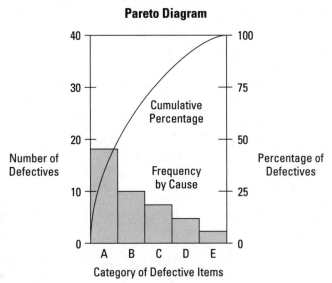

Pareto Diagram

Figure A-7:
A Pareto
diagram.

Kurtosis: Measures of the *heaviness of the tails* of a distribution. If the tails are heavier than in a normal distribution, kurtosis is positive, and a graph of the distribution appears to be relatively flat at its center — instead of the bell-shaped curve of a normal distribution. If the tails are *lighter* than in a normal distribution, kurtosis is negative, and a graph of the distribution appears to be relatively peaked at its center. The normal distribution has kurtosis of zero.

Acceptance sampling: Using sampling methods to determine whether the production batch or a shipment is of sufficient quality to be accepted.

Acceptance sampling plan: Defines a sampling procedure for a production batch or a shipment and gives decision rules for accepting or rejecting the goods, based on the sampling results.

Outlier: Sometimes a set of data has items with unusually large or unusually small values. These extreme values are called *outliers*. Outliers often arise from some mistakes in data-gathering or data-recording procedures, or from one-time-only failures of the process for known causes. The existence of an outlier means that a data point is extreme, not necessarily spurious.

Type I error: Rejecting the null hypothesis when it's true. The null hypothesis is often the reverse of what the experimenter actually believes and is put forward to allow the data to contradict it. An effect or event is statistically significant when the null hypothesis is false. The projected probability of committing a type I error is called the *level of significance.*

Type II error: Accepting the null hypothesis when it is false — failing to see a true difference as being statistically significant.

Analysis of variance (ANOVA): A statistical technique to determine whether three or more samples come from populations having the same mean. Assays of only two samples can be made using the ANOVA, but they are usually made with another statistic called the *Student's t distribution tests.* Taguchi uses this statistical procedure in his Design of Experiments to determine whether differences among the samples are caused by chance variation. ANOVA is a fairly common and relatively easy statistical technique to use, in most cases. Even Excel has an add-on Tool Pack that contains ANOVA.

Factor: In Design of Experiments, a factor is a categorical independent variable (*that is,* made up of sub-samples of the sample under study, each of which falls into its own specified category), as arranged by the experimenter. An experiment may have many factors.

Design of Experiments (DoE): In the realm of statistics, one of Taguchi's biggest contributions was in reducing the number of experiments required to control quality. Previously, experiments like Monte Carlo Simulations took hundreds and even thousands of iterations. The problem was that by the time the experimenter finished his calculations, the production process was way out of control and had produced many defective parts. DoE is a statistical model that specifies possible causal relationships between one or more dependent variables, $Y1, \ldots YN$, (but usually only one, in this context) and one or more independent variables (*that is,* causes of variation in the dependent variable), $X1, \ldots$ **XN**.

Analysis of covariance (ANCOVA): A slightly more sophisticated method of analysis of variance. ANCOVA includes the supplementary variables (called *covariates*) into the model, measuring the relationship between two ranges of data. If the two ranges of data move together, then you have a *positive covariance.* If the ranges move inversely, then you have a *negative covariance.* This lets you account for inter-group variation associated not only with the *treatment* itself but also with covariate(s). The Excel add-on Tool Pack's Covariance analysis returns an average of the product of deviations of data points from their means. Again, DoE uses this technique.

Bayes' Theorem: A formula for revising a priori probabilities after receiving new information. The revised probabilities are called *posterior probabilities.* This introduces the other side, the probability of something occurring versus the probability of its not occurring. Often, you can use formula 1 − (probability of the event occurring) to derive the probability of the not-occurring event.

Probability of Events

Probability of Event 1 plus Probability of Event 2, where the events are dependent upon each other:

Simple Probability = p(Event 1) + p(Event 2)

Probability of Event 1 plus Probability of Event 2, where the events are independent of each other:

Simple Probability = p(Event 1) × p(Event 2)

You are likely to see a decision tree as a graphic on some questions. The branches of the tree are composed of related events (but these are usually not dependent events in the sense of their joint probability).

You may see trick questions relating to opposites and be given some branches but not others. If so, you may have to subtract the "not" probabilities from 1 using the formula 1 − P(A). For example, the question may give you the fact that Branch A has a .7 probability of success. If the questions doesn't give you Branch B for the probability of failure, it's 1− P(.7) or .3. Another tricky question sets up a condition that is on the top branch or node. A question may give you two branches (Branch A and B are both .5 probabilities) at the lowest node as bins. The upper branch options are for defective (.3) or non-defective parts (.7). The question then asks you to determine the probability of selecting a defective part, given that you've already selected Branch B. That answer is that it's an independent action, and you don't have to calculate anything — because it's *already given* in the question that the probability of defective parts is .3.

Reliability for serial and parallel processes

The solutions to "combined probability" problems are a bit trickier. We give some examples shortly. You have a few concepts to remember here, including Bayes Theorem. If the question involves calculation of multiple probabilities, determine whether it's asking for a probability in series or in parallel. Each has different formulas . Here's an example of the series type: the question develops a manufacturing scenario in which a sub-assembly has two components. For example, a manufacturer of PC add-in boards has a new graphics card called Mojo Graphics 2002, using the new 3D graphics VRAM chip set called VirtualVision. The reliability of the VirtualVision 3D VRAM chip set is .95, and the reliability of the dynamic graphic memory chips is .95. The question then asks: What is the system reliability for this sub-assembly if the components are connected in series? What is the system reliability for this sub-assembly if the components are connected in series?

If the components are connected in series, the reliability is the intersection of the probability of A with the probability of B:

Reliability for Series = p(A) Intersection with p(B)

= 0.95 × 0.95 = 0.9025.

A similar example: In a two-step process, part A yields an 80 percent reliability, and part B yields 90 percent. The overall yield is therefore $0.8 \times 0.9 = 0.72$, or 72 percent. Remember that an overall process reliability involving a *series* of steps is always less than the lowest probability.

If the components are connected in parallel, the reliability is the intersection of 1 minus the probability of A with the probability of B:

Reliability for Parallel = $1 - p(A^*)$ Intersection with $p(B^*)$

$P(A^*) = 1 - p(A) = 1 - 0.95 = 0.05$

$P(B^*) = 1 - p(B) = 1 ¡V 0.95 = 0.05$

$= 1 - (0.05 \times 0.05) = 0.9975$

Now, you might think that this answer is intuitive for components that are connected in *series;* the reliability of both components taken together (0.9025) is slightly less than either alone (0.95). However, the answer is counterintuitive when the components are connected in parallel. You'd think that the reliability of both components taken together (0.9975) would be slightly less than taken separately (0.95). However, if you can take this to mean that if the first process doesn't fail, the second process is even less likely to fail. You can think of reliability in this case as more a condition of not-failing than of succeeding. To reinforce these concepts, see if you can replicate the answers in the table below. The *chain rule* applies when we have two functions with a connection: The independent variable of the first function is the dependent variable of the second.

Table A-1	Reliability for Serial and Parallel Processes		
Component A	**Component B**	**Series**	**Parallel**
0.9725	0.9725	0.9458	0.9992
0.95	0.95	0.9025	0.9975
0.9	0.9	0.81	0.99
0.89	0.89	0.7921	0.9879

Estimating Time Formulas

When referring to schedules or time, Expected Value is sometimes called Expected Time. It's also referred to as the *mean*. The exam uses these terms interchangeably.

To calculate Expected Value, you use different probability distributions based on the situation you encounter in a project. The PERT method of estimation uses a normal distribution, or beta distribution. You use this distribution when you have a larger sample size — for example, when historical information is available for estimating task. Remember the Central Limit Theorem: the larger the sample, the more normal distribution will be. You would use a triangular distribution when you base your task estimates on the subjective judgment of the team. The PERT method has a smooth bell-shaped curve characteristic of the normal distribution; the triangular has an abrupt peak at the top and slope away to look like a triangle.

Many project managers prefer the PERT approximation method for estimating similar tasks scheduled early in the project to a larger spread of variability. Use triangular methods when estimating tasks that are irregular or relatively unknown, as in R&D projects. Many IT application development projects fit here. This tends to minimize schedule risks because of the small variability of the Overall Schedule. In any case, the important perspective on probability distributions is Overall Schedule estimate.

Beta distribution using PERT-weighted average approximations

If the distribution is beta (normal), then the Mean or Expected Value = (Total Optimistic Estimate + 4 Times Most Likely Estimate + Total Pessimistic Estimate) divided by 6.

Mean = $(O + 4 \times M + P) \div 6$

O = Optimistic, M = Most Likely, and P = Pessimistic

Standard Deviation (approximate) = (Total Pessimistic Estimate minus Total Optimistic Estimate) divided by 6.

Standard Deviation or $\sigma = (P - O) \div 6$ or $\sqrt{\text{Variance}}$

Variance = Standard Deviation^2 or

$\sigma^2 = (P - O) \div 6^2$

O = Optimistic, M = Most Likely, and P = Pessimistic

Critical Path Method

CPM Hint: Use the *Most Likely* estimate only.

This trick question tests if you know CPM uses only the Most Likely estimate. If you are cruising at the speed of light on the exam, you're likely to overlook the fact that *CPM uses only the Most Likely estimate*. If you divide the CPM estimate by 3, as you would to determine the optimistic and pessimistic probabilities in a triangular distribution, you'll berate yourself for making a silly mistake when you check your results. The scratch paper comes in handy at this point: Write these formulas down during the 15-minute tutorial. And recheck your work if you finish early.

Triangular distribution

When the distribution is triangular, the formula for the mean is (O + ML + P) / 3, as shown in Figure A-8.

Mean = (O + M + P) ÷ 3

Standard Deviation σ = √ Variance

Variance = $[(P - O)^2 + (M - P)(M - 0)] ÷ 18$

Variance = $\sigma^2 = (P - 0) ÷ 3^2$

Figure A-8 shows a triangular distribution.

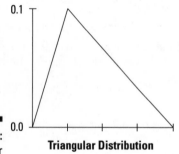

Triangular Distribution

Mean = (o+m+p)/3
Variance = [(b+a)²+(m−a)(m−b)]/18

1 Standard Deviation, 1 σ = 68.26%

2 Standard Deviations, 2 σ = 95.46 (95.5) %

3 Standard Deviations, 3 σ = 99.73%, or 2,700 defects per million parts.

6 Standard Deviations, or 6 σ = 99.99932 %, or 6.8 defects per million parts. (Six Sigma calls it 3.4, or one side of the mean.)

Probability of Completion

Probability of Completion questions ask you to find the mean, derive the standard deviation, and then determine where the measurement fits in the range. For example, a task has an optimistic duration of three days, a most likely duration of five days, and a pessimistic duration of ten days. The expected value, or mean, is 3 + (4 × 5) + 10 = 33; 33 ÷ 6 = 5.5 days. The Standard Deviation or 1σ = 10–3 = 7; 7 ÷ 6 = 1.17. You have an 84.15 percent probability of completing this task in 6.67 days. That's 1σ above the mean. Now the tricky part is this: Because 1σ on both sides of the mean represents 68.26 percent of the range of values, we're interested only in the portion above the mean — 68.26 ÷ 2 = 34.15%. Because the mean is defined to be 50 percent, just add 50 + 34.15 = 84.15%. You therefore have a probability of 15.85 percent of completion in 4.33 days, 97.73 percent in 7.84 days, and 99.87 percent in 9.01 days. This question format has a variant: What's the probability you won't complete the project in 9.01 days? The answer is: 1 – 99.87 = 0.13%.

Figure A-9 shows a Normal or Gaussian Distribution with probability intervals.

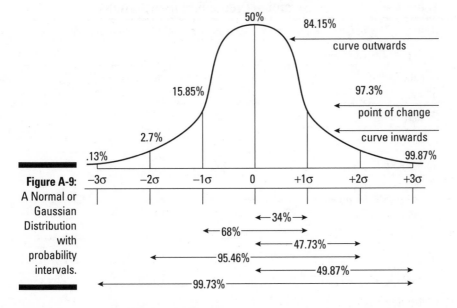

Figure A-9: A Normal or Gaussian Distribution with probability intervals.

Probability intervals on one side of the mean

   -3 Standard Deviations, –3σ =.13%

   -2 Standard Deviations, –2σ = 2.7%

   -1 Standard Deviation, –1σ = 15.85%

   Mean or expected value = 50%

   +1 Standard Deviation, +1σ = 34.13% — total on right side 84.15%

   +2 Standard Deviations, +2σ = 47.73% — total on right side 97.73%

   +3 Standard Deviations, +3σ = 49.87 — total on right side 99.87%

Some questions ask you to sum probability distributions. For these, you estimate the project totals, making several interim calculations on each individual activity. Calculate the mean, the standard deviation (sigma), and the variance for each activity. Remember that the correct formula depends on which distribution you're using, *in other words,* beta or triangular. Then you calculate the totals for the whole project. You calculate the project mean by summing down the column of each individual activity mean. You calculate the project variance by summing down the column of each individual activity variance. Now the trick is this: you derive the project standard deviation from the project variance, as its square root. Don't make the mistake of summing down the column of standard deviations! Make a mental note of the arrows in our example in Table A-2.

Table A-2		Summing Probability Distributions				
Activity	*Optimistic*	*Most Likely*	*Pessimistic*	*Mean*	*Sigma*	*Variance*
Triangular Distribution						
Feasibility Study	15	30	60	35	9	88
Requirements	30	60	90	60	12	150
Design	15	35	75	42	12	156
Construction	35	50	100	62	14	193
Testing	15	25	45	28	6	39
Acceptance Test	12	15	30	19	4	16
Deployment	5	<u>10</u>	30	<u>15</u>	5	<u>29</u>
		Sum↓		Sum↓	←	Sum↓
Estimated Project Totals	225			261	26	670
Beta Distribution						
Feasibility Study	15	30	60	33	8	56
Requirements	30	60	90	60	10	100
Design	15	35	75	38	10	100
Construction	35	50	100	56	11	117
Testing	15	25	45	27	5	25

Activity	Optimistic	Most Likely	Pessimistic	Mean	Sigma	Variance
Beta Distribution						
Acceptance Tests	12	15	30	17	3	9
Deployment	5	10	30	13	4	17
		Sum↓		Sum↓	←	Sum↓
		225		243	21	425

Total Standard Deviation (for the entire project) is the Square Root of the Sum of the Variances.

Variance = (Standard Deviation)^2

Notice that in both cases in Table A-2, the Project Mean is greater than the sum of the Most Likely estimates. If you mistakenly sum the row for the Standard deviations, you are way off — in the triangular, you get 64 instead of 26, and in the Beta, you get 51 instead of 21.

Process Capability Analysis

These are a group of simplified measurements for investigating the variability of a process and the spread of the specification limits. Notice this type of question refers to specification limits, not control limits! The engineering requirements for your products set the specification limits. Heed some warnings on their use: they don't measure specifically what's occurring in the process, and they're useful only when the underlying assumptions of the processes capabilities are satisfied. The main assumption is that the process must follow a normal distribution, where measurements fall between the traditional –3σ to +3σ. This accounts for 99.73% of all measurements.

Process capability refers to the normal variability of a process. It permits common-cause variability and indicates where you should investigate those disagreeable special causes resulting in out-of-control conditions. These indices compare the range of your process spread to the specification spread.

Generally three outcomes occur: a Capable Process, a Barely Capable Process, or a Not Capable Process. Here are the distinctions:

Capable process: When processes are capable, the tails of your process distribution fall inside the specification limits. It's therefore a reliable process, and it's in control. A capable process is the ideal of quality management because the product is consistent. It's described as 6σ < (USL – LSL). See Figure A-10.

Figure A-10:
Capable
processes.

Barely Capable process: In this outcome, the process spread just matches the control limits. When a process spread lands right on top of the specification spread, the process narrowly meets the specifications. The slightest variation could send the process spinning out of control. When processes are barely capable, the tails of your process distribution fall right on top of the control limits. It's described as $6\sigma = (USL - LSL)$. See Figure A-11.

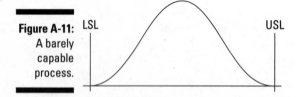

Figure A-11:
A barely
capable
process.

Not Capable process: When the tails of your process spread are wider than the specification limits, your process can't meet the specifications. This condition is described as $6\sigma > (USL - LSL)$. See Figure A-12. One of the purposes of quality management is to correct these conditions. This outcome represents an immediate *fix it* opportunity.

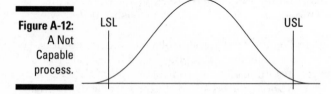

Figure A-12:
A Not
Capable
process.

Capability Index (Cp)

The simplest Capability Index, Cp, measures the ratio of the specification range to the process spread (which is six standard deviations, or 6σ — the traditional 3σ on both sides of the mean). Again, remember that this process is modeled on a normal distribution, so you should use 6σ in the divisor. When the process doesn't follow a normal distribution, the Cp is an inaccurate measure. It ignores the mean and measures the range of variability in the process. It relates more to current process performance — the precision of the process — than to potential capability.

Cp = USL – LSL ÷ 6σ

USL = Upper Specification Limit

LSL = Lower Specification Limit

Try this sample question: A project manager chooses a printing press to print documents bound into promotional booklets for marketing presentations. The project manager must have the paper cut 10 inches long, plus or minus 0.05 inches. The process has a standard deviation of 0.005 inches. What is the Process Capability Index of this process?

You calculate the Process Capability Index for this problem:

Process Capability Index Cp = USL – LSL ÷ 6σ

Cp = (10+0.05) – (10 – 0.05) ÷ 6 × (0.005) = 0.1 ÷ 0.03 = 3.33

You interpret reading the Cp indices this way: When Cp is less than 1, it's a *Not Capable Process,* and you have many defective parts. When Cp equals 1, it's a *Barely Capable Process,* and you have a few defective parts. When Cp is greater than 1, it's a *Capable Process*, and you have practically no defective parts at all.

Let's take a quick peek at what practically *no defectives* really means. When the Cp=1.00, about 2,700 parts per million (ppm) are nonconforming or defective. This 0.27 percent represents what the 3σ range doesn't cover (as in 1 – 99.73 percent). When the Cp = 1.33, about 64 ppm are nonconforming or defective. This .0064 percent represents 4σ. When the Cp = 1.67, about 6 ppm are nonconforming or defective. This .000057 percent represents over 5σ. That's the concept of Six Sigma — tighter limits and fewer defects.

Capability Ratio (CR)

The inverse of the Capability Index Cp is the Capability Ratio (CR). It's the percentage of the specification range occupied by the process range.

CR = Capability Ratio = 1 ÷ Cp ×100% = 6σ ÷ USL – LSL × 100%

Process Capability Index (Cpk)

A major weakness in Cp is that processes don't have to be centered on the mean, so the Process Capability Index (Cpk) was derived to estimate the relative position of the mean with the specification limits. It's one of those worst-case scenario estimates that compares the closest specification limit to the mean. Cpk relates to the accuracy of the process.

Cpk = *Minimum* (USL – μ ÷ 3σ *or* μ – LSL ÷ 3σ)

Remember two key points with Cpk. First, the limit closest to the specification limit is either the lower or the upper limit — but not both; it's an *either-or* condition. That's what the formula means by the *minimum*. Second, because we're working here on only one side of the mean, we use 3σ, not 6σ.

The related portions of Cpk are formulas for unilateral specification at the upper limit, Cpu, and for unilateral specification at the lower limit, Cpl:

$$Cpu = USL - \mu \times 3\sigma$$

$$Cpl = \mu - LSL \times 3\sigma$$

In the Cpu and Cpl formulas, the upper and lower specification limits refer to the allowable spread, while the 3σ denominator refers to the actual spread.

Risk Formulas

The three components of a risk include:

- Risk Event (R)
- Probability (P) of Risk Event
- Impact (I) of Risk Event. (Also called *Dollar Amount at Stake*, or *Risk Event Value*.)

$$Risk = P \times^* I$$

The Risk Probability of an identified Risk Event occurring is

Risk Probability = Frequency of Relevant Events ÷ Total Number of Possible Events

The financial impact (Dollar Amount at Stake) of an identified Risk Event equals the Cost of the Investment Lost (if a risk event occurs) plus the Cost to Restore Status Quo.

Impact (Dollar Amount at Stake) = Cost of the Investment Lost + Cost to Restore Status Quo

Expected Monetary Value is the product of an identified risk event's probability of occurrence and the resulting gain (or loss). If you have a 50 percent probability that a movie's daily shooting will be delayed due to rain, and this delay will result in a $10,000 loss, the expected monetary value of the rain event is $5,000 (.5 × $10,000). This can also be called *risk exposure* or *Risk Event Status*. You'll likely find these types of Risk Planning questions on the exam.

Expected Monetary Value = Risk Probability × Dollar Amount at Stake

Availability Formulas

Operational Availability is the Mean Time Between Maintenance (MTBM) divided by sum of MTBM plus Mean Down Time (MDT):

Operational Availability = MTBM ÷ MTBM+MDT

Inherent Availability is the period spent waiting for corrective action and maintenance. Inherent Availability equals mean time between failures (MTBF) divided by sum of MTBF plus mean time to repair (MTTR). Application of this formula assumes ideal conditions can be used to establish trade-offs between reliability (as measured by MTBF) and maintainability (as measured by MTTR)

Inherent Availability = MTBF ÷ MTBF+MTTR

Earned Value Analysis

Some EVA questions will almost certainly appear on your exam. Because many types of EVA word problems can be derived from a single scenario, these questions often appear in pairs or in sets. Remember that each of these questions may be separated by many other, unrelated questions, so as you encounter them, mark them on your screen for later recall, and remember where your calculations are on the scratch paper! Some data in one question might help you solve the others. Don't redo the calculations! Where terminology has changed as a result of revisions to the *PMBOK Guide,* know both the new term and the old term and be able to translate between them.

You can calculate EV using units in either dollars or in terms of labor — hours or days. You should also be able to translate labor hours into dollars. A question can give you the budget figures (Present Value, PV, or Earned Value, EV) as either $10,000 or 100 labor hours, and the expenditures (Actual Cost, AC) as either $12,000 or 120 labor hours.

✔ **Planned Value** (PV), formerly Budgeted Cost of Work Scheduled (BCWS): PV shows the work scheduled to be performed, as well as the authorized budget to accomplish the scheduled work. As the performance measurement baseline, PV indicates how much work should be done. It's a budgetary number that can't be spent.

✔ **Earned Value** (EV), formerly Budgeted Cost of Work Performed (BCWP): EV shows the physical work actually accomplished as well as the authorized budget for this work. It shows the *progress* the project makes. It's expressed in terms of the value of work completed as compared to your baseline budget. When the project is completed, EV equals PV (BCWP=BCWS). You can work in either dollars or hours. To convert labor hours, multiply the budgeted hours to complete a task by the budgeted labor rate. As with PV, EV is a budgetary number that can't be spent.

> ✔ **Actual Cost** (AC), formerly Actual Cost of Work Performed (ACWP): AC shows the real cost of the work the team has completed. This number will come from the organization's accounting system. This is a real expenditure — representing funds rather than PV or EV, which are budgets.

Figure A-13 shows the budget as an S-curve. Figure A-14 shows all the terms.

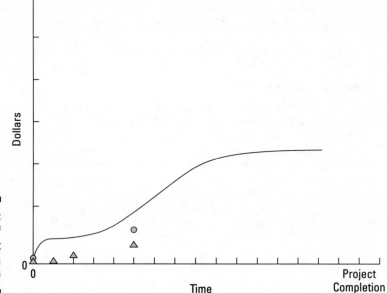

Figure A-13:
S-curve of
the budget
(spending
plan)

Cost Variance: Compares the Earned Value (Budgeted Cost of Work Performed) to Actual Cost of (Actual Cost of Work Performed). If it's positive, you're under budget. If it's negative, you're over budget — resulting in a cost overrun.

Cost Variance = EV − AC (BCWP − ACWP)

Variance = Planned − Actual

Schedule Variance: Compares what schedule progress the team has actually accomplished to what should have been accomplished according to the planned schedule. If SV is positive, you're ahead of schedule. If SV is negative, you're behind schedule; the work completed is less than what was planned.

Schedule Variance = EV − PV (BCWP − BCWS)

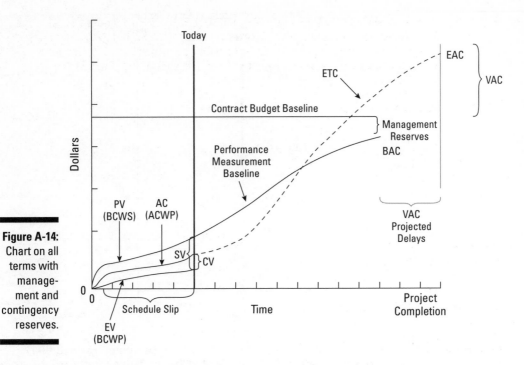

Figure A-14: Chart on all terms with management and contingency reserves.

Cost Performance Index (CPI): Tells how much (as a percentage) you're getting out of each dollar spent on the project. CPI is often expressed in terms of *cost efficiency* — the value earned per unit actual cost. It's often expressed in terms of the *efficiency of the budget.* If the result is greater than 1, the CPI is good: For example, you get $1.15 in return for every dollar spent. If it's less than 1, CPI is bad — the project is spending more funds than budgeted: For example, , you get only $0.85 in return for every dollar spent.

$$CPI = EV \div AC \ (BCWP \div ACWP)$$

Schedule Performance Index (SPI): Tells how much (percentage) you're getting out of each dollar spent on the schedule. SPI is often expressed in terms of *schedule efficiency* — the percent of work performed out of the total work scheduled. If the result is greater than 1, the SPI is good: For example, you get $1.15 in return for every dollar spent. If it's less than 1, CPI is bad: For example, you get $0.85 in return for every dollar spent.

$$SPI = EV \div PV \ (BCWP \div BCWS)$$

Figure A-15 shows EV in a Gantt chart.

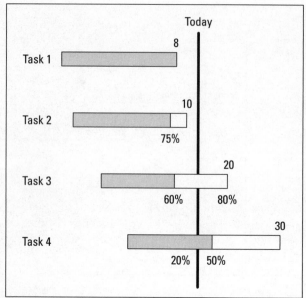

Figure A-15:
Gantt
chart EV.

This example shows how to figure the PV (BCWS) by summing the dollar costs of work scheduled at the point labeled Today. Tasks 1 and 2 were planned to be completed by today, so their PV is the top figure. Task 3 was planned to have completed only 80 percent of the $20 task, or $16. you determine the Earned Value (BCWP) by summing work actually accomplished, shown in gray shading. Task 2 earned 75 percent of the $10 task, or $7.50: and Task 3 completed only 60 percent of the $20 task, or $12. Task 4 is ahead of schedule.

PV (BCWS) = 8 + 10 + 16 + 6 = $40

EV (BCWP) = 8 + 7.5 + 12 + 15 = $42.5

AC (ACWP) = $35 (from Cost Accounting System)

Schedule Variance = 42.5 − 40=$2.5

Schedule Performance Index = 42.5 ÷ 40 = 1.06%

Cost Variance = 42.5 − 35=$7.5

Cost Performance Index = 42.5 ÷ 35 = 1.21

It appears that this sample project is ever so slightly ahead of schedule and under budget.

If the SPI is greater than 1.0, the project is ahead of schedule. If the SPI equals 1.0, then the project is right on schedule. If the SPI is less than 1.0, the project is behind schedule. SPI measurements are often used in forecasting project completion date.

Figure A-16 shows a project ahead of schedule. Figure A-17 shows a project behind schedule. Figure A-18 doesn't provide enough information.

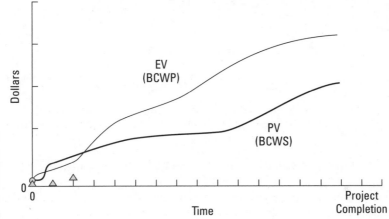

Figure A-16:
This project
is ahead of
schedule.

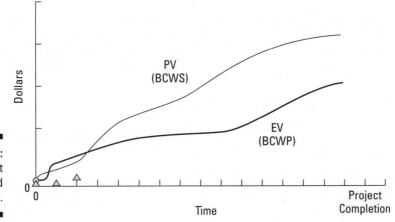

Figure A-17:
This project
is behind
schedule.

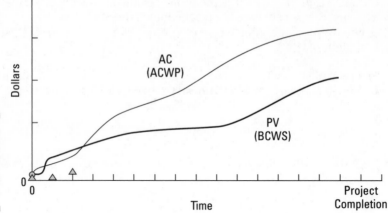

Figure A-18:
Can't tell
whether this
project in on
schedule.

Cost variance percentage: Indicates the percentage you're getting out of each dollar spent on the budget:

Cost Variance Percentage = CV ÷ EV × 100 (CV ÷ BCWP × 100)

Schedule variance percentage: Indicates the percentage you're ahead or behind schedule for the work the team accomplished:

Schedule Variance Percentage = SV ÷ PV × 100 (SV ÷ BCWS × 100)

Cumulative CPI: The sum of individual EV ÷ AC (BCWP × ACWP) is often used in calculating Estimate At Completion (EAC). Cumulative CPI rarely varies by 10 percent after a project is 20 percent complete. Many project managers use To Complete Performance Index (TCPI) to forecast final costs (see the further explanation of TCPI later in this section):

TCPI = (BAC − EV) ÷ (BAC − AC)

Variance At Completion (VAC): Compares what the project should cost to what the project is expected to cost:

Variance at Completion = Budget at Completion minus Estimate at Completion

VAC = BAC − EAC

Estimate at Completion (EAC)

Estimate at Completion (EAC): Is an educated guess. Several formulas have been proposed to derive EAC, which estimates final costs. It's based on project performance and risk quantification. Several estimating techniques are available:

> ✔ ACWP + Remaining Project Budget Modified (Divided) by a Performance Factor (Usually the Cost Performance Index).
>
> ✔ ACWP + New Estimate for All Remaining Work. Used when past performance indicates original estimates are fundamentally flawed. AC + ETC is used when you believe the original estimates are flawed.
>
> ✔ ACWP + Remaining Budget. Used when current variances are viewed as atypical.
>
> ✔ AC + BAC – EV is used when you don't expect future variances in the rate of work being performed.
>
> ✔ AC + ((BAC – EV) ÷ TCPI) is used when you expect future variances.

Budget at Completion (BAC): Tells how much is budgeted for the total project. BAC is the budget at completion, the total budgeted cost.

The ETC and EAC represent the funds required for work.

$$EAC = BAC \div CPI$$

Estimate to Completion (ETC) = EAC – AC or (BAC – EV) ÷ CPI

Variance at Completion (VAR) = BAC – EAC

Percent Spent = AC ÷ BAC

To Complete Performance Index

As stated in the previous discussion of Cumulative CPI, the TCPI formula is:

> To Complete Performance Index = (Budget at Completion minus Budgeted Cost of Work Performed) divided by (Estimate at Completion minus Actual Cost of Work Performed)
>
> TCPI = BAC – EV ÷ (EAC – AC)

TCPI compares the Work Remaining against the remaining budget, giving the efficiency that must be achieved to complete the remaining work with the remaining money. TCPI greater than 1 indicates a need to increase performance to stay within the budget. TCPI less than 1 indicates that either performance can actually decrease within the budget or you can improve quality.

> Percent Complete = Earned Value divided by Budget at Completion times 100. It compares Work Completed to Total Work.
>
> Percent Complete = EV ÷ BAC × 100
>
> Percent Spent = Actual Cost ÷ Estimate at Completion × 100
>
> Percent Spent = AC ÷ EAC × 100

Calculation of slack and Critical Path

The notion of slack (or *float*) is crucial to calculating The Critical Path in a network of interconnected tasks:

> Slack (Float) = Latest Time for Completion minus Earliest Time for Completion

> Slack = $T_l - T_e$

The Critical Path is the series of connected tasks for which Slack = 0; ($T_l - T_e = 0$).

If slack is greater than zero, some "extra" time is available. When slack equals zero, the early and late dates are the same, and the task is critical. When slack is less than zero (negative slack), you can't meet the scheduled completion date.

All variance and index formulas begin with Earned Value (BCWP).

> Variance uses the difference between plan minus actual.

> Index is always stated as a percentage. It's plan divided by actual.

> Cost formulas use AC (ACWP).

> Schedule formulas use PV (BCWS).

Material and Labor Variances

A number of formulas are available for calculating the variances in costs of labor and materials.

Material Price Variance

The Material Price Variance is defined as:

> Material Price Variance = Planned Price – Actual Price

A positive result is favorable; a negative result is unfavorable.

Total Material Price Variance is the difference between the planned and actual price (Material Price Variance) times the Actual Units used:

> Total Material Price Variance = Actual Units × (Planned Price – Actual Price)

A positive result is favorable; a negative result is unfavorable.

Material Usage Variance

The Material Usage Variance is defined as:

Material Usage Variance = Planned Usage − Actual Usage

A positive result is favorable; a negative result is unfavorable.

Labor Rate Variance

The Labor Rate Variance is defined as:

Labor Rate Variance = Budgeted Rate − Actual Rate

A positive result is favorable; a negative result is unfavorable.

A related measurement is Labor Efficiency Variance, which is the Labor Efficiency Variance equals Planned Labor Hours minus Actual Labor Hours.

Labor Efficiency Variance = Planned Labor Hours − Actual Labor Hours

A positive result is favorable; a negative result is unfavorable.

Total Labor Rate Variance is the difference in budgeted and actual labor rates (Labor Efficiency Variance) times the Actual Labor Hours used:

Total Labor Rate Variance = Actual Labor Hours × (Budgeted Rate − Actual Rate)

A positive result is favorable; a negative result is unfavorable.

Total Labor Efficiency Variance uses the Labor Efficiency Variance, which is the Planned Labor Hours minus the Actual Labor Hours.

Total Labor Efficiency Variance = Labor Efficiency Variance × Planned Labor Rate

A positive result is favorable; a negative result is unfavorable.

Total Material Usage Variance is Material Usage Variance (Planned Usage minus the Actual Usage) times the Planned Material Price:

Total Material Usage Variance = Material Usage Variance × Planned Material Price

A positive result is favorable; a negative result is unfavorable.

Communication paths

Communication channels, or paths, tell you how many different combinations of communication a group or project team has. See Figure A-19. The formula for the number of communication paths is

$n(n - 1) \div 2$

Where n = number of people

An example with 5 people in the team is

$5(5 - 1) = 5(4); 5(4) = 20; 20 \div 2 = 10$ channels

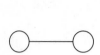

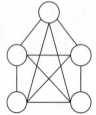

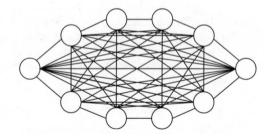

Figure A-19: Communication paths.

Equivalent worth

Equivalent worth describes several types of formulas that calculate the time value of money: Future Value, Present Value, Net Present Value, and Internal Rate of Return. These formulas all deal with the following variables:

- ✔ F = Future Amount
- ✔ P = Present Amount
- ✔ N = Periods
- ✔ n = Year from Date of Investment
- ✔ i = Interest Rate (Cost of Capital, Minimal Acceptable Rate of Return)

Equivalent Worth questions generally show a graphic with the numbers in a table, and then as you to apply them to a word problem. In doing so, you have to select one of the following formulas.

Future value

Future value (FV): The value at some future time of a present amount of money (or a series of payments) at a known interest rate. A typical question asks: You borrow $X for N years. How much do you need to repay at end year N?

> FV = Principal + (Principal $\times$ Interest)
>
> Future Value (FV) = $PV(1 + r)^n$

Alternatively, you can solve the problem as:

> FV = Amount $\times$ 1 $\div$ PV
>
> PV = Present Value
>
> n = Number of Periods
>
> r = Discount Rate or Interest Rate

Present value

Present value (PV): The total amount that a series of future payments is worth today using a specified rate of return.

> PV = FV $\div$ $(1 + i)^n$
>
> FV = Future Value
>
> n = Number of Periods
>
> i = Discount Rate

Net present value

Net present value (NPV): A variation of present value. When you've mastered PV, NPV is simple. NPV analysis discounts all expected future cash inflows and outflows to the present. To calculate the NPV, calculate the present value of future payments, and then subtract investments. If the result is positive, the investment should be favorably considered. If it's negative, forget it.

> **Net present value** = $CF_0 + CF_1 \div (1 + r)^1 + CF_2 \div (1 + r)^2 + CF_3 \div (1 + r)^3 + CF_n \div (1 + r)^n$
>
> CF_x = cash flow in period x. Initial cost (CF_0) is a negative number.
>
> n = Number of Periods
>
> r = Discount Rate

Internal Rate of Return

Internal Rate of Return (IRR): The interest rate when the sum of the Net Cash Flows for each year is divided by $(1 + i)^n$, equals the initial investment (Net Present Value = 0).

Initial Investment $= CF_1 \div (1 + r)^1 + CF_2 \div (1 + r)^2 + CF_3 \div (1 + r)^3 + CF_n \div (1 + r)^n$

CF_x = Cash Flow in Period x

n = Number of Periods

r = Internal Rate of Return or Discount Rate

This sample question deals with both NPV and IRR: What is the NPV for an Investment of $13,250 with cash flows of $4,000 for each of the next 4 years at 8 percent? What is the IRR?

NPV = [$4,000(0.926) + $4,000(0.857) + $4,000(0.794) + $4,000(0.735) − $13,250(1.0)]

NPV = $3,704 + $3,428 + $3,176 + $2,940 − $13,250

NPV = <$2>

Therefore, the IRR is slightly less than 8 percent.

Paybacks and benefits

Two types of formulas deal with assessing the desirability of investments: Payback analysis and benefit/cost ratio.

Payback Analysis

Payback period: The amount of time (years or months) to recoup the dollars invested in a project. Shorter payback periods are desired. The formula for Payback Period is straightforward:

Payback Period = Costs ÷ Annual Cash Inflow

Benefit/cost ratio

Benefit÷/cost ratio: The Expected Revenues ÷ Expected Costs. To apply this formula, you measure benefits, or the paybacks, to the total costs of the project. For PV of Revenue, assume the project end date, but the PV of Costs is in the initial period. It's also called *Savings Investment Ratio*. The higher the ratio, the better. If the ratio is greater than 1, benefits outweigh costs.

BCR=PV of Revenue ÷ PV of Costs

Sample question: What is the benefit/cost ratio for a project with $6,000,000 in revenue over 2 years with $4,500,000 in costs with an 8 percent rate?

BCR = $6,000,000 × 0.857 = $4,500,000

$5,142,000 ÷ $4,500,000 = 1.14

You can find the PV by multiplying using 0.857, the discounted interest rate for 2 years. Or, you can divide by $(1+.08)^2$ or 1.17.

Contracts

Several types of question assess the costs of contracts. Recall that some types of contracts provide financial incentives for the seller to perform. In the Cost-Plus-Incentive Fee (CPIF) contract type, you pay sellers for allowable performance costs along with a predetermined fee and an incentive bonus. If the final costs are less than the planned costs (because the seller has performed well), both the buyer and seller benefit from this cost savings. The amount of this cost saving is based on a pre-negotiated sharing formula, reflecting the risks of each party. The formulas give the amounts both parties split, the share that is the seller's performance bonus, and the total contract cost. The most complex contract type is Fixed Price-Plus-Incentive Fee (FPI), which provides stricter incentives to decrease costs. If costs exceed a ceiling, then the seller is penalized and receives no profits. The buyer pays no more than the ceiling price, called the *point of assumption*. For every dollar the seller reduces costs below this target cost, both the seller and buyer split the savings, according to the share ratio.

The Incentive Fee is a performance bonus to the seller; sometimes there are non-performance penalties that you need to subtract. When the project comes in under the contract, the buyer and seller often split the savings. This split is called the *sharing ratio*. The sharing ratio always lists the Buyer first and then the Seller. *Seller ratio* is the seller's portion of the sharing ratio. The Incentive Fee and Final Price calculations include: Target Cost, Target Fee, Target Price, Sharing Ratio (buyer–seller), and Actual Cost.

Incentive Fee = (Target Cost – Actual Cost) × Seller Ratio (%)

Total Fee = Fee + Target Fee

Final Price = Actual Cost + Total Fee

Figure A-20 shows contract risks.

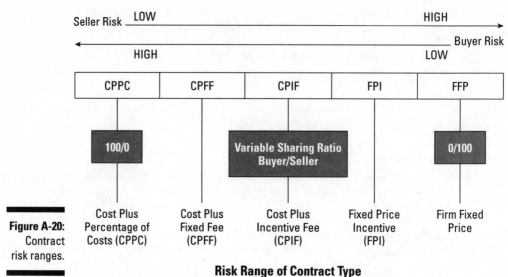

Figure A-20:
Contract
risk ranges.

Risk Range of Contract Type

Estimating Depreciation

One type of math question involves calculating depreciation, or the reduction in value of an asset over time.

The key cost accounting numbers in understanding depreciation are: useful life, period number, amount of depreciation, book (original) value, and residual value. You measure the useful life of the asset in terms of some number of years (*that is,* 1 year, 2 years, 5 years, 10 years, and so on). The useful life describes how long the asset can reasonably be expected to remain in service. For example, the useful life of an automobile might be three years, for accounting purposes. The useful life of a building might be 20 years. The period number is also measured in years. In Straight Line and Sum of the Years' Digits, you subtract a salvage, or residual, value. Declining Balance and Double Declining Balance use a ratio instead.

Straight Line Depreciation: A simple average. For each year, take the same amount of depreciation against the value of the asset:

SL = Book Value ÷ Life

Sum-of-the-Years'-Digits (SYD): Provides an accelerated depreciation method. In each year you depreciate the value of the asset by a fraction of the sum of the years.

Depreciation = (Book Value – Salvage Value) × Year ÷ Sum of the Years' Digits

For example, using a 3-year asset, the denominator would be 1 + 2 + 3 = 6. For 5 years, the denominator would be 1 + 2 + 3 + 4 + 5 = 15.

Declining Balance (DB): Provides another accelerated method. Instead of entering a salvage value, you enter the percentage of how much the asset depreciates each year. For the fastest acceleration method, use Double Declining Balance (DDB). In DDB just enter 200 percent for the rate.

DDB Double-Declining Balance = Book Value × Rate % ÷ Life

Appendix B

Practice Exam

Practice Exam Rules

▶ One hour time limit

▶ 35 questions correct to pass

▶ 49 questions

▶ Treat this exam as a closed book: Don't look ahead (to the answer) or behind (to the chapters)

*H*ere is a sample exam to help prepare you for Game Day.

The actual exam contains 200 questions, and you'll have four hours to complete them. That's how we derived one hour for 49 questions. The actual passing grade is 137 questions out of 200, or 69 percent. If you get 80 percent or better (40 questions) on the practice exam, you're in very good shape for the real exam. If you get 100 percent correct, we salute you.

These are the same *types* of questions that will likely appear on the exam, but you probably won't see these questions verbatim on the exam. (As we've coached repeatedly, beware of variants and pick out the key words so you understand the question's pattern.) If you miss a question, reread the section in the book that covers that topic. The answers guide you to the correct chapter and exam objective.

Like the actual exam, each question has only one correct answer. Choose the best answer, even if you think it is only the least incorrect. Always favor the PMI mindset over your own experience or interpretations.

Practice Exam

1 What is the mean of: 20, 80, 30, and 70?

A ○ 40

B ○ 45

C ○ 50

D ○ 60

2 What is the median of: 20, 80, 30, 70, and 40?

A ○ 40

B ○ 45

C ○ 50

D ○ 60

3 You are going to a Change Control Board meeting. What do you need to take with you?

A ○ Scope statement

B ○ Performance measurements

C ○ Corrective actions

D ○ Performance Reports

4 In developing the test plan, you determine whether your product meets the requirements. What do you use to figure out what's important?

A ○ Control charts

B ○ Statistical sampling

C ○ Pareto diagrams

D ○ Trend Analysis

5 Insurance is an example of risk____?

A ○ Avoidance

B ○ Transference

C ○ Mitigation

D ○ Acceptance

6 To make your deadlines, you reduce the scope of the project to eliminate a high-risk activity. What type of risk response strategy are you using?

A ○ Avoidance

B ○ Transference

C ○ Mitigation

D ○ Acceptance

7 In setting up your new software project, you determine that a module containing customer data needs to be delayed to another phase because the marketing staff needs to clean up errors in its customer lists. What type of risk response strategy are you using?

A ○ Avoidance
B ○ Transference
C ○ Mitigation
D ○ Acceptance

8 The PV (BCWS) is $100,500, the EV (BCWP) is $100,500, and the AC (ACWP) is $75,750. What can you tell about the project's performance?

A ○ Behind schedule, under budget
B ○ Over budget, ahead of schedule
C ○ On schedule, under budget
D ○ On budget, behind schedule

9 The sponsor wants you to take an aggressive schedule approach where you have a 20% probability of losing $100,000 and an 80% probability of making $25,000. What's the expected monetary value?

A ○ $0
B ○ $20,000
C ○ $40,000
D ○ $25,000

10 An Engineering manager counters with a conservative schedule by which you determine the project has a 40% probability of losing $60,000 and a 60% probability of making $50,000. What's the expected monetary value?

A ○ $0
B ○ $6,000
C ○ $30,000
D ○ $42,000

11 A task has an optimistic time of three days, a most likely time of five days, and a pessimistic time of ten days. What is the estimated time for this task with a Beta Distribution using PERT-weighted average approximations?

A ○ 5
B ○ 5.5
C ○ 6
D ○ 10

12 A milestone for developing technical requirements has an optimistic time of 30 days, a most likely time of 50 days, and a pessimistic time of 75 days. What's the probability of completing the requirements within 65 days?

   A ○ 95.5%

   B ○ 97.73%

   C ○ 99.73%

   D ○ 99.87%

13 A subassembly contains two parts. The reliability of the first part is .90%, and the reliability of the second part is .95%. What is the system reliability for this subassembly when the components are connected in parallel?

   A ○ 86%

   B ○ 92.5%

   C ○ 97.75%

   D ○ 99%

14 _____assesses whether you can make a new product with existing technology, human resources, skills, knowledge, and materials at a cost compatible with market expectations.

   A ○ Availability

   B ○ Producibility

   C ○ Reliability

   D ○ Operability

15 How many communication channels do you have with eight people on the team?

   A ○ 16

   B ○ 28

   C ○ 32

   D ○ 56

16 A task has an optimistic time of three days, a most likely time of five days, and a pessimistic time of ten days. What is the estimated time for this task using CPM? (Round up all fractional days.)

   A ○ 4

   B ○ 5

   C ○ 6

   D ○ 8

17 You observe the time that diners in Ace Mall restaurants take for meals. The table turnover rate at Ace Café is a normally distributed process with a mean of 48 minutes and standard deviation of 8 minutes. Estimate the percentage of guests who finish eating in 44 to 56 minutes.

A ○ 17%
B ○ 34%
C ○ 51%
D ○ 68%

18 You observe the time that diners in Ace Mall restaurants take for meals. The table turnover rate at Ace Café is a normally distributed process with a mean of 48 minutes and standard deviation of 8 minutes. Estimate the percentage of diners who take more than 45 minutes to finish their meals.

A ○ 48%
B ○ 68%
C ○ 71%
D ○ 84%

19 In implementing a preventative maintenance system at Universal Studios Hollywood, you find fittings for a part on the Jurassic Park ride are machined to a diameter of 2.0 inches, with a tolerance of 0.05 inches. Fittings with a diameter of greater than 2.05 inches are reworked at a cost of $5.00 each. Fittings with a diameter less than 1.96 inches are scrapped at a cost of $10.00. Measurements of 1,000 samples form a normal distribution, with a mean of 2.01 inches and a standard deviation of 0.05 inches. The supplier makes a batch of 1,000 fittings. Estimate the total cost of scrap and rework for your supplier.

A ○ $1,600
B ○ $2,400
C ○ $2,800
D ○ $3,200

20 As part of photographic processing at an imaging facility, you produce a quality control chart of color densitometry and gamma (contrast index) readings with a standard deviation of six units. Every hour three sample tests of the chemical process are taken, and you plot the mean. You are trying to determine if the developer is over- or under-replenished, if the film was over- or underdeveloped, and if the processing temperature was too high or too low. What is the standard deviation of the sample mean?

A ○ 2
B ○ 2.33
C ○ 3
D ○ 3.33

21 What is the benefit cost ratio for a project with $7,000,000 in revenue over two years with $4,500,000 in costs with an 8% rate?

A ○ 1.2
B ○ 1.24
C ○ 1.33
D ○ 1.56

22 A movie production requires a camera package rental for four months. You can rent the camera package for $20,000 per month. You have the option to prepay for the equipment rental, making a lump-sum payment when the camera rental trucks arrive at your location, or you can pay at the end of each month. Using a discount rate of 1% per month, what would be the maximum prepayment you'd make?

A ○ $76,056
B ○ $78,039
C ○ $80,000
D ○ $82,020

23 As a recently hired project manager, what should you rely on the most to improve your chances of success?

A ○ Project management methodology
B ○ Historical information
C ○ Following generally accepted practices
D ○ Following standards

24 In a Fixed Price plus Incentive Fee (FPI) contract, the target cost was $1,300,000, the actual cost was $1,900,000, and the ceiling was set at $1,500,000. The sharing ratio was set at 70/30, the target fee was $500,000, and the seller's fee was $250,000. What is the seller's profit?

A ○ $0
B ○ $500,000
C ○ $750,000
D ○ $2,250,000

25 The project manager finds that his sponsor and the customers have different views of the scope. How should the project manager proceed?

A ○ Perform a Business Needs Analysis.
B ○ Examine the scope statement for the project objectives and deliverables.
C ○ Use this as opportunity to negotiate requirement options along the lines of the triple constraint.
D ○ Use this conflict as an opportunity to educate both parties on project management.

26 Marketing has imposed a delivery date for your project. They want to show your new product at a trade show. This is an example of a _____.

A ○ Milestone

B ○ Deadline

C ○ Constraint

D ○ Risk

27 The concept of progressive elaboration of the project plan is called_____.

A ○ Requirements Analysis

B ○ Refinement

C ○ Iterative planning

D ○ Rolling wave planning

28 At a progress review meeting, you get a verbal report from the Engineering manager that critical analysis tasks have been completed. When you ask to see the results, the Engineering manager says that members of his team are moving forward with their results and documenting the analysis would delay them. How would the project manager best handle the situation?

A ○ Mark the tasks as 100% complete on the schedule.

B ○ Mark the tasks as 0% complete on the schedule. Check the task dependencies, and note this issue on Progress Reports.

C ○ Request documenting the analysis; if necessary, require them to recreate the analysis; mark the tasks as 50% complete on the schedule.

D ○ Request to inspect the analysis.

29 During the latter portion of your development phase, your metrics indicate your SPI is .91, and your CPI is 1.2. You also discover that unanticipated schedule delays will prevent you from completing the project on the agreed deadline. What should the project manager do?

A ○ Crash the schedule by providing overtime.

B ○ Reduce the product's scope.

C ○ Fast-track the schedule by performing the next phase's tasks in parallel.

D ○ Request schedule delays.

30 A problem has arisen on the project that requires the team's attention. What should you do first?

A ○ Authorize rework.

B ○ Issue a change request.

C ○ Meet with the sponsor for advice.

D ○ Take corrective action.

31 **Which of the following is not a cost of quality?**

A ○ Fixing software bugs
B ○ Application design omissions
C ○ Change requests
D ○ Rework

32 **Continuous Improvement is a key philosophical principle of _____.**

A ○ Zero defects
B ○ Quality Circles
C ○ Kanban
D ○ Kaizen

33 **Which of the following is not a Cost of Conformance?**

A ○ Training
B ○ Expediting
C ○ Process control
D ○ Process validation

34 **Which of the following is not a Cost of Nonconformance?**

A ○ Warranty repairs
B ○ Scrap
C ○ Product design validation
D ○ Expediting

35 **Which is not a stakeholder risk tolerance?**

A ○ Risk taker
B ○ Risk adverse
C ○ Risk neutral
D ○ Risk negative

36 **As project manager, you need to determine which risks have the greatest impact on the project. Which of the following should you use?**

A ○ Interviewing
B ○ Decision-tree analysis
C ○ Sensitivity Analysis
D ○ Simulation

37 **A warranty is an example of risk _____.**

A ○ Avoidance
B ○ Transference
C ○ Acceptance
D ○ Mitigation

38 Some activities will run over schedule. Your customer decides that the desired product features are more important to him than any schedule overrun. What type of risk response is the customer using?

A ○ Avoidance

B ○ Transference

C ○ Acceptance

D ○ Mitigation

39 QC audits, continuous-improvement targets, and personnel guidelines are examples of _____.

A ○ Organizational policies

B ○ Organizational procedures

C ○ Constraints

D ○ Preventive action

40 Which is not a tool and technique for Source Selection?

A ○ Weighting systems

B ○ Systems

C ○ Evaluation criteria

D ○ Contract negotiation

41 Which of the following is not an example of Team Building?

A ○ Increased responsibility

B ○ Promotions

C ○ Improved working conditions

D ○ A separate office

42 _____ describes what an element is and how the Quality Control process measures it.

A ○ Metrics

B ○ Quality management plan

C ○ Quality definitions

D ○ Quality Control Measurements

43 Which of the following is not a configuration management process?

A ○ Identifying and documenting the functional and physical characteristics of an item or a system

B ○ Controlling any changes to identified characteristics

C ○ Recording and reporting both the change and its status

D ○ Approving the product of the project or phase needs to be prepared

44 As project manager, the single most important factor in controlling *scope creep* is to_____.

A ◯ Don't exceed available resources.

B ◯ Insist on defining scope at the beginning.

C ◯ Insist that all changes be approved.

D ◯ Insist that all changes be made by a formal change request.

45 The amount of time an activity may be delayed from its early start date without delaying the project finish date includes all the following except_____.

A ◯ Slack

B ◯ Float

C ◯ Path float

D ◯ Lag

46 Schedule risk entails all the following except_____.

A ◯ Activity duration

B ◯ Duration along a path

C ◯ Resource leveling

D ◯ Points where parallel paths merge

47 Characters describing milestones include all except _____.

A ◯ They have a fixed duration.

B ◯ They provide kill points.

C ◯ They mark the start or end of a key event.

D ◯ They don't require resources.

48 The process that divides major project deliverables into manageable components is called____.

A ◯ Initiation

B ◯ Scope Planning

C ◯ Scope Definition

D ◯ Project Plan Development

49 The project plan is a composite document collected from the nine knowledge areas, which contain subsidiary management plans. In which Time process does the schedule management plan first appear?

A ◯ Activity Definition

B ◯ Activity Sequencing

C ◯ Activity Duration Estimating

D ◯ Schedule Development

Practice Exam Answers

1 **B,** 50. 20 + 80 + 30 + 70 ÷ 4 = 200 ÷ 4 = 50. See Appendix A for the mean formula.

2 **A,** 40. Reorder the list: 20, 30, 40, 70, 80. Take the middle number. See Appendix A for the median formula.

3 **D,** Performance Reports. This pattern asks for you to include an *input*. It tests your understanding of the relationship among facts, principles, and methods. See the information on Performance Reporting in Chapter 12.

4 **C,** Pareto diagrams. They help you rank by order of importance. This pattern asks for tools and techniques. It tests your understanding of methods. For more information on quality control, see Chapter 12.

5 **B,** Transference. This pattern asks for tools and techniques. It tests your understanding of risk methods. See *PMBOK Guide,* p. 142, and the information on Risk Response Planning in Chapter 10. This question is a tricky, because of the updates to *PMBOK Guide.* The older version didn't include Transference and put insurance under Mitigation.

6 **A,** Avoidance. The key word is *eliminate.* This pattern asks for tools and techniques. It tests your understanding of risk methods. See *PMBOK Guide,* p. 142, and the information on Risk Response Planning in Chapter 10.

7 **C,** Mitigation. You reduce a portion of the risk to an acceptable limit with a less complex process. The risk isn't totally avoided. This pattern asks for tools and techniques. It tests your understanding of risk methods. See *PMBOK Guide* p. 142 and the information on Risk Response Planning in Chapter 10.

8 **C,** On schedule, under budget. The question tests your understanding of EV methods and formulas. See Appendix A for the mean formula, and Table 12-1 in Chapter 12 for more information on schedule and budget performance.

9 **A,** $0. The expected monetary value is the probability of .20 × –100,000 = –20,000 plus the probability of .80 × 25,000 = 20,000; –$20,000 + $20,000 = $0. See Appendix A for the expected monetary value formula and *PMBOK Guide* p. 119.

10 **B,** $6,000. The expected monetary value is the probability of .40 × –60,000 = –24,000 plus the probability of .60 × 50,000 = 30,000; –$24,000 + $30,000 = $6,000. See Appendix A for the expected monetary value formula and *PMBOK Guide* p. 119.

11 **B,** 5.5 days. The calculation is: 3 + (5 × 4) + 10 = 33; 33 ÷ 6 = 5.5 days. The Mean or Expected Value = (Total Optimistic Estimate + 4 × Most Likely Estimate + Total Pessimistic Estimate) ÷ 6. See Appendix A for the Estimating Time Formulas.

12 **B**, 97.73%. Completion probability questions require you determine the mean and derive the standard deviation. The Mean or Expected Value = (Total Optimistic Estimate + 4 times Most Likely Estimate + Total Pessimistic Estimate) ÷ 6. The mean is 30 + (4 × 50) + 75 = 305; 305 ÷ 6 = 50.83. Standard Deviation σ = (P – O) ÷ 6 or √ Variance. Standard deviation is 75–30 = 45; 45 ÷ 6 = 7.5. A result of 65 days equals the mean of 50.83 days plus 2σ (15 days). The mean is 50% with + 2σ = 47.73, you have 97.73% probability of completion. This question asks you to determine the relationship among facts, principles, and methods. See Appendix A for the Estimating Time formulas.

13 **D**, 99%. Use the formula for the reliability for parallel processes:

$$P(A^*) = 1- p(A) = 1 - 0.90 = 0.1$$

$$P(B^*) = 1- p(B) = 1 \text{ ¡V } 0.95 = 0.05$$

$$= 1 - (0.1 \times 0.05) = 0.99.95\%. \text{ Rounded up to 99\%}$$

See Appendix A for the Reliability for Serial and Parallel Processes formulas.

14 **B**, Producibility. This is the simplest pattern; it asks for a straight definition. See Chapter 10 for more information on quality.

15 **B**, 28. Eight people are on the team: 8(8 – 1) = 8(7); 8(7) = 56; 56 ÷ 2 = 28. See Appendix A for the formulas for channels of communications.

16 **B**, 5 days. CPM uses only the Most Likely estimate. *This question is a trick.* If you wasted time doing a calculation, see Appendix A for the Estimating Time formulas.

17 **C**, 51%. The Standard Deviation, or σ, is 8. You have to figure out the areas on the left side of the mean and the right side of the mean. The mean is 48. On the left side of the mean, you have 48 – 44 = 4 or ½ of a standard deviation, which is 34%. Therefore, you have 34 ÷ 2 = 17% on the left side of the mean. On the right side of the mean, you have 56 – 48 = 8. This is exactly 1σ, or 34%,. so you have 17% on the left and 34% on the right — the proportion between 44 and 56 is 51%. See Appendix A for the probability formulas.

18 **C**, 71%. The second part of the question asks you to find a portion of the left side of the mean and the entire right side of the mean. Here's the trick. Since the mean contains the 50% level, you don't have to figure out the right side. You just have to figure out the left side. So 48 – 44 = 5; 5 ÷ 8 = .63 of 34% = 21; 21 + 50 = 71%. The proportion of all diners taking more than 45 minutes to eat is 71%. See Appendix A for the probability formulas.

19 **B**, $2,400. The portion 1σ from the right side of the mean is 2.01+ .05 = 2.06. The portion 1σ from the left side of the mean is 2.01 – .05 = 1.96. Between +/- 1SD, the parts are acceptable. This accounts for 68%. 50% is on the left side of the mean. The mean less 34% = 16%; 16% × 1,000 = 160 parts. These 160 parts are reworked at 160 × $10.00 = $1,600. On the right side of the mean, we have 50%, the mean plus 34% or 84%. That gives another 16% outside the acceptable upper limits. The calculation is 16% × 1,000 = 160 parts. These 160 parts are reworked at 160 × $5.00 = $800. The cost of scrap and rework is $1,600 + $800 = $2,400. See Appendix A.

20 **C,** 3. Process Standard Deviation σ = 6 units. Sample size = 3 units. Sample Standard Deviation σ = Process Standard Deviation σ ÷ (Sample size – 1). Process Standard Deviation σ ÷ (Sample size ¡V 1) = 6 ÷ (3 – 1) = 3. The (n – 1) as the divisor is an adjustment that corrects for the sample size (a statistic), approximating the population. You're likely to see answers of *2* and *3*. If you don't use the sample size adjustment (n – 1), you'll pick the wrong answer. See Appendix A for Process Standard Deviation formulas.

21 **C,** 1.33. Here's the math:

$$7,000,000 \div (1+8)^2 = 4,500,000$$

$$7,000,000 \div 1.17 = 5,982,905$$

$$5,982,905 \div 4,500,000 = 1.33$$

See Appendix A for more on Benefit Cost Ratio.

22 **B,** $78,039. The question asks, "What's the present value of the payment of $20,000 at the end of each month for 4 months?" Since the monthly discount rate is 1%, PV = the outflows PVs for each of the 4 months: PV1 (present value of 20,000 that is to be paid after 1 month) + PV2 (present value of 20,000 that is to be paid after 2 months) + PV3 (present value of 20,000 that is to be paid after 3 months) +PV4 (present value of 20,000 to be paid after 4 months).

$$PV1 = 20000 \div (1.01) = 19802$$

$$PV2 = 20000 \div (1.01)^2 = 19606$$

$$PV3 = 20000 \div (1.01)^3 = 19412$$

$$PV4 = 20000 \div (1.01)^4 = 19220$$

$$\text{Therefore, PV = PV1 + PV2 + PV3 + PV4} = \$78,039$$

With a monthly discount rate of 1%, you pay $78,039 now instead of $20,000 at the end of each month for 4 months.

23 **B,** Historical information. The key phrase in the pattern is *the most,* and the situation key is that you're *new.* While all these answers can improve the success of your project, the keys *most* and *recently hired* points you to B. Use of Historical Information is a mantra of PMI.

24 **A,** $0. In a Fixed Price plus Incentive Fee (FPI) contract, if costs exceed a ceiling threshold, the seller is penalized and receives no profits. FPI is the most complex contract type. It provides strict incentives to decrease costs. This question sets you up for a false pattern. You might have thought you'd need to do some calculations. If you did, review the different contract types. The question tests your ability to demonstrate your understanding of the relationship among facts, principles, and methods. See the information on contracts in Appendix A.

25 **C,** Negotiate along the lines of the triple constraint. This is one of those difficult situational questions. To answer it correctly, you have to identify the right pattern. In fact, the question is even more difficult because all these answers could be correct given different situations. A is a good choice; Business Needs Analysis should be done on all projects but should have been done already. It's an Initiation process; we're in a Planning process here. (It could also be Verification.) B is also good choice; a project manager should refer back to documents like the scope statement. Since we're in a Scope Planning process, the scope statement is a key output. Objectives and deliverables are keys to Scope Planning. But it doesn't go far enough and isn't specific enough because it suggests we're in Scope Planning. D is also good; PMI likes it when you take every opportunity to educate people on PM. That's its mission, but it doesn't go far enough and isn't specific enough. The pattern is asking you about a Scope Definition process. C is the best choice because it's further along; the process it covers is Scope Definition. A project manager facilitates, negotiates, and understands requirement options. The triple constraint provides a good way to identify, discuss, and define the scope tradeoffs. See Chapter 8 for information on Scope Definition and Chapter 14 for information on triple constraint.

26 **C,** A constraint. While A, B, and D are good choices, the best answer is C. Imposed dates are a classic example of constraints. Milestones can be a constraint. *PMBOK Guide* doesn't use the term *deadline*. For more information on schedule development, see Chapter 9 and *PMBOK Guide* p. 74.

27 **D,** Rolling wave planning. The concepts of iterative planning, refinement, and progressive elaboration are mantras of the PMI. See Chapter 8 for more information on using rolling wave planning.

28 **C,** A deliverable, like this analysis, is a tangible, verifiable work product. A verbal report is intangible and unverifiable. Eliminate A and B — A because the task is incomplete and you'd give a false impression on the schedule; and B because it's not proactive enough, and the functional manager will actively resist your ineffective control efforts. While the functional manager is clearly avoiding inspection, D is an incomplete answer. C is more complete because it covers schedule and inspecting the work product. C implies accepting a schedule delay so the responsible team can verify its results. This question tests your understanding of the relationship among facts, principles, and methods. See Chapter 8 for more information on the matrix.

29 **A,** Crashing the schedule by providing overtime. You can eliminate B and D as unacceptable options, although in some cases they are the correct *PMBOK Guide* answer as two aspects of the triple constraint. C could be a good choice, but the question doesn't indicate an additional phase. You could perform only *current* phase tasks in parallel to compress the schedule. This question tests your understanding of the relationship among facts, principles, and methods — here it's the Duration Compression Methods and earned value. The EV indicates the project is under budget (CPI = EV ÷ AC; CPI of 1.2 is under budget), so crashing the schedule by adding overtime is the best choice. See Chapter 8 for more information on developing the schedule and Appendix A for the earned value formulas.

30   **B,** Issue a change request. A is eliminated because work authorizations should be made after the change request is approved; if the change request is denied, another alternative needs to be determined. C is eliminated because the sponsor will usually request you recommend some alternatives. This pattern asks for you to analyze an *input* and determine the Component process, which is Integrated Change Control. See Chapter 13 for more information on handling change requests.

31   **C,** Change requests. A is an example of prevention costs. B and D are examples of failure costs. This is an exception pattern. It asks for you to analyze a tool and technique and determine the Component process, which is Quality Planning. See Chapter 10 for more information on Quality Planning.

32   **D,** Kaizen. Kaizen is the Japanese term for continuous improvement process. Deming said he'd rather have 1,000 improvements of 1 percent than one improvement of 1,000 percent. See Chapter 10 for more information on quality.

33   **B,** Expediting is a Cost of Nonconformance. Training, process control, and testing are costs of Conformance. This is the exception pattern. See Chapter 10 for more information on the cost of quality.

34   **C,** Product design validation is a Cost of Conformance. The rest are Costs of Nonconformance. This is the exception pattern. See Chapter 10 for more information on the cost of quality.

35   **D,** Risk negative. This is the exception pattern to the definition. See the information about stakeholder risk tolerances in Chapter 10.

36   **C,** Sensitivity Analysis. This is the match pattern to the definition. These are the four tools and techniques to Quantitative Risk Analysis. If you know the definition, they're easy to match up. Chapter 10 covers Quantitative Risk Analysis.

37   **B,** Transference. Transference deflects or shares risks like insurance or warranties. In the older *PMBOK Guide,* they were considered Mitigation techniques. This question tests your ability to demonstrate your understanding of the definition of risk techniques, as well as the relationship among facts, principles, and methods. See Chapter 10 for more information on Risk Response Planning.

38   **C,** Acceptance. This question tests your understanding of the definition of risk techniques, as well as the relationship among facts, principles, and methods. See Chapter 10 for more on Risk Response Planning.

39   **A,** Organizational Policies. Organizational Policies can be a constraint. The pattern is asking you to match input examples in Project Plan Execution. See Chapter 11 for more on Project Plan Execution.

40   **C,** Evaluation Criteria is an input in Source Selection. But, you say, Source Selection has only one tool and technique — contact negotiation. The others, weighting and screening systems, are a part of the technique.

41   **D,** A separate office. While having a separate office might be a status symbol and therefore part of a reward, it goes against Team building. Collocation, or placing the team in the same office location, is one of the tools. This is the exception pattern. See Chapter 11 for more on Team Development.

42 **A,** Metrics. These definitions are termed *Operational Definitions* or *metrics*. The pattern is asking for a definition of an input to Quality Assurance. See Chapter 11 for more on Quality Assurance.

43 **D,** Approving the product of the project or phase needs to be prepared. This is the definition of Formal Acceptance in Scope Verification. This is an exception pattern. See Chapter 12 for more on configuration management.

44 **D,** Insist that all changes be made by a formal change request. Eliminate the definitions in A and C because they're too narrow. Focus on B and D. This question is hard because either could be right. If B had added *properly* defining scope at the beginning, it might be the best choice. You could spend lots of time defining scope, but you could miss objectives — as when you don't use a WBS. As a general rule, the larger the number of change requests, the less planning went into the initial project planning stages. The pattern is the single most important thing a project manager should do is. See Chapter 14 for more on handling change requests.

45 **D,** Lag. This is the definition of float or lack. A, B, and C, are alternative definitions. A lag is a modification in the schedule that permits a delay in the successor task if slack is available. Think of lag as enforced waiting time like a coat of paint drying before you can paint another coat. See Chapter 9 for more on defining leads, lags, and float.

46 **C,** Resource leveling. A, B, and D are all schedule risks. D is called Convergence Bias. Resource leveling can alter the Critical Path. The exception pattern here is that resource leveling is a technique. See Chapter 9 for more on defining leads, lags, and float.

47 **A,** They have a fixed duration. Indeed, they have no duration and require no resources. See Chapter 6 for more on setting milestones.

48 **C,** Scope Definition. This pattern asks for you to know the definition of the process. See Chapter 8 for more information.

49 **D,** Schedule Development. It's created in the fourth process. This pattern requires you to know the order of events. The question tests your understanding of the relationship among facts, component processes, and methods. See Chapter 9 for more on developing the schedule.

Appendix C

About the CD-ROM

- -

On the CD-ROM

▶ Practice and Self-Assessment tests, to make sure you're ready for the real thing

▶ Evaluation on copies of Milestones Professional 2002

▶ Templates for your study plan, various project document templates

- -

System Requirements

Make sure that your computer meets the minimum system requirements listed below. If it doesn't, you might not be able to use the CD.

- ✔ A PC with a Pentium or faster processor.

- ✔ Microsoft Windows 98 or later, or Windows NT 4 or later.

- ✔ At least 16 MB of total RAM installed in your computer. For best results, we recommend at least 128 MB of RAM.

- ✔ A CD-ROM drive — at least a double speed (2X).

- ✔ A sound card for the PC.

- ✔ A monitor capable of displaying at least 256 colors (or shades of gray).

- ✔ A modem with a speed of at least 56Kbps.

Using the CD with Microsoft Windows

To install the items from the CD to your hard drive, follow these steps.

1. **Insert the CD into your computer's CD-ROM drive.**

2. **Click Start⇨Run.**

3. **In the dialog box that appears, type** D:\Start.EXE.

   Replace *D* with the proper drive letter if your CD-ROM drive uses a different letter. (If you don't know the letter, see how your CD-ROM drive is listed under My Computer.)

4. **Click OK.**

   A license agreement window appears.

5. **Read through the license agreement, nod your head, and then click the Accept button if you want to use the CD — after you click Accept, you'll never be bothered by the License Agreement window again.**

   The CD interface Welcome screen appears. The interface is a little program that shows you what's on the CD and coordinates installing the programs and running the demos. The interface basically enables you to click a button or two to make things happen.

6. **Click anywhere on the Welcome screen to enter the interface.**

   Now you are getting to the action. This next screen lists categories for the software on the CD.

7. **To view the items within a category, just click the category's name.**

   A list of programs in the category appears.

8. **For more information about a program, click the program's name.**

   Be sure to read the information that appears. Sometimes a program has it's own system requirements or requires you to do a few tricks on your computer before you can install or run the program, and this screen tells you what you might need to do, if necessary.

9. **If you don't want to install the program, click the Back button to return to the previous screen.**

   You can always return to the previous screen by clicking the Back button. This feature allows you to browse the different categories and products and decide what you want to install.

10. **To install a program, click the appropriate Install button.**

    The CD interface drops to the background while the CD installs the program you chose.

11. **To install other items, repeat Steps 7–10.**

12. **When you've finished installing programs, click the Quit button to close the interface.**

    You can eject the CD now. Carefully place it back in the plastic jacket of the book for safekeeping.

In order to run some of the programs on this *PMP Certification For Dummies* CD-ROM, you may need to keep the CD inside your CD-ROM drive. This is beneficial because you don't have to install a large chunk of the program on your hard drive.

Dummies Test Prep Tools

The CD contains questions related to the PMP Certification exam. Most of the questions cover topics that you can expect to appear on the exam.

Practice test

The practice test contains over 300 questions similar to what you'll find on the exam. You can select questions from any of the content domains to focus on your weak areas or you can take the entire test. You can also randomize the questions to keep it interesting! Each correct answer includes a brief explanation and references the appropriate chapter for review.

Web site links

We've also created a link page, a handy starting place for accessing the large amount of information we have on our Web site about the Certification test. You can find the page at D:\Links.HTM. Send us e-mail about your progress. We'll see where we can help you pass the exam. Surf to our Web site at www.projectmania.com.

Commercial Demos

Milestones Professional 2002, from KIDASA Software, Inc.

This package from KIDASA Software, Inc., is a great way for you to present key milestone information to customers, sponsors, and other stakeholders. Using this program on your own study plan and posting the various earned value reports where you can see them will help motivate you. It's easy to learn and to use. It handles data bi-directionally from Microsoft Project, so you can share data between programs. It's also great for reporting on actual project data from MS Project. The milestone chart examples in this book were created using this program. (We also have these sample files on the CD.) For more information about Milestones Professional 2002, visit the KIDASA Software Web site at `www.kidasa.com`.

Template Files

We've included on the CD some templates for a simplified Study Plan. This Study Plan enables you to practice the same methodology that the exam tests for. If you use these tools and follow our practical steps, you'll already have "done it" when you sit for the exam. These templates are merely data files that allow you to customize your PEPP Study Plan to suit your individual needs. Please review the Study Plan templates. Create your Study Plan's Scope Statement as a word processing document, develop your WBS by decomposing all of your exam deliverables using WBS Chart Pro, sequence your activities and work through the network using PERT Chart EXPERT, plan and track your milestones using Milestones, create the schedule baseline and track your progress using Microsoft Project, plot out your budget baseline to see it's S-curve in Excel, and, finally, print out your EV metrics using Milestones. At the end of each chapter, monitor and control your Study Plan using Earned Value measurements. Post your EV metrics like SV, CV, SPI, and CPI near your study materials — next to your computer monitor. If you follow this study method, you'll have so much practice with the methodology that you'll ace the exam.

If You Have Problems with the CD

We tried our best to compile programs that work on most computers with the minimum system requirements. If your computer differs, some programs may not work properly.

The two likeliest problems are that you don't have enough RAM for the programs you want use, or you have other programs running that are affecting the installation or the running of a program. If you get error messages like *not enough memory* or *setup cannot continue*, try one of the following fixes and then try using the software again:

- **Shut down all running programs.** The more programs you have running, the less memory is available for other programs. Installation programs typically update files and programs. If other programs are running, installation might not work properly.

✔ **Turn off any antivirus software that you have on your computer.** Installation programs often mimic virus activity because they need to overwrite or replace system files. So, installation programs drive antivirus programs crazy. Your antivirus software may incorrectly believe it's being infected, so turn it off temporarily — but don't forget to turn it back on when the installation is done.

✔ **In Windows, close the CD interface and run demos or installations directly from Windows Explorer.** The Windows interface often ties up system memory, which can conflict with certain kinds of interactive demos. Use Windows Explorer to browse the files on the CD and manually run the installation programs.

✔ **At your local computer store, install more RAM to your computer.** RAM is cheap. It can speed up your computer and enable more programs to run at the same time.

If you still have trouble with the CD, please call the Customer Care phone number: (800) 762-2974. Outside the United States, call 1 (317) 572-3994. You can also contact Customer Service by e-mail at techsupdum@wiley.com. Wiley Publishing Inc. will provide technical support only for installation and other general quality control items; for technical support on the applications themselves, consult the program's vendor or author. You can also check ProjectMania.com, the author's Web site.

Index

• A •

abstract, 76
acceptance sampling, 341
acceptance sampling plan, 341
accidental project managers, 10
activity definition
  defined, 160
  inputs, 160
  outputs, 161
  tools and techniques, 160
activity duration estimating
  defined, 168
  inputs, 169–170
  outputs, 170
  tools and techniques, 170
activity list, 147
activity sequencing
  arrow diagramming method (ADM), 163–164
  conditional diagramming methods, 163
  defined, 161
  inputs, 162
  network diagrams, 163, 165–168
  outputs, 163
  precedence diagramming method (PDM), 162–163
  tools and techniques, 162–163
activity-on-node (AON), 162–163
actual cost (AC), 183, 354
actual cost of work performed (ACWP), 354
ADM (arrow diagramming method), 163–164
administrative closure, 304, 306
advertising, 51
alignment (of projects with business goals), 70
alternatives identification, 124
analysis of covariance (ANCOVA), 342
analysis of variance (ANOVA), 342
analysis questions, 23
answer key for practice exam, 379–384
AON (activity-on-node), 162–163
application process
  CE Number, 15
  educational requirements, 15
  eligibility letter, 16
  experiential requirements, 15
  online application, 317

application questions, 22
approvals (written), 193–194
archiving project records, 304
arithmetic mean, 336
arrow diagramming method (ADM), 163–164
assumptions, 105–106
audits, 307
authority
  coercive authority, 102, 246
  expert authority, 102, 246
  formal (legitimate), 102, 246
  referent authority, 102, 246
  reward authority, 102, 246
authorization (for a project), 102–103, 194
availability formulas, 353

• B •

BAC (budget at completion), 184, 359
balancing the interests of stakeholders, 52–53
Bayes' Theorem, 342
BCWP (budgeted cost of work performed), 353
BCWS (budgeted cost of work scheduled), 353
behavior diagram, 124
benefit/cost analysis, 124
benefit/cost ratio, 129, 364–365
bidder conferences, 237
boundaries (of a project)
  acceptance criteria, 90
  assumptions, 105–106
  constraints, 104–105
  definition, 127
  documentation, 107
  expectations, 74, 84
  future decisions, 75–76
  measuring project benefits, 89–90
  milestones, 91–92
  needs, 74
  organizational policies, 75
  planning, 121–125
  prep test, 96
  prep test answers, 97

boundaries (of a project) *(continued)*
  product deliverables, 90–91
  product scope, 90, 122–123
  project objectives, 90–91
  project scope, 90, 122–123
  project scope management, 122
  purpose of, 72
  quick assessment, 82–83
  requirements, 74–75
  scope management plan, 72, 122–123, 125
  scope statement, 90–91, 122, 124–127
  scope statement updates, 127, 146–147
  stakeholders, 84–89
budget
  constraints, 104
  cost baseline, 181
  cost budgeting, 180–182
  time-phased budget, 181
budget at completion (BAC), 184, 359
budgeted cost of work performed (BCWP), 353
budgeted cost of work scheduled (BCWS), 353
business case, 66–67
business requirements document, 76

• *C* •

calculation of slack, 360
Capability Index (Cp), 350–351
Capability Ratio (CR), 351
CAPM Exam. *See* Certified Associate in
    Project Management (CAPM) Exam
CAQ Exam. *See* Certificate of Added
    Qualification (CAQ) Exam
cause-and-effect diagrams, 200, 202
CCM (critical chain method), 173
CD-ROM
  installing items on your hard drive, 385–386
  license agreement, 384
  Microsoft Windows, 385–386
  Milestones Professional 2002 (KIDASA
    Software, Inc.), 385–386
  practice test, 385
  Self-Assessment Test, 385
  study plan, 18, 388
  system requirements, 385
  technical problems, 388–389
  Web site links, 387
  Wiley Publishing, Inc. Customer Service, 389

CE Number, 15
Central Limit Theorem, 335
Certificate of Added Qualification (CAQ)
    Exam, 14–15
Certification Board Center, 11
Certification Handbook, 15, 317
Certified Associate in Project Management
    (CAPM) Exam
  application process, 14
  question structure, 14
  who should take it, 14
change control, 260–264, 275–277
change requests, 277, 286–287
CHAOS Report, 113
charter, 76–77, 102–103
closeout process
  administrative closure, 304–306
  contract closeout, 307–308
  knowledgebase, 303
  post mortem, 303–304
  prep test, 310–311
  prep test answers, 312–313
  quick assessment, 300–301
  releasing resources, 309
  repeating at each phase, 302–303
  rewards, 309
  work package evaluation, 303
code of accounts, 144, 146
coercive authority, 102, 246
commercial software demos
  Milestones Professional 2002 (KIDASA
    Software, Inc.), 387–388
common-cause variation, 337
communication paths, 197–198, 362
communication skills, 106
communications
  defined, 72
  feedback loop, 247
  horizontal communication, 247
  sender-receiver model, 247–248
  stakeholder communications, 194
  stakeholders, 195–197
  vertical communication, 247
communications management, 194–197
communications planning
  communications management plan
    (CMP), 196
  inputs, 195–196
  outputs, 196

stakeholder analysis, 196
tools and techniques, 196
compliance
integrated change control, 262–264
measuring, 267–268
prep test, 278–279
prep test answers, 280
professional responsibility, 50–51
quality control (QC), 264–266
quick assessment, 260–261
scope change control, 275–277
scope verification, 272–275
component process interactions, 323
component processes, 40
conducting feasibility studies, 67
confidence interval, 337
conflict management, 246–247
conflicts of interest, 54
constraints
budget, 104
defined, 104
duration, 105
organizational planning, 151
procurement planning, 155
resource availability, 104–105
target date, 104
task predecessor, 105
triple constraint, 287
continuing education requirements, 12
contract administration, 234, 239–241
contract closeout, 307–308
contracts
consideration, 157
cost reimbursable contracts, 158
delegation of procurement authority, 239
direct costs, 158
fixed-price contracts, 158
indirect costs, 158
legal capacity, 157, 365–366
letter contract, 159
offer, 157
purchase order (PO), 159
risks, 159
unit price contracts, 159
control charts, 267–268, 338–340
control gate, 124
controlling processes
change requests, 286–287
corrective action, 287
cost control, 290–291

overall change control, 262–264
performance reporting, 292–294
prep test, 295–296
prep test answers, 297
quality control, 264–266
quick assessment, 282–283
risk monitoring and control, 284–285
schedule control, 288–289
scope change control, 275–277
scope verification, 272–275
core processes. *See also core processes
by name*
defined, 40
illustration, 41
Corporate Reform Bill, 49
corrective action, 287
cost, 72, 158
cost account, 146
cost baseline, 181
cost budgeting
baseline cost, 180
budget estimates, 180
contingency reserves, 180
cost baseline, 180–181
defined, 180–182
inputs, 181
management reserves, 181
outputs, 181
tools and techniques, 181
cost control, 290–291
cost control system, 146
cost estimating, 177–179
cost metrics, 253
cost of quality, 93, 201, 204–205
cost performance index (CPI), 184, 355
cost performance measurements, 270–272
cost reimbursable contract, 158
cost variance, 183, 354
cost variance percentage, 184, 358
covariance, 342
Cp (Capability Index), 350–351
CPI (cost performance index), 184, 355
Cpk (Process Capability Index), 351–352
CR (capability ratio), 351
crashing, 175
critical chain method (CCM), 173
critical path, 166–168, 360
critical path method (CPM), 166, 174, 345–346
Critical Tools, Inc.
Web site, 387

Crosby, Philip, quality guru, 209–210
cultural differences, 54–55
cumulative CPI, 358
customer satisfaction, 93, 106, 202
customer service Wiley Publishing, Inc.
   (for CD-ROM problems), 389

• D •

DCF (discounted cash flow), 128, 131–134
decision models, 71
declining balance (DB), 367
decomposition, 127, 146
delegation of procurement authority, 239
deliverables
  decomposition, 146
  defined, 37
  examples, 37
  milestones, 91–92
  project charter, 76
Deming, W. Edwards, quality guru
  Out of the Crisis, 207–208
  System of Profound Knowledge, 208
demo software
  Milestones Professional 2002 (KIDASA
    Software, Inc.), 385–386
depreciation, 366–367
descriptive statistics, 334
design of experiments (DoE), 201, 211, 342
direct costs, 158
discounted cash flow (DCF), 128, 131–134
documentation
  archiving project records, 304
  assumptions, 105–106
  audits, 307
  communication skills, 106
  constraints, 104–105
  importance of, 99, 106, 307
  lessons learned, 304, 306
  life-cycle processes, 99
  performance measurement, 304–305
  project charter, 76–77, 102–103
  project plan, 118–121
  project records, 106–107
  scope, 107
  scope statement, 125–127
  supporting details, 118, 125
  trade-off decisions, 106
  written approvals, 193–194
DoE (design of experiments), 201, 211, 342

downloading the Certification Handbook, 317
duration
  constraints, 105
  estimating, 168–173

• E •

EAC (estimate at completion), 184, 358–359
earned value (EV), 183, 353
earned value analysis (EVA)
  actual cost (AC), 183, 354
  actual cost of work performed (ACWP), 354
  budget at completion (BAC), 184, 359
  budgeted cost of work performed
    (BCWP), 353
  budgeted cost of work scheduled
    (BCWS), 353
  cost performance index (CPI), 184, 355
  cost variance, 183, 354
  cost variance percentage, 184, 358
  cumulative CPI, 358
  earned value (EV), 183, 353
  estimate at completion (EAC), 184
  estimate to completion (ETC), 184
  inherent availability, 353
  operational availability, 353
  percent spent, 184
  planned value (PV), 183, 353
  planning, 182–183
  schedule performance index (SPI), 184,
    355–358
  schedule variance, 183–184, 354
  schedule variance percentage, 184, 358
  variance at completion (VAC), 184, 358
earned value (EV), 183, 353
earned value management (EVM), 117, 182
eligibility letter, 16
Equal Employment Opportunity (EEO), 54
equivalent worth, 362–364
estimate at completion (EAC), 184, 358–359
estimate to completion (ETC), 184
estimating
  activity duration, 169–173
  budgets, 180
  costs, 177–179
Ethics Resource Center, 53
EV (earned value), 183, 353
EVA (earned value analysis). *See* earned value
  analysis (EVA)
EVM (earned value management), 117, 182

exam day preparations
  dress, 326
  before the exam, 325
  identification required, 318, 325
  note-taking during exam, 329–330
  registration, 326
  schedule appointment, 317
  tools you can use, 327
  tutorial, 327–328
exam fees, 15
exception patterns (in questions), 24
executing processes
  contract administration, 234, 239–241
  information distribution, 234, 248–250
  prep test, 254–255
  prep test answers, 256
  project plan execution, 234, 236
  quality assurance, 234, 250–252
  quick assessment, 232–233
  solicitation, 234, 236–237
  source selection, 234, 238–239
  team development, 234, 242–248
expected monetary value, 352
expected value, 340, 344–345
experiment, 334
expert authority, 102, 246
expert judgment, 71, 124, 149

• F •

facilitating processes
  defined, 40
  illustration, 41
factor, 342
fast tracking, 37, 175
feasibility study
  business case, 66–67
  conducting, 67
  defined, 66
  feasibility report, 66
  financial projections, 67
  market potential, 67
  outcomes, 67
  potential economic justification, 67
  project manager, 67
  purpose of, 66–67
  team composition, 67
  technical practicality, 67
  work plan, 67
feature gold plating, 88, 199
fishbone diagrams, 200, 202

fixed price contracts, 158
Fleming, Quentin, project management
    expert, 182
float, 168
formal (legitimate) authority, 102, 246
formulas
  availability, 353
  benefit/cost ratio, 129, 364–365
  budget at completion (BAC), 184
  calculation of slack, 360
  communication paths, 362
  To Complete Performance Index (TCPI), 359
  cost performance index (CPI), 184
  cost variance, 183–184
  Critical Path, 360
  declining balance (DB), 367
  depreciation, 366–367
  discounted cash flow (DCF), 128, 131–134
  earned value, 183–184
  earned value analysis (EVA), 353–358
  equivalent worth, 362–364
  estimate at completion (EAC), 184, 358–359
  estimate to completion (ETC), 184
  estimates, 170–173
  future value (FV), 131–132, 363
  internal rate of return (IRR), 134–135, 364
  Labor Rate Variance, 361
  Material Price Variance, 360
  Material Usage Variance, 361
  memorizing, 324
  net present value (NPV), 132–134, 363
  payback analysis, 129–131
  payback period, 364
  percent spent, 184
  present value (PV), 132, 363
  risk, 352
  schedule performance index (SPI), 184
  schedule variance, 183–184
  Straight Line Depreciation, 366
  Sum-of-the-Years'-Digits (SYD), 367
  time, 344–349
  time value of money (TVM), 128
  variance at completion (VAR), 184
function analysis, 124
functional manager
  functional organization, 94
  matrix organization, 94–95
  projectized organization, 95
functional organization, 32, 94
future decisions, 75–76
future value (FV), 131–132, 363

• G •

general management, 32
goals
  feasibility study, 67
  project mission statement, 68–69
  scope, 68
  strategic plan, 69
gold plating, 88, 199
graphical evaluation and review technique
  (GERT), 174
Guide to the Project Management Body of
  Knowledge
  importance of, 12
  limitations, 13
  study tips, 30
  versions, 12

• H •

Herzenberg's theory, 245
hierarchy of needs, 243–244
histogram, 340
historical information, 70
human resources, 72

• I •

identification required for exam day, 318, 325
identifying stakeholders, 84–86
indirect costs, 158
information distribution, 234, 248–250
initiation process
  discovery phase, 66
  documentation, 99
  failure likelihood, 63
  feasibility study, 66–67
  historical information, 70
  importance of, 63, 69
  inputs, 70
  needs analysis, 66
  planning processes, 66–67
  prep test, 78–79
  prep test answers, 80
  product description, 71
  project management office (PMO), 66
  project phases, 74
  project scope, 68
  project selection criteria, 70–71
  quick assessment, 64–65, 100

  scope initiation, 69
  strategic plan, 70
inputs
  activity definition, 160–161
  activity duration estimating, 169–170
  activity sequencing, 162
  administrative closure, 304–305
  communications planning, 195–196
  contract administration, 240
  cost budgeting, 181
  cost control, 290
  cost estimating, 177–178
  defined, 42
  information distribution, 249
  initiation, 70
  initiation process, 70
  integrated change control, 263
  organizational planning, 151
  overall change control, 263
  performance reporting, 292
  procurement planning, 155
  project plan development, 117
  project plan execution, 235
  qualitative risk analysis, 219
  quality assurance, 250–251
  quality control (QC), 264–265
  quality planning, 200
  quantitative risk analysis, 221–222
  resource planning, 148–149
  risk identification, 216–217
  risk management planning (RMP), 214
  risk monitoring and control, 284
  risk response planning, 223–224
  schedule control, 288
  schedule development, 173–174
  scope change control, 276
  scope definition, 127
  scope verification, 274
  solicitation, 237
  solicitation planning, 156
  source selection, 238–239
  staff acquisition, 153
  team development, 242
installing CD-ROM demos and templates,
  383–384
integrated change control, 116, 262–264
integration, 72, 116, 119
internal rate of return (IRR), 134–135, 364
Ishikawa diagrams, 200, 202
Ishikawa, Kaoru, quality guru, 212
ISO (International Organization for
  Standardization), 198

• J •

joining the Project Management Institute (PMI), 15
Juran, Joseph M., quality guru, 208–209

• K •

kaizen, 203–204
KIDASA Software, Inc.
  Milestones Professional 2002, 387–388
  Web site, 387
knowledge areas
  communications, 72
  component processes, 40–43
  cost, 72
  defined, 38–39
  human resources, 72
  illustration, 39
  integration, 72
  matrix, 43
  memory aid, 73
  procurement, 73
  quality, 72
  risk, 73
  scope, 72
  time, 72
  work breakdown structure (WBS), 145
knowledgebase, 303
KPMG's 2000 Organizational Integrity Survey, 53
kurtosis, 341

• L •

Labor Rate Variance, 361
lags, 167
leads, 167
legitimate authority, 102, 246
letter of engagement, 76
level of significance, 341
license agreement for CD-ROM, 386
life-cycle processes, 73
lower control limit (LCL), 338

• M •

management tasks
  communications management, 194–197
  general management, 32

quality management, 93
  scope management, 122, 125
  stakeholder management, 85
Maslow's hierarchy of needs, 243–244
match patterns (in questions), 24
Material Price Variance, 360
Material Usage Variance, 361
math
  difficulty of questions, 333
  tips for mastering, 324, 333
matrix organization, 32, 94–95
McGregor's Theories of X and Y, 244
mean, 336, 344
measuring
  compliance, 267–268
  profitability, 128
  project benefits, 89–90
median, 336
Member Code of Ethics, 48
memory aids
  for integration, 119
  for knowledge areas, 73
  for scope processes, 123
  on the Website, 23
methodology, 31
metrics
  aesthetics, 91
  conformance, 91
  control charts, 267–268
  cost metrics, 253
  cost performance measurements, 270–272
  durability, 91
  features, 91
  monthly progress indicators, 252
  Pareto diagrams, 268
  performance, 91
  phase gate indicators, 253
  progress measurements, 269
  progressive elaboration, 90
  project completion indicators, 253
  purpose of, 269
  reliability, 91
  risk metrics, 253
  scope metrics, 253
  serviceability, 91
  time metrics, 253
  weekly progress indicators, 252
Microsoft Project, 144
milestones, 91–92
Milestones Professional 2002 (KIDASA Software, Inc.), 387–388
mission statement for a project, 68–69

mnemonics, 23
mode, 336
monthly progress indicators, 252
motivational theories
  Herzenberg's theory, 245–246
  Maslow's hierarchy of needs, 243–244
  McGregor's Theories of X and Y, 244
  Ouchi's Theory Z management, 245

• N •

National Business Ethics Survey, 53
needs analysis, 66
net present value (NPV), 132–134, 363
network diagrams, 165–168
nine knowledge areas, 38–39, 43
normal distribution, 335
note-taking during exam, 329–330

• O •

OBS (organizational breakdown
    structure), 148
ongoing operations, 33
opening a project
  assumptions, 105–106
  authorization, 102–103
  constraints, 104–105
  documentation, 104–107
  prep test, 108–109
  prep test answers, 110
  project charter, 103
  project manager selection, 103
  project records, 106–107
operational availability, 353
opportunity cost, 128
organizational breakdown structure
    (OBS), 148
organizational charts, 34–35
organizational planning
  defined, 150–151
  inputs, 151
  outputs, 152
  project interfaces, 151
  tools and techniques, 152
organizational policies, 75
organizations
  culture, 32
  functional organization, 32, 94
  matrix organization, 32, 94–95

project manager's authority within, 93–94
  projectized organization, 32, 95
  structure, 32, 93
Ouchi's Theory Z management, 245
Out of the Crisis, W. Edwards Deming, 207
outliers, 341
outputs
  activity definition, 161
  activity duration estimating, 170
  activity sequencing, 163
  administrative closure, 306
  communications planning, 196
  contract administration, 241
  cost budgeting, 181
  cost control, 291
  cost estimating, 179
  defined, 42
  information distribution, 250
  integrated change control, 264
  organizational planning, 152
  overall change control, 264
  performance reporting, 293–294
  procurement planning, 155–156
  project plan development, 118
  project plan execution, 236
  qualitative risk analysis, 220
  quality assurance, 251
  quality control (QC), 266
  quality planning process, 201
  quantitative risk analysis, 222
  risk identification, 218
  risk management planning (RMP), 215
  risk monitoring and control, 285
  risk response planning, 224–225
  schedule control, 289
  schedule development, 176–177
  scope change control, 277
  scope definition, 127
  scope verification, 275
  solicitation, 237
  solicitation planning, 157
  source selection, 239
  team development, 243
overall change control, 116, 262–264

• P •

Pareto diagram, 265, 268, 341
passing scores for the PMP Exam, 14, 17
patterns in questions, 18, 23–25, 321–322,
    328–329

payback analysis, 129–131
payback period, 364
PDM (precedence diagramming method),
    162–163
PDSA (Plan-Do-Study-Act), 269
percent spent, 184
performance measurement, 304–305
performance reporting, 292–294
PERT (program evaluation and review
    technique), 171–172, 175, 345
phase gate indicators, 253
phase review, 303–304
phone numbers
  Prometric Test Center, 16
  Wiley Publishing, Inc. Customer Service, 389
Plan-Do-Study-Act (PDSA), 269
planned value (PV), 183, 353
planning
  bottom-up approach, 121
  earned value analysis (EVA), 182–183
  importance of, 113
  initiation process, 66
  integrated change control, 116
  organizational planning, 150–152
  prep test, 136–137
  prep test answers, 138
  procurement planning, 154–156
  project plan development, 116–121
  project plan execution, 116
  quick assessment, 114–115
  resource planning, 148–149
  rolling wave planning, 120
  scope, 121–125
  solicitation planning, 156–157
  top-down approach, 121
PMBOK Guide
  importance of, 12
  limitations, 13
  study tips, 30
  versions, 12
PMI (Project Management Institute)
  Certification Board Center, 11
  chapter meetings, 12
  chapters, 13
  continuing education opportunities, 12
  exam sponsorship, 1
  joining, 15
  membership (by country), 13
  membership (in numbers), 10–11
  Role Delineation Study, 2
  seminars, 12
  symposium, 13
  Web site, 13
PMI ID number, 16
PMIS (project management information
    system), 117, 119
PMO (project management office), 66
PMP Certification Exam. *See* Project
    Management Professional (PMP)
    Certification Exam
PMP Code of Professional Conduct
  business pressures, 49
  organizational behavior, 49
  regulation, 49
  Responsibilities to the Profession, 48, 50–52
  Responsibilities to Customers and
  the Public, 52–55
policies
  organizational policies, 75
  quality policy, 200
post mortem, 303–304
power. *See* authority
practice exam
  answer key, 379–384
  CD-ROM version, 387
  length (in minutes), 367
  questions, 368–376
  scoring, 367
precedence diagramming method (PDM),
    162–163
present value (PV), 132, 363
prevention over inspection, 93
probability density, 335
probability distributions, 348–349
probability of completion, 346–348
probability of events, 343
process capability analysis, 349–350
Process Capability Index (Cpk), 351–352
process flow charts, 200
process interactions, 322–323
processes. *See also processes by name*
  defined, 36
  life-cycle, 73
  product-oriented processes, 37
  project management processes, 36,
    38–41, 43
procurement
  buyer's side, 236
  contract administration, 239–241
  contracts, 157–159
  contract-type selection, 155

procurement *(contnued)*
  defined, 73
  make-or-buy analysis, 155
  solicitation, 236–237
  solicitation planning, 156–157
  source selection, 238–239
  staff acquisition, 153
procurement planning
  defined, 154
  inputs, 155
  outputs, 155–156
  tools and techniques, 155
product analysis, 124
product description, 70–71
product scope, 90, 122–123. *See also* scope
product-oriented processes, 37
professional responsibility
  compliance, 50–51
  conflicts of interest, 54
  cultural differences, 54–55
  Member Code of Ethics, 48
  number of exam questions about, 45
  personal integrity and professionalism,
    53–54
  prep test, 56–58
  prep test answers, 59–60
  professional advancement, 50–52
  Professional Code of Conduct, 48–55
  professional practices, 50–51
  quick assessment, 46–47
  stakeholder interests, 52–53
profitability, measuring, 128
program evaluation and review technique
    (PERT), 171–172, 175
programs
  defined, 33
  examples, 34–35
progress indicators, 252
progress measurements, 269
progressive elaboration, 36, 90, 107
project abstract, 76
project charter, 76–77, 102–103
project closeout process
  administrative closure, 304–306
  contract closeout, 307–308
  knowledgebase, 303
  post mortem, 303–304
  prep test, 310–311
  prep test answers, 312–313
  quick assessment, 300–301
  releasing resources, 309

  repeating at each phase, 302–303
  rewards, 309
  work package evaluation, 303
project completion indicators, 253
project execution
  contract administration, 234, 239–241
  information distribution, 234, 248–250
  prep test, 254–255
  prep test answers, 256
  project plan execution, 234, 236
  quality assurance, 250–252
  quick assessment, 232–233
  solicitation, 234, 236–237
  source selection, 234, 238–239
  team development, 242–248
project initiation process
  discovery phase, 66
  documentation, 99
  failure likelihood, 63
  feasibility study, 66–67
  historical information, 70
  importance of, 63, 69
  inputs, 70
  needs analysis, 66
  planning processes, 66–67
  prep test, 78–79
  prep test answers, 80
  product description, 70–71
  project management office (PMO), 66
  project phases, 74
  project scope, 68
  project selection criteria, 70–71
  quick assessment, 64–65, 100
  scope initiation, 69
  strategic plan, 70
project management
  defined, 33
  software, 149
project management information system
    (PMIS), 117, 119
Project Management Institute (PMI)
  Certification Board Center, 11
  chapter meetings, 12
  chapters, 13
  continuing education opportunities, 12
  exam sponsorship, 1
  joining, 15
  membership (by country), 13
  membership (in numbers), 10–11
  Role Delineation Study, 2
  seminars, 12

symposium, 13
Web site, 13
project management office (PMO), 66
project management processes
  component processes, 40
  core processes, 40–41
  defined, 36
  facilitating processes, 40–41
  knowledge areas, 38–39
  matrix, 43
  memorization trick, 39
  relationships between, 38
Project Management Professional (PMP)
    Certification Exam
  application process, 15–16, 317
  continuing education requirements, 12
  fees, 15
  history, 10, 12
  length (in hours), 12, 14
  passing scores, 14, 17
  PMI ID number, 16
  question breakdown by section, 17, 28–29
  question number, 328
  question structure, 14, 16–17, 321–324, 328
  retaking, 17
  scheduling, 16, 317
  scoring, 14
  study plan, 18–20, 318–319, 386–387
  study tips, 18
  time clock, 328
  tutorial, 14, 327–328
project management software, 149
project manager
  authority within various organizations,
    93–94
  feasibility study, 67
  role, 88–89
  selection criteria, 103
  team development, 242
  title, 1
project metrics, 90–91
project mission statement, 68–69
project organization, 85
project plan
  change control, 193
  communications planning, 194–197
  development, 118–121
  execution, 234–236
  project management information system
    (PMIS), 119

qualitative risk analysis, 218–220
quality planning, 198–201
quantitative risk analysis, 220–222
risk identification, 216–218
risk management planning (RMP), 213–215
risk response planning, 223–225
rolling wave planning, 120
subsidiary plans, 192–193
updates, 192
written approvals, 193–194
project scope, 90, 122–123. *See also* scope
project selection criteria, 70–71
projectized organization, 32, 85, 95
projects
  costs, 38
  defined, 33
  deliverables, 37
  examples, 33–34
  fast tracking, 37
  kill point, 37
  life cycle, 37
  metrics, 269–272
  phases, 37
  processes, 36–41, 43
  progressive elaboration, 36
  ramp-down periods, 37
  ramp-up periods, 37
  risks, 37–38
  uncertainty, 74
  uniqueness, 34
Prometric Test Center, 16
purchasing
  buyer's side, 236
  contract administration, 239–241
  contracts, 157–159
  contract-type selection, 155
  defined, 73
  make-or-buy analysis, 155
  solicitation, 236–237
  solicitation planning, 156–157
  source selection, 238–239
staff acquisition, 153
PV (planned value), 183, 353
PV (present value), 132, 363

• **Q** •

QC (quality control), 264–266
qualified seller lists, 237
qualitative risk analysis, 218–220

quality
  assurance, 234
  cost, 93
  cost of quality, 201, 204–205
  customer satisfaction, 93, 202
  defined, 72, 92, 198, 213
  gold plating, 199
  improvements, 199
  kaizen, 203–204
  management, 93
  management responsibility, 93
  prevention over inspection, 93
  quality planning process, 198–201
  quality policy, 200
  Six Sigma, 203
  standards, 92
  Three Sigma, 203
  total quality management (TQM), 204
  zero-defects philosophy, 203, 209, 212
quality assurance, 250–252
quality by design, 211
Quality Circle movement, 212
quality control (QC), 264–265
quality function deployment, 124
quality gurus
  Crosby, Philip, 209–210
  Deming, W. Edwards, 206–208
  Ishikawa, Kaoru, 212
  Juran, Joseph M., 208–209
  Shingo, Shigeo, 212
  Taguchi, Genichi, 211–212
quality theory, 203
quantitative risk analysis, 220, 222
question sets, 26
question structure
  CAPM Exam, 14
  extraneous details, 25–26
  PMP Exam, 14, 16–17, 328–329
  repeated patterns, 18, 23–25, 321–322,
    328–329
  type variations, 323–324
question types, 22–23

• R •

RAM (responsibility assignment matrix),
    86, 147–148
recall questions, 22
recognition, 243, 309
referent authority, 102, 246

registration at the test center, 326
regulations, 33
reliability for serial and parallel processes,
    343–344
repeated patterns in questions, 18, 23–25,
    321–322, 328–329
request for proposal (RFP), 237
request for quotation (RFQ), 237
resource availability
  constraints, 104–105
  defined, 147
resource leveling, 168
resource leveling heuristics, 175
resource planning, 148–149
resources
  defined, 147
  histogram, 148
  releasing after closeout process, 309
responsibility assignment matrix (RAM),
    86, 147–148
retaking the PMP Exam, 17
reward authority, 102, 246
rewards, 243, 309
RFP (request for proposal), 237
RFQ (request for quotation), 237
risk
  contracts, 159
  defined, 73, 213
  opportunities, 213
  threats, 213
risk controls
  change requests, 286–287
  corrective action, 287
  triggering event, 286
Risk Event Status, 352
risk exposure, 352
risk formulas, 352
risk identification, 216–218
risk management planning (RMP), 213–215
risk metrics (RM), 253
risk monitoring and control, 284–285
risk response planning, 223–225
Role Delineation Study, 2
rolling wave planning, 120
rule of 7s, 268, 338–339

• S •

sample, 335
sampling distribution, 335

Savings Investment Ratio, 364
schedule
    activity definition, 160–161
    activity durations, 168–170
    activity sequencing, 161–166
    coding structure, 176
    crashing, 175
    critical path, 166–168
    critical path method (CPM), 174
    development of, 173–177
    duration compression methods, 175
    fast tracking, 37, 175
    float, 168
    graphical evaluation and review technique
        (GERT), 174
    lags, 167
    leads, 167
    network diagrams, 165–168
    program evaluation and review technique
        (PERT), 175
    resource leveling heuristics, 175
    slack, 168
schedule control, 288–289
schedule performance index (SPI), 184,
    355–358
schedule variance, 183–184, 354
schedule variance percentage, 184, 358
scheduling a time to take the PMP Exam,
    16, 317
scope
    acceptance criteria, 90
    assumptions, 105–106
    constraints, 104–105
    definition, 127
    documentation, 107
    expectations, 74, 84
    future decisions, 75–76
    measuring project benefits, 89–90
    milestones, 91–92
    needs, 74
    organizational policies, 75
    planning, 121–125
    prep test, 96
    prep test answers, 97
    product deliverables, 90–91
    product scope, 90, 122–123
    project objectives, 90–91
    project scope, 90, 122–123
    purpose of, 72
    quick assessment, 82–83

    requirements, 74–75
    scope management plan, 72, 122–123, 125
    scope statement, 90–91, 122, 124–127
    scope statement updates, 127, 146–147
    stakeholders, 84–89
scope change control, 275–277
scope creep, 275, 286
scope initiation, 69
scope metrics (SM), 253
scope verification, 272–275
SD (standard deviation), 336–337
sequencing of activities
    arrow diagramming method (ADM), 163–164
    conditional diagramming methods, 163
    defined, 161
    inputs, 162
    network diagrams, 163, 165–168
    outputs, 163
    precedence diagramming method (PDM),
        162–163
    tools and techniques, 162–163
Self-Assessment Test, 385
service and supply contracts, 157–158
Seven Deadly Diseases, 207–208
Shingo, Shigeo, quality guru, 212
Six Sigma, 203, 340, 351
skewness, 340
SM (scope metrics), 253
SMART (Specific, Measurable, Achievable,
    Realistic, and Time-specific), 76
software demos
    Milestones Professional 2002 (KIDASA
        Software, Inc.), 387–388
solicitation, 234, 236–237
solicitation planning
    defined, 156
    inputs, 156
    outputs, 157
    procurement documents, 157
    tools and techniques, 157
source selection, 234, 238–239
SOW (statement of work), 76, 125, 156
special-cause variation, 337–339
Specific, Measurable, Achievable, Realistic,
    and Time-specific (SMART), 76
SPI (schedule performance index), 184,
    355–358
sponsor
    characteristics of a good sponsor, 86–87
    conflicts with, 88

sponsor *(continued)*
  defined, 85
  feature gold plating, 88
  responsibilities, 86
  role, 86–87, 89
  working with, 87–88
staff acquisition
  defined, 152
  inputs, 153
  outputs, 153
  tools and techniques, 153
staff management plan, 150
stakeholder management, 85
stakeholders
  balancing interests of, 52–53
  buy-in, 88
  communications, 106, 194–197
  consensus, 88
  customer, 85
  defined, 35
  external stakeholders, 85
  functional manager, 85–86
  identifying, 84–86
  individual contributors, 85
  information sources, 86
  internal stakeholders, 85
  performing organization, 85
  project accountant, 86
  project champion, 85
  project influencer, 86
  project manager, 85
  project organization, 85
  project plan development, 117
  project team members, 85
  responsibility assignment matrix (RAM), 86
  risk tolerances, 214
  sharing findings with, 196–197
  sponsor, 85–89
  steering committee, 85
standard deviation (SD), 336–337
standards, 33
statement of work (SOW), 76, 125, 156
statistical terms
  acceptance sampling, 341
  acceptance sampling plan, 341
  analysis of covariance (ANCOVA), 342
  analysis of variance (ANOVA), 342
  arithmetic mean, 336
  Bayes' Theorem, 342
  Central Limit Theorem, 335

confidence interval, 337
  control chart, 338–340
  descriptive statistics, 334
  Design of Experiments (DoE), 342
  expected value, 340, 344–345
  experiment, 334
  factor, 342
  histogram, 340
  kurtosis, 341
  level of significance, 341
  mean, 336, 344
  median, 336
  mode, 336
  normal distribution, 335
  outliers, 341
  Probability of Events, 343
  reliability for serial and parallel processes, 343–344
  sample, 335
  sampling distribution, 335
  Six Sigma, 340, 351
  skewness, 340
  standard deviation (SD), 336–337
  statistics, 334
  type I error, 341
  type II error, 342
  variance, 336
  variation, 337–338
statistics, 334
Straight Line Depreciation, 366
strategic plan, 70
study plan, 18–20, 318–319, 388–389
study tips
  budgeting your time, 29–30
  color-coding, 18, 30
  extraneous details, 25–26
  memory aids, 23
  mnemonics, 23
  motivation, 319
  PMBOK Guide, 30
  question sets, 26
  repeated patterns in questions, 18, 23–25
  wall chart, 30
  what to focus on, 319–321
subsidiary plans, 192–193
Sum-of-the-Years'-Digits (SYD), 367
sunk cost, 128
supporting details, 118, 125
System of Profound Knowledge, W. Edwards Deming, 208

system requirements for CD-ROM, 385
systems engineering, 124

• T •

Taguchi, Genichi, quality guru, 211–212
target dates, 104
TCPI (To Complete Performance Index), 359
team development
  authority (types of), 246
  collocation, 243
  communication paths, 197–198
  communications, 247–248
  conflict management, 246–247
  defined, 234
  external feedback, 243
  input for performance appraisals, 243
  motivation techniques, 243–246
  performance improvements, 243
  performance reports, 243
  project manager's role, 242
  project staff assignment, 242
  recognition, 243
  rewards, 243
  staffing management plan, 242
  team-building activities, 243
  training, 243
technical support for CD-ROM, 387
telephone numbers
  Prometric Test Center, 16
  Wiley Publishing, Inc. Customer Service, 389
terminology, 11, 27
test centers, 326
Theories of X and Y, 244
Theory of Constraints (TOC), 173
Theory Z management, 245
Three Sigma, 203
time, 72
time formulas
  Critical Path Method, 345–346
  expected time, 344
  expected value, 344–345
  mean, 344
  PERT method, 345
  probability distributions, 348–349
  probability of completion, 346–348
  triangular distribution, 346
time metrics (TM), 253
time value of money (TVM), 128

time-phased budget, 181
To Complete Performance Index (TCPI), 359
TOC (Theory of Constraints), 173
tools and techniques
  activity definition, 160
  activity duration estimating, 170
  activity sequencing, 162–163
  communication planning, 196
  contract administration, 241
  cost budgeting, 181
  cost control, 291
  defined, 42
  information distribution, 249
  organizational planning, 152
  overall change control, 263–264
  performance reporting, 293
  procurement planning, 153
  project plan development, 117
  project plan execution, 235–236
  qualitative risk analysis, 219
  quality assurance, 251
  quality control, 265
  quality planning, 200–201
  quantitative risk analysis, 221–222
  resource planning, 149
  risk identification, 217–218
  risk management planning, 215
  risk monitoring and control, 284
  risk response planning, 224
  schedule control, 288–289
  schedule development, 174–176
  scope change control, 276–277
  scope definition, 127
  scope planning, 124
  scope verification, 275
  solicitation, 237
  solicitation planning, 157
  source selection, 239
  staff acquisition, 153
  team development, 243
total quality management (TQM), 204
trade conventions, 13
triangular distribution, 171, 346
triple constraint, 287
tutorial, 327–328
TVM (time value of money), 128
type I error, 341
type II error, 342

• U •

upper control limit (UCL), 338

• V •

value analysis, 124
value engineering, 124
variance, 336
Variance at Completion (VAC), 358
variation, 337–338

• W •

wall chart, 30
WAS (work authorization system), 194
WBS. *See* work breakdown structure
Web sites
  Critical Tools, Inc., 387
  helpful Website links page on CD-ROM, 387
  KIDASA Software, 387
  Project Management Institute (PMI), 13
  Prometric Test Center, 16
weekly progress indicators, 252
Wiley Publishing, Inc. Customer Service, 389
work authorization system (WAS), 194
work breakdown structure (WBS)
  activity definition, 160–161
  activity durations, 168–170
  activity list, 147
  activity sequencing, 161–166
  code of accounts, 144, 146
  cost account, 146

cost budgeting, 180–182
cost control system, 146
cost estimating, 177–179
critical path, 166–168
decomposition, 146
defined, 142, 145
illustrations, 142–143
knowledge areas, 145
labeling, 144
network diagrams, 165–168
organizational breakdown structure
  (OBS), 148
prep test, 185–186
prep test answers, 187
purpose of, 144
quick assessment, 140–141
resource planning, 148–149
resources histogram, 148
responsibility assignment matrix (RAM),
  147–148
schedule development, 173–177
scope statement updates, 146–147
staff acquisition, 152–153
staff management plan, 150
templates, 127
views, 144
WBS dictionary, 146
work package, 144, 146
written approvals, 193–194

• Z •

zero-defects philosophy, 203, 209, 212

Wiley Publishing, Inc.
End-User License Agreement

READ THIS. You should carefully read these terms and conditions before opening the software packet(s) included with this book "Book". This is a license agreement "Agreement" between you and Wiley Publishing, Inc."WPI". By opening the accompanying software packet(s), you acknowledge that you have read and accept the following terms and conditions. If you do not agree and do not want to be bound by such terms and conditions, promptly return the Book and the unopened software packet(s) to the place you obtained them for a full refund.

1. **License Grant.** WPI grants to you (either an individual or entity) a nonexclusive license to use one copy of the enclosed software program(s) (collectively, the "Software" solely for your own personal or business purposes on a single computer (whether a standard computer or a workstation component of a multi-user network). The Software is in use on a computer when it is loaded into temporary memory (RAM) or installed into permanent memory (hard disk, CD-ROM, or other storage device). WPI reserves all rights not expressly granted herein.

2. **Ownership.** WPI is the owner of all right, title, and interest, including copyright, in and to the compilation of the Software recorded on the disk(s) or CD-ROM "Software Media". Copyright to the individual programs recorded on the Software Media is owned by the author or other authorized copyright owner of each program. Ownership of the Software and all proprietary rights relating thereto remain with WPI and its licensers.

3. **Restrictions On Use and Transfer.**

   (a) You may only (i) make one copy of the Software for backup or archival purposes, or (ii) transfer the Software to a single hard disk, provided that you keep the original for backup or archival purposes. You may not (i) rent or lease the Software, (ii) copy or reproduce the Software through a LAN or other network system or through any computer subscriber system or bulletin- board system, or (iii) modify, adapt, or create derivative works based on the Software.

   (b) You may not reverse engineer, decompile, or disassemble the Software. You may transfer the Software and user documentation on a permanent basis, provided that the transferee agrees to accept the terms and conditions of this Agreement and you retain no copies. If the Software is an update or has been updated, any transfer must include the most recent update and all prior versions.

4. **Restrictions on Use of Individual Programs.** You must follow the individual requirements and restrictions detailed for each individual program in the "What's on the CD" appendix of this Book. These limitations are also contained in the individual license agreements recorded on the Software Media. These limitations may include a requirement that after using the program for a specified period of time, the user must pay a registration fee or discontinue use. By opening the Software packet(s), you will be agreeing to abide by the licenses and restrictions for these individual programs that are detailed in the "What's on the CD" appendix and on the Software Media. None of the material on this Software Media or listed in this Book may ever be redistributed, in original or modified form, for commercial purposes.

5. **Limited Warranty.**

    (a) WPI warrants that the Software and Software Media are free from defects in materials and workmanship under normal use for a period of sixty (60) days from the date of purchase of this Book. If WPI receives notification within the warranty period of defects in materials or workmanship, WPI will replace the defective Software Media.

    (b) WPI AND THE AUTHOR OF THE BOOK DISCLAIM ALL OTHER WARRANTIES, EXPRESS OR IMPLIED, INCLUDING WITHOUT LIMITATION IMPLIED WARRANTIES OF MERCHANTABILITY AND FITNESS FOR A PARTICULAR PURPOSE, WITH RESPECT TO THE SOFTWARE, THE PROGRAMS, THE SOURCE CODE CONTAINED THEREIN, AND/OR THE TECHNIQUES DESCRIBED IN THIS BOOK. WPI DOES NOT WARRANT THAT THE FUNCTIONS CONTAINED IN THE SOFTWARE WILL MEET YOUR REQUIREMENTS OR THAT THE OPERATION OF THE SOFTWARE WILL BE ERROR FREE.

    (c) This limited warranty gives you specific legal rights, and you may have other rights that vary from jurisdiction to jurisdiction.

6. **Remedies.**

    (a) WPI's entire liability and your exclusive remedy for defects in materials and workmanship shall be limited to replacement of the Software Media, which may be returned to WPI with a copy of your receipt at the following address: Software Media Fulfillment Department, Attn.: *PMP Certification For Dummies,* Wiley Publishing, Inc., 10475 Crosspoint Blvd., Indianapolis, IN 46256, or call 1-800-762-2974. Please allow four to six weeks for delivery. This Limited Warranty is void if failure of the Software Media has resulted from accident, abuse, or misapplication. Any replacement Software Media will be warranted for the remainder of the original warranty period or thirty (30) days, whichever is longer.

    (b) In no event shall WPI or the author be liable for any damages whatsoever (including without limitation damages for loss of business profits, business interruption, loss of business information, or any other pecuniary loss) arising from the use of or inability to use the Book or the Software, even if WPI has been advised of the possibility of such damages.

    (c) Because some jurisdictions do not allow the exclusion or limitation of liability for consequential or incidental damages, the above limitation or exclusion may not apply to you.

7. **U.S. Government Restricted Rights.** Use, duplication, or disclosure of the Software for or on behalf of the United States of America, its agencies and/or instrumentalities "U.S. Government" is subject to restrictions as stated in paragraph (c)(1)(ii) of the Rights in Technical Data and Computer Software clause of DFARS 252.227-7013, or subparagraphs (c)(1) and (2) of the Commercial Computer Software - Restricted Rights clause at FAR 52.227-19, and in similar clauses in the NASA FAR supplement, as applicable.

8. **General.** This Agreement constitutes the entire understanding of the parties and revokes and supersedes all prior agreements, oral or written, between them and may not be modified or amended except in a writing signed by both parties hereto that specifically refers to this Agreement. This Agreement shall take precedence over any other documents that may be in conflict herewith. If any one or more provisions contained in this Agreement are held by any court or tribunal to be invalid, illegal, or otherwise unenforceable, each and every other provision shall remain in full force and effect.

FOR DUMMIES®

The easy way to get more done and have more fun

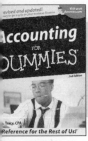

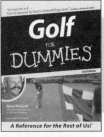
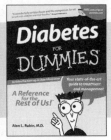

FOR DUMMIES®

A world of resources to help you grow

HOME, GARDEN & HOBBIES

Feng Shui
0-7645-5295-3

Gardening
0-7645-5130-2

Guitar
0-7645-5106-X

Also available:

Auto Repair For Dummies
(0-7645-5089-6)

Chess For Dummies
(0-7645-5003-9)

Home Maintenance For Dummies
(0-7645-5215-5)

Organizing For Dummies
(0-7645-5300-3)

Piano For Dummies
(0-7645-5105-1)

Poker For Dummies
(0-7645-5232-5)

Quilting For Dummies
(0-7645-5118-3)

Rock Guitar For Dummies
(0-7645-5356-9)

Roses For Dummies
(0-7645-5202-3)

Sewing For Dummies
(0-7645-5137-X)

FOOD & WINE

Cooking
0-7645-5250-3

Cookies
0-7645-5390-9

Wine
0-7645-5114-0

Also available:

Bartending For Dummies
(0-7645-5051-9)

Chinese Cooking For Dummies
(0-7645-5247-3)

Christmas Cooking For Dummies
(0-7645-5407-7)

Diabetes Cookbook For Dummies
(0-7645-5230-9)

Grilling For Dummies
(0-7645-5076-4)

Low-Fat Cooking For Dummies
(0-7645-5035-7)

Slow Cookers For Dummies
(0-7645-5240-6)

TRAVEL

Italy
0-7645-5453-0

Hawaii
0-7645-5438-7

Las Vegas
0-7645-5448-4

Also available:

America's National Parks For Dummies
(0-7645-6204-5)

Caribbean For Dummies
(0-7645-5445-X)

Cruise Vacations For Dummies 2003
(0-7645-5459-X)

Europe For Dummies
(0-7645-5456-5)

Ireland For Dummies
(0-7645-6199-5)

France For Dummies
(0-7645-6292-4)

London For Dummies
(0-7645-5416-6)

Mexico's Beach Resorts For Dummies
(0-7645-6262-2)

Paris For Dummies
(0-7645-5494-8)

RV Vacations For Dummies
(0-7645-5443-3)

Walt Disney World & Orlando For Dummies
(0-7645-5444-1)

Available wherever books are sold. Go to www.dummies.com or call 1-877-762-2974 to order direct.

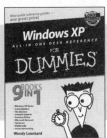

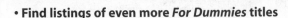

FOR DUMMIES®

Helping you expand your horizons and realize your potentia[l]

INTERNET

0-7645-0894-6

0-7645-1659-0

0-7645-1642-6

Also available:

America Online 7.0 For Dummies
(0-7645-1624-8)

Genealogy Online For Dummies
(0-7645-0807-5)

The Internet All-in-One Desk Reference For Dummies
(0-7645-1659-0)

Internet Explorer 6 For Dummies
(0-7645-1344-3)

The Internet For Dummi[es] Quick Reference
(0-7645-1645-0)

Internet Privacy For Dum[mies]
(0-7645-0846-6)

Researching Online For Dummies
(0-7645-0546-7)

Starting an Online Busin[ess] For Dummies
(0-7645-1655-8)

DIGITAL MEDIA

0-7645-1664-7

0-7645-1675-2

0-7645-0806-7

Also available:

CD and DVD Recording For Dummies
(0-7645-1627-2)

Digital Photography All-in-One Desk Reference For Dummies
(0-7645-1800-3)

Digital Photography For Dummies Quick Reference
(0-7645-0750-8)

Home Recording for Musicians For Dummies
(0-7645-1634-5)

MP3 For Dummies
(0-7645-0858-X)

Paint Shop Pro "X" For Dummies
(0-7645-2440-2)

Photo Retouching & Restoration For Dummie[s]
(0-7645-1662-0)

Scanners For Dummies
(0-7645-0783-4)

GRAPHICS

0-7645-0817-2

0-7645-1651-5

0-7645-0895-4

Also available:

Adobe Acrobat 5 PDF For Dummies
(0-7645-1652-3)

Fireworks 4 For Dummies
(0-7645-0804-0)

Illustrator 10 For Dummies
(0-7645-3636-2)

QuarkXPress 5 For Dumm[ies]
(0-7645-0643-9)

Visio 2000 For Dummies
(0-7645-0635-8)